M000310040

# The Meaning of Movement

# The Meaning of Movement

## Developmental and Clinical Perspectives of the Kestenberg Movement Profile

**Janet Kestenberg Amighi**

**Susan Loman**

**Penny Lewis**

and

**K. Mark Sossin**

with invited contributors

**Routledge**
Taylor & Francis Group

NEW YORK AND LONDON

Copyright © 1999 OPA (Overseas Publishers Association) N.V. Published by license under the Gordon and Breach Publishers imprint.

All rights reserved.

No part of this book may be reproduced or utilized in any form or by any means, electronic or mechanical, including photocopying and recording, or by any information storage or retrieval system, without permission in writing from the publisher.

Published by
Routledge
711 Third Avenue
New York, NY 10017

Published in Great Britain by
Routledge
2 Park Square
Milton Park, Abingdon
Oxfordshire OX14 4RN

First issued in paperback 2014

*Routledge is an imprint of the Taylor and Francis Group, an informa business*

Body–Mind Centering™ denotes a patented system of movement therapy created by Bonnie Bainbridge Cohen. For purposes of the clarity and design of this book, the trademark symbol has been omitted from the term "Body–Mind Centering" when it appears in the text. However, this term is a registered trademark owned by Bonnie Bainbridge Cohen and is fully protected under U.S. law.

British Library Cataloguing in Publication Data

The meaning of movement : developmental and clinical
   perspectives of the Kestenberg Movement Profile
   1. Kestenberg Movement Profile
   I. Kestenberg Amighi, Janet
   152.3

ISBN 13: 978-90-5700-528-2 (hbk)
ISBN 13: 978-1-138-00630-0 (pbk)

# CONTENTS

# PREFACE

It is an intriguing challenge to the student of human behavior to develop a system for the meaningful interpretation of movement patterns. We propose that a formalized system of movement notation and analysis, drawing upon years of study by Dr. Judith Kestenberg and her colleagues, offers a remarkably useful tool for the coding and interpretation of movement. This system can be applied in methodological research inquiry, therapy and everyday life. It can greatly supersede intuition in providing a valuable and coherent approach to the understanding of meanings attributable to specific patterns of movement.

The primary objective of this book is to present the Kestenberg Movement Profile (KMP)—a multi-tiered system for the notation of observed movement patterns, classification of these patterns, and analysis of an individual's movement repertoire. The KMP offers a comprehensive "way of seeing" movement, and of gleaning a deeper understanding of the individual through his or her nonverbal behavior. Despite its richness and complexity, we will attempt to elucidate the KMP system using a simple and accessible style of presentation. The authors and invited contributors to this book are all students of Judith Kestenberg; they have backgrounds in diverse fields of study, including clinical psychology, psychoanalysis, child development, creative arts therapy—including dance/movement therapy—anthropology and social work. Their interests converge on study and utilization of the KMP as a bridge toward an awareness of development and meaning of movement behavior. We have each felt our professional work has been enhanced, and our lives enriched, through this pursuit.

For those who use nonverbal information in their work, the KMP can provide a formal system of observation, notation and analysis of movement with a theoretical framework for interpretation of the meaning of movement. The framework is developmental; it focuses on the way movement patterns develop throughout the life span. The KMP helps train observers to see patterns of movement, including those not readily apparent, and to define, quantify and interpret a fairly comprehensive range of movement qualities.

For those who are not movement specialists, the KMP offers a new perspective, capable of being integrated into other clinical or educational assessment systems and treatment plans for clients. The reader may not use the Profile as a whole; an educator, for example, may choose to focus most on those diagrams—clusters of movement qualities—particularly central to learning processes.

For parents and other students of human behavior, the study of movement may provide an underutilized avenue of access fundamental to understanding not only individuals but interrelationships as well.

Of equal importance, for all students of the KMP—parents, creative arts therapists, educators, anthropologists, ethologists, communication specialists, and clinical, developmental and social psychologists—KMP training enhances awareness of one's own movement repertoire and how it can affect relationships with others both professionally and personally.

Before describing the contents of this book, we offer readers an extended anecdote as an introduction to the KMP and an invitation to membership in the KMP community of learners.

In 1962 a group of researchers, the Sands Point Movement Study Group, composed of child psychiatrists and movement specialists, began a long-term collaboration seeking to elucidate the role and meaning of movement in child development. Judith Kestenberg, a child psychoanalyst with a background in neurology, invited the others to join with her in the quest to tease out the intimate connections between mind and body and develop them into a theoretical framework to guide parents, researchers and therapists working with children and families.

Hershey Marcus (1996 personal communication), one of the group members, relates his early experience with Judith Kestenberg:

At the time I was the Director of Child Psychiatry at Hillside hospital. Dr. Judith Kestenberg was one of the supervisors of our fellows and we heard strange stories about how she would describe a specific movement and its meaning in order to understand a child better. When I finally got to sit down and speak to Judith about children I was a bit stiff. She already had a huge reputation as a child analyst, but I was a young psychiatrist then, a bit full of myself and arrogant. She said, 'Hershey, let's crawl. You have to experience how to crawl in order to understand a child. You cannot sit in a chair or stand up and understand it.' I looked at her and she started to crawl, so I started to crawl too and there went my dignity.

There began a journey into understanding the meaning of movement. The Sands Point Movement Study Group met every Friday for nearly twenty years observing children and adults, moving together, eventually opening their own Center for Parents and Children. In addition, they invited numerous specialists as guests to their meetings and studied the work of Rudolph Laban.

As part of the group learning process, the dancers Forrestine Paulay and Irmgard Bartenieff taught the "klutzy" child psychiatrists how to move and the analysts helped enrich the psychological interpretations of movement that came to them from dance/movement therapy. Through the combination of observing children, moving themselves, clinical practice, and theoretical interchange among themselves and with others, "The Profile unfolded in front of our eyes." (Arnhilt Buelte, 1990, p. 17)

This book invites the reader to an *approximation* of the study group experience by utilizing a conversational style throughout the first section, short side excursions into cross-cultural domains intriguing to the authors, and movement exercises to experience the feeling of movement patterns. In the second and third sections, the reader will find more theoretical multidisciplinary approaches by various authors.

The introduction covers movement qualities of the KMP, its historical development, and issues of reliability and validity. Also presented is a detailed overview of the whole Profile. The first section of the book, chapters 1–9, takes the reader through the nine main categories of movement covered by the KMP. Chapter 1 tells the story of development from earliest infancy through six years of age, as revealed by observation of rhythms of movement or tension flow rhythms. The reader is shown how early childhood rhythmic preferences are played out in adult patterns of behavior and personality. Relationships between movement constellations and personality constellations begin to emerge. In chapter 2, movement patterns reflecting individual temperament and emotional characteristics of the mover are introduced. Chapter 3 covers a category of movement qualities, "pre-efforts," people use when learning new tasks, facing anxiety-provoking situations, and in defenses against unwanted impulses.

The study of efforts, movement qualities used by individuals when coping with the external environment, is presented in chapter 4. Rudolph Laban developed the concept of "efforts" and used it to help workers develop more effective approaches to their tasks. In chapter 5 we look at bipolar shape flow movements through which people express self-feelings and their relationship to the general environment. Chapter 6 describes the ways in which people respond to attractive or repulsive stimuli. These patterns reflect how individuals feel about people and things in their environment. More effective and mature ways of defending oneself evolve based on these patterns.

Chapter 7 gives a brief outline of an ongoing investigation of movement designs within the kinesphere—the bubble of space surrounding the body—that tends to vary considerably among people of different cultures. Directional movements are described in chapter 8. These are simple movements reflecting complex processes involved in defenses against people and objects. They are also used in labeling and defining, as well as in creating bridges to others. Of special interest to educators, these movement qualities are often associated with styles of learning, patterns of cognition, and speech. In chapter 9 we explore shaping in planes, motions that reflect complex styles of thinking and through which a mover relates to others in multidimensional ways. From these chapters, the reader will gain insight into a wide variety of ways in which movement and thought, feelings, and personality configurations are integrated.

Section II contains chapters with examples of applications of the KMP. In chapter 10 K. Mark Sossin, a clinical psychologist and psychoanalyst, describes the ways in which infant–parent therapy can be informed by the KMP. He offers examples of integrating the KMP into clinical work with parents and children. Dance/movement therapists Susan Loman and Hillary Merman (chapter 11) present numerous clinical examples of the integration of KMP approaches into assessment, treatment planning and intervention in dance/movement therapy.

In chapter 12, Penny Lewis interweaves KMP-derived insights with Jungian perspectives and techniques of depth psychotherapy, drama therapy, and dance/movement therapy to help clients overcome effects of early trauma. Chapter 13 describes how the KMP and the Body–Mind Centering (BMC) approach developed by Bonnie Bainbridge Cohen support and enrich each other as systems of developmental movement. Susan Loman, Amelia Ender and Kim Burden describe how study of reflexes and basic neurological patterns within BMC complement KMP phases of development.

Three chapters on theoretically linked ways of interpreting the Kestenberg Movement Profile conclude the book in the third and final section. In chapter 14, K. Mark Sossin covers principles of KMP interpretation and illustrates them with an example of the KMP of an adult. His theoretical orientation is psychodynamic. Janet Kestenberg Amighi and Susan Loman (chapter 15) use the case of a three-and-one-half-year-old boy to illustrate the process of interpreting a KMP of a child. They base their interpretations on a developmental and movement-based framework. Chapter 16 by Penny Lewis provides a clinical outline of the KMP movement qualities, offering interpretations relevant to adults based on the Recovery Model.

# ACKNOWLEDGMENTS

We are deeply indebted to Judith Kestenberg for her mentorship, love, support and for being the source of this creative work and our constant inspiration.

We also thank the contributors to this book, the Sands Point Movement Study Group and those who helped greatly in formation of the KMP and its body of knowledge: Irmgard Bartenieff, Jay Berlowe, MD, Arnhilt Buelte, Martha Davis, PhD, Judith S. Kestenberg, MD, Ellen Goldman, CMA, Warren Lamb, Hershey Marcus, MD, Forrestine Paulay, ADTR, Islene Pinder, Esther Robbins, MD, and Martha Soodak, ADTR.

Our appreciation to the Antioch New England Graduate School, Allegheny University, Laban/Bartenieff Institute for Movement Studies and all KMP students who provided feedback on the manuscript.

Special thanks to Carolyn Moore and Carol Hollander for their wonderful editing abilities and to Nava Lotan for her support and for computerizing the KMP.

Finally, we thank Antioch New England Graduate School and Child Development Research for their support and encouragement. We are grateful to our KMP students, spouses, family and partners for their support as well as stamina and patience.

# CONTRIBUTORS

**Kim Burden**, MA, MS, DTR has masters degrees in both dance/movement therapy and dance science and is a certified practitioner of Body–Mind Centering. She is currently working with adolescents at "Acting Out" in Keene, New Hampshire, a psychodrama program, and teaching dance at the Putney School Summer Program in Vermont. She utilizes dance/movement therapy in her work with individuals with developmental disabilities.

**Amelia Ender**, MA, DTR, CMA teaches Body–Mind Centering at the School for Body–Mind Centering and at Antioch New England Graduate School, Keene, New Hampshire, and also teaches for the Department of Performing and Visual Arts at Springfield College. She was a student of pioneer dance/movement therapist Blanch Evan and assisted Yael Daniel at the Group Project for Holocaust Survivors and Their Families. She has worked extensively with children and adults in both psychiatric and educational settings and maintains a private practice in Northampton, Massachusetts.

**Janet Kestenberg Amighi**, PhD, MSS, MLSP applies anthropological principles through the field of social work. She is currently working as an advocate for the rights of farm workers in Pennsylvania and has done research in Iran and Bali. She has taught courses in anthropology at West Chester University, Pennsylvania and wrote a book called *Zoroastrians of Iran*. The daughter of Judith Kestenberg, she has co-taught the KMP for more than ten years at the Laban/Bartenieff Institute for Movement Studies.

**Penny Lewis**, PhD, ADTR, RDT/BC is a KMP trainer, a member of the Academy of Dance/Movement Therapists, and a board certified registered drama therapist. She is the author of *Theoretical Approaches in Dance Movement Therapy*, vols. I & II and *Creative Transformation: The Healing Power of the Arts*; editor of *The Choreography of Object Relations*; and co-editor with Susan Loman of *The Kestenberg Movement Profile: Its Past, Present Applications and Future Directions*, all of which apply KMP concepts in therapy. She is currently a senior associate faculty member at Antioch New England Graduate School, an international workshop leader, and has a private practice in supervision and depth psychotherapy in Amesbury, Massachusetts.

**Susan Loman**, MA, ADTR is director of the Masters Program in Dance/Movement Therapy with a minor in counseling psychology, and associate chair of the Department of Applied Psychology at Antioch New England Graduate School. She serves on the editorial board of *The Arts in Psychotherapy* and is chair of the Education, Research and Practice Committee on the board of the American Dance Therapy Association. The co-editor of two

KMP books, *The Kestenberg Movement Profile: Its Past, Present Applications and Future Directions* and *The Body Mind Connection in Human Movement Analysis*, and author of many articles on KMP, she teaches the KMP system of movement analysis at Antioch New England Graduate School, the Laban/Bartenieff Institute of Movement Studies in New York City and provides workshops nationally and internationally.

**Hillary Merman**, CSW, ADTR, CMA, graduate of the KMP system, has worked with children and adults integrating Kestenberg concepts in dance/movement therapy assessment, practice, supervision, teaching and writing in the United States and abroad. Publications include articles on KMP in *The Kestenberg Movement Profile: Its Past, Present Applications and Future Directions* and *Motortherapeutische Arbeit Mit Hyperaktiven Kindern*. She currently practices individual psychotherapy and dance/movement therapy in New York City.

**K. Mark Sossin**, PhD, is an associate professor of psychology at Pace University in New York City, where he is also co-director of the Pace Parent-Infant/Toddler Research Nursery. He serves on the faculties of Adelphi University's Derner Institute for Advanced Psychological Studies' postdoctoral programs in adult psychoanalysis and psychotherapy and in child psychotherapy, and of the New York Freudian Society's Institute for Psychoanalytic Training's program in parent-infant psychotherapy. He serves as vice-president on the board of Child Development Research (CDR), and is active in the New York Association for Early Childhood and Infant Psychologists. He is co-author of *The Role of Movement Patterns in Development, Vol. II* with Judith Kestenberg and is author of several articles related to the Kestenberg Movement Profile. He began studying with Judith Kestenberg in 1976, and later served as supervising psychologist at the Center for Parents and Children on Long Island where he was a leader of CDR's Father's Project. He has taught about the KMP and developmental aspects of movement at the Laban/Bartenieff Institute for Movement Studies. In addition to his teaching and research roles, he currently maintains a private practice in clinical psychology in New Hyde Park, New York.

# Introduction

The quest for the understanding of movement begins with everyday observations and experiences. The challenge of extracting the rules and meanings from the seemingly obvious invites us on a fascinating journey. Though often outside of our awareness, we regularly rely on nonverbal cues to assess the feelings and personality traits of others. We each have our own informal "lexicon" of movement patterns that becomes an untaught, yet essential, reference guide, enabling us to respond and adjust to others. Can this level of understanding be transformed into a more systematic and reliable methodology which would have far reaching applications? Given the breadth of information which bodily movements potentially reveal to us, it is not surprising that a wide variety of methods have been used in scientific and artistic fields to decipher the meaning of movement.

Many questions arise. To what extent does a person's style of moving offer worthwhile clues as to the person's nature or state of mind? In what ways are movement patterns reflective of cultural influences? Seeking attunement with another, how do we know which patterns would harmonize, and which would clash? In clinical situations, to what extent are an individual's movements relevant to assessment and treatment planning? Are movements an uncensored expression of one's unconscious and thus revealing of hidden meanings?

In some contexts, movement patterns may be fashioned under conscious control. Dancers and choreographers use movement in precise ways to elicit predictable, and sometimes powerful reverberations in their audience. Actors use facial expressions as well as master gestures and other body movements to define a character's affective state and to convey intention and personality. Ekman (1985) has studied the ways in which individuals censor their nonverbal behavior in attempts to disguise feelings and mislead others.

However, in most contexts, movement patterns have the potential to reveal a host of non-verbalized feelings and states. Freud (1905) pointed out that patients unconsciously reveal inner anxieties and feelings through body movements: "If his lips are silent, he chatters with his fingertips, betrayal oozes out of him at every pore" (p. 95). Lowen maintained that "Even when a person tries to hide his true feelings by some artificial postural attitude, his body belies the pose in the state of tension that is created. The body does not lie" (Lowen, 1971, p. 100).

The use of movement analysis for psychological assessment and treatment rests on our understanding of the mind, emotions and body as closely integrated, mutually interacting systems. This link, this holistic connection, means that not only does the body reflect the psyche, but the body can affect the psyche as well. We have learned, for example, that mental imagery can improve movement skills and that movement can affect cognitive and emotional patterns (Eddy, 1992). "When traumatic events or obstacles impede the normal growth process, maladaptive [and adaptive] experiences get stored in the body and are reflected in body movement" (Loman and Foley, 1996, p. 4). A person who feels rejected may develop a hollow, narrowed body attitude which expresses and reinforces such feelings. A small child whose caregiver has a hollowed torso may accommodate to it and develop a similar body attitude and associated feelings.

Because both physical and emotional experiences leave long-term traces upon the way people hold themselves and move, the study of movement opens a door to the study of patterns of early development, coping strategies, and personality configurations. Intriguing studies have considered the inherent/biological and cultural/experiential factors influencing the development of one's nonverbal "style."

To the extent that movement analysis serves as a source of information about the mind, it also can serve as a guide for a movement-based form of therapy and/or re-training. Those focused on infant–parent relationships, as well on adult relationships often highlight the efficacy and signaling power of nonverbal communication. Mental health professionals regularly use the facial expressions and body movements of those they treat as indicators of affects and motives that may not be verbalized (or conscious), and they may use their own movement patterns and paralinguistic features (consciously or unconsciously) to construct and sustain a working, trusting relationship. One may also attend to the ways in which movement patterns of two individuals clash and harmonize, creating positive or negative "chemistry" between partners and forging or disrupting relationships.

Those interested in pursuing the study of nonverbal behavior range across many disciplines and backgrounds, including parents who study parenting manuals seeking insights into their children's nonverbal development, as well as social, developmental, and clinical psychologists, anthropologists, educators, and animal behaviorists, as well as students of semiotics, communications, linguistics, creative art therapies, kinesiology, dance, drama, and child development.

In order to pursue their interests, members of academic and therapeutic disciplines require coding and classificatory systems for describing and analyzing nonverbal behavior. Although several formats have been developed, some are quite broad, utilizing gross movement categories, while others are fairly specialized and thus may not be suitable for interdisciplinary work. Of value to the broad field of nonverbal behavior is a system which is sufficiently detailed and specific to capture subtle yet important distinctions and individual variations, and yet comprehensive enough to be applicable to diverse interests.

Our purpose in this book is to present the Kestenberg Movement Profile (KMP), which provides: (1) a Laban derived method of labeling and categorizing elementary movement qualities, (2) a system for psychological assessment through the observation and analysis of movement, (3) a theoretical framework which guides the interpretation of movement repertoires in developmental terms, and (4) a framework for the prevention and treatment of a wide variety of psychological, physical, and cognitive problems. Movement qualities coded using the KMP reflect individuals' styles of learning and cognition, expression of needs and feelings, modes of relating, styles of defense, and dynamics for coping with the environment. The psychoanalytically-oriented analyst can use the KMP to access information about drives, object relations, ego development, the superego, and defense mechanisms. However, the KMP is equally accessible to those with other orientations and can be used to pursue varied research goals.

This text also includes an up-date of approaches to interpretation and presentation of several recent applications of the KMP. For the reader, we hope to make the KMP a more understandable and usable tool, and through the KMP, we hope to make processes of human movement more understandable.

## A Portrait of the KMP

The Austrian choreographer and movement educator, Rudolf Laban, conceived of and generated a system of dance notation and movement analysis (1960, 1966). The Laban system provides a systematic means of perceiving and describing elementary components of movement, both qualitatively and quantitatively (Bartenieff and Lewis, 1980). Labanotation and Labananalysis (effort/shape) are applicable to many fields of study for it was the process that was fundamental for Laban "not the end product or goal of the action" (Bartenieff and Lewis, 1980, p. ix). The movement components described by Laban are readily observable and the interpretive scheme is logical and accessible to the lay person willing to learn.

Reflecting their essentially developmental and psychological interests, Kestenberg and her colleagues elaborated upon the Laban system so that it reflected the ways in which movement patterns evolve within the context of development. In order to facilitate the use of this new profile for psychological assessment, they initially sought to highlight the correspondences they discovered between movement qualities and Anna Freud's developmental scheme (1965).

Based on long term movement observation of children, clinical practice, and research, Kestenberg and the original study group amended Laban's description of efforts into four distinct movement clusters: tension flow rhythms (which reflect unconscious needs) tension flow attributes (which reflect temperament and affects), pre-efforts (which reflect immature ways of coping, often used in learning and defensive behaviors), and efforts (used in coping with space, weight, and time elements) (Koch, 1997). Similarly, they differentiated shape flow into bipolar shape flow (movements which reflect self feelings) and unipolar shape flow (involved in responses to specific stimuli). They added movement qualities which relate to how we move and gesticulate in the kinesphere around us (shape flow design) and developed a developmental and psychological understanding of shaping in directions (used in defenses and learning) and shaping in planes (used in complex relationships).

What emerged was a movement-based profile, consisting of qualitative information and nine diagrams which display more than ninety different possible qualities of movement in an individual's movement repertoire.[1] These nine frequency diagrams of movement quality clusters are arranged to reflect developmental sequences and the alternation of mobilizing and stabilizing qualities in development (see Laban, 1960).[2] Comparing diagrams within the profile can illuminate how movements qualities are used in varied harmonious and clashing combinations.

Once a Kestenberg Movement Profile is completed, it serves as a movement portrait upon which to base a developmental assessment, and in clinical contexts, a treatment plan. As described above, it can also be used to assess learning styles, personality characteristics, styles of relationships, creative intelligence; or by comparing two profiles, one can discover areas of accord and conflict between individuals.

The original and primary arena for KMP study has been "primary prevention." This has involved the appraisal of parent and child movement patterns, contributing to the identification of risk and to the development of facilitative and interventive methods appropriate for particular child-rearing situations.

Movement observations based on the KMP can extend the perspectives of developmental theories, highlighting drive and defense (e.g., Anna Freud, 1965), object relations (e.g., Margaret Mahler, 1974), psychosocial influences (e.g., Erikson, 1950), patterns of dyadic interaction (e.g., Stern, 1985, 1995), and phase development. For example, her study of movement resulted in Kestenberg's effort to revise the classic schema of phase development. Characterized by distinct movement patterns, additional phases were postulated, each of which has distinct psychological correlates. One of these phases, the "inner genital phase," an early childhood phase linked to functions of maternality, is characterized by long gradual rhythms which facilitate nurturing, relationship building, and integration (Kestenberg, 1967, 1975). The movement and psychological constellations which typify children in this phase occur among boys as well as girls suggesting the biological, maturational preconditioning of both genders for parenting capabilities.

The scope of KMP interpretations and applications has grown over the many years since its germination, and it appears that there is great potential for the KMP to be employed in further clinical, developmental, interactional and inter-cultural research. The next generation of KMP students, dance/movement therapists, clinical and developmental psychologists, educators, anthropologists, and parents, are exploring ways in which the KMP can be integrated with diverse theoretical frameworks and thus offer a bridge to diverse disciplines and interests.

## History of the Development of the KMP

This section looks at the early influences on Judith Kestenberg, originator of the KMP, and traces the work of the Sands Point Movement Study Group and more recent students of the KMP.

Notably, nonverbal behavior was the "hobby horse" of Charles Darwin, who began collecting his observational notes as a young man, drawing upon his infant son as well as other subjects for observation (Fridlund, 1994). Before publishing his text *The Expression of the Emotions in Man and Animals* in 1872, Darwin had asked colleagues to answer queries about cultures he himself had not observed. He asked sixteen questions that do not sound terribly dated: they include:

When a man is indignant or defiant does he frown, hold his body and head erect, square his shoulders and clench his fists? ... When considering deeply on any subject, or trying to understand any puzzle, does he frown, or wrinkle the skin beneath the lower eyelids? (Darwin, 1872/1965, p. 15–16).

Consider his conclusions:

The movements of expression in the face and body, whatever their origin may have been, are in themselves of much importance for our welfare. They serve as the first means of communication between the mother and her infant, she smiles approval and thus encourages her child on the right path, or frowns disapproval. We readily perceive sympathy in others by their expression; our sufferings are thus mitigated and our pleasures increased, and mutual good feeling is thus strengthened. The movements of expression give vividness and energy to our spoken words. They reveal the thoughts and intentions of others more truly than do words, which may be falsified (Darwin, 1872/1965, p. 364).

Further insights have been offered since publication of Darwin's work. In 1911 Diderot suggested that gesture expresses thought more clearly than verbalization (quoted in Kendon, 1984). Allport and Vernon (1933) and Reich (1949) suggested that individual differences in movement patterns are a reflection of aspects of personality.

Judith Kestenberg, then studying medicine in the Neurologische and Psychiatrische Klinik in Vienna in the 1930's, developed an interest in the body/mind relationship. Psychiatrists and psychoanalysts who studied brain damaged adults and children in the clinic could not help but be impressed by the intimate interconnections of thought processes, neurological functioning, and movement. Freud (1905) had recognized the confluence of somatic and psychic processes when he spoke of the "... tension by which a person indicates somatically the concentration of his attention and the level of abstraction at which his thinking is at the moment proceeding" (p. 193).

Following her training in Vienna, Kestenberg maintained a focus on psyche-soma relations and on the methods by which they could be studied. She emphasized the art of observation of movement through "kinesthetic identification" which she noted was a principle understood by Freud (1905), who commented, "I have acquired the idea of ... carrying the movement out myself or by imitating it and through this action I have learned the standard of this movement" (p. 191). One can see examples of the use of kinesthetic identification in the notator's development of observational skill, the clinician's understanding of a patient's behavior from nonverbal cues, the parent's empathy with a child and the infant's manner of relating to the parent in transforming early reflexes into modes of coping.

Another major influence on Kestenberg's thinking was the work of Schilder (1935) who wrote *The Image and Appearance of the Human Body* and who found consistency between neurological and psychoanalytic findings and perspectives. Schilder (1931) suggested that

... rhythmic tendencies are in close relation to the system of emotions and the affective life ... [while] ... Deliberate action ... has a much closer connection with the cortical region ... (pp. 28–29).

In 1937, Kestenberg, pursuing further medical education, came to New York as a student of Schilder. When she discovered that verbal data was insufficient for understanding psychic processes in young children, she turned to the study of movement patterns. However, there were few models to follow. Fries (1958) had suggested that early motor behavior was related to later psychic functioning, but she offered no method for investigation and substantiation of this concept. As Kestenberg (1967) pointed out:

Papers concerned with rhythmic and nonrhythmic patterns of motor discharge have been few. Although both academic and psychoanalytic developmental psychology are based in good part on observation of motor behavior, no systematic study of rhythms of motor discharge has been attempted ... (pp. 2–3).

In 1953, Kestenberg undertook a longitudinal[3] study of three newborn infants for the purpose of developing a method of movement notation which would replace the "... impressionistic descriptions of nonverbal transactions between mothers and infants" (Kestenberg, 1975, p. xviii). Initially, she watched the babies move and began to move with them, translating observed changes in muscle tension into her own body and then onto paper in tracings which resembled electrocardiograms. While she recognized that the tracing captured some aspect of movement, she had no theoretical framework with which to interpret the lines.

At this point, the dancer, Maria Piscator, recommended that Kestenberg study Rudolf Laban's Effort/Shape system with Laban's students, Irmgard Bartenieff in New York and Warren Lamb in London. Effort/Shape offered not only clear symbols with which to notate, but also a structured way of looking at movements.

Rudolf Laban was intrigued by observations of patterns of movement employed in work. His understanding of the relationship of movement to space, weight, and time (i.e., efforts) evolved from a program he developed in Europe which trained workers to approach their tasks more effectively, given their particular movement styles (North, 1972). Laban connected preferences for certain movement patterns with specific ways of thinking and acting. For example, he suggested that people who use an abundance of deceleration[4] tend to approach tasks with measured consideration. As Laban (1960) pointed out, we can see "... in other people's movements what they feel and even how they think..." (p. 115). The richness of Laban's work, and the applicability of it to work with children, struck Kestenberg like lightning (in the language of efforts: direct, strong, accelerated).

In 1962 in Sands Point, New York, the Sands Point Movement Study Group (Hershey Marcus, Jay Berlowe, Arnhilt Buelte, Martha Soodak, Ester Robbins and Judith Kestenberg) began working with a vast array of movement specialists including Irmgard Bartenieff, Warren Lamb, Forrestine Paulay, Marion North, Jody Zacharias, Islene Pinder, among others. Their study focused on the work of Laban and Lamb and extended their applications into the realm of child development. Lamb, a student of Laban, not only enriched the group's knowledge of Laban's work, but also introduced them to his own formulations of effort-shape correspondence, flow, and posture. Originally, it was Lamb who identified the free hand tracings that Kestenberg drew as changes in muscle tension rather than changes in efforts as Kestenberg originally believed.

It took many years of collaboration to complete work on the format of the KMP. Along the way, many researchers in the field of psychoanalysis left their imprint on the theoretical underpinnings of the KMP, e.g. Anna Freud (1965), Winnicott (1965), Hartmann (1939), Spitz (1950), Erikson (1950), and Mahler (Mahler, Pine and Bergman, 1974). Over the course of later years, Kestenberg thoughtfully compared and contrasted her evolving works to those of many others, including Phyllis Greenacre, Heinz Kohut, Margaret Mead, and more recent infant researchers and theorists such as Daniel Stern. Her interest in determining the universality of her observations led her to consult with Mead who agreed that a gradual swaying rhythm, common in nagging, typified women in many cultures.[5]

Before presenting the profile to a larger audience the Study Group sought verification of the validity of the use of movement observation to create a psychological profile of a mover. In 1965 Kestenberg visited the Hampstead Nursery in London directed by Anna Freud. She observed and notated children attending the nursery and constructed KMPs. Comparing these profiles with Anna Freud's developmental assessments of the same children revealed significant correspondence between Anna Freud's clinical data and Kestenberg's movement-based data.

In succeeding years, Kestenberg worked to collect more data for the establishment of developmental norms and further corroboration of the interpretative scheme. In 1969 and 1970 she visited several Israeli kibbutzim, notating the movement patterns of over one hundred and fifty infants and children. The Sands Point Movement Study Group also visited the newborn nursery and the well baby clinic of Long Island Jewish Hospital and the Merklee Nursery in Port Washington, NY. In 1972, The Center for Parents and Children (CDR), a research-oriented, primary prevention center for children birth to four years and their parents, was founded to provide further research opportunities.[6] Kestenberg and her colleagues applied concepts based on their Movement Profiles to all family members in their methods of prevention and interventions with parents and children.

Kestenberg and her colleagues continue to encourage further research and integration of materials from the work of other students of development and movement. In this volume, several authors describe the ways in which the KMP can be integrated with other perspectives. For example, Loman, Ender, and Burden discuss the ways in which the Body–Mind Centering approach can compare with and enrich the KMP. Lewis integrates Jungian and Recovery theory into a clinical interpretation of the KMP. Loman and Merman discuss how dance/movement therapists can use the KMP as a tool for movement assessment and intervention. In an earlier volume on the KMP, Martha Eddy (1992), the developer of Body–Mind Dancing, reports on the use of the KMP in her approach:

It [the KMP] reveals richer details of rhythm, movement patterns, group interactions and emotional expression. My students say that working with KMP imagery is emotionally involving, fun and meaningful and stimulates the natural developmental flow of movement (p. 208).

Since the 1960's there have been many new developments and refinements of the KMP based on a body of research that is rich in case study material. Hundreds of children and adults have been profiled. In an on-going project, developmental and gender-based norms are being derived from collected profiles, and new applications are evolving. Recently there has been an attempt to simplify the methodology and terminology of the Profile. Nava Lotan has created a computer program to simplify the mathematics and plot the diagrams of the KMP. It is available, via the internet, on the KMP home page[7] (Lotan and Tziperman, 1996).

Psychologists, dance/movement therapists, educators, anthropologists, and others who do not work within the theoretical framework of psychoanalysis have been discovering that movement data can be evaluated and interpreted either developmentally or in relation to other research questions. In order to facilitate the use of the KMP with a variety of different theoretical frameworks, most of the original Freudian terms have recently been replaced with movement descriptors, though the names for development phases have been retained. Those who use psychodynamic models and interpretations may still use the original terminology.

## The KMP Within the Spectrum of Other Current Work

There is considerable diversity among perspectives in the study of nonverbal behavior. How does the KMP fall within this varied spectrum? It shares an interest in the application of mind/body linkages to therapeutic goals with the neuroscientist/psychoanalytical researchers and dance/movement therapists. While many in the field of psychoanalysis have moved away from the study of the nonverbal, currently a few clinicians and theorists are attempting to synthesize psychoanalysis and neuroscience (e.g. Levin, 1991). In doing so they are returning to an historically earlier interest in the nonverbal.

Neuroscience may once again offer the impetus. In acknowledging the relevance of unconscious emotional processing in everyday life, the neuroscientist LeDoux (1996) commented:

... we may not have a very accurate picture of the sophistication of unconscious processing. Most of the work done so far has used verbal stimuli to analyze conceptual processing, but the unconscious mind may work more fluently in nonverbal modalities [my emphasis] (p. 312).

Gedo (1991), in his preface to Levin's book wrote:

In psychoanalysis, as in all of life, the verbal and nonverbal realms are closely linked ... therapeutic success is more fundamentally dependent on the nonverbal components of the transaction than on its lexical content (p. xviii).

Neuroscience has the potential to further elaborate on and substantiate the mind/body connections found through clinical practice and movement observation. Particular focus on the body aspect of the mind/body link is seen in Kestenberg's (1975) investigation of the correlations of psychic organization in adolescence (phases of growth, differentiation, and consolidation), with anatomic and neurohormonal changes. Bonnie Bainbridge Cohen's (1989) Body–Mind Centering work also takes the investigator further into physiological processes in her study of reflexes and cellular level functioning. Such studies are setting a framework for the reintegration of specialized disciplines and interests which have undercut the understanding of mind/body linkages.

Dance/movement therapists share the Laban-anchored "movement language" perspective with the KMP, the focus on coding elementary qualities of movement, and therapeutic goals. They are attracted to the developmental focus of the KMP and its heightened differentiation of movement qualities. Warren Lamb (Movement Pattern Analysis) and Action Profilers both use such language to assess capacities of professionals for industry and personal evaluation (Lamb and Watson, 1987; Ramsden 1973). The KMP can benefit from their attention to issues of methodology and reliability.

While the KMP has been applied primarily for the purposes of individual assessment, many students of the nonverbal focus on interpersonal interaction. Scheflen's (1973) "context analysis" was notable for the way in which it codes key features of the movements of therapist and patient. Following on this work, Martha Davis (1983) and colleagues are developing nonverbal coding systems for use in therapy contexts as well as primary research. Applying the Davis Nonverbal States Scales (DNSS) (e.g. Davis and Hadiks, 1990), and then the Nonverbal Interaction and States Analysis (NISA) (Davis and Hadiks, 1994) to studying patient-therapist interaction and attunement, investigators have found "... support for the assumption that body movement patterns are physical manifestations of intrapsychic and relational processes." (p. 403). Using "signature analysis," Davis (1995) has extended such sophisticated movement analysis into the research of credibility and political presentation.

Many nonverbal researchers in fields such as psychology, communications, and ethology, focus primarily on the communicative or "display" role of the nonverbal in every day life and less on therapeutic applications. There is a general conception of a universal substrate to nonverbal displays upon which cultural and experiential factors may be laid. This is found both in the biologically-rooted perspective of ethology (Eibl-Eibesfeldt, 1975) using naturalistic conditions, and in the differential-emotion theory perspective of psychology emphasizing universalities in facial expressions (Tomkins, 1962, 1963; Izard, 1977; Ekman, 1977, 1984; Ekman and Friesen, 1975). A similar approach has evolved in developmentally-relevant research focused on adult perceptions of infant affect (Emde, Osofsky and Butterfield, 1993).

The KMP also has centered upon the intrinsic meaning of movement patterns, but linking them primarily to developmental processes and psychological experiences. Its focus has been primarily the intrapersonal, and only secondarily to communication. The distinctiveness of the KMP approach is further evidenced in the vocabulary used to describe movement units and the movement units themselves. In other research into nonverbal behavior, description of appearance changes are often exemplified by "brows drawn down and together" or by "mouth rectangular shaped" (Izard and Dougherty, 1982). Similar descriptors are used in some infant–parent research as well (cf. Beebe and Stern, 1977; Tronick and Cohen, 1989), where the focus is relative attunement and coordination. In contrast, Laban-derived units of study are more elementary than such descriptions, yet not on the microlevel found in some of Ekman's work (e.g. Ekman, 1975).

In sum, the KMP is unique in its inherently developmental layout. Building on Laban's work, it is process oriented. Primarily, it seeks to inform us about dynamics and structure within an individual. Though present application and research has been primarily intrapersonal, new applications may further extend the use of the KMP to explore ongoing patterns of interpersonal interaction. Martha Davis (1984) has discussed the challenge of developing therapeutically relevant and applicable nonverbal research. In Sections 2 and 3 of this book, the reader is offered examples of such efforts by investigators and clinicians of the KMP.

## Issues of Validity and Reliability

### *Validity*

Given the multifaceted nature of the KMP, issues of validity can be raised on many levels. We can question the validity of the KMP as a stand-alone descriptive tool, as a framework for interpreting developmental processes, as a framework for interpreting dynamic processes, and with regard to the significance of each plot-pointed pattern or frequency, of each movement quality. Does each reflect the drive, affect, defensive pattern, learning pattern, adaptational process and/or relational manner that has been ascribed to it over many years of observation and analysis?

The complexity of conducting such validational work is remarkable. Hard data regarding the KMP methodology has lagged behind its conceptual growth and utility in assessment, primary prevention, and clinical application. The original Sands Point Movement Study Group was composed of clinicians and primary-preventionists who saw validation in their experience-near work and confirmed their findings amongst themselves. Kestenberg's own blind comparison of KMPs and their interpretation with Anna Freud's Hempstead Developmental Profiles lent more validation and encouragement. Accelerated in their pursuit, no one had a proclivity for decelerating and doing the more rigorous and tedious validational work required. Although no comprehensive study has been undertaken, there are studies by KMP students and from other related fields which support the validity of some general and specific aspects of the KMP. We are encouraged too because negative findings have so far not emerged.

In general, as we have seen earlier in this introduction, there is considerable support for various forms of mind/body connections and the utility of the nonverbal domain for the understanding of infants and children. Levin (1991) describes information coding and decoding in our brains "... occurring ... outside of our conscious awareness and control and access to that coding lying in the nonverbal domain (p. 151). Numerous studies have indicated that rhythmic "melodies" of interaction, along with expressive facial and body gestures and postures, are especially meaningful and essential in interaction between infant and parent (e.g. Freedman and Fajardo, 1981, see also Chapter 10). After all, the body is the primary vehicle by which the infant relates to her environment and herself.

More specifically, there is considerable support mounting for some of the KMP formulations of correspondences between cognitive processes and body gestures. Rimes (1983) summarized studies that suggest that restricting body movement interferes with a subject's ability to organize and verbalize thoughts. Other studies suggest that movement facilitates the translation of thought into speech by helping the speaker focus on and then symbolize cognitive patterns (Freedman, 1977). Du Nann Winter and colleagues (1989, 1992) found significant correlations between certain movement qualities in the Laban-derived Action Profiling system (Lamb and Watson, 1987) and cognitive styles revealed during verbal communication sessions and the Myers-Briggs test. Support from communication theorists for more specific KMP formulations are described in more detail in Chapter 8. Du Nann Winter (1989) has also demonstrated the validity of the interpretative scheme for movements called "integrated postures" (see Chapters 4 and 9).

Of particular significance, several studies have supported specific lines of developmental sequencing postulated under the KMP (e.g. Blake and Dolgoy, 1993, Zinober and Martlew, 1985). There has been some preliminary work comparing the Kestenberg Movement Profile with other diagnostic tests. In an earlier KMP volume, Ellen Goldman (1990) compared an Action Profile and a KMP profile on the same subject and described their common findings. She noted that there is little discrepancy between the general conclusions on the subject, but that the KMP offers a much wider range of information and thus a direct correspondence cannot readily be detailed. Mark Sossin (1993) compared a KMP with a standard battery of psychological tests and found, similarly, that such different approaches demonstrate interesting parallels. Thus, further studies using psychological tests, such as the Rorschach, may further offer support for KMP validity.

### *Reliability*

Studies of interobserver reliability by users of Laban derived systems such as Action Profiling have met with moderate to good levels of success. Ruttenberg, Kalish, Wenar and Wolf (1975) drew upon Labananalytic principles in the development of a body movement scale of the Behavior Rating Instrument for Autistic and other Atypical Children (BRIAAC). They have shown highly satisfactory interrater reliability (0.85–0.95). Satisfactory reliability (interrater and test-retest) utilizing the Action profile system was also reported by Ramsden (1973, 1982) and Winter (1987). McCoubrey (1984) found good to satisfactory levels of reliability in the observation of efforts, but low interrater reliability in flow factors.

Sossin (1987), working specifically with the KMP, found satisfactory reliability using experienced raters, with correlations per cluster (diagram) ranging from 0.70 to 0.80. However, Burt (1995), working with advanced student raters, found good reliability for shape flow, but low reliability for tension flow. Working with very novice profilers, Koch (1997) found satisfactory levels of interrater reliability on two (tension flow and bipolar shape flow) of three KMP diagrams (and three of the six measures chosen for a preliminary study (1997). She points out that, given the complexity of the KMP, a one semester course is clearly not sufficient to achieve reliability for clinical work. Clearly, there is need for further study and development of improved reliability training.

### The Issue of Context

There has been a basic assumption that individuals use a core movement repertoire that is based on individual personality with its history of previous experiences and impressions. Because of the movement observer's goal to capture such a context-independent portrait, the KMP has historically underplayed the influence of context. However, it is inarguably true that the way we move may be significantly influenced by context. An individual may interact differently with objects than with people, may respond differently in public or private arenas, and may in fact use different movement patterns with men or with women in social interactions.

Bronfenbrenner (1977) criticized developmental psychology when he wrote, "Developmental psychology as it now exists is the science of strange behavior of children in strange situations with strange adults..." (p. 19). Martha Davis, critiquing movement analysts, decried the study of static poses, single body parts, and artificially contrived movements (1984).

The Kestenberg Movement profiler is not limited to controlled laboratory-like settings nor is the mover required to engage in any prescribed movement. Instead, movement can be observed naturalistically at home, outdoors, in a clinical setting or at play. However, profilers face the following dilemma: How can one attend to context while at the same time seek to construct a profile which reflects a core configuration of movement styles minimally influenced by contextual factors? It is hoped that by observing a child engaged in several different activities in a naturalistic way one can extract a cross-context, or relatively context-independent, movement profile.

Therefore, we now suggest that an individual mover be observed in varied activities and preferably in more than one setting. Prior to the beginning of a notation session, the profiler should include a short description of the context and setting of each observation. Moreover we anticipate that future studies will compare movement patterns demonstrated in different contexts. For example we might examine KMPs of individuals in sport, parenting, and work roles specifically to identify which patterns are relatively persistent throughout all contexts.

## Advantages and Disadvantages of the KMP system

The KMP is a nonverbal system which can be used where a mover is preverbal or nonverbal or to complement studies based on verbal responses. It is observation-based and not dependent on self reports. Movement qualities observed are readily quantified and lend themselves to simple statistical analysis (Koch, 1997).

Because the KMP can be used in a naturalistic setting without requiring the mover to undertake any specific tasks or actions, the method is less intrusive. Subjects can be observed and notated live or can be videotaped for more careful scrutiny.

The focus on elementary qualities of movement contributes to the KMP's range of application. Because the terminology describes universal qualities of movement it is applicable across cultural boundaries and with individuals of diverse backgrounds. It does not classify movement according to culturally specific labels though the meanings attributed to movement patterns may be culturally influenced. The study of elementary qualities of movement also permits discovery of subtle variations in meaning and in an individual's style of completing an action. For example, it is often suggested that crossing one's arms closes oneself off or distances oneself from others. Describing a gesture using more elementary qualities would allow us to differentiate individual ways of performing the same action. For example, using a straight arm in a linear movement with high levels of tension in the arm (bound flow) may be distancing, while the use of relaxed (low levels of) tension with a curving arm may have an embracing quality.

However, the same complexity that enriches the KMP also challenges the beginning student. The details which illuminate subtle differences also require careful study. The very breadth and comprehensiveness of the KMP in its variety of movement qualities and interpretations make it more difficult to validate and test in terms of reliability than systems developed within narrower frameworks.

## An Overview of the Profile

### The Structure of the KMP

The Profile is composed of nine diagrams placed on one page (see Figure 1 below). The nine diagrams are arranged to reflect a developmental progression. The diagrams placed at the top of the KMP page are composed of clusters of movement qualities which are present

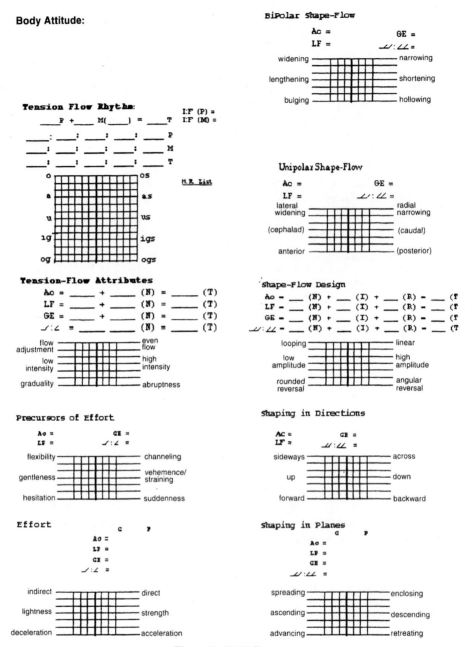

**Figure 1.** KMP Form.

earliest in child development. These movement qualities lay the foundation for the development of later, more mature patterns found further down on the profile page. The diagrams placed at the bottom of the KMP page are composed of movement qualities which are the most mature of those portrayed. Thus, looking from top to bottom, one can trace the development and maturation of specific psychological and movement qualities.

Each diagram itself is designed to show developmental sequencing. The top line of the diagram portrays movement qualities which come to the fore in the first year of life. On the second line of the diagram, those movements which become more prominent in the second year of life are portrayed, and so forth.

On the left side of the profile page are four diagrams of System I documenting a line of development beginning with rhythmic movement patterns available to the fetus and newborn and evolving into more mature patterns relating to environmental challenges.[8] More specifically, System I patterns give a movement portrait of (1) needs, (2) feelings and temperament, (3) defenses, and (4) coping strategies.

On the right side of the profile page are the five diagrams of System II. They document a line of development beginning with movement patterns which reflect and express (1) self feelings, (2) responses to stimuli in the environment, (3) use of designs in space, (4) use of directional movements, and (5) complex relationships with others (Loman, 1990). Movement qualities on the right side of the KMP and the left side of the KMP combine sometimes in harmonious, and at other times in clashing, ways in the service of survival patterns and adaptation.

### The Method of Movement Notation

The KMP uses two distinct types of movement notation. One is based on **Laban Movement Analysis (LMA)**. The KMP uses Laban symbols to represent effort and shape movement qualities following Laban and Lamb. We also use these symbols in modified form to notate a wider range of movement qualities. The system of notation used is explained fully in the KMP Manual. The second type of movement notation is called **flow writing** (referring to the notation of tension-flow and shape-flow-design). To begin tension-flow writing, the notator observes changes in the muscle tension of a mover and then attempts to kinesthetically attune with the mover. Kinesthetic attunement is the process of translating movement qualities observed in another person into one's own body. It is easiest to attune to the muscle tension of another person through the use of physical contact. For example, when shaking someone's hand, one can attune to the other person's grasp, using about the same degree of pressure as the other party. However, one can also "feel" another person's muscle tension through observation. While watching an ice skater fly over the ice, the exhilaration of the skater can be felt kinesthetically and thus shared.

The translation of changes of observed muscle tension into one's own hand and then onto paper requires considerable training and practice. The method consists of drawing a line downward from a midline in correspondence with observed increases in muscle tension (bound flow) and drawing a line upward in correspondence with observed decreases in muscle tension (free flow) (see Figure 2).

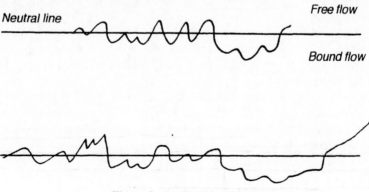

**Figure 2.** Tension Flow Lines.

### *The Qualitative Descriptions*

## I. The Setting

As described earlier in this introduction, the notator should describe the setting, the persons present, and changes which take place over the course of the notation session. Differences in ways of interacting with particular individuals or objects should be noted. Information about the broader context (i.e., cultural background, recent events) should also be included where possible.

## II. The Body Attitude

The Body Attitude includes the characteristic movement qualities of the mover which can be readily detected without formal notation. This includes body alignment and characteristic movement styles (see Chapter 16).

## The Nine Diagrams

The nine diagrams graphically depict the relative frequencies of different movement qualities.

### *Diagram 1. Tension Flow Rhythms*

The flow of muscle tension is inherent in all movement. The rhythmic patterns created by the changes in muscle tension have been identified as **tension flow rhythms**. Most rhythmic movements consist of alternations between what is called **bound** and **free flow**. When the antagonistic muscle tightens and resists the movement of the agonist muscle, movement is restrained or, in KMP terminology, demonstrating bound flow. When the agonists are less restrained by the antagonist or opposing muscle, the movement is unhampered, or demonstrating free flow.

Kestenberg began to discern definite patterns or rhythms of tension flow changes in the free hand tracings she made while observing babies. These rhythmic patterns were not recognizable as patterns when simply observing movements, but were revealed in the free hand tracings. The earliest of such rhythms to be identified was the oral or sucking rhythm. This rhythm was used by small infants not only when sucking milk or pacifiers, but also during other activities such as stroking mother's back while nursing, vocalizing, or soothing themselves to sleep. Nine more rhythms also associated with biological functions were later identified. The ten rhythms are: **sucking**, **snapping/biting**, **twisting**, **strain/ release**, **running/drifting**, **starting/stopping**, **swaying**, **surging/birthing**, **jumping**, and **spurting/ramming**.

Although all ten of these rhythms are present from birth or even before birth, as development progresses particular rhythms tend to become more predominant. For example, during the first half of the first year, the sucking rhythm becomes clearly defined and prominent. As teething begins during the second half of the first year, the child bites and chews on hard surfaces to relieve the pain, and snapping/biting rhythms become more prominent. Preferences for particular rhythms reveal preoccupation with particular needs. For example, individuals with a frequent use of biting rhythms often enjoy taking in and biting down on crunchy foods. Associated with this predilection one often finds a person who enjoys taking in new knowledge or ideas, but tends to view things critically or sarcastically. Such a person tends to make "biting" comments.

Thus, the pattern of rhythms used reflects stage of development (in small children) and dominant needs throughout life. However, in all typical children and adults all the rhythms are present, reflecting the universal presence of biological functions such as sucking, biting, defecating, and urinating. Our interpretations are based on the relative frequency of use of specific movement patterns and examination of the overall configurations found.

### Diagram 2. Tension Flow Attributes

Kestenberg and the Sands Point Movement Study Group (1975) discovered that they could identify not only rhythmic patterns, but also particular attributes in the line tracings. There might be a segment which is entirely **even** or one which has little **flow adjustments**. The lines may be drawn far away from the neutral line, indicating **high intensity** muscle tension or may be drawn close to the neutral line, indicating **low intensity**. The change in intensity may be **abrupt** or **gradual**. While all these qualities are normally present, some are usually more pronounced than others. Each of these six attributes reflects qualities of emotions or affects. As a whole, this configuration reflects individual temperament. For example, some people use a lot of abruptness and may disconcert others who are more comfortable doing things in a gradual manner. A gradual person may be very taken aback by someone who departs abruptly, while the latter might be irritated with prolonged, gradual goodbyes. One may be able to characterize a person as generally low intensity (calm) and on an even keel (rarely changing levels of emotional expression). When moods change, they do so gradually. These movement attributes underlie the core of temperament and tend to persist throughout one's life (Kestenberg, 1975).

In addition to the six attributes of tension flow listed above, quantities of bound and free flow are also included statistically in the diagram. These flow factors are scored separately in **animated** and in **neutral flow**. Bound flow, as discussed above, refers to movements which are restrained. Free flow refers to movements which are relatively unrestrained. Neutral flow pertains to movement which has lost elasticity and tone in comparison with animated flow, which describes the flow of muscles which have greater elasticity and tone.

What do these tension flow changes represent psychologically? Bound flow is frequently associated with caution, anxiety, or anger whereas free flow is often associated with feeling safe, carefree, and at ease. The ratio of the free to bound movements used by individuals offers an indication of how restrained or how unrestrained they are. Too much restraint inhibits functioning. Too much free flow signals a deficiency in control. A fairly even balance is the most desired ratio.

What is neutral flow? Neutral flow was discovered in the process of scoring tension flow. It was found that tension flow levels of some movements are of so low intensity that they barely rise above or fall below the midline (or neutral line) of the graph. Such neutral flow is associated with a state of deanimation found in people who are very tired, depressed, or undertaking very repetitive mechanical tasks. When found in high proportions, neutral flow is indicative of disordered states of mind. Sometimes we find neutral flow in one part of a person's body only, such as the face, which appears vacant—empty of feeling or thought.

Bound flow, free flow, and neutral flow are amongst the earliest types of regulations and defenses that a baby can use. Bound flow may freeze motion (being cautious), free flow is used for flight, and neutral flow deadens feelings and movement (e.g., playing dead). In sum, tension flow rhythms and attributes are among the earliest types of movement patterns found in newborns. Rhythms are the expressions of needs and attributes reveal affects or emotions.

### *Diagram 3. Pre-Efforts*

Following Laban's work, Kestenberg and associates observed movements which could be identified as efforts, which are movements which deal with space, weight, and time. They found that infants moved in ways reminiscent of efforts (North [1972], called them early efforts), but which seemed to have important differences from efforts. For example, "strength" in Laban terms deals with the conquest of weight. Infants generally cannot use strength, but they may attempt to move an object. How do they do it?

It was discovered that during processes of learning, and often in anxiety provoking circumstances, a mover becomes inwardly oriented and relies on tension flow attributes to accomplish tasks rather than directly dealing with space, weight, and time (Kestenberg, 1975). For example, children attempting to move heavy objects might tense their muscles with high intensity bound flow (straining). These children will make little impact on weight because so much energy is bound up in the contracting muscles. To highlight its role as a precursor of strength we call straining a "precursor of effort" or a **pre-effort**. There are six pre-efforts: **channeling** and **flexibility**, **straining/vehemence**[9] (pre-effort of strength), and **gentleness, suddenness** and **hesitation**.

Pre-efforts are helpful in the learning stage. However, once an activity is learned, efforts themselves should emerge. Over dependence on pre-efforts renders actions less effective.

Pre-efforts are also used as defenses against impulses. The three indulging pre-efforts counterbalance the three fighting pre-efforts. In order to prevent giving in to distractions, one may *channel* one's attention. In order to avoid sticking to an unpleasant task or feeling, one may turn away with *flexibility*. In order to overcome one's fear of an aggressor, one may become *vehement*, putting on a tough front. To control one's aggressive impulses, one might use *gentleness*, being especially careful not to hurt. When one is afraid to enter the doctor's office, one may, instead of moving with acceleration into the office, jump in *suddenly* to overcome fear. To defend against impulsivity, one may delay by *hesitating*.

### *Diagram 4. Efforts*

The study of efforts reveals more effective and mature ways of coping with the forces of space, weight, and time. Laban identified six different approaches or attitudes towards the environment (i.e., space, weight, and time). One can use space **directly** or **indirectly**. Weight can be approached with **strength** or **lightness**. The passage of time can be fought with **acceleration** or indulged in with **deceleration**.

Not only are these six efforts used in physical tasks, but in cognitive tasks as well. A person using lightness will touch lightly on topics, while someone using a lot of strength will tend to delve more deeply and decisively into a topic.

These four diagrams (rhythms, attributes, pre-efforts, and efforts) form a developmental sequence. They are all dynamic patterns which arise from changing forces within the individual.

## SYSTEM II: THE RIGHT SIDE OF THE PROFILE: RELATIONAL DEVELOPMENT

The diagrams on the right side of the profile (System II) show the frequency of movement qualities which reflect self feelings and relationships to others. System II also provides the form and structure for the dynamic movement qualities in System I.

### Diagram 5: BIPOLAR SHAPE FLOW

**Bipolar shape flow** refers to patterns of growing or shrinking in a symmetrical fashion. The shape of the body grows and shrinks with breathing. Growing shapes are ways of opening up and generally reflect good feelings or feelings of comfort. Shrinking shapes are ways of closing oneself off and generally reflect feelings of discomfort. We grow and shrink in three dimensions: the **horizontal**, **vertical**, and **sagittal**. In the horizontal, one can **widen** (open) to take in the world; bask in the warm sun, feel generous or expansive or one can **narrow** (close) to shut out the world; respond to coldness, discomfort, or constriction of space; or express self-containment. In the vertical, one can **lengthen** or **shorten**. In the sagittal one can **bulge** or **hollow**.

We often evaluate the feelings of others on the basis of their bipolar shape changes, particularly in the face, but in the torso as well. A smile is produced by bipolar widening; a worried look or frown by bipolar narrowing.

Growing and shrinking are used in internal body processes, such as breathing, or in response to the outer world, such an infant's curling up and stretching out. Growing and shrinking in a caregiver's supporting arms helps develop a sense of trust.

As in all other movements, we like to see a balance. It is not only necessary to be able to grow and express comfort and pleasure, but it is also important to be able to shrink to express discomfort and attract the nurturance of others.

### Diagram 6: Unipolar Shape Flow

**Unipolar shape flow** movements are asymmetric and grow and shrink toward one direction or dimension rather than toward two. They are made in response to specific stimuli. We lean on a friend (widening), we reach towards a desired object (lengthening), or bulge back into mother's lap. In response to negative stimuli, we shrink away, by narrowing, shortening, and/or hollowing.

Bipolar and unipolar shape flow follow a developmental sequence. From the global qualities of growing and shrinking emerge more specific responses to people and objects in the environment. Infants are born with a tendency to grow toward an attractive stimulus and shrink way from a noxious one. Rather than just feeling generalized comfort or discomfort, unipolar responses involve feelings related to specific things in the environment.

### Diagram 7: Shape Flow Design

**Shape flow design** focuses on the way movements create designs in space moving away from the body (centrifugally) and toward the body (centripetally). This system of notation was created by Kestenberg and Paulay while Paulay was working with Lomax and Bartenieff on their choreometric study of ethnic groups (Lomax, Bartenieff and Paulay, 1967). Through Paulay's influence, it was recognized how strongly shape flow design is affected by cultural differences. However, it also reflects individual preferences seen from birth on.

Within personal space, movements may be in a **near**, **reach**, or **intermediate** space. Outside of reach space movements enter general space. These movements reflect sociopsychological definitions of space that are often culturally specific.

There is a typical developmental progression from the primary use of near space in infants, to the use of intermediate space in latency children to the focus on reach space among adolescents.

One also notates whether the movement proceeds in **lines** or in **loops**, with **high** or **low** **amplitude**, and with **angular** or **rounded reversals** (Kestenberg and Sossin, 1979). Shape flow design is notated using free hand tracings as with tension flow. To date, interobserver reliability is low because of the difficulty of capturing three-dimensional movement on a two-dimensional flow line. We therefore do not use this diagram on a regular basis.

### Diagram 8: Shaping in Directions

Evolved from growing and shrinking movements, directions help children locate objects in space. An infant may bulge toward mother; a more mature child may point to her, locating her in space directionally.

**Directional movements** are movements which trace lines in space. They not only locate people and objects, but are also used in learning new skills and in defending against people and objects. For example, a student may close herself off from distractions by bringing one arm across her body in front of herself. There are six directions notated: **sideways** and **across**, **up** and **down**, and **forward** and **backward**.

### Diagram 9: Shaping in Planes

Students of Laban are familiar with **shaping in planes**, which derives from Laban and Lamb's work (Lamb and Watson, 1987). Shaping movements carve space in a multidimensional fashion traversing one or more planes. The shape that is carved through space reflects complex relationships between people.

Using the horizontal plane ("table" plane) one may **spread** one's arms, inviting and including many people, or one may **enclose** a few people, keeping the space more closed and confined. In the first year, the infant uses all planes but focuses on the horizontal, enclosing space for a focused exploration, or spreading to open up to diverse places and things. Movements in the horizontal plane facilitate exploration.

The vertical plane ("door" plane) is the plane for presentation and confrontation. With **ascending** movements one can present ideas, objects, hopes, and aspirations. With **descending** movements one can confront others, demand explanations, or challenge them. The toddler in the second year confronts people with his or her demands for autonomy or climbs up and down picking up things and presenting them for approval or explanation.

The sagittal plane ("wheel" plane) is the plane for anticipation. **Retreating** is used for withdrawal from a situation or a relationship. **Advancing** is used to engage in a relationship or situation. Children in the third year practice advancing and retreating. When they play ball, they are able to anticipate the movements of the ball, retreating or advancing towards its path.

Observing how shaping in planes is used, we come to understand more about the ways a person relates to other people. Looking back at the diagrams of the right side of the profile, we see a pattern of maturation, from the use of bipolar shape flow to unipolar shape flow to directions and finally to shaping in planes.

## Postural Movements

All of the movements described above are **gestural** movements. This means that the movement occurs in parts of the body rather than as a movement in which the whole body participates in unison. **Postural** movements imply total emotional, cognitive, and psychological commitment to a concept or behavior. They have received considerable attention by Action Profilers and Movement Pattern Analysts in particular (Lamb, 1965). They are also considered in the KMP.

### Matching and Mismatching: Clashes and Affinities

Although we interpret movement qualities individually, it must be recognized that these interpretations are very preliminary. A proper interpretation requires evaluation of configurations rather than of individual movement qualities.

Each diagram offers a configuration showing the relative frequency of movement qualities in one category of movement. For example, within efforts, we can compare the frequency of the use of strength versus lightness or how well the fighting qualities are balanced by the indulging qualities.

We can look at the KMP developmentally, tracing the progression from tension flow attributes to pre-efforts to efforts, for example.

We can also evaluate the match between related diagrams in Systems I and II. Diagrams in System I are associated with affined diagrams in System II which are located horizontally across. Thus tension flow attributes (Diagram 2) are structured by and closely related to unipolar shape flow. The movement qualities of System I and System II work together in patterns of survival and adaptation. When qualities which are matched or **affined** are combined this reflects a well integrated response. When qualities which are mismatched (**clashing**) are combined this either reflects underlying conflicts or creates conflicting feelings. When clashing combinations are used habitually, they may come to feel natural.

Finally, the profile as a whole must be interpreted.

### Conclusion

By studying the Kestenberg Movement Profile one learns to observe and notate[10] basic qualities of movement and understand their psychological, cognitive, and emotional correlates. Following the exercises in the text, the reader becomes familiar with movement by moving as well as by reading about movement. Gradually, the eye and the rest of the body become trained to be aware of (observe/feel) many qualities of movement.

The intention of this overview has been to intrigue the reader to learn more and continue on to the following chapters. The next nine chapters will elaborate each of the points raised in the overview, offer more examples, and clarify ideas. We will discuss aspects of child development as related to each of the movement qualities and we will also devote more space to general movement-based interpretations. Where data exists, cross-cultural comparisons are also offered.

### Notes

1. Various numbers have been given in other publications. The exact number of movement qualities or components measured in the KMP varies depending on whether one includes only the qualities which are in the frequency diagrams or whether one includes a number of other qualities described but not diagramed. If one also includes ratios which are used as part of the interpretative scheme, over one hundred aspects of

movement are included in the KMP. Any one movement can be described in terms of at least 28 facets or qualities of that one movement.

2.  Laban (1960) described the alternation of mobility and stability in movement. The Sands Point Movement Study Group found that this alternating pattern also reflected the process of development. (cf. Kestenberg, Buette, 1983).

3.  This study was conducted with three newborn babies, one African-American and two white.

4.  "Deceleration" and "acceleration" are KMP terms. Laban used the terms "sustained" and "quick." KMP has kept most Laban terms, but has made a few changes which will be noted when they occur.

5.  Margaret Mead and Gregory Bateson had developed study of body language in their early work in Bali (1949), and so Mead was intrigued with Kestenberg's interest in movement as a reflection of both cultural universals and cultural influences. Later, Kestenberg discovered that such "swaying" rhythms typify three year olds, both boys and girls (1975).

6.  The Center ran from 1972 to 1990. It was co-directed by Judith Kestenberg and Arnhilte Buelte.

7.  The internet address of the KMP home page is
    http://www.weiemann.ac.il/ESER/people/Eli/KMP/home.html

8.  Fetal rhythms have been collected by pregnant mothers in research conducted at the Center (Loman, 1992).

9.  Vehemence is based on high intensity free flow while straining is based on high intensity bound flow. Since this is their only difference, and they are both pre-efforts of strength, they are counted as one pre-effort for diagraming purposes.

10. The system of notation is explained in greater detail in the Kestenberg Movement Profile Manual (Berlowe, Kestenberg, *et al.*, 1995).

# SECTION I

# CHAPTER 1

# Tension Flow Rhythms

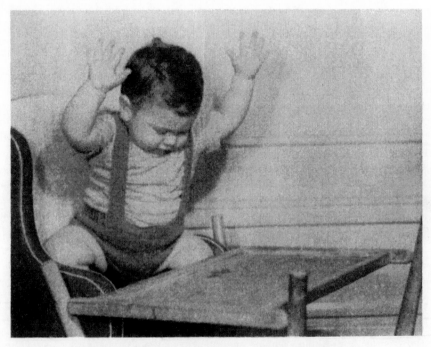

The boy is using "outer genital rhythm" with his upper body.

Movement is everywhere. A bouncy walk and smiling lips or a sunken chest and downcast eyes all give the observer material for interpretation. Changing levels of muscle tension are ever-present movement qualities which can be quite revealing. Observers often rely on tension flow changes to get a general "feel" for the other. Putting a hand on someone's shoulder one may sense their anxiety or ease. Watching a person tighten up in pain, an observer may "feel" what the sufferer feels.

Muscles can tense or relax in broad rhythms of change which are discernible in other human beings. When one child eagerly crunches a piece of candy and another one languidly licks it, they create distinct rhythmic patterns of muscle tension change. Based on these rhythms, onlookers often make judgments such as, "he's a greedy child" or "she's taking her time, nothing can faze her."

Through the use of the KMP system, observers can attune to movers, notate their movements, and then analyze large as well as minute fluctuations in muscle tension. These tension flow rhythms offer an important avenue for understanding development and personality. Kestenberg and associates have used the knowledge gained from observing tension flow patterns in children to modify and elaborate on our understanding of child development.

Tension flow rhythms comprise the first movement category or diagram of nine diagrams within the Kestenberg Movement Profile. In the course of describing the ten tension flow rhythms that comprise Diagram 1, we introduce the reader to the basic components of rhythms (free, bound, and neutral flow) and to phases of child development as seen from a movement perspective. In each phase of development, movement plays an important role both in shaping and reflecting psycho-social changes. This chapter sets forth an understanding of development as informed by movement study and by Anna Freud's developmental theory. Interwoven into the discussion of development from birth to six years of age which follows, the reader will find short sections on parent–child attunement and clashing, father–child relations, and other related topics.

## The Components of Tension Flow Rhythms

Periodic alternations in muscle tension create discernible patterns called **tension flow rhythms**. Very simple repetitive rhythms used in hammering, rocking back and forth, tapping a foot impatiently, or jumping up and down to a drum beat can be easily observed and kinesthetically felt. They can be notated by an observer using tension flow writing system developed by the Sands Point Movement Study Group. Kestenberg and her colleagues discovered that particular tension flow rhythms typically emanate from specific biological zones and are adaptively associated with specific biological functions. For example, a sucking rhythm originates in the mouth and is suited to ingestion of soft foods. These rhythms appear to spread from the zone of origin and become used for various other functions throughout life, i.e., the sucking rhythm can often be seen in self-soothing rocking and caressing movements. The strain/release rhythm originates in the anal sphincter and supports defecation. It also can be seen in throwing a ball, rising with difficulty, or holding onto a secret. The constellation of tension flow rhythms an individual uses reflects his or her predominant needs as well as the influence of developmental phase and external environment. In an adult, the deficit of a particular rhythmic pattern may reflect early traumas, the influence of a caregiver, or other events which led to the avoidance of a need-satisfying pattern. For example, an infant who experiences a consistently disturbing nursing environment may not develop a well-structured oral rhythm, integral to self-soothing abilities in later life. The study of tension flow rhythms offers a unique pathway into the understanding and assessment of development and personality.

### The Basic Components of Tension Flow: Free and Bound Flow

"A feeling of ease and its polarity, a feeling of unease, are the simplest affective patterns representing the basic dichotomy between life-giving and aggressive drives" (Kestenberg and Sossin, 1979, p. 32).

Tension flow rhythms are created by patterned changes in muscle tension, or alternation between two basic elements of movement: free and bound flow. When an agonist muscle contracts it initiates movement: an arm swings forward during ambulation or a child runs forward. The agonist[1] muscle moves the body with little opposition and thus the movement flows easily or freely, with an accompanying pleasant feeling in the release of movement. Such fairly unrestrained movements use the quality of **free tension flow**. For each agonist muscle there is a paired antagonist muscle which contracts, limiting the action of the agonist. The greater the contraction of the antagonist, the more the movement is restrained. With the contraction of the antagonist muscles, the swing of the arm slows or stops; the child may freeze in place. There is an accompanying feeling of inhibition and constraint. Such restrained movements use the quality of **bound tension flow** (Kestenberg and Sossin, 1979).

With a high degree of free flow (minimal contraction of the antagonist muscles) movement becomes uncontrolled, leading a small child to swing wildly, fall over, or smash into something. With a high degree of bound flow (strong contraction of the antagonist muscles), motion is immobilized (Kestenberg, 1967). The controlled movement used to pick up a vase, for example, generally employs more moderate levels of bound tension flow.

Many everyday movements such as walking, hammering, sucking, and breathing consist of rhythmic alternations of bound and free flow. These movements reflect the importance of both mobilization of motion and control. The changes in tension flow from free to bound which typify rhythmic movement are notated as displayed in Figure 2 (see Introduction). The observer with pen in hand kinesthetically attunes with a mover, allowing her hand to rise above the middle line as tension flow of the mover becomes more free and move downward as the tension flow of the mover becomes more bound.

### Animated Versus Neutral Flow

**Animated** movements range from high to low levels of intensity of bound and freeflow reflecting the elastic nature of living tissue. A person who uses animated flow looks alive and reasonably alert. However, sometimes people use movements which have only minimal changes of bound and free flow. The mover appears inanimate, either limp like a rag doll or stiff like a robot. This quality of movement with reduced elasticity is called **neutral flow**. People tend to use neutral flow when they are exhausted, depressed, or engaged in routine "mindless" tasks. It is easiest to recognize neutral flow in facial expressions. An individual may appear dazed, "out of it," or unfocused. This is because neutral flow reflects an absence of vitality and a numbing of emotions and thoughts.

### Rhythmic Patterns

The changes from free to bound to free, etc., often fall into rhythmic patterns. Jumping, walking, chewing, patting, wringing the hands, and many other activities are formed by rhythmic alternations of bound and free flow. The rhythms differ in intensity, duration, and uniformity of level (curvature). A jumping rhythm generally uses high intensity and has short duration, while a swaying rhythm is of long duration with less intensity. Ten rhythmic patterns associated with specific biological functions and developmental phases have been identified. Their roles and relationships to each phase will be discussed below.[2]

### Rhythms and Development: The Biological Origin of Rhythms

An infant is born with a large variety of rhythmic patterns. As biological functioning and associated zones develop and mature they organize and enhance the use of specific rhythmic patterns. These rhythms spread from the zone of origin to other parts of the body, creating a constellation of associated behaviors typical of each phase of development. For example, the sucking rhythm of infants spreads from their mouths (the oral zone) to their hands, which caress the nursing mother in the same self-soothing pattern. This caress serves not only to stimulate the flow of milk, but also to reinforce the feeling of mutuality with mother initiated by nursing. Likewise, the twisting contractions of the anal sphincter (anal zone) in the one-year-old spread twisting rhythms to the whole pelvis area, hands, and face. This facilitates crawling, climbing, and the playful teasing characteristic of many one-year-olds (see Table 2 below for specific biological correlates).

Specific rhythmic patterns can pervade not only the voluntary musculature, but also involuntary functioning, enhancing the body/mind synthesis. Both voluntary and involuntary functioning are regulated and coordinated by the hypothalamus. The hypothalamus not only regulates the rhythmicity of organs, zones, and body systems, but also the secretion of hormones. This explains the correlation between secretory and motor rhythms as seen, for example, in the interrelation of adrenaline secretion and a vigorous motor discharge. A co-functioning of voluntary and involuntary muscle systems is also exemplified in the interaction between eating and gastric contractions (Kestenberg, 1975; Bainbridge Cohen, 1989; see also Chapter 13). The constellations of behaviors (voluntary and involuntary) and emotional qualities (soothing, playful) are the ingredients of each developmental phase and are interrelated with each other through their shared rhythmic pattern.

This developmental scheme focuses on the biological zones and associated rhythmic patterns as they mature and become predominant in each phase. However, biological zones, rhythms, and developmental tasks are not restricted to specific phases of development; they are present and relevant to all phases of life (see also Stern, 1985). For example, self-soothing rhythms may be dominant in the first few months of life, but they continue and are used throughout life. It is useful to see both the continuities and the predicted preferences specific to each phase. This chapter focuses on the issues and modes of coping which tend to come to the fore during each phase of development.

## Phases in Development

Elaborating on the Freudian theory of development, the KMP scheme delineates five developmental phases based on maturing biological zones, psychological constellations, and rhythmic patterns found in the first six years of life. They are the oral, anal, urethral, inner genital, and outer genital (phallic) phases of development (see Diagram 1).

Each of these phases has two subphases consisting of indulging and fighting rhythms as shown in Table 1 and in Diagram 1.

The first, an **indulging** subphase, is based on rhythms which have an indulging, accommodating, mobilizing quality. The second, a **fighting** subphase, is based on rhythms which are more aggressive and differentiating. They support the consolidation of gains. In each subphase an individual typically (1) has an associated body attitude[3] or typical way of holding herself and moving, (2) focuses on specific developmental tasks, (3) uses associated rhythmic patterns, and (4) has associated cognitive and emotional attitudes.

Two phases, the urethral and inner genital phases, were identified by the KMP group based on movement observation. Today the KMP still uses Freudian terminology to refer to phases, but refers to phase-associated rhythms with simple movement terms.[4] However, the KMP is not bound to any specific theoretical framework and can be used as a survey of movement patterns organized along developmental lines.

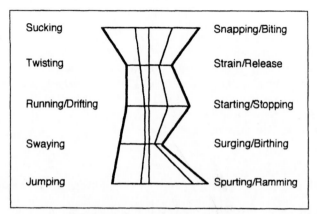

**Diagram 1.** Tension Flow Rhythms

**Table 1** Tension Flow Rhythms.

| Phase | Indulging Rhythms | Fighting Rhythms |
|---|---|---|
| Oral | Sucking | Snapping/Biting |
| Anal | Twisting | Strain/Release |
| Urethral | Running/Drifting | Starting/Stopping |
| Inner Genital | Swaying | Surging/Birthing |
| Outer Genital | Jumping | Spurting/Ramming |

## The Ten Rhythms and Their Developmental Phases

### Early Semi-Rhythmic Patterns

#### Prenatal Life

Until recently the fetus had been depicted as a passive life form. However, there is now evidence that by six months of gestation the fetus can see, hear, taste, dream, and even learn *in utero* (Verney, 1981; Emde, 1981). The fact that the fetus can interact with its environment suggests that communication with it is possible, and that the behavior and feelings of expectant mothers and possibly fathers can affect their unborn children. Many cultures have long recognized such early parental influences. For example, many Iranians believe that if a mother is frightened, her fetus will be adversely affected. Some people, such as the Yanomamo (Lizot, 1986) and the Mundurucu of Brazil (Murphy and Murphy, 1985) believe that fathers' behavior may also affect the unborn fetus. Fathers are therefore subject to food and/or behavioral taboos while their wives are pregnant. Such customs, termed *couvade*, aid in paternal bonding and underscore the importance of paternal roles (Broude, 1988).

Kestenberg and Loman (1992) have observed that fetal movements fall into semi-rhythmic patterns which can be discerned by mothers, fathers, and others. Through attending to these rhythms one can come to know and attune to the baby before birth. One can also engage in elementary forms of communication through gentle pressure on the mother's abdomen which often elicits a response (parent–fetal interactive play). However, no distinct rhythms patterns have been identified as characteristic of the prenatal phase.

## The Neonate

When babies are born they are obviously no stranger to movement. The infant exhibits all of the basic KMP rhythmic qualities, though these movements are not clearly organized into pure rhythmic patterns. Patterns may be mixed, interrupted, and disrupted by outside stimuli. As neonates move in response to stimuli, their own movements serve as new stimuli because they do not yet fully differentiate between themselves and the outside world. The developmental task of the neonate is to integrate the various disorganized rhythmic segments into functionally adaptive forms.

## The Sucking Rhythm (o) in the Oral Indulging Phase[5]

Although all rhythms are present in the developing infant, the indulging **sucking** rhythm generally predominates in the first five or six months of life. The oral cavity, the lips, the inside of cheeks, and the tongue are all sources of pleasurable sensations for infants. They seek their mother's nipple with their mouths. Later other objects (or their own fists) are sucked and mouthed as non-nutritive sources of pleasure. Hands learn to explore in the mouth and then extend to explore outside spaces. Eyes also explore (Kestenberg, 1975). Pacifiers, fingers, toys, blankets, etc., all serve as pleasurable oral objects (Loman, 1994).

The sucking rhythm (originating in the oral zone) spreads to the whole alimentary system via the peristaltic rhythm. This rhythm spreads further, pervading all parts of the body, particularly peripheral parts such as fingers and toes. All body parts seem ready to assist in the functioning of digestion and the related processes of incorporation (Kestenberg, 1967).

The sucking rhythm consists of a smooth alternation of free flow and bound flow as depicted in Figure 3. It is never abrupt in its pure form. It tends to occur in a series of monotonous repetitions like a heart beat.

It begins as a reflex action which only gradually comes under conscious control. While still *in utero*, infants became familiar with the sucking rhythm through hearing and feeling the rhythmic heart beat of the mother and through use of the sucking reflex. This steady, smooth, repetitive rhythm, with neither high nor low intensity, has a calming, almost hypnotic effect.

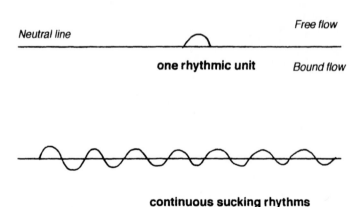

**continuous sucking rhythms**

**Figure 3.** The Sucking Rhythm.

---

**Exercise**

Try sucking on a piece of candy and then hum and rock gently for a few minutes to capture the feeling of the rhythm. This is a slow rhythm. Use about twelve repetitions in fifteen second time period.

With a partner, try rocking back to back or holding hands and squeezing in a gentle, sucking rhythm. Can you feel a comfortable attunement with the other person?

---

As infants suck several processes help them to develop a clearly defined and adaptive rhythm. The mother breathes more slowly than the infant, but the rhythm is similar. The milk flows from the mother's breast in waves which approximate the sucking rhythm. Maternal hormones, which circulated in the infant *in utero* still linger, encouraging inner genital (gradual) rhythms, longer than but similar to sucking rhythms. Mothers may also reinforce this calm, steady rhythm by rocking gently or humming to the child. Not only does the steady rocking rhythm of a caregiver help the infant develop adaptive sucking rhythms, but this also helps establish regular breathing rhythms.

Reciprocally, the infant may evoke sucking or similar rhythms in the mother as he rhythmically touches the mother's breast while nursing. His other arm, if unrestrained, will enclose mother in the back, and may also pat her using the sucking rhythm. Infant and mother thus form a reciprocal unit, attuning to one another in their mutual embrace. This dyadic attunement may be fundamental to Mahler's (1975) symbiotic phase.

Sucking rhythms are used in other contexts as well, such as nodding, dabbing or patting, and finger play. These movement patterns can be seen as rehearsals which keep the sucking rhythm in readiness when needed for obtaining nourishment, self-soothing, and bonding.

### *Attunement*

In the early part of the oral phase, the sucking rhythm promotes attunement between an infant and nursing mother. **Attunement** is the blending or adapting of rhythms to those of another person. It allows the mother and infant to converse in harmony. "Complete attunement is based on mutual empathy ... a sameness of needs and responses, but also a synchronization in rhythms" (Kestenberg, 1975, p. 161). Attuning to or sharing the same or affined tension flow rhythms creates the foundation for empathy and communication (Kestenberg and Buelte, 1977). Birdwhistle (1970), Condon (1988) and others have shown that both infants and adults thrive, feel joined, congruent, and better understood when their rhythmic sequences or melodies are attuned (see Lewis, Chapter 16). Eckerman, Davis and Didow (1989) describe how toddlers imitate each other's movement patterns and thereby maintain social contact. Using KMP terminology, we would speak of attunement in rhythms and adjustment in shape flow (see Chapter 5). Loman (1994) suggests that with attunement, needs and feelings are responsively duplicated on the level of physical sensation. She points out that attunement can take place through the use of touch or visual cues translated into kinesthetic sensations.

Breathing patterns reinforce a sense of connection. When parent and infant both inhale simultaneously, they literally grow closer together and a feeling of trust develops (see Chapter 5). As parent and infant both exhale and grow apart, the foundations for separation and differentiation begin to form. However, the main focus in the first months of life is still on feelings of unity, empathy, and symbiosis.

Mahler, Pine, and Bergman (1975) describe the infant's narcissistic experience of being undifferentiated from a loving, need-satisfying environment during symbiosis. This self-object unity (Kohut, 1977) promotes a sense of feeling full and satisfied. Bowlby (1977) and Ainsworth (1973) explain that the attachment-seeking behavior of infants (smiling, rooting, gazing) leads to the development of mother-infant bonds. The KMP focuses on rhythmic attunement as one of the major foundations for the symbiosis and bonding described by other theorists.

## The Role of the Father

Because fathers rarely act as the main caretakers of infants, symbiosis between father and infant was rarely considered until recently. Most studies depict fathers as offering a distinct style of interaction with their infants, generally described as more intermittent, more focused on playful interaction, and more socially stimulating than interaction with mother (Parke and Sawin, 1976; Lamb, 1981). Fathers tend to orient infants away from the embrace of the mother to the outside world (Applegate, 1987; Stiver, 1991). However, Pruitt (1983) found that when fathers were the primary caregivers there appeared to be a "... very literal 'taking in' of these babies by the fathers..." analogous to incorporation, and that there was a biorhythmic synchrony reminiscent of that found in mother–infant dyads (p. 269; see also Abelin, 1975). Cross-cultural studies also call into question the view that fathers universally rough-house with their infants and orient them to the outside world (e.g., Hewlett, 1992).[6] As fathers and others become more involved in infant care in the U.S., child development researchers are finally beginning to look beyond the mother–infant dyad to include a larger radius of relationships and interactions in their analysis as early theorists have suggested (Erikson, 1959; Broffenbrenner, 1977).

## Bonding and Attunement in Non-Western Cultures

Rhythms of interaction and patterns of attunement are affected by cultural influences. Freedman and Fajardo (1977) found that African-American, Anglo, and Native American mothers used different rhythms as they interacted with their infants.[7] In many non-Western cultures, e.g., Japan (Caudill and Weinstein, 1969), and in much of sub-Saharan Africa (LeVine, 1977), infants are almost continuously held in close physical contact by a member of the family. In contrast, in Western industrialized areas such as the United States, separation training begins early; infants are often physically separated from caregivers, i.e., bottle fed[8] and placed in cribs, high chairs, and cradles. What are the effects of these differences? Does longer time spent in physical contact lead to a greater ability to attune or to a higher level of attunement? Does more contact with inanimate objects in Western cultures enhance ability to relate to things as opposed to people? Does a stage of merging and symbiosis have greater duration in high contact non-Western societies?[9] Do members of high contact cultures understand others more through kinesthetic clues, while members of low contact cultures rely more on visual and verbal clues?[10] Japan is an example of a culture in which mothers and infants have a high amount of physical contact and where understanding of nonverbal cues is highly developed. The Japanese call this *ishin denshin* or "intuitive sense." It is used to create a synchrony of movements (*aizsuchi*) and a sensitivity to others' needs or empathy for others (*omoiyori*) based on subtle nonverbal cues

(Ramsey, 1984). From a Western perspective, one might ask how separation develops with this high degree of embeddedness in the relationship. In response, a non-Westerner might question how Westerners achieve connectedness. The KMP focus on balance suggests that in all cultures successful parenting involves mutual attunement counterbalanced by some degree of separation between infant and caregiver (see also Sossin and Romer, 1989).

### Extremes of Attunement and Clashing

Attachment theorists have pointed out that bonding between mother and infant improves the infant's chances of survival and that good attachment is a good prognosis for future ability to cope and interrelate with others (Bowlby, 1977; Ainsworth *et al.*, 1973). Nonetheless, however desirable bonding and attunement may be, complete attunement and blending of self and other is not always desirable (Kestenberg, 1975). The mother and infant may find themselves so absorbed in one another that separating becomes difficult and the mother is unable to give attention to others. This may occur with "motherly" mothers who are successful with all infants. They intuitively seem to know how to bold a baby, when it is hungry, etc. They have an above average ability to regress to early rhythms both empathetically and in motor performance. Although this can be an asset with infants, it may be a liability with older children. An older child may have difficulties in doing things on her own that require new patterns (Kestenberg, 1975). Her typical response may be, "I cannot do it—you do it with me."[11] If continued throughout infancy and toddlerhood, complete attunement may lead to a loss of boundaries and merging (Lewis, 1993).

A high degree of attunement may also occur in the case of the baby who is remarkably pliable. These "good" babies adapt to the needs of their caregivers and household routines. They readily adjust to new schedules, and can be taken most places without problems. They are less need-centered and more people-focused. They observe their caregiver's facial expressions and feel changes in her body tension. Such pliable children are closely influenced by the mood of the people they care about and their behaviors are geared toward meeting other peoples' needs rather than their own (Kestenberg, 1975). Some current research (Jordan *et al.*, 1991) indicates that mothers will encourage this behavior more in their daughters than in their sons.

### Clashing Patterns: Lack of Attunement

In all relationships, there are periods when rhythmic patterns of individuals clash rather than blend. The clashing of rhythms indicates differentiation between self and other, and may be stimulating or foster creativity. Frequent recoveries from a clashing pattern reinforces the dyad's confidence that they can re-establish attunement and repair conflicts (see also Tronick and Cohen, 1989; Newman and Newman, 1991). However, a predominance of clashing rhythms may reinforce or create dysfunctional patterns both in relationships with people and with the material environment. This is especially true when the mother's pattern is not adaptive for the developmental tasks of the child. For example, an inexperienced mother may clash with her infant's nursing rhythms, interjecting abruptness and preventing him from taking in milk in a smooth fashion. She may have a lot of high intensity in her movements, which excites the baby and interferes with relaxed nursing. On the other hand, a mother may have such low intensity in her rhythms that her nursing infant falls asleep before becoming satiated.

Infants may also experience an internal clash caused by a predilection for rhythms which jarringly mix with the sucking rhythm, making nursing more difficult. For example, some infants suck with gusto; they gulp and either take in a lot of air and need to be burped often, or may occasionally choke on the gulped milk. Other infants might suck with such low intensity that they get little milk, tire eventually, and fall asleep without having taken in enough nourishment.

Caregivers can encourage more adaptive rhythms in the infant and in themselves through rocking, patting, humming, and breathing in a sucking rhythm or a rhythm in synchrony with the sucking rhythm. The average mother and baby unconsciously encourage a good sucking rhythm in each other and functional nursing and attunement evolves. A father, mother, grandmother or other caregiver bottle feeding an infant may also adapt to and encourage the smooth, rocking quality of the sucking rhythm.

### Body Attitude and Alignment in the Oral Indulging Phase

The body attitude of the early oral phase infant is complementary to its indulging quality. The body is soft, flexible, and malleable. This facilitates attunement, symbiosis, and incorporation. Together with mother, the body tends to grow "wide as the whole world." When separated from the mother, the child narrows, reflecting its aloneness. The fluctuating body attitude is a response to the relationship with the need-satisfying caregiver (Kestenberg, Marcus, Robbins, Berlowe, and Buelte, 1975).

The primary alignment in the first year of life is in the horizontal (table) plane. The horizontal plane fosters communication and exploration (see Chapter 5).

### The Sucking Rhythm in Later Development

The sucking rhythms which predominate in infants in the oral indulging phase continue to be used by growing children and adults with a high frequency relative to all other rhythms. The pleasure an individual derives from oral sensations in eating and drinking extends to other activities. Oral rhythms spread and are used throughout the body, reflecting and reinforcing the urge to take-in, incorporate, and find succor.

In individuals who demonstrate particularly strong preferences for particular rhythmic patterns, we often find a common constellation of behaviors and preferences. We have found that people with a relatively high predominance of sucking rhythms tend to particularly enjoy taking in food, knowledge, new sights, sensations, and experiences. They tend to be curious and greedy for life. Their orality may also be expressed in an enjoyment of talking, communicating and conversing with others, singing, and other orally satisfying and self-soothing behaviors. They tend to have "soft" body boundaries and feel comfortable joining in with others as opposed to holding themselves apart. They may also tend to be more dependent than independent, enjoying regressing to the early merging stage of development.

However, these tendencies may be counterbalanced by other qualities. A person may at times be dependent and merging and then at other times become more independent. Environmental factors, developmental history, and individual proclivities all play a role.

Note that throughout this book, the potential influences of particular movement pattern preferences will be discussed, however, it is not our intention to imply simple one-to-one relationship between one movement pattern and the complex constellation we call personality. One must examine the full constellation of movement qualities to begin to understand the full constellation of personality (see Section III).

### *Summary*

The oral indulging phase is the first part of the oral phase (aged birth to five or six months). Its qualities of accommodation and receptivity can be seen in the soft pliable body boundaries of the young infant and the baby's tendency to mold to others.

**Phase of Incorporation**: In the oral phase, the individual's need to incorporate, which begins as a nutritive need, extends to the rest of the body. The baby sucks with its mouth and with its hands in the oral rhythm. It might be suggested that the process of "taking in" is integral to the development of attachment to others. Through the mouth, nose, hands, eyes, and ears, the infant takes in pleasurable sensations associated with nursing. Gradually the taking in of a wide range of such stimuli may become imbued with pleasure in and of itself, apart from the nursing context. An infant may mature to a person who finds particular pleasure in the process of incorporation.

## Oral Snapping/Biting Rhythms (os) in the Oral Fighting Phase[12]

This phase develops with teething and predominates in infants in the second half of the first year. When the process of teething begins at about five or six months, those places in the mouth which had been such a source of pleasure for the infant now become a source of pain as well. Babies find relief from pain in the gums by **snapping** and **biting** down. Both are used for masticating food, and thus function in the process of taking in and incorporating.

The snapping rhythm is a tapping-like rhythm. It is biphasic (alternating free and bound flow) like the sucking rhythm, but has sharp transitions as it reverses directions (see Figure 4). The biting rhythm is similar but has a short holding portion instead of a sharp transition. It is used in chewing and grinding food.

Snapping and biting rhythms spread from the mouth into other parts of the body. Babies often use the snapping rhythm in patting, clapping, rocking, or pulling hair. For example, infants will often push themselves up on all fours, and having gained this stable stance, they will rock back and forth in the snapping rhythm. Both rhythms have a measured pace, being neither abrupt nor gradual.

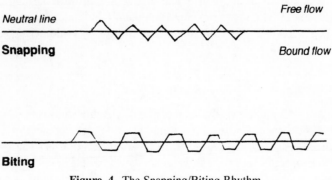

**Figure 4.** The Snapping/Biting Rhythm.

## Exercise

Snap down as you might bite down on nuts or cut into a carrot. Feel sharp, snappy transitions. Try patting your belly, clapping your hands, and then patting the ground in an even rhythm of about twelve claps per fifteen seconds. Keep the sharp transitions typical of a snap of the fingers.

In the biting rhythm the teeth hold the tension briefly to grind the food and then the pressure is released. Try pinching or pulling hair. Keep the rhythm of "grab, hold, release." One can clap using this rhythm also, using a "clap, hold, release" pattern.

### The Subphase of Differentiation

Through the use of snapping rhythms, the periphery of the body becomes more clearly defined, encouraging self-definition, distinct body boundaries, stability, and differentiation from the primary caregiver. Mahler has termed this early differentiation "hatching" (1975). In patting one's body with the snapping or biting rhythm, one can experience oneself as a separate, distinct being with boundaries. In patting the ground, one can establish its otherness.

Children in this teething stage love taking things into their mouth and snapping or biting on them. As the rhythm spreads to the hands, the hands "snap or bite" by poking or pinching. Children this age also spend time staring with briefly held attentiveness. The short, evenly held portion of the biting rhythm serves as an early foundation for sustained attention and concentration.

In the first few months of life outside the uterus, the infant's attunement with mother or other primary caregiver reached a peak; now the snapping and biting rhythms promote individuation and separation. Infants in this oral fighting stage of development are more outwardly directed. Their behaviors often initiate acceptance and support of increased separation on the part of the caregiver. An infant biting on its mother's nipple may cause her to pull back. The infant in turn may stiffen and jerk backward, turning away from the caregiver to explore the outer environment. Mahler suggests that the initial differentiation of self and mother occurs first with respect to the infant's body boundaries or outer shell (Mahler *et al.*, 1975).

Fighting rhythms not only promote the infant's self boundaries, but also discourage the caregiver from giving the same degree of physical contact offered previously. Cognitive and motoric development spurts in the second half of the first year (eating solid foods, pre-crawling, rocking, sitting up unassisted, and expressing likes and dislikes) also encourage more outward exploration on the part of the infant. Seeing these new behaviors in their children may encourage parents to separate from them a little more. Thus several developmental factors collaborate to move the infant from a focus on symbiosis to a growing sense of selfhood.

### Sense of Self

What this sense of self might be is the subject of considerable controversy. Stern (1985) has pointed out that Westerners tend to see maturation as the development of a differentiated, and individualized sense of self. However, in Japan, maturation is seen as the process of learning how to connect; a sense of self is understood as a self in relation to others. Jordan *et al.* (1991) note that the importance of connections and relationships is undervalued and underestimated in America due to the cultural focus on individuation. This valuable insight encourages us to emphasize that maturation offers the foundations for both connection and individuation in all phases of development. Although there is a growing interest in exploration in the oral fighting phase, it is not an exclusive orientation. There are strong lines of continuity underlying the phase pattern of development.

New developments may lead to the reconfiguration of earlier patterns rather than their displacement. Physical separation and a more separate sense of self does not necessarily preclude connection. As the infant explorer moves outward, she may turn back, meeting the caregiver's eye. The briefly held look can form a bridge between infant and adult (Mahler *et al.*, 1975) and may encourage verbal and visual forms of interaction. Though tactile connection may diminish, new forms of connection and communication emerge.

### Body Attitude and Alignment in the Oral Fighting Phase

Body boundaries tend to be more clearly defined in the oral fighting phase and the body attitude, rather than pliable, is solid and stable. The upper body is vertically aligned in the sitting position.

### The Snapping/Biting Rhythm in Later Development

The snapping/biting rhythm is a fighting rhythm. At its oral source, it is a response to pain. Snapping/biting rhythms continue the function of incorporation begun with the sucking rhythm, but they process what has been incorporated by cutting and breaking down. Cognitively, the snapping rhythm promotes delineating, and differentiating. Psychologically, the snapping rhythm promotes differentiation between self and other. The evenly held tension of the biting rhythm creates the foundation for the ability to hold apart and concentrate. These two functions, separation of self and concentration, are mutually reinforcing. A certain degree of separation of oneself from external stimuli is necessary for concentration; concentration in turn accentuates separation.

What are the characteristics of adults who exhibit a high frequency of biting rhythms? Pleasure is derived from biting down; this may be expressed in tastes for hard, crunchy foods, biting humor, and critical perspectives. With snapping/biting rhythms, the oral urge to take in and incorporate becomes taking in in order to break down. Thus, people with a preference for biting rhythms may be eager to take in new knowledge and experiences, but tend to respond in a critical fashion. Intellectually, they are more inclined to differentiate and delineate one idea from another than to integrate or blend ideas.

The snapping/biting rhythms also influence social relationships. While a sucking rhythm promotes snuggling and merging, a person who hugs with a snapping rhythm offers a pat or tap on the back promoting separation. Of course, as mentioned previously, people are not pure types, but rather combine various qualities based on different constellations of needs.

### Summary

In the oral fighting phase the infant's urge to take in becomes increasingly wider in scope, leading to an interest in a variety of external stimuli. Thus, oral rhythms come to play a role in the development of attention and exploration, tasks which evolve with the support of more mature movement qualities (see Chapters 3 and 4).

The oral sucking rhythm with its associated molding body attitude supports the development of the ability to attune to others which in turn creates the foundation for kinesthetic identification and empathy. The oral snapping/biting rhythm with its associated firm body boundaries supports an early sense of separateness and differentiation. Separation combined with feelings of connection lays the foundation for the more complex task of communication (Kestenberg, 1975).

## The Twisting Rhythm (a) in the Anal Indulging Phase

This phase comes to the fore at about nine or ten months of age. In the second part of the first year, we see twisting rhythms begin to vie with sucking and snapping/biting rhythms for prominence in the infant's movement repertoire. While the short holding pattern of the biting rhythm permits longer contact with an object, the twisting rhythm is an initiator of play (Kestenberg and Sossin, 1979). The fussy teether changes to a smiling, playful, teasing charmer (Kestenberg, 1975).

The twisting rhythm originates in the anal sphincter, which twists with small adjustments in intensity as it releases. This rhythm is adaptive to the biological function of passive defecation (see Figure 5).

The twisting rhythms emanating from the anal sphincter encourage the infant to move from the pelvis: crawling, climbing, and rising up to a wobbly vertical position. Verticality offers a new presentational perspective on life, and rising up offers the child a different relationship to gravity.

Gradually, the twisting rhythm spreads from the lower spine area to the rest of the baby's body. The playful child teasingly crawls away from mother or father and then looks back, smiling flirtatiously; or returns back to a parent for refueling ("Go away and come back"). In Mahler's terms this is the practicing subphase of the larger phase of separation/individuation (Mahler, Pine, and Bergman, 1975). Here we also see the use of "transitional objects" which help a child retain a connection to the parent even while separating (Winnicott, 1989).

As the teasing, twisting rhythm spreads into the hands, children enjoy playing with soft, messy things, such as food or mud that responds to their fingers. Sometimes they will play with a bowel movement if it falls out of their diapers. They may feel pride in this product that they have created and dislike having it taken away. This is a pre-bowel training mindset.

The foundations for generosity are being laid, but at this stage the child is still teasing. She may offer food and then retrieve it, give a toy and then want it back. She is playing at

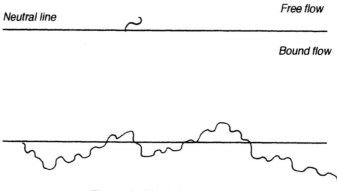

**Figure 5.** The Twisting Rhythm.

being able to give something away. Such actions are generally carried out with twisting rhythms.

Playing with hands also involves exploration, but this is quite different from the exploration in the earlier oral phase. Whereas the six-month-old was interested in locating things in space ("where is it?"), the one- to two-year-olds are interested in substance ("what is it?"). They pick things up and turn them around, appraising them. One- to two year-olds enjoy the sense of touch, feeling the texture or weight of things. In the indulging anal phase, they particularly like little things, like pieces of thread or fabric, and enjoy the lightness of them. The valued object may then be presented to a parent or caregiver for admiration. As objects are offered up for the parents to admire, the child practices the process of presentation.

---

## Exercise

Try crawling, feeling how your pelvis twists (or watch a child crawling). Squirm around to get comfortable in a chair, smile flirtatiously, or pick up small objects and turn them about in your hand to admire them. The twisting rhythm is also typical of the short whining or lilting vocalization patterns of this age group. Try a child-like whine. Hear the flow adjustment and twist in the tone.

---

### Body Attitude and Alignment in the Anal Indulging Phase

The body attitude of the anal indulging phase is flexible and twisting, offering little stability. The body is in transition to vertical alignment. Adults with such a flexible body attitude may feel afraid to "fall" if they do not have others to hold onto or depend on.

### The Twisting Rhythms in Later Development

Twisting rhythms which are freely moving (with free flow) encourage "feelings of the joy of rhythmic playfulness" (Kestenberg and Sossin, 1979, p. 33). They are often used in association with a humorous outlook on things, teasing playfulness, flirtatiousness, and charm. Adjustable and thus adaptable, such rhythms support improvisation, change, evaluating in an offhand and perhaps humorous way.

On the other hand, twisting rhythms also underlie ambivalence and vacillation. Use of twisting rhythms undermines attempts to stick to one plan or idea, assert oneself, or make definitive judgments. A person with an abundance of twisting rhythms may be very dependent on others for structure and support. Such a person may also tend to be messy and disorganized.

Sometimes twisting rhythms are constrained (bound flow) and associated with displeasure, used, for example, when a child is whining or squirming restlessly. In adulthood it is seen in people who are constantly dissatisfied and complaining, unable to find pleasure in anything.

### Summary

The twisting rhythm is an indulging rhythm. By twisting, the crawling child or beginning toddler can mobilize and move away from a secure base. With a twisting rhythm she may turn back to reconnect and refuel (Mahler *et al.*, 1975). The twisting rhythm forms a basis for adaptability.

### The Strain/Release Rhythm (as) in the Anal Fighting phase

This phase comes to the fore at about eighteen months of age, evolving from the lower pelvis. It builds in intensity, then holds for a long time and then releases (see Figure 6).[13]

The **strain/release** rhythm is used in active defecation and its mastery signifies a child's readiness for bowel control. Not only has the child mastered the physical process of straining and releasing but also the psychological processes of holding, pushing, and then letting go. Children of this age are finally able to give something away without wanting to get it back.

---

### Exercise

Try using the strain/release rhythm to rise from a sitting to a standing position. With legs planted firmly on the ground, tense the muscle of the thighs and back and stand up. Note how authoritative this stance feels. You may also try holding onto something and not letting go (perhaps a partner wants to have it). Hold on tightly to retain the object, but then relax your hold and let go.

---

The strain/release rhythm is evident in babies who, straining with bound flow, get red in the face while defecating. It is also seen in toddlers who spend more and more time pulling up to a standing position with a high intensity of tension. They hold onto things and to themselves, seeking stability, but may fall or sink down abruptly. Parents, couches, even small objects are held in an attempt to help develop the stability which will eventually come from within.

### *Issues of Autonomy in the Anal Fighting Phase*

The straining, or holding part of the rhythm, helps the child gain stability. As the rhythm spreads from the lower pelvis, it tends to create a single solid body attitude which can

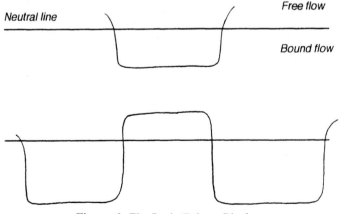

**Figure 6.** The Strain/Release Rhythm.

support an erect posture. As the child rises into the vertical plane and stands firmly, she gains a feeling of self-assurance, the desire for greater autonomy, and (building on other movement qualities) a willingness to confront others (usually parents).

The strain/release rhythm also contributes to the development of a need to engage in clearly defined and structured behaviors. A child in this phase tends to feel comfortable with orderliness and structure in his life. Erikson (1975) has suggested that the need for order is one of the three social drives in children. However, the need for order comes from within the child in this phase and he may not find it easy to adapt to the structures imposed by others. This is particularly the case if the rules imposed by parents keep changing. Assertiveness over his own autonomy may lead the child into a series of parent–child confrontations.

The degree to which parent–child battles emerge in this age period depends both on the child's individual temperament and the style of parenting used. In traditional Middle Eastern, Native American, and Asian families, where children are given a considerable degree of autonomy (usually until age five or six) there may be few conflicts. Ironically Euro-American culture tends to encourage individual autonomy as an ideal, but in practice it focuses more on control of children. This contradiction may intensify control issues in dealing with the one-and-a-half to two-year-old and the adolescent.

When parents, concerned about control issues, unconsciously match the high level of excitement of the child, battles often erupt. Note that the rising intensity of the first part of the straining rhythm is often associated with rising excitement. The shared excitement may be pleasurable and rewarding for all parties. The attunement, even in mutual rage, creates a connection between parent and child. In order to avoid such intense confrontations, a parent or other caregiver may attune selectively to the evenly held part of the strain/release rhythm (rather than to the high intensity), using it to quietly reinforce consistent boundaries and rules and provide stabilization. Rather than attempting to control the child (and encroach on his new-found autonomy) one can suggest permissible behaviors and set boundaries beyond which the child may not go. In the releasing part of the rhythm we find a prototype for letting go sometimes and giving the child a chance to do it his own way when possible. Thus the child is offered both a structured environment and also space to develop some autonomy (Kestenberg, 1975).

### The Strain/Release Rhythm as a Valuable Resource

The strain/release rhythm is a fighting rhythm and many of the behaviors associated with it are in the service of assertiveness. Parents may label the assertiveness as stubbornness and disobedience and see it as a behavior to be admonished, particularly in children with a predisposition towards this rhythm. However, not only is assertiveness an important resource for survival, but also other important skills including controlled defecation develop on the foundation of the strain/release rhythm. The holding part of the rhythm, although often associated with stubbornness, is an important element of torso stability and concentration. Concentration is needed to accomplish tasks. Interruptions or distractions are particularly unwelcome in this stage and can eventually disturb the ability of the child to stay focused.

Many other activities involve the use of somewhat less sustained holding in the strain/release mode. For example, the toddler often enjoys pushing, shoving, lifting, and throwing things. Through these activities motor skills and strength are developed and the ability to give things up (the release part of the rhythm) is practiced. As children strain to lift, shove, or rise up, they feel the weight of things and of their own bodies, too. This gives them a sense of themselves as beings who can throw their weight around or refuse to be pushed around (Kestenberg, 1975). Feeling and understanding the weight of things is an important component of the process of evaluation as we discuss in Chapter 4 in relation to the development of the efforts of strength and lightness. Thus the strain/release rhythm can be seen as an important resource rather than as an obstacle in child rearing.

### Issues of Connection in the Anal Phase

Prideful presentation of oneself as "so big" and "so strong" plays a role in the development of feelings of autonomy. However, it also plays a role in building connections. Children present themselves to parents in order to be admired. As in the earlier anal indulging phase, they continue to present objects for admiration. Parental admiration makes the object valuable and disapproval makes it unworthy and expendable. All objects act in part as transitional objects because they belong to both child and parent (Winnicott, 1989). The valued object can represent parental approval and worthiness, and thus come to represent mother or father themselves. Presentation of objects creates bridges back to the parents without the surrender of autonomy. Of course, autonomy is often surrendered voluntarily. The sometime assertive toddler can still dissolve into a parental lap. Mahler speaks of "rapprochement" within the phase of separation–individuation (Mahler *et al.*, 1975).

### Body Attitude and Alignment in the Anal Fighting Phase

The body attitude of the one-and-a-half to two-year-old is sturdy, stable, and wall-like, fully established in the vertical plane. A firm body supports a sense of growing autonomy (which occasionally collapses), self-assertiveness, and strength. The vertical plane encourages stability, confrontation, and presentation.

### The Strain/Release Rhythm in Later Development

The strain/release rhythm encourages such qualities as assertiveness, strong will, stubbornness, a need for order, and the ability to concentrate. People who use an abundance of strain/release rhythms are often neat, well-organized, controlled, and sometimes controlling. They generally find it easy to concentrate on a problem or issue and do not tolerate distractions well. They tend to fix on an idea or principle, seeing things as clear-cut (i.e., good or bad, right or wrong) and are not easily swayed.

Strain/release rhythms encourage holding onto things, feelings, ideas, and/or people. People with a preference for strain/release rhythms are likely to hold onto feelings, remember past wrongs or past events, keep secrets well (unlike the twisting person who often gives them up), hold onto relationships, ideas, judgments, or belongings.

This discussion has focused on the straining (holding) portion of the rhythm which underlies inflexibility. The releasing portion is equally significant. In most cases, stubborn people will suddenly give in when faced with the right circumstances. The straining/holding portion is associated with holding back, yet generosity may emerge when the fear of loss of control is placated. A person who strains frequently may be holding in anger. The release might come as a violent outburst, though some people are adept at letting go in more appropriate ways. When someone is attempting a difficult task, he may strain and strain and then give up. Understanding the sources of this pattern may help bring out its strengths.

If strain/release rhythms become too dominant, compulsive behavior may develop. Erikson *et al.* (1986) describe how a well-developed sense of autonomy may result in a renewed sense of willfulness in old age. However, empowering people may actually make it easier for them to give in or compromise.

### Summary

The strain/release rhythm underlies the development of stability, self-assertion, and autonomy. It also supports the ability to concentrate, to hold on, and to give up or relinquish the products of one's labor.

During the anal phase, which coincides roughly with the second year of life, we see the development of intentionality and the ability to confront and present oneself and objects. Cognitively, children learn to represent objects in symbolically meaningful forms. These developmental tasks of the anal phase are supported by anal rhythms, but rely on the more mature pattern (efforts) for their development.

### Running/Drifting Rhythm (u) in the Urethral Indulging Phase

The **running/drifting** rhythm become prominent in children when they are beginning their third year of life. It originates in the bladder and the urethra opening. It is characterized by very gradual increases or decreases of muscle tension of low levels of intensity. A tracing of the tension flow takes a linear form, often with slight vibrations, resembling dribbling urine or water (see Figure 7). It is the rhythm of passive urination.

Before they reach this phase, children may have tried to control urination by using the straining rhythm (holding and then releasing) but now they begin to give in to the outpouring of urine, letting it flow. One can see a similar process in their own bodily movement which seems to drift and flow like liquid (Kestenberg, 1975).

At the end of the second year, the willful toddler becomes more pliable and agreeable. Use of the straining rhythm diminishes, the hard body shell softens as does the confrontational self. Children orient in the sagittal plane, bulging forward and letting this bulge carry them off in a mobile, drifting, fluid manner. They also dribble, dawdle, and wander aimlessly without boundaries. Two-year-olds feel that, like liquid, they can flow over or "take a spill." Like liquid also the child bubbles with ideas and words, speaking in run-on sentences that replicate run-on mobility. Words, ideas, and even they themselves drift and flow with little control.

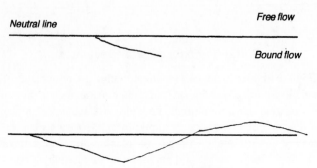

**Figure 7.** The Running/Drifting Rhythm.

Although children enjoy playing with liquids now, they lack control and often make a mess. While playing a child may forget to run to the bathroom, or only drifts toward it too late, urine spilling down on clothes or the ground.

---

### Exercise

Try to slowly collapse onto a couch or chair. Enjoy the relaxed reverie of the feeling. Rise up slowly and wander somewhere without much thought of where you are going and when you will get there. Note the timelessness of the movement.

---

The mobility and softened boundaries of the running/drifting rhythm are associated with less structure and more reliance on others. The child may run away from a parent and then run back, landing lovingly in a lap or wrapping herself around the legs of a caregiver. Slowing down, speeding up, meandering, and playing with time, children easily get lost as space and directions become irrelevant. They may dissolve into tears, discovering that they are lost and no caregiver is there. The running/drifting child needs help with boundaries, help to keep from spilling and falling down, help with controlling the free flow of motor impulses. Children need containment systems to offer support when they are over-mobilized.

Conflicts with caregivers now center around time more than wants. A parent, trying to hurry, becomes frustrated with a child who seems to have no concept of time (but who is actually practicing playing with time). The two-year-old dawdles and delays interminably, then rushes out the door way ahead of the adult. Conflicts also involve parental attempts to control the child's running, which propels him forward in a seemingly erratic way. Yet like water spilling, the child has little control over stopping. Parents can provide boundaries and directions without impeding the movement itself. This is applicable to urine training. Children of this age may still make many toilet training mistakes, and spill things often. This is partly because they do not have sufficient control and partly because they seek autonomy over timing, wanting to indulge in time even when the urine is pressing to come out. Stern points out that issues of autonomy pervade all stages of life (1985).[14]

### *Body Attitude and Alignment in the Urethral Indulging Phase*

The body attitude of the child in the urethral indulging phase is fluid, at times languid and at times energetic. The body tends to align in the sagittal or wheel plane. The child walks with forward motions now (rather than side to side) but without sufficient control to make definitive stops and starts.

### *Urethral Rhythms in Later Development*

The running/drifting rhythm encourages a feeling of letting go, relaxing, drifting, meandering. Reminiscing tends to follow a drifting rhythm. When using such a rhythm it is difficult to keep focused on one goal or on time limits. People who have a preference for the running/drifting rhythm tend to prefer moving or thinking at their own pace in an unstructured fashion. They may often drift about, losing or misplacing things or getting lost themselves. Like fluid, the rhythm dribbles and flows, not allowing one to adhere to a strict schedule or to attend much to the element of time.

### The Starting/Stopping Rhythm (us) in the Urethral Fighting Phase

At about two-and-a-half-years of age, a **starting/stopping** rhythm begins to come to the fore, offering children more control over starting and stopping, and thus more control over urination. This rhythm is characterized by sharp transitions (see Figure 8).

Urine can now be shot out, stopped, and aimed. Body movements such as coordinated running also come under greater control. Children learn to bulge forward and run, then hollow back and stop. It is a great achievement to be able to stop yourself at will. With greater control over themselves and timing, they develop many new abilities. They can anticipate the need to find a bathroom, follow directions to get there, aim properly (boys), and finish definitively. Children of this age have short attention spans, are interested in going here and there and interrupt themselves and others with impatience.

Now instead of embodying spilling water, they become like a stream of water shot out of a fire fighter's hose. They love stop-and-go games, rushing forward and winning races, darting from one place to another, shooting water guns and role-playing firefighters using hoses to put out many fires.

---

#### Exercise

Imagine that you are waiting for a friend to find her car keys so that you can both go. Try tapping your foot impatiently while waiting. When out of patience, you go to find the key yourself; you run around the house, looking here and there, finally find the keys, grab a notebook (which you might need), and race outside, showing your friend how fast you were.

There are several important elements in this exercise. Note that there is a schedule of events, that a task is undertaken and completed from start to finish, that there is a competitive element.

---

Mastering time allows children in their third year to anticipate things, such as when mother or father will come home or the concept of eating dessert after dinner. This supports the development of object constancy in time (Kestenberg, 1975). Whereas in the earlier phases, children learned the concept that an object is likely to be where it was last seen (object constancy in **space**), that objects have weight and mass which remain consistent (object constancy in **weight**), now they are able to conceptualize that the object retains an identity over time, even when it is no longer in its place (object constancy in **time**). Thus, in the third year a child can anticipate a parent's return and more easily accept a parent's absence (see also Vaughn, Kopp, and Krakow, 1984).

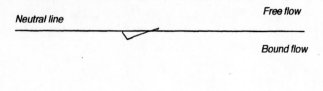

**Figure 8.** The Starting/Stopping Rhythm.

Gaining greater control over a sense of time as well as their own timing, children can follow a sequence of activities. At times they become bossy and like to tell others what they should do next. They like to choose which color paper to use or which game to play. They can follow games with simple rules and carry out tasks but they may get derailed. They begin to make decisions, choices, anticipate consequences, and follow through on them. The developmental task of the urethral phase is to develop the ability to anticipate, plan, and make decisions that serve as the foundation for carrying out operations.

### Body Attitude and Alignment in the Urethral Fighting Phase

The body is a mobile, elastic unit in this subphase. It is sagittally oriented and projects forward.

### The Starting/Stopping Rhythm in Later Development

Starting/stopping rhythms encourage mobility, bursts of energy, and impatience with any delay. Using this rhythm people initiate action but may interrupt themselves, which creates feelings of urgency or irritability.

People exhibiting a large number of starting/stopping rhythms tend to be doers who are often goal-oriented, ambitious, and competitive. They also tend to be "work ethic" people, who value themselves and others in terms of what they accomplish. Their concern with fighting the passage of time is reflected in social and recreational patterns as well as work. "On the go" people who are dominated by starting/stopping rhythms often have little time for relaxed social interaction. They are list-makers who put many tasks on their agenda. Socializing is frenetic or limited and often work-related. Even vacations are fully planned and spent rushing about, with a full schedule of sights to see and activities to do. In describing a stage he terms "initiative versus guilt," Erikson suggests that this willingness to go after things (as described above) continues throughout life, evidenced in work, recreation, and creativity. It reflects " ... an energetic involvement with diverse aspects of the world" (Erikson, Erikson, and Kivnick, 1986, p. 173).

However, the starting/stopping rhythm does not promote a clearly structured organization. Using this rhythm, one often rushes from one job to another without necessarily finishing one before starting the next. Such drive needs to be guided by a more structured rhythm, such as the strain/release described above. Industrial regions such as the urban northeast of the United States encourage the use of the starting/stopping rhythm and its associated approach to life. While indulging in time with the running/drifting rhythm is often devalued in American culture, the starting/stopping type pattern has been appreciated and admired. There appears to be a changing trend today, however, among some segments of the population who are experiencing a renewed interested in "taking time" to appreciate life (see also discussion of acceleration in Chapter 4). Is this change related to downsizing and a "slowing down" economy?

### The Swaying Rhythm (ig) in the Inner Genital Indulging Phase[15]

The **swaying** rhythm comes to the fore in the three-year-old and generally remains prominent until about age four. The swaying rhythm consists of wave-like contractions of gradually increasing and decreasing intensity (see Figure 9).

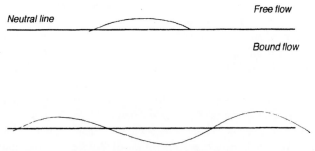

**Figure 9.** The Swaying Rhythm.

The area of origination for this rhythm is in the inner genitals: the inner vagina and uterus in females and the prostate and tunica dartos (scrotum cover) in males. The inner genital contractions are stimulated by an influx of estrogen in girls, and by a slight reduction of testosterone in boys of this age (Kestenberg, 1975). Early swaying rhythms are forerunners to various aspects of later reproduction, including release of the sperm by the prostate in males[16] and light menstrual and vaginal contractions in females. Some men report sensations of pleasure emanating from contractions in the tunica dartos.

---

### Exercise

Try walking in an undulating, swaying rhythm. It is languid and graceful. Try rocking a doll or baby to sleep. An adult's rock is often a large swaying movement in contrast to the short and sharper rock of the biting rhythm typical of six- or seven-month-old. Caressing a friend, walking arm in arm, or playing with baby animals often call forth the use of this nurturing rhythm in three-year-olds. Contrast the swaying rhythm with the running/drifting rhythm which flows aimlessly like spilling water.

---

### Behavioral Patterns in the Inner Genital Phase

To what extent does the heightened presence of the swaying rhythm in three-year-olds help account for some of the common behavioral patterns of this age? Let us begin by describing the three-year-old. One of the tasks facing the child aged two-and-a-half to four is the transition from being a baby/toddler to becoming a big girl or boy. The pride in becoming more grown up is counterbalanced by the pleasures of remaining a baby in mother's lap. Children of this age often vacillate, at times regressing and wanting to be a baby, coddling and sucking their thumbs, having toilet accidents, tantrums etc., and then at other times behaving very grown up and helpful, like mother's or father's friend. They also vacillate between feeling comfort and discomfort; at times they complain of tummy aches or are unaccountably disgruntled. They whine, nag, and cling, though at times they are proud, self-confident, and creative. This time of regressing and growing up offers children a second chance to resolve issues from earlier phases.

Children's use of imaginative role plays often helps them deal with old problems and confront new ones, such as the conflict they feel between remaining a baby and growing up. Sometimes three-year-olds imagine that they have a baby.[17] If they themselves cannot be babies, they can at least be like mothers and have babies. Children (including boys when not discouraged) will play with baby dolls and mother them. Boys who do not play with dolls will play in a maternal fashion with other toys, such as trucks. Boys and girls will sometimes play at being pregnant and having a baby inside their tummies. Children do not usually disclose this pregnancy fantasy. However, it can be intuited when observing children in play with pillows stuffed under a shirt or when they draw circles with little squiggly things inside, which are subsequently identified as little babies. Imagining a baby inside is an ingenious solution to the conflict surrounding growing up.

Three-year-olds often ask many questions such as, "What happens to the train when it goes in the tunnel? Where do people go when they die? Where do the lights go when you turn them off?" Parents note with pride that these are "scientific" questions. However, these questions are repeated over and over in a nagging fashion. It appears that the children want to ask something, but don't know how to frame the question. Therefore, no answer is satisfying.

Is there a relationship between these behavioral patterns and the inner genital rhythms experienced by both girls and boys of this age? One can imagine the perplexity and discomfort of feeling inner sensations which come and go without explanation, are not defined by caregivers, and do not have clear modes of response or satisfaction. At earlier ages, if a child felt inner sensations, appropriate responses could be found (eating in response to hunger pangs, urinating in response to a full bladder). Both one's body and social milieu reinforced the appropriateness of the response. In this stage, masturbation is sometimes tried, but it does not lead to a resolution of the sensations. Criss-crossing waves of contractions come and go, seemingly independent of any action taken by the child.

It seems appropriate and reasonable that children would sometimes feel dissatisfied, whiny and tummy-achy, that they would pose innumerable questions about things which are and then are not. They may have pregnancy fantasies, fear of monsters, and interest in death, all of which may relate to the appearance and disappearance of internal sensations. It seems reasonable that children might imagine that the something inside them could be a baby (particularly if mother is pregnant). Both girls and boys in this phase will often say that when they grow up they want to become mothers. The inner sensations they experience may become associated with feelings of love for self and other. When the sensations disappear, the child may feel concerned or anxious (Kestenberg, 1975).

The specific qualities of the inner genital rhythm also may have important influences. The swaying rhythms spread through the body, creating soft, flowing movements that can be seen in a languid, swaying walk in both girls and boys. This long rhythm is useful for integration of various impulses and of needs associated with the past, present, and future. The distresses and problems which accumulate in the first three years of life can be processed under the wing of the swaying rhythm. For example, the starting/stopping rhythm, which may reflect irritation and conflicts in the two-year-old, may now be smoothed out with the swaying rhythm. The harshness of the strain/release rhythm, the twists of the twisting rhythm may be ameliorated by the swaying gradual rhythm which allows time for reintegration. Likewise, a very languid, drifting quality inherited from the early two-year-old stage may become energized and organized by the swaying inner genital rhythm. The integration of movement qualities presumes a corollary integration of psychological qualities associated with these movements (Kestenberg, 1975).

Finally, this phase promotes a surge of creativity in the child. Many children enjoy drawing and artistic expression, which they can sustain for long periods of time. They become adept at drawing circles and faces. Their dances become flowing and rhythmic, often including turns. Storytelling, playing with dolls, dress up, and playing house all become favorite activities if not negatively sanctioned by others.[18]

The main tasks of the inner genital phase are integration of earlier patterns and maturation from babyhood to childhood. Movement qualities and associated behaviors reveal that as part of the process of maturation, the child is given early preparation for the ability to nurture and parent. This understanding of development differs from that most commonly found in the literature. Most developmental schemes portray childhood as a period of growing autonomy and differentiation (e.g., Erikson, 1960; Mahler *et al.*, 1975) with "little preparation for the intimacy of the first adult stage" (Gilligan, 1979, p. 9) or for developing fathering qualities in boys. In fact, Chodorow suggests that boys find their identity in separating from mother, their primary caregiver, and thus have a "more emphatic individuation and a more defensive firming of experienced ego boundaries" than girls (Chodorow, 1978, p. 150).

However, based on movement observations, KMP analysts describe a stage of maternality or paternality at age three to four when gender identity is being established. During this stage inner genital rhythms develop nurturing patterns in a child which derive both from the movement quality itself and from identification with mother. This would suggest that where early separation and differentiation of boys from mother takes place, it does so in response to cultural pressures which conflict with developmental tendencies. This perspective would more clearly explain evidence of nurturing fathering styles described earlier among some American men and more commonly in men of several other cultures. For example, in Iranian culture definitions of masculinity include nurturing behavior and displays of physical affection towards children, boys may play with and care for small children, and later as fathers may be comfortable relating to and interacting with infants (Kestenberg Amighi, 1992). Thus, if not counteracted by socialization pressures, the inner genital phase creates the foundations for paternality and maternality and perhaps more generally, a nurturing orientation towards others in later development.

### Body Attitude and Alignment in the Inner Genital Indulging Phase

In this phase children begin to take on the form and movements of gendered children rather than toddlers. A waistline appears and hips sway as the child walks.

### The Swaying Rhythm in Later Development

Undulating or swaying rhythms promote easy-going, nurturing movement patterns and feelings. With mounting intensity, they may create persistent nagging feelings, whining, and complaining behavior. Because they are long rhythms they support the ability to integrate diverse ideas or unite people with conflicting views. As described previously, the swaying rhythm blends well with others, smoothing out abruptness and sharp edges. It is a rhythm for creating relationships, nurturing, and integrating diversity.

Using the swaying rhythm, one can follow through on a theme and develop imaginative, creative ways of thinking. However, for the child, the rhythm has a mysterious internal origin. When it leads to creativity it is often a personal, intimate art form which the artist is not propelled to thrust forth and exhibit. The product of one's artistic endeavors may feel like a baby which the creator only shyly displays to others, feeling not yet ready to separate from it. The inner genital rhythm encourages no urgency about completion, competition, or exhibition. The swaying rhythm is the rhythm of the earth mother/father.

### The Surging/Birthing Rhythm (igs) in the Inner Genital Fighting Phase

Very large in scale, the intense **surging/birthing** rhythm gradually builds to high levels of intensity (see Figure 10).

This is the rhythm used in the strong contractions of the uterus during childbirth and in a milder form during menstrual and prostate contractions. Outside of these circumstances, it is rarely expressed in its entirety. As a childbirth rhythm it might seem to exclude male involvement, but in some societies males are encouraged to participate in the act and rhythm of childbirth. A man becomes involved in this rhythm when he holds, massages, or breathes with his female partner while she is giving birth, e.g., as in the Lamaze Method.[19]

At age three-and-a-half to four or so, towards the end of the inner genital phase, we see short segments of this rhythm in pure form or longer segments in mixed form. Expulsive contractions may be associated with strong stomach aches, a heartfelt but whining "no ... ooo", or the pushing away of a no longer valued baby doll, toy, or parent.

The movements can be seen as symbolic of throwing away the baby, expelling it from the womb, and giving up the fantasy of having a baby. Often the child begins to seem more aware of the inanimate qualities of the baby doll. The world of fantasy becomes more distinct from the world of reality.

Saddened by the loss of the fantasy, the child may blame the mother. Not surprisingly, fairy tales about witches eating children and cruel stepmothers are popular at this age. Where are the cruel stepfathers and male witches? In these fantasies, the male is rarely implicated in either the birth or death of children. The father role in many Euro-American fairy tales is that of an accessory or passive observer, to whom surprisingly no blame is attached for their failure to rescue the child.[20]

At the close of the inner genital phase, parenting and babies become less of a focus for the child. The doll baby is gradually given up, replaced by the non-maternal and more explicitly sexually developed dolls and action heroes which become popular with the four- and five-year-olds in the outer genital phase.

### *Body Attitude and Alignment in the Inner Genital Fighting Phase*

The body attitude in this phase is often rounded in the belly region. Children often enhance this look by putting soft objects like pillows under their shirts. The body is in a

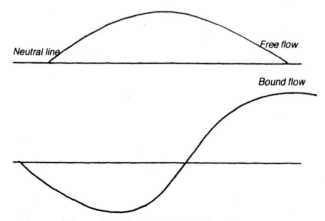

**Figure 10.** The Surging/Birthing Rhythm.

state of preparation for spiraling turns and is full of dramatic intensity, theatrical and overwhelming.

### The Surging/Birthing Rhythm in Later Development

The process of giving birth to an idea or creating a work of art may follow the rhythm of birth, building up to an intense pressure in the effort of creation, and then followed by a strong but gradual release necessary to actually deliver the product of one's labor. Perhaps without such intensity many potential creative works are retained within, never to be forced out to see the light of day.

The intense surging/birthing rhythm is also involved in falling deeply in love and gradually coming out of it to a calmer stage. It is involved in various activities and feelings which develop great intensity very gradually and abate just as gradually. This rhythm may resemble the processes sometimes used in giving up grown up children or mourning someone who was loved (Kestenberg, 1975). Conversely in many cultures, it may be the rhythm of passionate family reunions.

The length and strength of the rhythm encourages the process of integration and organization. Such a long-lasting rhythm can subsume other rhythms into its course (Kestenberg and Sossin, 1979). Various parts of the past can integrate, diverse interests can be merged. The surging/birthing rhythm also supports a deep commitment which may be a long time in unfolding and evolving, giving time for integration and compromise despite the depth of passion involved.

However, a surging/birthing rhythm can be overwhelming and suffocating. A child would need a lot of strength to achieve some independence from such an overpowering parenting style. The backstage parent who is more deeply committed than the performing child is an example. When used in creativity, such rhythms support large scale projects which require perseverance to truly give birth to a new concept or structure.

### Summary

The developmental task of the inner genital phase is integration of the past in preparation for further maturation. The rhythm supports reproductive functions and their emotional correlates, feelings of love and nurturance. This phase begins with periods of regression to babyhood often followed by the fantasy of having a baby. As children work through the problems of earlier development and past experiences, they "give birth" to their baby, giving up the fantasy as well as the wish to regress to babyhood. They now identify with mother in her role as an adult as well as a parent.

### The Jumping Rhythm (og) in the Outer Genital Indulging Phase

Towards the end of the fourth year, there is a shift (in association with a rise in testosterone in boys) from gradual rhythms to abrupt rhythms with smooth transitions (see Figure 11).

These rhythms are usually, but not always, of high intensity. Contractions in the outer genital zones (the penis in boys and the clitoris in girls) create an overflow of energy and excitement which functions in the service of externalizing immature sexual feelings.

This is a boisterous, **jumping** rhythm. Children move in a single body unit, shaped much like the graph of the rhythm. For example, when children swing at a ball, their whole body participates in the swing, when they jump, they look like bouncing balls.

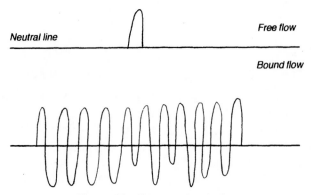

**Figure 11.** The Jumping Rhythm.

This is sometimes called a narcissistic phase in which children experience much joy in themselves. They are often exhibitionists, "on stage," performing, declaring, "Look at me!" and finding pleasure and pride in what they can do.

---

### Exercise

Jump joyously and with abandon. As you fly through the air, feel the glory in yourself, big and tall. Also try swinging your arms and letting your whole body participate in the swing. Note that there is little control in these movements. If you bump into someone you may hurt them, but it would be unintentional.

---

Gesell called this phase a "high drive, combined with a fluid mental organization" (1940). The "high drive" can be seen in the rigorous, high intensity play at gymnastics (tumbling), jumping rope, hopscotch, vigorous dancing, and ball games. A fluid body organization is associated with the rounded transitions of the movement, which blend together different movements rather than differentiate them. While chasing, jumping, running, or throwing balls, children bump into things and into each other accidentally. They have little control and little regard for boundaries of themselves or of others. Their bodies disdain limits and seek to penetrate new domains. They fall over in high-pitched giggles and laughter, expressing their excitement and pleasure. The smooth transitions of this rhythm reflect the pleasurable, non-aggressive quality of the movements.

There is also a correlated fluid mental organization. In their patterns of thought as well as in the roles they play, four-year-old children do not make strong distinctions and differentiations. They blur the difference between inside and outside, true and false, kind and cruel. They play the role of the chaser and then the role of the chased, the giant slayer and the slain, alternating passive and active roles.

The abruptness of the rhythm (see Figure 11) is reflected in quickly shifting mood swings. Children often fall from happiness into despondency about an injury or about feeling rejected. From sadness they recuperate, bouncing into pleasure.

Most societies have offered sports activities to children (especially boys) as an outlet for the expression of such high intensity energy. Children with a quiet disposition, or those discouraged from such physical expressions of exuberance (most often girls), could express their excitement verbally, gushing, interrupting, or shouting. Many cultures such as Eskimo (Briggs, 1970), or Morrocan (Davis, 1993) define small children as those "who have no sense yet" thereby freeing them from proscriptions against undue exuberance.

We see waves of sexual excitement emerging in this phase. When Freud (1905) discussed infantile sexuality, many objected, preferring to see childhood as a state of innocence. However, adult sexuality, like all other behaviors, has its precursors. In this subphase sexuality is not highly focused or differentiated. It expresses itself in masturbation, rubbing against things and bumping into people, penetrating gestures, and interest in the process of procreation (not how babies emerge, but how they get planted).

This is a stage in which fathers often find a bond with their children in their shared interest in sports, cars, and other things involving bursts of energy. Children identify with and want to be like their fathers, who often are the focus of a passionate attachment (Stiver, 1991).

### Body Attitude and Alignment in the Outer Genital Indulging Phase[21]

The body attitude of this subphase is that of a long, thin, springy, single body unit.

### The Jumping Rhythm in Later Development

The jumping rhythm introduces dynamics to gestures, body movements, emotions, and thought processes. Using a jumping rhythm a person flies forward with exuberance to greet a visitor. Jumping rhythms are the dynamic behind abrupt and intense mood swings, or ideas which come with a sudden flash of insight.

People with an abundance of jumping rhythms are outgoing and energetic and like to show off. They may wholeheartedly plunge into undertakings or adventures, but they may just as easily jump right back out. They may provide the impetus and stimulation for getting a job started, but they may need direction and organization from others for the completion of tasks.

Jumpers and bounders can be intrusive and disruptive. However, because the jumping rhythm is indulging (the movements end in rounded rather than sharp transitions) its intrusiveness is not aggressive. People are often charmed by the enthusiasm of the "intruder" whose glory in himself evokes the admiration of others. A childish vulnerability (deriving from the alternation of active and passive roles) often marks those who frequently use the jumping rhythm.

Although many cultures offer special dispensation for children, there is considerable cultural variation in the degree to which jumping rhythms are accepted or rejected among adults. Successful speakers, teachers, or preachers in the African-American community often use a mixed jumping rhythm to energize the audience, who responds interactively. The jumping rhythm blended with the inner genital swaying rhythm can be very involving.

### The Spurting/Ramming Rhythm (ogs) in the Outer Genital Fighting Phase

As children reach their fifth birthday, the jumping rhythm becomes defined by sharp transitions (see Figure 12).

Movements become more sharply differentiated. Rather than boisterously rambunctious, five-year-olds become more purposeful, aggressive, penetrating, and focused. If they ram into a friend, it is more often done deliberately rather than by accident. The sharp transitions

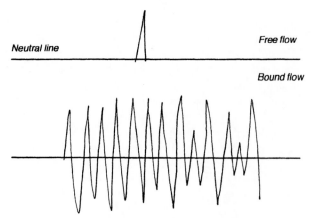

**Figure 12.** The Spurting/Ramming Rhythm.

and high intensity make **spurting/ramming** the most aggressive and potentially violent of all the rhythms.

By five years of age, children no longer move as a single global unit, but rather can use considerable differentiation in arms, legs, and torso. As their limbs are used in differentiated fashion, fine manipulations improve.

---

### Exercise

Try a karate chop. Remember to keep the sharp transition which gives the movement an aggressive, fighting quality. Hammer a nail, pound the gavel with authority, reach forward to grab something aggressively, or lunge forward. The movement is purposeful and aimed.

---

The spurting/ramming rhythm gives a child's movements decisiveness, assertiveness, penetration, and clarity. This does not mean that the child's exuberance, exhibitionism, and sexual excitement are tamed, but rather that they are more clearly aimed and focused.

As the five-year-old's body movement becomes more clarified so does her process of thinking. "Good guys" are distinguished from "bad guys," fantasy from reality. Winning versus losing becomes an important issue. Roles are less flexible and more defined. The chaser chases, the bad guy is bad.

Gender identity also becomes more clearly differentiated. The majority of boys try hard to act like boys and segregate themselves from girls, who mostly try to act like girls. There are exceptions, for example, children who tend to be more androgynous or who have trans-sexual identification. Most societies, however, begin marking gender roles by the age of five or six, intensifying the differentiation process (Whiting, 1963). Girls look more to their mothers as role models and boys to their fathers. In the U.S., dolls and action figures emphasize male and female "ideal types" (stereotypes), as do many of the traditional fairy tales with active heroes and passive heroines. Stiver (1991) suggests that when fathers are absent or have limited relationships with their children, idealization of fathers may continue into adulthood. However, this does not mean that children with absent fathers have no familiarity with qualities often associated with the masculine role. Both girls and boys experience these as they pass through the indulging outer genital phase and as they interact in the social environment. The fighting outer genital rhythm serves to clarify the gender role differences as they evolve.

As movements and thought processes become more differentiated, children learn the use of opposite movements as preparations. For example, they begin an action by bending the knees as a preparation for jumping up or they move an arm backward to throw a ball forward. The concept of using opposite movements will develop in the next phase into more complex patterns, such as using gentleness to deal with vehemence and aggression, or suddenness to get over feelings of hesitation (Kestenberg, 1975).

### *Body Attitude and Alignment in the Outer Genital Fighting Phase*

The body attitude of this subphase continues to be long and thin but is differentiated, sharp, and tends to be vertically and sagittally oriented like a rocket in a forward trajectory.

### *The Spurting/Ramming Rhythm in Later Development*

The spurting/ramming rhythm tends to produce explosive, aggressive, ballistic, and penetrating movements which are often accompanied by an assertive attitude. A person with a preference for spurting/ramming rhythms may pursue a goal in a highly motivated fashion, hammering away at a task until it is completed (note: this is different from the evenly-held straining rhythm type of persistence). We can envision here a hyper-involved, competitive sports coach, a dynamic but aggressive speaker and leader, or a parent who unremittingly pressures a child to excel.

### *Summary*

As the inner genital phase gave children the experience of nurturing, the outer genital gives them the opportunity to express a narcissistic pleasure in themselves and their achievements. While the inner genital rhythms are more inner-directed, the outer genital ones provoke externalization: expressing emotions, embarking on adventures, dynamic interactions. Each individual integrates these experiences in unique ways within the larger context of family and society. The developmental goal of the outer genital phase is to synthesize divergent drives and clearly differentiate wants and needs. As the use of the body becomes more clearly differentiated so also does the child's understanding of the world around him.

## Pure and Mixed Rhythms

The ten pure rhythms described above are associated with specific biological zones and are adapted to meeting the needs served by those zones. They come to be used for varied functions which may be quite unrelated to their biological role, as shown in Table 2.

Rhythms are often used in blends and combinations which are termed **mixed rhythms**. Mixed rhythms modify pure rhythms and often reflect individual personality characteristics. Some play adaptive roles in meeting needs while others disrupt and derail. One mixed rhythm which has been recognized and named is the Hershey Rhythm.

### The Hershey Rhythm: A Mixed Rhythm of Adult Sexuality

The **Hershey Rhythm**, named for Hershey Marcus and shaped a little like a chocolate kiss, is created by a blend of the swaying rhythm and the jumping rhythm (see Figure 13).

**Table 2**  Pure Rhythms and Associated Functions.

| Rhythm | Biological Function | Other Functions |
| --- | --- | --- |
| **First Year** | | |
| Oral sucking | Sucking, nursing | Soothing, bonding |
| Oral snapping | biting, snapping | Pinching, patting, differentiating |
| **Second Year** | | |
| Anal twisting | Passive defecation | Crawling, messing, snuggling, teasing |
| Anal strain/release | Controlled defecation | Climbing, holding on, standing up, throwing, creating order |
| **Third Year** | | |
| Urethral running/drifting | Passive urination | Relaxing, running on, dreaming |
| Urethral starting/stopping | Controlled urination | Stopping, starting, competing, darting, interrupting |
| **Fourth Year** | | |
| Inner genital swaying | Nurturing | Integrating, creating caressing, nagging |
| Inner genital surging/birthing | Birthing | Giving birth to ideas, internalizing |
| **Fifth Year** | | |
| Outer genital jumping | Sexual excitement | Showing off, externalizing |
| Outer genital spurting/ramming | Sexual penetration | Attacking, penetrating |

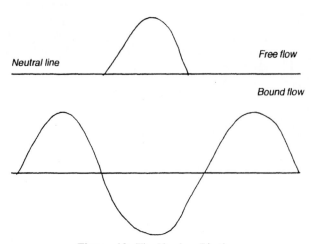

**Figure 13.** The Hershey Rhythm.

The integrating quality of the swaying rhythm mixes with and smooths the abruptness the jumping rhythm. The jumping rhythm gives more intensity to the swaying rhythm. This blend is often used in adult sexual acts, dancing, and in other mature patterns of social interaction. The Hershey rhythm (igog) is one example of the many mixed rhythm combinations possible.

Mixed rhythms reveal the existence of diffuse rather than purely differentiated needs. They are used for sublimation and for changing or redirecting needs by fusion with other needs. Because mixed rhythms are so revealing, we list them along the side of the diagrams. Some examples of interpretations of mixed patterns are given in the interpretation section (see especially Chapter 15 and the Appendix).

## Conclusion

As individuals pass through the developmental phases, not only do biological zones mature, but cognitive and psychological processes develop as well. Having some familiarity with phase related movement qualities facilitates understanding of the developmental processes being experienced by an offspring, student, client, or patient. With adults, the prevalence of specific rhythmic patterns reflect phase related issues with which the person is concerned or which have become focal aspects of one's personality.

However, the pattern of development depicted here is not a simple linear one, in which one phrase replaces the previous one, though models by virtue of their simplicity tend to suggest such pattern. Stern (1995) has cautioned that while qualities may emerge or begin at a certain general age during infancy, they are not limited to specific phases, but continue throughout life. Nor, as Erikson (1950) pointed out, is development a process of successive mastery of skills, "... secured once and for all at a given stage." (p. 173). Such a view is a projection of our success ideology on our understanding of child development (Erikson, 1950).

Instead, hopefully we have shown how issues emerge, are struggled with, and reoccur. For example, balancing the need for both attachment and differentiation is a life-time struggle which is approached in various ways throughout life influenced by developmental phase, individual proclivities and experiences, and broader context. Nevertheless, there are certain universal maturational tendencies. Rhythmic patterns, all available from birth, become more organized and gain or lose prominence with each developmental subphase, contributing to the formation of an individual style. As we have depicted them here, they offer individuals the opportunity to experience a diverse range of behaviors and feelings. As development moves us in a spiraling pattern from indulging to fighting to indulging subphases, we experience and practice adapting and resisting, indulging and fighting, mobility and stability, connecting and separating.

These processes do not end with the phases described here. They continue throughout life in phases whose movement correlates remain to be further investigated and portrayed by later students. Kestenberg (1976) has described developmental phases of pregnancy and Loman (1997) has proposed that an inverse pattern of rhythmic preferences may parallel the process of aging in later adulthood.

In contrast to the multiple experiences offered by maturation, many cultures sustain gender, class, age, and other differences by emphasizing certain elements of the spectrum of qualities offered to us by developmental processes and experiences. For example, a culture may stress individuation and differentiation for some members of society or may devalue female assertiveness and male pliability. Although societal pressures often restrict the opportunities for balance that biological development offers us, we can help children embrace those qualities which provide wholeness, knowing the potential is there. Like-wise, knowing phase-related movement patterns and behaviors and how they relate to development allows us to guide children in ways concordant with both individual proclivities and general processes of development.

# Notes

1. An agonist muscle is one which is paired with an antagonist muscle. The contraction of the antagonist limits the action of the agonist muscle with which it is paired.
2. Rhythmic patterns are present before birth, but they have not been subject to this kind of study and categorization. There may be common rhythmic patterns associated with later phases in the life cycle, but these also have not been subjected to a KMP analysis. Further research is encouraged.
3. For an extended discussion of "body attitude" see Chapter 16.
4. In past years the phase terminology was also used to refer to associated rhythms. For example, in the second part of the oral phase, the rhythms were referred to as oral-sadistic rhythms. Some profilers who are psychoanalytically oriented or have studied the KMP in previous years still use that terminology. This text however refers to all rhythms by simple descriptive terminology. Thus we would say that in the second half of the oral phase, infants use a predominance of snapping/biting rhythms.
5. Note that in earlier KMP publications (Kestenberg and Sossin, 1979; Kestenberg, 1965) the indulging phases were labeled "libidinal" and the fighting phases were labeled "sadistic," reflecting Freudian terminology. In an effort to use terminology which is not linked to one specific school of thought, the terms "indulging" and "fighting" are now utilized. The name of the rhythm is based on movement terms which are pedagogically useful. The abbreviations are based on the name of the phase in the case of indulging rhythms and the name of the phase plus the rhythm in the case of fighting rhythms.
6. Hewlett found that Aka pygmy fathers spent long periods of time in quiet holding of their infants (1992).
7. African-American mothers used rhythms with a relatively high level of intensity compared to Anglo mothers, who in turn were more intense than Native American mothers (Freeman and Fajardo, 1977).
8. When parents bottle feed their infant, they can still attain feelings of merging and attunement by holding the infant so as to maximize a mutual embrace (see Chapter 5, also Kestenberg and Buelte, 1977).
9. The study of the use of multiple caregivers in many non-Western cultures may offer insights into this practice now becoming more popular in the United States. Mead has suggested that in extended family settings, the infant develops diffuse feelings of affection for caregivers. In movement terms does this mean that the infant develops the ability to attune with diverse rhythmic patterns to diverse attachment figures?
10. Tharp's (1994) studies with Navajo children suggest importance of nonverbal kines-thetic cues in learning in contrast to reliance on verbal instruction.
11. Of course this is more a concern in cultures or families where individual rather than cooperative activities are stressed.
12. In earlier KMP publications the Freudian term "sadistic" was used. Most KMP ana-lysts have now replaced this word with the term, "fighting" to reflect movement qualities rather than psychodynamic theory.

13. The small holding section of the snapping rhythm described above, may be seen as a precursor of the more sustained holding seen in the strain/release rhythm.

14. Stern (1985) criticizes the concept of developmental phases as focal points for dealing with clinical issues such as autonomy and attachment. He suggests that they are issues for the life span. From the KMP perspective, indeed issues of autonomy are not confined to one phase, but movement analysis suggests that striving for autonomy takes different forms in different developmental stages. In the urethral stage children often seek autonomy in relation to time.

15. The inner genital phase was originally termed the feminine phase because it was believed that it occurred exclusively in girls. It was renamed when it was discovered that boys also experience inner genital sensations and are involved in phase-related behaviors.

16. The prostate gland is a homologue of the uterus and therefore it is not surprising that they share similar rhythmic forms of contraction.

17. Boys and girls as early as one year of age may express interest in having a baby (Parens *et al.*, 1977), but this intensifies in the inner genital phase.

18. Children in this age love hearing and telling long stories. Through the stories and games of imagination children can work through problems from earlier times which resurface during the inner genital phase.

19. Men are sometimes discouraged from certain activities during their female partner's pregnancy and/or postnatal period, notably hunting activities. Is this because hunting is associated with death or is there an avoidance of outer genital penetrating rhythms, in contrast to undulating rhythms used in birthing and nurturing?

20. In contrast to the blameless role of passive fathers in Euro-American fairy tales, in real life mothers who stood by while their daughters were sexually abused by stepfathers (or fathers) are often blamed for their inactivity. This suggests that men, despite their greater strength and dominant role in most families, are less often blamed for misfortunes of children. Even in the Oedipus myth, the focus is on the son's murder of his father, rather than the father's earlier attempt to have his son killed. This suggests that children generally recognize the mother as the primary caregiver and protector.

21. This phase was originally termed the phallic phase when it was believed that it was primarily characteristic of boys and stemmed from sensations in the penis. When it was discovered that girls also experience heightened sensations in their outer genitals (clitoris) in this phase and engage in other phase specific behaviors, it was renamed the "outer genital phase."

# CHAPTER 2

# Tension Flow Attributes

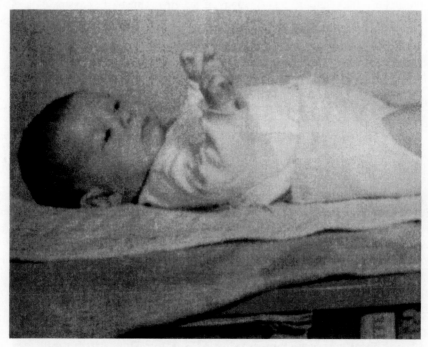

The baby is using "even tension flow" in his hands as well as in his staring eyes.

Tension flow rhythms arise in response to psychological as well as biological needs. However, people do not usually follow the textbook form of rhythmic patterns; personality and emotions shape the way needs are met. Even small infants exhibit individual differences in the qualities or **attributes** of tension flow used. One child may eat with gusto and impatience, snapping up even ice cream with **abrupt high intensity** movements, while another languidly chews with **graduality** and **low intensity**. Some children tend to hold a prized toy with a steady, **even** tension; others tend to hold the toy teasingly or shyly, making subtle **flow adjustments**.

This chapter examines tension flow attributes, their movement qualities, and role in development and in the expression of emotions or affects. The fundamental components of tension flow, bound versus free flow and animated versus neutral flow, are reintroduced followed by a description of the six diagramed attributes which reflect individual temperament. The last section of the chapter is devoted to discussion of related issues including resiliency, tension spots, and cultural influences.

Tension flow attributes have several significant qualities. First of all, they express attributes or qualities of emotions and reflect the core temperament of an individual. They are important developmentally because it is through the use of individual preferences or proclivities in tension flow attributes that an individual develops a small measure of control or regulation over the expression of needs (rhythms). As attributes come to exert more influence on the way needs and feelings are expressed and satisfied, they create individual styles of doing, feeling, and thinking. Thus for example, an individual's calmness (low intensity) or passion (high intensity) affects the way her needs are met.

Tension flow attributes are also significant developmentally because they stem from an early stage in development which is primarily inward-oriented. The use of particular tension flow attributes reflect subjective evaluations of the environment. For example one individual may move in a carefree fashion (using free flow) because he *feels* safe. Another person in the same environment might feel unsafe and thus move with restraint (bound flow).

Of all the movement qualities studied, the tension flow attributes have the most long-term persistence from infancy to adulthood (Kestenberg, 1967). It has been repeatedly observed that low-key infants tend to grow up to be low-key adults. The passionate high intensity child also tends to maintain the same temperament in later years. Furthermore, as Kestenberg and Sossin (1979) point out:

specific affect [qualities], experienced in infancy, play a role in the choice of later modes of adaption to external reality (efforts). For instance, an abrupt, impulsive baby...will be inclined to grow into an impatient, hurried adult who tends to beat time by acceleration (p. 57).

Harmonious or clashing attribute patterns play an important role in creating positive or negative chemistry between people. The study of tension flow attributes thus is particularly relevant for an understanding of interpersonal relationships within the context of the family, a therapy session, work, or other settings. These attributes are also important in the study of cross-cultural interactions, as each culture tends to value and devalue attribute patterns in different ways. Therapists working with people from different cultural backgrounds should be aware of the influence of both culture and individual temperament in constructing modes and styles of interaction as revealed in tension flow attributes.

## Fundamental Components of Tension Flow Attributes: Bound and Free Tension Flow

Tension flow reflects the elasticity of living tissue. The flow of muscle tension (tension flow) can range from extremely contracted in high intensity bound flow to extremely unconstrained in high intensity free flow. In the ordinary course of moving, a person's muscles contract and release in patterns related to the task at hand, individual temperament, and to the individual's feelings of ease or unease in a particular environment.

**Bound flow** is associated with feelings of restraint and caution which accompany more specific emotions of anger, fear, anxiety, or displeasure. In bound flow, both the antagonist muscles and the agonist muscles contract, tightening, constraining, and restricting movement.

Isometric exercises exemplify the inhibition of movement which occurs in bound flow. A high intensity of bound flow immobilizes movement; a low intensity of bound flow constrains movement. The use of bound flow introduces the element of control and thus is used in stopping movements and/or being cautious and careful. It arises in response to feelings of danger, insecurity, anxiety, and in turn can create such feelings. It also is typically used in attempts to restrain expression of emotions which may be deemed dangerous, such as anger.[1]

**Free flow** is associated with feelings of spontaneity and ease which accompany more specific emotions of happiness and pleasure. Free tension flow emerges when the agonist muscles move relatively unopposed by the antagonists. Free flow increases pleasant sensations when used in many recreational physical activities, including relaxation exercises. The mobilization and release of tension is associated with freedom from anxiety and caution, i.e., it arises from feelings of safety, pleasure, and ease and in turn creates such feelings.[2]

Rhythmic movements usually alternate between free and bound flow. Free flow is used when a movement impulse is released from control. Bound flow is used to control or stop the movement.

---

### Exercise

Tense your face, arm, and torso muscles tightly. What feelings accompany this high intensity bound flow? Are they specific emotions or a general emotional state? Try tensing just an arm or just your jaw. Use of bound flow in different parts of the body may arouse different kinds of feelings. Now try moving freely. Let your arms swing through the air. The movements are unconstrained and free of tension. What feelings accompany these movements?

If you feel nothing at all, it may be because you are a little uncomfortable with these exercises and are going into neutral flow in the central part of your body as a defense against emotional involvement (see below) or maybe because of physical exhaustion. Try again, engaging your face and whole torso in the movement.

---

The control achieved through bound flow protects and the release achieved through free flow liberates. Bound and free flow are responses to feelings which arise out of conditions which are perceived as dangerous/threatening or safe/reassuring. Thus bound and free flow are responses to both internal emotions and external reality, but with an emphasis on internal reality or subjective experience. The broader context of culture, family, and individual experience shapes our perceptions of what is dangerous or safe, pleasurable or unpleasurable. For example, imagine walking along the edge of a cliff. Would one use more bound or free flow? The choice would depend on one's perceptions of danger or safety. One person may be unafraid of heights and thus may use a lot of free flow, which would add to the feeling of being carefree and at ease. Another person who is afraid of heights might tense up in bound flow, focusing on the danger and feeling anxiety both from the height and from the bound flow itself.

### *Animated Versus Neutral Flow*

A person moving with **animated** flow, sometimes referred to as "regular flow," looks "alive." Movements which are animate have the elasticity of living tissue. Levels of intensity of bound and free flow exist above a certain minimum. In contrast, one may see a person who appears de-animated, sleep walking, or dazed. There is only a minimal level of intensity of bound and free flow in the movements used. This we term **neutral flow**. Neutral flow is often seen in people who are numb, exhausted, detached from their environment and their own feelings. Their faces often take on a vacant look.[3]

Even though movements in neutral flow have little elasticity, they still utilize changes in bound and free flow. Thus we can speak of various levels of intensity within neutral flow: very low intensity neutral (deadened) and high intensity neutral (mildly de-animated). We can also differentiate between free flow and bound flow in neutral flow.

A person in neutral free flow, (neutral flow in free flow) is limp like a rag doll with movements which tend to flow like molasses. Such an individual may appear tired, depressed, or listless. In neutral bound flow a person's body looks rigid and wooden. Movements are like those of a mechanical toy, robot, or have the lifelessness of a rock. Such an individual may appear mindless, unresponsive, and without feelings.

Neutral flow can pervade the whole body or can be localized in one body part such as the hands or face.

---

### Exercise

Try various exercises in neutral flow. Let your hands lie limply in your lap. Imagine that they are de-animated and no longer a part of you. Note that you can still move them and even use them to pick something up while retaining this de-animated quality (Note: for many people this is quite disturbing).

Also try a more pervasive neutral flow. While sitting, sink down into yourself, letting most of the tension go out of your body. You may feel yourself in a state resembling the feeling of falling asleep. Imagine that you are a blob of nothingness.

Once you have sustained this state for a minute or so, attempt to think about something complex or feel strong emotions. It is almost impossible.

---

The condition of neutral flow, especially a deep neutral (very low intensity), deadens feelings and thoughts. It occurs in most people when exhausted, depressed, ill, or in shock. When it is frequently present it may indicate serious depression.

A light state of neutral flow (on the upper edge of the neutral zone) is more of an everyday experience. Sleep often takes place in neutral flow though there are usually some periods of greater animation. When engaging in every day routine tasks that do not engage feelings or thoughts, people sometimes slip into neutral flow. Movements may take on a mechanical quality as one mindlessly puts dishes away or straightens up a room. Many people slip into neutral flow during a daily commute on familiar territory. One may arrive at one's destination without remembering how one got there. Driving in neutral flow is not safe because responsiveness to outside stimuli is diminished. A temporary memory lapse may also be an indication that one has been in neutral flow. Neutral flow is often involved when one goes into a room and cannot remember what the purpose was.

When one uses neutral flow in social situations, this emotionally disconnected state is disconcerting to others. A small degree of de-animation may lead an observer to judge the mover as tired, sad, or emotionally disinterested. Neutral flow is most often used when emotional communications are irrelevant, such as when one is working with inanimate objects.

The discovery that animate flow animates thoughts *and* feelings and neutral flow mutes both, supports the view held in many non-Western cultures that feelings and thoughts are not completely distinct entities. The people on the island of Ifaluk, for example, speak of feeling/thoughts (Lutz, 1988, see also Goleman, 1995).

### Free, Bound, and Neutral as Protective Mechanisms

By numbing thoughts and emotions, neutral flow acts as a protective mechanism or defense against unpleasant thoughts/feelings or circumstances. Neutral flow may numb pain and in extreme form, (i.e., fainting), it provides an escape from a painful or stressful situation. It may protect a person from fully experiencing a trauma, such as child facing abuse, or fear of the abuse. Some animals play dead, thus using neutral flow as a defense against predators. However, an over-reliance on neutral flow reduces the ability to use other adaptive responses and shuts one off from social relationships.

Bound flow also may be used as a protective mechanism or defense. Its prototype is immobilization or freezing in response to fear or anger. For example, rather than hitting someone, one may go into high intensity bound flow, constraining the active expression of anger. Here anger is not muted as it would be if one fainted, but rather the response to it is restrained. When people see someone tensed up with a tightened, clamped jaw they often infer that the person is angry, even though she is probably trying to hold back the expression of anger. In cultures, such as Bali, which disapprove of the display of anger, people often defend against expressing anger with low intensity bound flow, which ironically is used by others to infer the presence of anger (Kestenberg-Amighi, Pinder and Kestenberg, 1992).

One may also freeze in bound flow in response to fear. Bound flow serves to restrain movement and thus prevent further incursion into a dangerous situation. Becoming motionless may also help avoid detection by an enemy. Note that high intensity bound flow characterizes responses to both fear and anger. Other movement qualities help observers distinguish between these two emotions (see Chapter 5). Bound flow is valuable in the service of defense, but used in exaggerated form it can be debilitating. Too much bound flow creates so much inhibition that movement is stopped, pleasurable feelings are suppressed, and social relationships are cut off.

Free flow, by forming the basis for mobilization, can also serve as a protective mechanism. For example, one may use free flow to fling oneself away from an unpleasant situation towards safety. Note that although free flow is used in the service of escaping unpleasant situations, it usually contains the element of heading towards safety and more pleasant situations. Thus with free flow one escapes towards safety, whereas with bound flow one freezes in the face of danger.

However, too much free flow means a loss of boundaries and control. Feelings soar without mediation. Due to lack of caution, movements flow unchecked, inviting injury or damage to others.

### Gender, Class, and Culture

In North American culture, the use of bound flow as a response to danger (i.e., "hold your ground") and suppression of emotions has often been associated with the male gender. Our society has expected and encouraged females to use free flow (escape) or neutral flow (collapse) in response to anxiety-provoking situations. Such dichotomization of gender roles and movement patterns in the United States is perhaps declining, but not as significantly as some have expected (Faludi, 1991).

In many Asian and Anglo-Saxon cultures individuals considered to have a high status are held to stricter standards of suppression of emotions than are lower status individuals. However, the means by which emotions are suppressed varies in accordance with cultural display rules and individual tendencies. In Bali, for example, smiling with neutral flow is a common masking device (Kestenberg-Amighi, Pinder and Kestenberg, 1992; Wikan, 1991) while in the United States bound flow is a preferred way of suppressing feelings. The Balinese value "softness" and are thus less disturbed by a face with neutral flow than one with bound flow. As is revealed by an analysis of commonly used American English phrases, the American public has a certain level of understanding that movement qualities and emotions or attitudes are often closely associated. The use of such terms as "tense" and "uptight" reflects the recognition of an emotional correlate of bound tension flow. "I felt numb. I couldn't think or speak," is a phrase which reflects the sensations which accompany neutral flow. It also appears to be understood that tension spots in particular parts of the body may have body-specific meanings. For example, we speak of a person who is "tight-assed" and picture someone with a lot of bound flow in their lower hips. This implies an inhibition of comfortable social/sexual relationships. In earlier "tense and constrained" decades people used the term "loose woman" pejoratively to define a woman with a lot of free flow and thus relaxed boundaries. Now in freer times, we may say, "Hang loose," or "Don't be uptight."

### Localized Tension Spots

As noted above, bound, free, and neutral flow do not necessarily pervade the whole body, but often are localized. In some cases a tension flow pattern may be frozen in one body part. Typically these are either bound flow tension spots or areas of neutral flow. Tension spots can develop around an injury as a form of protection of that area. Later, if the bound tension flow persists, it becomes a source of discomfort or pain. Work habits and postures can lead to painful tension spots, for example, in the lower neck and shoulder area.

Neutral areas may arise from an inhibition in part of the body. A woman may deaden her chest in response to feelings of self-consciousness. This deadening inhibits full breathing patterns and circulation. One sometimes observes children or adults with neutral flow in their hands. This may result from inhibition of some form of exploratory behavior. Breathing exercises can relax and/or animate bound and neutral tension spots and are particularly effective in some cases of asthma.

### The Six Tension Flow Attributes

Six additional attributes (bound and free flow are also considered attributes), even flow, flow adjustment, high and low intensity, abruptness and graduality help define the qualities of emotions. For example, happiness can be held at an even level or fluctuate in levels of intensity based on flow adjustments. Happiness can be of high intensity (deeply felt) or low intensity (mildly felt). It can appear and disappear abruptly or gradually.

Diagram 2 displays the frequency of the six tension flow attributes in an observed individual. On the right side of the diagram are the fighting attributes and on the left side are the indulging ones. The two attributes on the top line of the diagram, flow adjustment and even flow, become prominent in the first year of life. The two attributes on the second

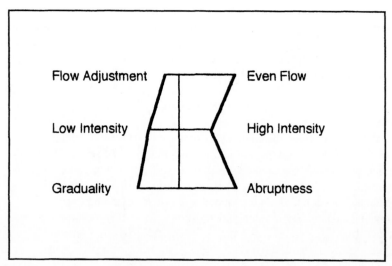

**Diagram 2.** Tension Flow Attributes

line of the diagram become prominent in the second year of life, and the third line reflects patterns common in the third year of life. All patterns are present from birth, but their frequency levels depend on stage of development, context, and individual preferences or temperament.

**Even flow** consists of evenly held levels of tension. The use of even flow sustains emotional states and supports the ability to concentrate. A short duration of even flow exists in the biting rhythm. A pinch, a bite or a short intent look use a short duration of even flow. Even flow of longer duration is an integral part of the straining rhythm which comes to the fore in the second year. Holding on, pressing, defecating, sustaining attention and concentration are based on the use of longer durations of even flow.

Even flow is considered a fighting attribute because it forms the basis for an unyielding response to frustrating stimuli. Evenness represents the dedication to hold on, persist, keep focused, and remain on track despite distractions or interruptions.

The use of even flow helps perpetuate a mood or feeling. The evenness of the flow steadies feelings and keeps them on an even keel. Infants who stay calm and quiet, often staring at nearby objects and people for long periods of time, are using even flow. Strong emotions can also be sustained. For example, when an infant screams one can often hear an even holding of the sound and the anguish behind it.

Children and adults with a predominance of even flow appear poised both in terms of movement and emotionality. They are generally even-tempered, steady, and not particularly spontaneous or capable of shifting from one emotion to another. Individuals using even flow may be able to keep focused despite distractions, but they generally find interruptions disturbing.

Although composure is often associated with even flow, many other moods or emotions can be evenly held. The particular emotion expressed is not revealed by a single attribute. The complexity of emotions are expressed through complex combinations of movement qualities, including attributes, bound, free, and neutral flow components, as well as shape flow discussed in Chapter 5. For example, even flow in combination with free flow presents a picture of an easily held, unruffled equanimity. In contrast, with bound flow, the evenly held steadiness is constrained, maintained through control (i.e., bound flow). If there is only low intensity bound flow, this may look like a preparation for concentration. With higher levels of bound flow, one may perceive held in anger, fear, or sternness.

Even flow in neutral creates a state of suspended animation. A person using this combination looks dazed or blank, and has muted thoughts and feelings.

---

### Exercise

Compare the effect of three different styles of speaking. One is stern and controlled (even bound flow). Another is unflappable and poised, but pleasant (even free flow). The third is monotonous and wooden (even neutral flow). All three will be monotonal and thus hard to listen to after a while. Because a person with even flow does not show a change in affect, she may appear emotionally isolated and disinterested and thus not very interesting (like many text books). Try moving and speaking in even flow combining free, bound, or neutral flow.

---

**Tension flow adjustment** consists of small adjustments in tension flow which reflect and create subtle changes in feelings and moods. Tension flow adjustments form part of the twist in the twisting rhythm. In the first year of life infants frequently make little adjustments to the body of a person holding them, snuggling and fitting in. They also may become restless and squirm to free themselves from being held when they want to explore. These small adjustments in tension flow may be used in seeking comfort (using free flow) or adjusting away from discomfort (using bound flow). Infants typically use flow adjustments in turning over and in chewing.

Tension flow adjustments move one from one level of intensity of feeling to another. The use of flow adjustments thus promotes little shifts in moods, feelings, or attitudes. A person with a high frequency of tension flow adjustments rarely sustains a single feeling for a long time, but rather is more apt to be emotionally variable.

Tension flow adjustment has an indulging quality. It promotes adaptability and playful and coy behaviors. The combination of flow adjustment and free flow intensifies the indulging quality of the movement, while the combination with bound flow counteracts it. Thus people who use a predominance of free flow with flow adjustment tend to have an accommodating temperament and people who use a predominance of bound flow, tend to adjust, but with caution and restraint. For example, flow adjustment with free flow may express itself in uncertainty about two equally attractive options, while bound flow may express itself as a resistant uncertainty. "I'm not sure, maybe ... no, I don't want to." Children and adults generally use flow adjustments with bound flow when there is difficulty in fitting in and free flow when there is an easy acceptance.

Flow adjustment in neutral flow, particularly bound neutral flow is seen in various neurological disorders. In neutral free flow it is more commonly seen in sleep.

---

### Exercise

Try making yourself more comfortable in your chair. Most often free and bound flow alternate when making these adjustments. However, try settling into a chair with a predominance of free flow. Do you experience a pleasurable feeling? Free flow gives the quality of lightheartedness; free flow with flow adjustment often becomes playful.

Now try finding a comfortable position using more bound flow. What differences do you feel?

Finally, try flow adjustment with neutral flow. When flow adjustment is within the neutral flow zone it leads to the co-occurrence of deanimation with minute adjustments of tension flow. We may see small restless movements intrude on the placid inertia of neutral. Such movements are associated with certain pathologies.

---

**High intensity** consists of extreme levels of intensity of tension flow (very free or very bound). It reflects intensely and deeply held feelings. High intensity is an integral part of the surging/birthing rhythm, and is found in jumping and spurting/ramming and often in straining rhythms. Infants lying prone may use high intensity to raise their heads and later to push up to a crawling or standing position.

In combination with free flow, high intensity movements are wild and unrestrained. Imagine a child doing a running somersault with free flow high intensity. Watching, one can feel the excitement, but may also be concerned with the child's safety. Feelings, like movements, in high intensity free flow are exuberant and uncontrolled. They can range from ecstatic and wildly happy to disturbingly upset, as in a flailing, out of control temper tantrum.

In combination with bound flow, high intensity movements become tense, strained, and sometimes completely immobilized. Imagine a person bound up with rage. High intensity bound flow creates and reflects intensely felt anger, anxiety, pain, or fear. A person combining three fighting elements, bound, even, and high intensity may experience intensely unpleasant emotions which are strongly and evenly controlled, like a time bomb ready to explode.

High intensity in the neutral zone is not very far from low intensity in the animated zone. It can be interpreted as a slight muting of emotions or an expression of intense feelings in a numbed state.

Adults and children with a high frequency of high intensity tension flow attributes have powerful emotions. If they tend to combine high intensity with free flow, they are likely to be exuberant, sometimes out of control. If they tend to use more bound flow, they may be deeply passionate, angry, fearful, and/or distraught. In any case, their emotional lives will be intense.

---

### Exercise

Try leaping up with high intensity free flow and coming down with high intensity bound flow. Try the reverse. Note how each change to the movement configuration changes the emotional quality of the movement.

Try putting yourself into neutral flow. Once you feel the de-animated, numbed sensation of neutral flow, attempt to recall strong feelings about something. Do you sense a veiling of the emotion?

---

**Low intensity** consists of low levels of intensity in tension flow. Low intensity is typical of many (though not all) twisting, running/drifting and swaying rhythms. Low intensity reflects low-key feelings. It is seen in mild, quiet, reserved, shy behavior. It is typical of the one-year-old who delights in the delicacy of things, picking up little toys or fluffs of thread from the carpet.

An indulging quality, low intensity, in combination with free flow creates a mild and relaxed feeling. It characterizes someone who does not experience strong, deeply felt sentiments, but rather takes things easily and calmly. With the addition of flow adjustment, easy acceptance emerges. "It'll be all right. We'll work it out" (the "no problem" personality).

If an individual frequently combines bound flow with low intensity this creates a mood of mild caution and restraint. We see someone who tends to be measured in her responses and feelings. The addition of even flow introduces modulated, steady feelings and ideas. People with low intensity are often uncomfortable when with deeply emotional people. Perhaps they are also unaccepting of strong feelings of their own.

Emotions are deadened or muted greatly by a collapse into low intensity neutral flow. Low intensity neutral flow is equivalent to deep neutral with the most minimal flow changes. Low intensity neutral free flow is rag doll-limp and inanimate. Low intensity neutral bound flow is wooden, robotic, and inanimate.

---

## Exercise

In order to experience the differences between low and high intensity, try expressing an emotion (happiness, anger, surprise) in words and gestures first in low intensity and then in high intensity. Note the differences, not only in the impression you make in front of others, but also in the way you feel as you use lower or raise levels of intensity.

Also note how free flow enhances the pleasant quality and bound flow contributes to the unpleasant quality of a movement or a speaker's voice.

---

**Abruptness** consists of swiftly changing levels of intensity. Abruptness is an inherent quality of jumping and spurting/ramming rhythms and often, though not always, is part of the starting/stopping rhythm. We see abruptness in the starting/stopping pattern of the two-and-a-half-year-old, in the bounce of a four-year-old, in the startle response of a baby hearing a loud noise, and in the rapid drumming of a dance band. Abruptness gives emotions the quality of rapid change. Many different emotional qualities emerge as various attributes combine with abruptness. Below is a sampling of the great variety of emotional responses associated with abruptness. A person using an abrupt increase in free flow with low intensity appears skittish, capricious, and impulsive. With high intensity abrupt, she would appear explosive, eruptive, or ecstatic. She may use an abrupt decrease of free flow in collapsing, fainting, or falling or in conjunction with sharp disappointment.

In stiffening, becoming alert, irritable, and/or impatient, one uses an abrupt increase in bound flow in low intensity. When a person erupts with a sudden flash of anger, fear, or pain he generally does so with an abrupt increase in bound flow in high intensity. An abrupt decrease in bound flow is associated with feelings of relief. In neutral flow, abruptness may be seen in tic-like movements.

High intensity abruptness in general is associated with a temperamental personality; someone who is described as mercurial, volatile, quick to anger or to frustrate (Berlowe, Kestenberg *et al.*, 1995).

An individual who uses abruptness frequently is often startling, surprising, dynamic, and undiplomatic. In every day speech in English, we speak of someone as "an abrupt person" because she spends little time on preliminaries, but rather "jumps right in."

## Exercise

Select patterns described above (e.g., flash of anger, sigh of relief) and act them out with a focus on the emotion. Then repeat the movement, identifying the tension flow attributes which you used.

---

**Graduality** consists of gradual changes in tension flow. Graduality is an integral part of the running/drifting, swaying, and surging/birthing rhythms. Graduality is often seen in the two-year-old who indulges in time, in the three-year-old caressing a toy, or in adults relaxing, lifting heavy weights, or walking languidly. Emotionally, it is seen in the gradual build up or diminishment of feelings.

Graduality is characteristic of people who move into new feelings, thoughts, and activities with measured transitions, i.e., the kind of person who is slow to anger (bound flow) and slow to get over it, or slow to reach a peak of happiness (free flow) and slow to lose it. Such people tend to move away from frustration and towards gratification with a gradually changing pace.

A gradual increase of intensity in free flow is freeing, both bodily and emotionally. It signals growing pleasure, wakefulness (after sleep), enthusiasm, or excitement (with high intensity). A gradual decrease of intensity in free flow is associated with diminishment of those feelings, i.e., calming down.

Gradually increasing intensity in bound flow steadies and restrains movements. It reflects and creates the gradual building up of unpleasant feelings (such as concern, anxiety, fear or anger) like a slow-burning fuse. The gradual decrease of intensity in bound flow leads to an easing of restraint associated with feelings of unwinding from a tense time, relaxing, yielding, letting go.

Gradual changes in neutral are seen most often in the process of falling asleep. One moves gradually into loss of animation.

---

## Exercise

Go through the descriptions above, acting out each pattern of gradually rising and falling tension levels. Try the combinations with free and bound flow. Do the descriptions match your experience of the movement patterns?

---

The attributes of abruptness and graduality are closely related to time. A predominance of graduality or abruptness shows up most clearly in the transitions a person makes from one activity, thought, or mood to another. With abruptness transitions tend to be rapid (for example, saying goodbye and immediately leaving). With graduality, the transition from one focus to another is drawn out or smoother.

If no early trauma occurs, these six tension flow attributes are among the most stable of all movement patterns, often maintaining a similar configuration or style for an individual from the time *in utero* through adulthood. Looking at the pattern of attribute use, one can detect a personality or temperament configuration. It is the whole pattern that is revealing, rather than the particular emphasis on one or another movement quality. The analyst looks for a balance which indicates that an individual is able to express a wide range of emotions in varied ways.

It is in the area of attributes that one often finds clashes in personality. A person who does things abruptly may be quite disconcerting to someone who prefers to move gradually into emotions and activities. On the other hand, a person with an abundance of abruptness may have little patience for the drawn out development of feelings, decisions, and actions taken by a much more gradual person. A person with a lot of high intensity, may judge a person with a lot of low intensity as shallow, bland, or lacking in feelings. In contrast, a mild person may view an intensely passionate one as too emotional, too intense, and too visceral.

The remainder of this chapter will discuss rebounds, measures of emotional resiliency, and the general topic of emotion as it relates to the KMP.

A **rebound** is the diminishment of a quality in order to renew it. A person who hammers a nail will quickly become exhausted if she maintains a consistent high level of intensity. Instead she must slow down and lighten up a bit before resuming her high energy level. Rebounds offer respite and are a source of replenishment of energy. The pattern and frequency of rebounds in tension flow attributes is used as a measure of resiliency.

---

### Exercise

Try using high intensity bound flow to push a heavy object. After a few moments, taking a breath, you may decrease the intensity (or let up slightly) to gain a respite and then be able to bounce back with yet higher intensity.

---

The rebound supports a renewed attempt with refreshed energy. The ability to diminish a quality of movement momentarily in order to renew it is an important asset in many tasks and in dealing with emotions. Picture, for example, a child sobbing hysterically, who pauses momentarily, only to resume sobbing more loudly.

Two kinds of rebounds have been identified: **upbeat** and **tripartite**. In the upbeat, the rebound begins with the expression of a quality which is followed by an intensification of that same quality. For example, one may be somewhat abrupt in initiating departure from a party; this may be followed by a greater degree of abruptness necessary for actual departure. The first part of the phrase acts as a preparatory movement.

In the tripartite rebound, there is a three part sequence of "abrupt, less abrupt, even more abrupt." The diminishment of abruptness is in service of greater abruptness. At this same party, the guests are trying to leave with some abruptness. "The baby sitter called, we have to go now!" Then they may back off slightly, "Great party!" (less abrupt), followed by, "but we must leave now!!" (even more abrupt).

In the KMP system rebounds do not involve going into the opposite movement quality, rather they are only a diminishment of a quality. For example, if one loses high intensity so much that one goes into low intensity, this is not a rebound. Losing a quality completely does not offer renewal to the extent that a diminishment does; in fact, shifting into a different attribute may lead to a loss of momentum. We study rebounds as a measure of a person's ability to persist at a task be it emotional or physical. A person who has a high level of intensity might be able to work up considerable passion for an activity, but become easily worn out and thus not be the effective proponent of a cause that one would have expected. Likewise, in emotional relationships, the person with little rebounds may "run cold or hot" not being able to adapt to the usual ups and downs a relationship requires.

## The Role of Tension Flow Attributes in the Expression of Emotion

Tension flow attributes work as mood-regulating mechanisms. For example, anger with high intensity becomes deeply felt; with low intensity it becomes diminished. Using even flow a person can hold onto a feeling or, using abruptness, one can quickly change the feeling. Thus tension flow attributes or combinations of attributes give specific qualities to emotions, but they do not determine the emotion itself. A similar situation exists with bound and free flow. Bound flow is usually used when a person is feeling wary, fearful, or angry. Free flow is usually used when a person is feeling elated, relaxed, or simply pleased. There is no clear specificity or one: one correlation between use of a tension flow attribute and expression of a specific emotion. We cannot distinguish between such related emotions as fear and anger just on the basis of tension flow attributes.

In a similar fashion the chemical/hormonal basis of emotions does not appear to differentiate specific emotions clearly. For example, adrenalin is released in both aggressive and fearful responses (both ergotropic responses) (Laughlin, 1993).

However it is possible that such general emotional responses can be given greater specificity on both a neuro-chemical and a movement basis. The differential or discrete emotions theory (Tomkins, 1962; Izard, 1980; Ekman and Friesen, 1975) suggests that there are fundamental emotions which operate like innate programs with a neural substrate, specific neuromuscular-expressive patterns and specific subjective qualities. These theorists have defined 7–12 discrete emotions which they attribute to innate sources. By looking more carefully at combinations of movement qualities in the KMP system, we should be able to develop more specific movement-based definitions of emotions. Meijer (1989) also notes that only a general attribution of emotions can be made on the basis of one feature, but more specific determinations can be made on the basis of combinations. For example, it appears that the specific area of the body in which a tension flow attribute is localized may help define the emotion experienced and expressed by the mover. When a person is startled, high intensity, abrupt, bound flow localizes in the chest and neck region. This is often associated with an abrupt intake of breath and backward retreat. In contrast, a person who is angered tends to localize bound flow high intensity in the jaw, brows, shoulders and hands. Perhaps this serves to restrain primitive aggressive patterns, biting and hitting. Secondly, changes in body shape, such as a forward bulging chin or chest or clenched fists may not only help communicate specificity of emotions to others, but through kinesthetic feedback help shape and sustain an emotion in the mover. The role of body shape changes and directional movement in affect communication and expression will be discussed further in Chapters 5 and 7.

## Cross-Cultural Comparisons

In order to further substantiate the existence of innately based discrete emotions, Ekman and his associates (1989) attempted to demonstrate there are basic emotions which are expressed in universally recognizable fashion. When they showed photographs of human faces to a sample group of people in several European and one non-European culture area (New Guinea), the test group were remarkably consistent in their identification of six "basic" emotions. The validity of the results of this study would be strengthened if people with more diverse cultural backgrounds were included and if more consideration was given to the problems of translation of feeling terms. As Sossin and Kestenberg (1994) have pointed out, a label may be used to include a wide variety of subjective experiences.

However, Ekman and other followers of discrete emotions theory do not dismiss the affects of cultural influences. It is fairly well recognized that the way each person experiences and expresses emotions is affected by individual temperament, experience, and cultural background. The general public often make generalizations about the emotional expressiveness or repressiveness of people from cultures other than their own. Ekman and Friesen (1975) themselves have noted that the way that emotions are expressed is governed by culturally specific "display rules." Izard (1980) makes a similar point when he suggests that there are some underlying universals but that "... expressive cues that convey emotion in every day life are frequently embedded in complex expressions which are not uniform cross-culturally" (p. 203). Thus, evaluators of a tension flow attribute diagram must take cultural context into consideration and culturally based norms must be developed.

Cultural differences in use of attributes may create significant interpersonal misunderstandings and clashes. For example, Mitchell (1988) describes how his low intensity gestures made him stand out as a "goy" (non-Jew) in a Jewish ghetto. Residents interpreted his gestures to mean that he was not emotionally engaged with them. After his Jewish friends trained him in high intensity movements and jumping rhythms (though he didn't use our categories) he became more accepted by the community he was studying. Edward T. Hall (1977), a cross-cultural trainer, has stressed the role of discordant types of transitions in culture clashes. For example, in cultures where time is commonly measured in discrete units and highly valued, abruptness often characterizes transitions. Meetings, therapy sessions, and classes both begin and end with a certain precision and differentiation of one activity from another. Where time is subordinated to social goals, beginnings and endings are usually not so clearly defined. A Western spectator at a village dance in another part of the world may feel unnerved by the degree of graduality with which a performance begins.[4] In many cultures punctuality, which relies on abrupt transitions, connotes emotional distance while delaying, based on graduality, often results from emotional connectedness.[5]

Particular tension flow attributes may characterize a culture or a distinct subgroup. For example, in many stratified cultures, members of the upper class attempt to maintain a refined, poised manner based on low intensity, even flow, and graduality, e.g., the Fulbe of West Africa (Reisman, 1989), the Balinese of Indonesia (Wikan, 1991; Geertz, 1973),[6] Spaniards, (Ellgring, 1984), and Japanese (Ramsey, 1984). This cultivated poise conveys emotional control and imperturbability, and thus someone who is beyond animal instincts. High intensity displays are viewed as a sign of emotional disorder or lack of "class." One can see this same class differentiation in many subcultures of the United States. Much more data is still required for the culturally sensitive therapist and student of human behavior.

### Tension Flow Attributes and Emotional Intelligence

Several psychologists have questioned the concept of I.Q. as a singular entity. Howard Gardner (1983) for example, suggests that we should speak of multiple intelligences, including musical ability, mathematical, literary, mechanical, etc. Daniel Goleman (1995) has focused on what he calls "emotional intelligence," or the ability to use and control a complex array of emotions. One component of emotional intelligence is the ability to regulate emotions to facilitate adaptive functioning. In the KMP, we have several indices including social intelligence, creative intelligence (in coping skills), and emotional intelligence. The degree to which emotions are regulated is revealed by comparing the number of tension flow attributes with the number of tension flow rhythms notated. The more a child (or adult) engages in repetitive rhythmic behavior, the less her impulses and emotions are being controlled. The more she uses tension flow attributes, the more she modulates her impulses perhaps in adaptation to changing contexts. For example, a person might jump up and down many times as an expression of happiness or might keep greedily gulping down food in response to hunger. In these cases, rhythms predominate. However, a more mature (or more regulated) response might be to modulate such behavior according to the larger context. The use of a pause in even flow to check the responses of others, the use of graduality to allow the food to be thoroughly chewed, are adaptive regulations of rhythms.

The presence of a greater number of attributes indicates that rhythms are being regulated. It does not indicate that this is necessarily an adaptive or intelligent pattern of regulation. That can only be judged within context. However, we can use another index, called the **load factor**, to evaluate the complexity with which the task is undertaken. If a person uses two or three different tension flow attributes in various combinations, this offers them a larger range of response and has the potential to produce more adaptive behavior than if someone only uses one attribute at a time. Following Goleman, we might call this an "emotional intelligence" measure (see Notes 3 and 4 below for further explanation).

## Conclusion

Tension flow attributes introduce a measure of control or regulation over the expression of needs (rhythms) through the influence of feelings and temperament. As attributes come to exert more influence on the way needs and feelings are expressed and satisfied, they create individual styles of doing, feeling, and thinking. One individual may characteristically be evenly poised (even flow) and mild (low intensity) and have moods which shift gradually (gradual flow change) while another may easily become anxious, shift moods abruptly, and express intense emotions.

Tension flow attributes supply important components in the experience, expression, and communication of emotions. Their contributions are recognized to some extent as English language expressions such as "tense," "up tight," and "intense" indicate. However, they are not always readily observable and often go unlabeled. Patterns of tension flow in movers can be recognized through the process of kinesthetic attunement and can be captured most accurately through tension flow writing as described in the introduction.

## Notes

1. The predominance of bound flow can be associated with functioning of the ergotropic system, our so-called fight or flight responses (Laughlin, 1993).
2. As the observant reader will note, different kinds of emotion may be associated with one attribute. For example, we describe bound flow as associated with caution, fear, anger, or anxiety. Which one of these variants it will be partially depends on the various movement qualities which are used in combination (some of which have not yet been discussed). For example, bound flow in combination with shortening is associated with anger, while bound flow and hollowing are more associated with fear.
3. The vacant look in a person's face who is in neutral flow may also reflect the use of neutral shape flow discussed in Chapter 5.
4. In rural Bali, Mexico, Iran, and many other places of the world a foreign observer is often told that a dance performance which has been advertised as beginning at 8:00 p.m. may not actually "start" until 11:00 p.m. However, this is a misunderstanding of the

process. Long before eleven o'clock, the preparations begin; a musician arrives, a stage piece is set up. Still, to Western eyes "nothing" has happened yet. However, there has been a gradual assemblage of actors and equipment. The phase of preparation blends gradually into the beginning of the dance. Western observers ask amazed, "How did everybody know it was time to start?"

5. Hall (1966) pointed out that Americans kept waiting for an appointment interpret this as a personal insult while many Mexicans regard time as expandable and of less emotional import.

6. Although the Balinese stress emotional control, they see themselves as much more emotionally connected than the American tourists with whom they come in contact. They probably judge capacity to attune as an expression of emotion while Americans tend to see emotions primarily in high intensity displays.

# CHAPTER 3

# Precursors of Effort: Pre-Efforts

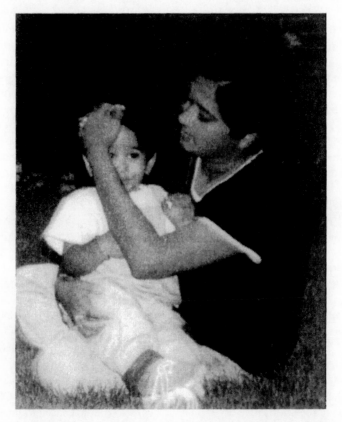

This mother is stroking her child's head in a "gentle" manner. What other qualities do you see?

Although a student dancer may twirl across the stage with technical precision, there is often something missing from the performance that marks her as not having quite mastered the dance. Although the dancer attempts to be light, the buoyant feeling does not develop. Although she twirls quickly, the exhilaration usually associated with acceleration is missing.

Rudolf Laban (1960) focused on movement qualities which effectively respond to environmental forces of space, weight, and time. He noted that one can use directness or indirectness in relation to space; strength or lightness to cope with weight; and acceleration or deceleration to cope with time. He labeled these movement qualities "efforts"(see Chapter 4).[1] However, some actions, like the steps of the dance student, although oriented towards space, weight, and time and resembling efforts, are in some way distinguishable from efforts.

These distinctions can be seen in the movements of young children as they attempt to cope with space, weight, and time elements in the environment. For example, when adults reach down to pick up a small object, they may simply reach directly down, while a small child may have to move carefully in order to keep her hand on course. An adult may move a heavy object with a strong shove, while a child may strain trying to muster strength. Marion North (1972) labeled such movements in children "early efforts." Kestenberg and her colleagues (1979) saw them as developmental precursors of efforts or **pre-efforts.**

Kestenberg and colleagues observed that the qualities found in these immature movements of children could also be found in the movements of adults who were engaged in learning new tasks, like the dancer described above. Whereas efforts are movements which are oriented outwards, pre-efforts have a mixture of inner and outer orientations because learning how to move in a new way involves inner concentration as well as outer awareness.

Kestenberg and her associates found that the inner concentration leads to dependence on tension flow attributes in the service of action. Thus a student dancer seeking to be light concentrates on low intensity of muscle tension; seeking acceleration, she abruptly changes muscle tension. When a person relies on tension flow attributes to manipulate the external environment, her movement takes on an affect-laden quality. Thus, a person using pre-efforts often appears intent, anxious, careful, or distressed. The difference between low intensity and lightness or abruptness and acceleration is a significant distinction. The Sands Point Movement Study Group found it important to distinguish (in both adults and children) the movements used in learning (pre-efforts) from the movements used in effective coping skills (efforts) (Kestenberg and Sossin, 1979).

Because of their important role in learning new tasks, pre-efforts may be of particular interest to educators. In this chapter, and in Chapter 8, we attempt to show how these movement patterns can be used to evaluate and guide learners into more adaptive and successful learning styles.

Pre-efforts are also of interest to psychologists because they present the motoric counterparts of an individual's use of defense mechanisms. There is often a connection between the use of pre-efforts in the process of learning and in the process of defending against undesirable impulses. A person may employ a pre-effort defensively to cope with overwhelming feelings which tend to derail learning. In order to learn something new, one may have to control anxieties and fears, steady a shaking hand, or hold back an aggressive impulse. Therefore we can define pre-efforts as affectively charged ways of attempting to manipulate the external environment and defend against intrusive impulses (Sossin and Loman, 1992; Kestenberg, 1977). The use of pre-efforts may occur on both a conscious or unconscious level.

In sum, pre-efforts play an important role in (1) development, (2) learning and/or attempting tasks, and (3) in defenses against inner impulses. In this chapter we present the six pre-effort elements which comprise the third diagram of the KMP. After a discussion of the development of pre-efforts and further elaboration of the role of pre-efforts in defenses and learning, we turn to a discussion of each element and its specific role in development, learning, and defense.

**Table 3** The Developmental Line System I.

| Tension Flow Attributes | Pre-Efforts | Efforts |
|---|---|---|
| Even flow | Channeling | Direct |
| Flow adjustment | Flexibility | Indirect |
| High intensity | Vehemence/Straining | Strength |
| Low intensity | Gentleness | Lightness |
| Abruptness | Suddenness | Acceleration |
| Graduality | Hesitation | Deceleration |

## The Development of Pre-Efforts

In the neonate, tension flow attributes reflect and regulate the internal environment of feelings and needs. By toddlerhood, a child is attentive to the external environment and sometimes able to cope directly with space, weight, and time. How do we develop from the primarily inner-focused newborn to the more outer-focused child? Pre-efforts represent the bridge between an internal focus and the more mature ability to cope with the realities of the outside world.

Within the first few months of life outside the womb, the infant gradually begins to regulate the selection of tension flow attributes. She can hold her muscle tension evenly or change it slightly in the service of accomplishing a task. When a satiated infant wants to avoid the breast, she may squirm and wrinkle up her face slightly. She has both an external focus on the breast and avoiding it and an internal focus on adjusting her flow (flow adjustment) to accomplish her goal. By the time a child is three years old, we expect to find all the pre-efforts in her movement repertoire.

Table 3 shows the developmental line from tension flow attributes to pre-efforts to efforts.

### Pre-Efforts in Learning

As stated above, pre-efforts are not only the immature movements of a small child; they also play an important role in the process of learning throughout life. When adults or children learn a new task, they are concerned not only with completing the task, such as riding a horse, but also with "doing it right." This triggers an internal focus. A novice archer focuses as much on holding a steady arm and concentrating (control of self) as on hitting the target (outer goal). The inner focus allows the learner to regulate tension flow (often called "practicing") until new movement or cognitive patterns have become automatic.

---

### Exercise

One way to feel the difference between pre-efforts and more mature and more externally-oriented efforts is to attempt a difficult task.

Open a window or move a heavy object. What movement patterns did you use? You may just give the window a shove, focusing on the window and using the effort of strength and acceleration. In contrast, try to open a window that you know is stuck shut. If you are concerned about whether or not the window can be opened or uncertain about how to use strength in an upward movement, you will probably bring your focus inward and try very hard, straining in high intensity bound flow (pre-effort of straining). Because bound flow partially immobilizes action, straining is not a very effective approach and the stuck window will probably not open very much.

---

## Pre-Efforts Used Defensively

Movement observation led to the discovery that pre-efforts are often used defensively against feelings of anxiety or uncertainty (Kestenberg, 1985). Imagine a man walking along the edge of a rooftop, knowing that with a misstep he will fall. He will keep an inner focus, carefully controlling his fear and accompanying flow fluctuations so that they do not lead to a fall. He may also be controlling an impulse to jump down. Pre-efforts here are effective means of dealing with both the internal and external aspects of an anxiety-provoking situation.

The reader may recall the earlier discussion of free, bound, and neutral flow as early defenses (see Chapter 2). Pre-efforts are more mature forms of defense which build on the earlier ones. For example, with bound flow a person can freeze his movement, but with the pre-effort channeling he can give the movement focus. For example, if the man on the edge of the roof freezes with bound flow in response to his fear, this simple defense is protective, but perhaps not the most effective or adaptive one. A person may build on the simple defense of bound flow. He may bind his flow moderately (bound flow) and hold it steady (even flow, low intensity) and then apply that inner flow regulation to reaching an outward goal (a safe spot). The movement becomes the pre-effort of channeling. The pre-effort of channeling in this case involves an inner control which is both emotional and physical.

The Sands Point Movement Study Group found that the process of learning tasks often involves the use of pre-efforts both in the service of trying to do new things and in defending against intrusive emotions. The urge to avoid a hard problem, inner distractions, fear of failure, or concern about "doing it right" may seriously interfere with the learning process and require simultaneous and integrated use of pre-efforts as defenses as well as learning tools.

## Pre-Efforts as Impediments

However useful pre-efforts may be in the initial stages of learning, eventually the inner focus limits the outer effectiveness. Once the dance steps are mastered, the dancer can perform to the audience; once the archer has become experienced, she can focus more completely on the target. However, if the experienced dancer is still plagued by fears of not achieving lightness, if the archer is still "trying too hard" to be steady, the inner focus impedes the goal of mastery.

Likewise defenses may derail learning rather than support it. One may defend against the fear of failing by avoiding, one may defend against an aggressive impulse to be critical by instead being superficial, or defend against an urge to delay work by rushing through it too fast.

The individual diagrams reflect the relative frequency of the use of different types of pre-efforts. Interpreting the whole KMP (discussed in Chapters 14–16) gives us indications of how well the defenses integrate into the larger movement repertoire. For example, we can compare the pre-effort and effort diagram to see to what extent the pre-efforts coordinate with (or overshadow) movements which allow one to cope effectively with space, weight, and time.

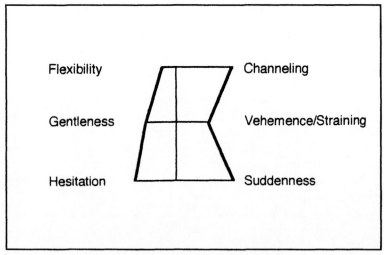

**Diagram 3.** Precursors of Effort

## The Six Pre-Efforts

There are six identified pre-efforts: **channeling** and **flexibility**, **vehemence/straining**[2] and **gentleness**, and **suddenness** and **hesitation**.

Diagram 3 of the KMP, displays the six pre-effort elements:

Following the same structure as the tension flow attributes diagram, the indulging pre-efforts are on the left side of the diagram and the fighting pre-efforts are on the right. Likewise, the pre-effort elements on the top line predominate in the first year, those on the second line come to the fore in the second year, and those on the third line are more prominent in the third year of life. We begin from right to left.

### *Channeling*

**Channeling** develops out of even flow and is the precursor of the effort of direct, which is used to cut precisely through space (Kestenberg, 1967). One can see channeling develop as an infant learns to successfully bring her thumb into her mouth. After some period of lack of success, the infant attempts to keep the tension flow even to restrict flow fluctuations and to channel the arm steadily towards the mouth. Eventually, the skill of directly bringing hand to mouth becomes automatic. The child can use the effort direct to effectively move through space without needing to focus on tension flow regulation. Adults use channeling when they try hard to concentrate or focus or when attempting a challenging task such as handing over a full cup of hot coffee to a friend.

As Kestenberg (1967) described:

Such aim-directed control of tension flow is accomplished through taming of impulses to move every which way. It differs from earlier types of regulation...as it is specifically concerned with adjusting the body to function in space (p. 67).

---

### Exercise

Try walking while carrying a tray of breakable glasses filled to the brim. Feel how much your focus is on your own body and keeping it steady or even. You may keep your arm steady and focus your eyes on the glasses by using even flow. This epitomizes the process of channeling.

---

As a mode of learning, channeling helps to create steadiness and an undistracted, evenly held focus which serves as a precursor to direct attention. When trying to pay attention to a speaker one may fix one's eyes on the speaker in an attempt to stay focused.

Channeling is also used for dividing, separating, and isolating. One may use channeling to carefully cut a cake into two equal pieces, or use channeling cognitively to separate one idea from another. For example, when trying to distinguish two concepts, such as pre-efforts and efforts, a person may cognitively channel a line dividing them and their meanings. Thus channeling underlies the cognitive processes of defining, discriminating, and pinpointing issues.

---

### Exercise

Try speaking in a precise way, carefully making distinct points. Feel the even bound flow in your voice. Note the hand gestures you use. You can hear or see the even flow which underlies the pre-effort of channeling as movement patterns and cognitive processes work together to support the expression of carefully focused ideas.

---

As a mode of defense or protective mechanism, channeling is also used to isolate and separate oneself from undesirable needs, feelings, or aggressive actions. For example, students who are distracted by the temptation to daydream or by feelings of frustration may isolate or channel out those inner urges.

When a person uses channeling excessively it reduces his adaptability and flexibility. He may tend to maintain a single-minded focus. Sometimes a person may channel a line segregating feelings from "objective" thought and work. He may act rigidly and impersonally and defend such behavior as a matter of principle. In the social domain, protectively isolating feelings through channeling may segregate a person from close relationships with others. It is interesting that many great thinkers and activists have limited relationships with their families. They isolate distractions such as love for their family from their single-minded goals. Their single-minded focus isolates them from any deviation.

On the positive side, the use of channeling aids a person in the achievement of specified goals, supports important cognitive processes such as differentiation and delineation, and protects against internally motivated diversions and distractions. It supports persistence.

### *Flexibility*

**Flexibility** develops out of tension flow adjustment and is the precursor to the effort indirect, which indulges in free forms in space. A person may use flexibility in her hand, wrist, ankle, shoulders, torso, parts of her face, and her pelvis. Flexibility arises in the joints and allows a person to shift from one spatial plane to another. For example, a small child may use the pre-effort of flexibility when trying to fit a wooden puzzle piece in its proper place. Rather than moving through space to place the piece where it belongs, she may turn the piece about, rotating her wrist this way and that way until she finds the right fit. Although small tension flow adjustments may accidentally bring the puzzle piece in the right place, with flexibility there is control of tension flow in the service of a task.

Note that there is always an inner as well as outer attitude when using pre-efforts. For example, in twisting to avoid stepping on or bumping into people when finding a seat in the theater, one is both aware of the other people and of one's own body contortions used to avoid them.

As a learning strategy, flexibility can be used in learning how to fit things into place or trying to fit in socially. With flexibility one may go back and forth examining an idea from different points of view. Flexibility can be used both to adapt to new ideas and avoid unpleasant ones. Using flexibility, a child may turn his attention from a math problem to baseball statistics and then to after school baseball practice.[3]

A flexible person is one who is often willing to adapt to another person's wishes. This involves both turning towards what is wanted by the other and turning away from an aggressive "stick to your guns" stance. In other words, flexible people are those who avoid being confrontational or persistent.

Flexibility can used as a defensive or protective mechanism for avoiding unpleasant or frustrating situations or feelings. While talking to a less-than-fascinating person at a gathering, one may find oneself twisting away, looking for an excuse to leave. Twisting away is an avoidance gesture which brings one closer to oneself and does not venture out into space. In contrast, a bored party guest using the effort indirect might scan the room taking in space and other people.

---

### Exercise

Flexibility can be used to twist about a little to avoid an uncomfortable lump on a couch or to avoid stepping on someone while climbing over seated people in a crowded theater. Alternatively, you might try debating with yourself out loud about whether you should go to a dentist appointment or just live with the pain. When asking, "Should I go, shouldn't I go?" your hand or torso may twist back and forth, mimicking the verbal/cognitive pattern.

---

A person can use flexibility excessively. One might too readily adapt to any situation, thereby rarely fulfilling one's own needs. There are also those people who turn eagerly to any new idea or task. Such people are unlikely to follow through on any of them, like the proverbial "jack of all trades and master of none;" by always turning to new things, they avoid persistence in anything.

When individuals have a good balance between flexibility and channeling they can use one to counterbalance the other. A person can use channeling as a defense against an urge to be too accommodating (too much flexibility) and use flexibility as a defense against an impulse to persist blind to "distractions" (too much channeling).

### *Vehemence/Straining*

**Vehemence** is based on the combination of high intensity with free flow and **straining** develops out of the combination of high intensity with bound flow. Both movement patterns develop from high intensity and both are considered precursors of the effort of strength. They are counted together to create one plot point on the pre-effort diagram.

"Deliberate increase of flow intensity to accomplish a purpose is a precursor and component of organized actions in which we cope with weight (i.e., effort of strength)" (Kestenberg, 1967, p. 67). In other words, when one applies high intensity (extreme levels of bound or free flow) in order to try to be strong, the inner focus on high intensity to accomplish an end makes the movement into a pre-effort of vehemence/straining.

We may see a child using vehemence in flailing temper tantrums with loss of control (free flow), in trying to persuade with enthusiasm, or in throwing himself into a task with passionate dedication.

In trying to be strong, one often lacks the authority or effectiveness that comes with strength. An adult yelling loudly with vehemence (high intensity free flow) but no strength will not exude much authority. The feeling is expressed, but not the determination to act. One may be intimidated by the strong feelings, but not by a sense of power. However, as the vehemence becomes less inner-oriented ("I really want to do it very much") and more oriented to external reality ("I'm going to do it"), determination and the effort of strength emerge.

Likewise, in the more physical sphere vehemence is not as effective as strength. A small child who flails out in anger may injure someone, but the force of the impact is reduced by the child's dual focus on his feelings as well as the object of his rage.

As a learning mode, vehemence may bring high levels of excitement and passionate involvement. A child may fling herself into a task, attacking the problem in order to solve it. Vehemence is used by those who feel deeply about an issue and then use the passion to develop strong dedication to the cause. Feelings and points of view tend towards the extreme; ideas seem great/terrific or terrible/horrible.[4]

Vehemence can be used as a defense against feelings of weakness and vulnerability. For example, people who have been oppressed can become vehemently aggressive to attempt to overcome the feelings of fearfulness they have learned. An abused child who feels impotent in relation to his family may become vehement with others to make himself get past feeling small and vulnerable. This pattern is sometimes termed "identification with the aggressor."

Vehemence can also be a defense against aggressive impulses. For example, with vehemence a person can let off steam without actually physically damaging others.

---

### Exercise

Try throwing an object across the room, focusing on propelling it with high intensity free flow rather than on its weight. Does the movement have much strength? Probably not. There is more focus on the feeling.

Imagine yourself trying to get a point across that seems obvious and yet is being disputed. You might wave your hand in a vehement gesture for emphasis, thus demonstrating a feeling while avoiding an aggressive act.

---

Persistent use of vehemence can be exhausting and ineffective, like beating one's head against a wall. A reasonable level serves as a useful bridge in the translation of strong feelings into effective acts.

If one combines high intensity with bound flow in an attempt to accomplish a task, it becomes **straining.** A person may strain to lift a heavy object or to try to coerce or convince others.

In learning new tasks, a child may strain hard to understand, to concentrate, or to demand an explanation. Straining may serve to focus intense feelings on a task. However, trying very hard to learn something or do something, one may confront frustration, but not necessarily conquer it.

Straining (like vehemence) may also be used defensively to overcome fears of weakness or feelings of inadequacy. Knowing in advance that a task will be difficult, one may approach it with both caution and dedication. Straining may help one go on despite obstacles.

---

### Exercise

While imagining pushing a heavy piece of furniture, concentrate on contracting your muscles. Feel the high intensity bound flow. How effective is the push? With straining, energy is bound rather than put to work. The inner orientation limits the outer effectiveness.

---

However, frequent straining with high intensity bound flow is exhausting and immobilizing. The child may remain stuck at one "unsolvable" problem, never progressing beyond it. It is easy to imagine that a parent or teacher may believe that the child, who after all is trying very hard, simply doesn't have the ability. The problem may be that the process of trying so hard (too much straining) may interfere with the learning process.

Both vehemence and straining are high intensity approaches to problems. They may be particularly effective in the initial phase of getting to the depth of an issue and applying intense feelings to a task. They are involved in supplying sufficient intensity to conquer problems.

### *Gentleness*

**Gentleness** develops out of low intensity tension flow and is the precursor of the effort of lightness which is a buoyant response to the force of gravity. A small child, attempting to pat a large dog or a new sibling, may decrease the intensity of tension so that the caress is gentle.

Gentleness also plays a role in learning to be light. For example, a piano student may be instructed to play with a light touch, but uncertain how to do it, the student focuses on low intensity and becomes gentle instead. The inner focus may help in the process of learning to be light, but does not allow the mover to actually achieve it. While the correct notes may all be played, the sound produced is mild or not heard, rather than buoyant. However, as the player becomes more at ease and adept, lightness may emerge.

In a cognitive learning mode, a person may approach a problem or a task gently, being careful not to delve too deeply. Treating the matter gingerly, one skims over it and remains on the surface level of understanding.

There may be a defensive element involved in learning gently. Caution (fear of learning too much, getting into something too deeply, or of arousing deep feelings) may hold back in-depth learning. This approach to learning characterizes many students. Because they are chastised or anticipate chastisement for making critical evaluations, they often may treat the material with "kid gloves" (i.e., gently) and unquestioningly. They learn "the facts" but do not probe. Perhaps such students could benefit from looking at concepts from different angles (flexibility) and teaching styles which encourage some passion (vehemence).

In the interpersonal mode, the pre-effort of gentleness is often used when someone is trying to be tactful or trying not to be too intense. Gentleness is an appropriate movement quality for caressing and soothing someone. Using gentleness one does not probe or hurt and can deflects one's own aggression. At times gentleness serves the defense mechanism of "reaction formation" by "nice" behavior which masks undesirable angry or hostile feelings.

---

### Exercise

Imagine consoling the child who is crying bitterly, having just accidentally broken the dish your grandmother gave you before she died. What pre-efforts do you use in your attempts to console when you would probably like to express your anger? Gentleness (based on low intensity) subdues the anger, allowing you to comfort the child.

---

However, gentleness, if too prevalent, keeps one on the outskirts or periphery of a relationship. One can caress with gentleness, but one cannot give much of a hug. Perpetual gentleness may be perceived as artificially nice. Of course, the mild, benign quality of the gentle person is usually appreciated and may be very appropriate for initial stages in learning and relationships, for giving comfort, and for diminishing aggression.

A person's use of the pre-effort gentleness can create an effective counterbalance to the use of pre-efforts vehemence/straining. One may use fighting qualities to defend against an impulse to be weak or too gentle and use gentleness to defend against one's aggressive impulses.

### *Suddenness*

**Suddenness** is based on abrupt tension flow changes and is the foundation for the effort of acceleration, which resists the passage of time. A startle or flash of movement is sudden. An individual may use a sudden movement to start in high speed or to stop abruptly and try to fight time. However, suddenness creates an instantaneous change and does not continue on in time. Therefore, it can not fight time as effectively as the effort of acceleration does. A small child who is summoned home may jump up suddenly, but if there is no acceleration, the sudden movement does not bring the child home any more quickly. It only gives the sensation of speed.

---

### Exercise

In order to differentiate between a sudden movement and an acceleration, try acting them out. An arm gesture can begin slowly and then gain speed, thus accelerating. In contrast, focus on the inner feeling of abruptness, for example, when some one calls your name unexpectedly. What kind of movement results? Note that it does not cope with time.

---

When one applies abruptness to learning a task, one seeks a quick answer, a sudden flash of insight or intuition. If the insight is good, its sudden appearance may suggest that its originator is a brilliant thinker. A student with a predominance of suddenness does not wait for a gradual understanding, but rather looks for the initial gut feeling or insight. Decisions are made quickly and impulsively. It is common that people who make snap decisions often withdraw just as suddenly, avoiding the consequences of potential errors. A person can learn to develop a more steadily progressing pace by following procedures and steps which lead toward the effort of acceleration.

People may also use suddenness as a defense or protective mechanism to escape danger. When combined with forward motion it is sometimes used as a counter-phobic defense. A person may rush into danger to overcome his fear of it. Just as a child might jump into an ice cold lake to overcome his hesitation, a learner may plunge into a hard task to conquer her reluctance.

A person using a lot of suddenness with free flow may appear flighty and impetuous. If a person is frequently in bound flow, suddenness may take the form of nervous or jerky movements. A person with an abundance of suddenness may feel anxious that things are not being done fast enough and falsely believe that rushing around, darting here and there, is an effective method to fight time.

### Hesitation

**Hesitation** is based on the gradual change of tension flow and is the foundation for the effort of deceleration, which draws out time. The small child, in an attempt to slow down (decelerate), hesitates, proceeds, then pauses again before having mastered the process of deceleration.

As a learning mode, hesitation creates a pause in the learning process. This may come from a reluctance to proceed. It can be helpful when one is struggling with a problem and needs to pause and go back over it again. However, too much hesitation may impede moving forward if the learner pauses repeatedly out of anxiety. Offering students simple procedures or ritualistic steps to take often helps them to move forward and progress. Hesitation may develop into the effort deceleration, i.e., slowing down and taking deliberate steps rather than pausing or hesitating during the learning process.

As a defense or protective mechanism, the use of hesitation delays progression towards an unpleasant or anxiety-provoking situation or feeling. In response to anxiety about a visit to the dentist, a child may pause or dawdle and an adult may postpone the appointment. One may also hesitate in order to delay a sudden onslaught of feelings. For example, when faced with provocation, a person may defend against an urge to retaliate immediately by pausing to reconsider.

---

### Exercise

Imagine approaching a cluster of strangers at a social gathering. Walk towards them uncertainly. Do you hesitate as you get closer? Note the combined inner and outer focus.

---

People who use hesitation frequently may constantly postpone decisions and actions with questions, concerns, and other delay tactics. When used excessively, it can promote a lifestyle of procrastination and be debilitating. On the positive side, an individual can use hesitation to delay impulsive actions and create pauses in a decision-making or learning process.

A person with a good balance of hesitation and suddenness is able to defend against too much delay by the use of suddenness and can defend against impulsiveness with hesitation.

## Discussion

The modes of learning and defenses people employ depend to a great extent on culture, personality, and past experience. Let us begin with a consideration of cultural and contextual factors and then turn to individual temperament and personality.

### *Cultural and Contextual Influences: The Reliance on Pre-Efforts*

Tharp (1994) has suggested that learning processes vary considerably across cultural boundaries. His studies suggest that Navajo children use more kinesthetic information (understanding through bodily attunement with others) than is found in Western cultures. Navajo children often observe an adult behavior and then apparently, without a practicing or instructional phase, move directly into performance. It appears that as the child observes (a visual mode), the information becomes incorporated into her body (a kinesthetic process) and this substitutes for the practicing stage[5] as we think of it. Does this mean that the child has worked through the pre-efforts stage largely through the process of imagination of the movement and therefore has the confidence and ability to go directly to efforts when she embarks upon the task?

This process of imagination or visualization of a sequence of movements in one's mind apparently has been proven an effective learning strategy. Visualization is coming to play an important role in American coaching techniques. It may be used by people in the United States on an unconscious level in informal learning contexts, though formal instruction in the U.S. generally mandates practice (i.e., pre-efforts) as the primary learning strategy.

Cultural preferences may also exert an influence on the kind of pre-efforts used. Mainstream American culture encourage rushing forward to confront danger rather than hesitantly waiting for backups. American presidents are criticized more for "waffling" than for making bad choices. It is not surprising that slang expressions for someone who is intelligent include "sharp," "whiz bang," "crackerjack," and "quick-witted."

This mindset seems to indicate a cultural confusion between suddenness and acceleration between making "snap" decisions and developing the speed to carry through an operation or endeavor. Many Americans seem to believe that by focusing on suddenness, they accelerate. However, suddenness gives a fast start, but it has no duration.[6]

### *Individual Differences*

Individual preferences and context shape the kind of pre-efforts which a mover will choose to use. For example, when faced with an unpleasant task, people who tend to move gradually are likely to respond with hesitation while those who use an abundance of abruptness are more likely to use suddenness to overcome their reluctance. Some people might effectively channel off distractions while at work, but at home find that they are more likely to indulge in whims, turning with flexibility to hobbies or family and away from work brought home. We might find that some people usually approach others gently (perhaps also with hesitation) but are quite passionate and vehement when dealing with ideological issues. Furthermore, people may begin with one strategy, but then later switch to others when the first becomes ineffective. For example, one might delay (using hesitation) and avoid (using flexibility) unpleasant tasks, but if forced by deadlines to get something done, the same person might overcome her reluctance by jumping right in with suddenness. Because there is always an inner focus in the use of pre-efforts, one can say that there may be a certain degree of consciousness of the defenses one uses.

No one has a perfectly balanced set of movement qualities nor is it likely that anyone has a total absence of any movement quality unless he is severely disturbed. We look for a general balance and adequate amounts of movement qualities, understanding that there are always individual and cultural influences and styles.

## Summary

Because learning how to move in a new way involves inner concentration as well as outer awareness, Kestenberg differentiated the movements used in this process from efforts described by Laban (Kestenberg, 1975). Pre-efforts serve diverse though interrelated functions in (1) the maturation from tension flow attributes to efforts, (2) in learning, and (3) in defenses against one's own undesirable wishes. By the time children are three years of age, we expect to find all pre-efforts in their movement repertoire.

There is a line of development from specific tension flow attributes (such as flow adjustment) to each effort (such as indirectness). However, when efforts (the more mature qualities) develop, the precursors of effort do not disappear, but continue to be employed throughout life (Kestenberg, 1967).

## Notes

1. Laban used slightly different terminology than described here. This issue will be further discussed in Chapter 4.
2. Vehemence is the pre-effort to strength which uses free flow. Straining is also a pre-effort to strength, but it is based on the use of bound flow.
3. The issue of indirect attention and imaginative thinking processes will be given more direct attention in Chapter 4.
4. This simplistic style of thinking is also typical of people who use predominantly one pre-effort element at a time rather than combining two or three.
5. Recently coaches have found that visualization (creating an visual image) of a behavior enhances performance of that behavior more so than practice alone.
6. Often cultures offer complex or contradictory messages. While mainstream American culture avowedly values free expression of emotions and impulsivity (free flow, vehemence, suddenness), it also expects moderation (graduality), goal-oriented behavior (channeling), and stoicism (i.e. restraint of emotions: channeling, gentleness, and bound flow).

# CHAPTER 4

# Efforts

The child on the right is moving through space with the effort of "direct".

The availability of a full range of efforts in a person's movement repertoire indicates that the person is able to effectively cope with environmental challenges. Rudolf Laban (1947) identified six **effort** elements with which we contend with the forces of space, weight, and time: **direct, indirect, strength, lightness, acceleration** and **deceleration**. People use effort elements in many everyday movements, but efforts are most clearly seen in exertions connected with physical work, sports, and performance arts: swinging a hammer, slashing wheat, wringing out clothes, gliding over ice, or dancing airily through space. Laban pointed out that cognitive tasks also draw upon the use of efforts. This is particularly evident in his description of inner attitudes. For example, Laban taught us to think of the effort of strength as including the mental attitude of determination and the effort of directness to encompass direct attention (Laban, 1960). He suggested that efforts are composed of three parts: (1) the mechanical aspects of the movement, (2) the movement sensations that accompany it, and (3) the mental attitude which instigated it (or follows from it) (Laban, 1960).

Physical or cognitive tasks are most effectively accomplished by the use of an appropriate combination of effort elements. Thus, a person who is adept in combining effort elements tends to be more successful in solving problems. The KMP uses the average complexity or loading of effort actions as a measure of "creative intelligence."

This chapter will present the six effort elements described by Rudolf Laban and the psychological and developmental aspects which Kestenberg and her associates elaborated upon. Those familiar with Laban's work will note that the KMP has modified some of his terminology and conceptualizations though the basic framework of Laban's work remains intact. The chapter begins with a short introduction to efforts and then turns to the analysis of each effort element. Following the main body of the chapter, the reader will find a discussion of clashing and affined movement qualities and a partial list of the effort combinations described so vividly by Laban. These are particularly helpful to students learning to recognize efforts. Following the conclusion of the chapter is a short synopsis of the developmental progression from tension flow rhythms to efforts, System I of the KMP.

## An Introduction to Efforts

Rudolf Laban, an artist, architect, choreographer, and avid observer of movement, studied martial arts, ceremonies, and dance to analyze work and movement of ordinary people in everyday life. He offered advice to workers in England on ways to move which would relieve the stress of physical labor (Laban and Lawrence, 1947). Laban was also very interested in the cognitive aspects or mindset reflected in the effort patterns most commonly used by individual movers.

The Sands Point Movement Study Group (Kestenberg and associates), having studied effort theory under Laban's students Warren Lamb and Irmgard Bartenieff applied Laban's framework to the study of child development. However, as described in earlier chapters, they found that the newborn infants or neonates are not capable of organized action and their motor behaviors bear little relation to the external environment. They concluded that true efforts did not exist at birth.

By about three months of age, building on tension flow attributes and pre-efforts, the infant begins to develop enough control to use a few movements which affect the external environment. They found that effort elements mature gradually on the foundations of tension flow attributes and pre-efforts (Kestenberg, 1967, 1975; Kestenberg and Sossin, 1979). Thus efforts are the culmination of a developmental progression of increasing control over movement leading to the ability to focus on and cope with the outside environment.

When notating movement, an observer must distinguish between pre-efforts which have both an inner focus (on tension flow attributes) and an outer focus (on the external environment) and efforts which are focused on problem solving and outer reality (Bartenieff, 1980). Efforts are qualities which individuals can use to make an impact on the environment (Kestenberg, 1967). Examples and exercises given below will hopefully further clarify the differences between efforts and pre-efforts. Table 4 shows the developmental line from specific pre-efforts to specific effort elements.

## The Six Effort Elements

The term "effort" in ordinary speech refers to the use of energy. In KMP terms it is defined as the use of motion factors (a) to cope with space, weight, and time, (Bartenieff, 1980)

**Table 4**  The Developmental Line from
Pre-Efforts to Efforts.

| Pre-Effort | Effort |
|---|---|
| Approaching **space** with | |
| Channeling | Direct |
| Flexibility | Indirect |
| Approaching **weight** with | |
| Vehemence/Straining | Strength |
| Gentleness | Lightness |
| Approaching **time** with | |
| Suddenness | Acceleration |
| Hesitation | Deceleration |

and (b) to express changes in attitude towards space, weight, and time (Laban, 1960). The six effort elements in the KMP are: indirect and direct, lightness and strength, and deceleration and acceleration.[1]

In the first year of life (first line of the diagram) there is the strongest development of the two polarities, direct and indirect with which an individual relates to space. Using direct movements, one can cut clearly through any plane of space; using indirect movements, one passes through more than one plane and thus can take in a variety of stimuli. An individual uses direct and indirect movements or attitudes in the service of paying attention. In the second year of life (second line of the diagram) a child develops a focus on weight along the polarities of strength and lightness. Using strength, one contends with weight; using lightness, one can indulge in gravity and feel buoyant. Children enjoy feeling the lightness or heaviness of objects or their own bodies. Coping with weight elements helps develop intentionality (an ability to weigh the importance or lack of importance of things and thus determine what one wants). In the third year of life (the third line of the diagram) a child tends to focus on time. A person can relate to time along the polarities of acceleration and deceleration. One can fight time by accelerating or indulge in time by decelerating and yielding to its passage. Coping with time elements helps shape decision making qualities (see Diagram 4).

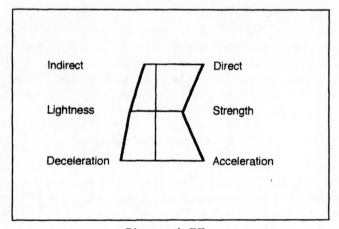

**Diagram 4.** Effort

### *Indulging and Fighting Qualities*

As with the previous movement qualities, efforts can be divided into indulging and fighting polarities. Indulging efforts respond to reality by accepting, yielding, and accommodating. Fighting efforts respond aggressively to reality: confronting, contending, and/or resisting.

## *Direct*

With the use of a **direct** approach to space, one can divide space along the path of one plane;[2] one can cut geometric forms in space. One can use directness as a basis for focused attention.

Whereas an infant or small child may channel a line to reach an object (visually or with a gesture), the direct gaze or reach of the more practiced child cuts precisely through space. Rather than being guided by and focusing on even flow, the child is oriented outward into space. With a direct attitude toward space, a trail blazer charges ahead, directly cutting a path for others to follow. Direct movements are effective for precise and clear-cut tasks. When hammering a nail, one's arm should sweep downward directly to effectively reach its target. Direct motions divide, conquer, and cut space.

In the cognitive domain, direct may be used in a similar fashion. If a person pays attention directly, he sees each point or detail clearly and with focus. He attends to the specifics of an issue, getting directly to the point, or "hitting the nail on the head." In a garden he will tend to see the trees and then the flowers rather than the landscaping as a whole.

The combination of direct attention and channeling may provide the basis for making abstractions. Direct attention provides the information ("See the Hemlock trees") and channeling can then be used to isolate out the essence of the information (defining them as evergreens).

Socially, directness is associated with blunt speech, coming directly to the point, and giving clear-cut directives. A direct approach cuts through diplomatic niceties and subtleties.

Of course, as discussed in earlier chapters, these descriptions do not reflect the complexity of real behavior. In practice, individuals use combinations of movement qualities rather than a single quality, and these combinations modify the effect and meaning of their movement patterns.

---

### Exercise

Hammer, punch, and tap. Cut directly and precisely through space without being concerned with the movement patterns you use. Can you recognize in yourself a direct orientation to space?

Give orders to someone. Explain very precisely what you want done. Note how hand gestures accompanying such speech cut directly through space.

---

### Direct Versus Channeling

With channeling (the pre-effort of direct), one has both an inner and outer focus. The inner focus impinges on the effectiveness of the movement in coping with space, weight, and time. For example, an early walker, practicing carefully, may pay attention to where he is walking. However, his outward attention (or attitude towards space) is limited by his focus on controlling flow fluctuations so he does not fall down. In contrast, the accomplished walker moves easily, focused on moving through space directly. His attention is focused outward.

## Indirect

With the use of an **indirect** approach to space one can indulge in free forms, carving wavy shapes in space and traversing planes (i.e., passing across more than one plane). A person using indirect efforts tends to pay attention in a multi-focused manner. The gaze of an infant may wander from here to there, tracing intricate designs in space and taking in a variety of sights. A person who is listening to surrounding sounds tends to use indirect attention. In the garden, an indirect gaze takes in the flow of the landscape, how the plants blend and interrelate. Walking through a garden with indirect attention, one can easily gaze down various side paths to new places, and perhaps to new thoughts and concepts. Indirect attention thus means that one yields attention to a variety of things and ideas.

In the cognitive domain, the effort of indirect is used when tracing one idea as it leads to another or in the process of making generalizations. Indirect thinking makes it easy to find associations, metaphors, and wander creatively to new imaginations.

---

### Exercise

Try gazing around a room, taking in all its dimensions. Note how your gaze makes wavy lines through space, traversing planes, using the effort of indirect. You may try flicking a bunch of crumbs off your sleeve. Did you use indirect or direct?

Repeat sentences such as: "One idea will lead us to another." "You can see many different beautiful flowers in this garden." Observe movement qualities used by yourself and other speakers when expressing various ideas.

---

The use of indirect has numerous repercussions in the social domain. It fosters diplomacy, ritualized forms of greeting, and various polite expressions common in many formally stratified societies. In upper class traditional Persian culture, for example, it was preferable to state thoughts and orders indirectly and to reach goals indirectly. Not surprisingly, Persian literature consists of more poetry than prose. The poetry is replete with metaphors and allusions which are based on indirect processes of thinking. In contrast, American culture tends to value directness. Americans have a reputation for being "up front," "speak your mind" types with little patience for diplomacy and rituals.

A person's relative frequency of use of direct versus indirect efforts depends not only on personality and culture, but also on context. One who is dominant is in a better position to be direct than one who is subordinate. Direct contends, while indirect has an indulging, yielding quality. In American culture, typically, though not always, an effective order is direct, a question or suggestion tends to be indirect.

A person who uses an abundance of indirect will find it easy to attend to a variety of ideas or goals, but may find it difficult to stay focused on one particular idea. A professor using a lot of indirect may offer a variety of anecdotes and examples to illustrate a point, capturing the interest of the students, who leave the class intrigued but confused about the main point of the lecture. A camp counselor with a lot of indirect movements will be able to monitor children playing while chatting with a peer but may lose track of the goal of the play session.

## Flexibility Versus Indirect

It is important to note the distinction between flexibility (the pre-effort of indirect) and indirect. Both indirect and flexibility may turn a person from one task or idea to another, but there are important differences: (1) Flexibility is based on a rotation of the joint. A flexible rotation of the wrist does not carve shapes in space. (2) Flexibility (focused on the joints and the use of the tension flow attribute, flow adjustment) has an inward focus as well as an outward one. The effort of indirect has only an outward orientation. (3) Flexibility as a learning strategy and as a defense is used to turn from unpleasantness towards pleasant sights, thoughts, feelings, or tasks. In contrast, paying attention indirectly is not so much a learning strategy as a way of thinking. Imagine attempting to solve a geometry problem. With flexibility one turns from one technique to another, trying to find one that works. With indirect, one broadens one's perspective or generalizes. With flexibility one is saying, "Should I do it this way, should I do it that way, maybe this, maybe that?" Indirect movements or cognitive patterns do not have the defensive, indecisive quality of flexibility, but rather lead one to attend to the full range of possibilities.

This is an important distinction. If someone frequently avoids work, problems, or ideas or turns frequently from one to another (flexibility), this may create a learning problem. If someone frequently uses imagination to develop new perspectives this is generally seen as a positive feature. With an indirect effort, integrated thinking may emerge, while with flexibility integration cannot occur. At times it may be difficult to distinguish between flexibility and indirect approaches when working with a student. Observation of movement qualities may facilitate evaluation of cognitive processes.

## Movements With No Attitude Toward Space

Pre-efforts of channeling and flexibility are used when a person is attempting to relate to space. With the efforts of direct and indirect one develops specific orientations towards space. However, there are movements or ways of thinking that have no relation to space at all. For example, a person running "blindly" through a field, dancing rhythmically at a disco, or floating aimlessly on a wave has an attitude of inattention to space. She does not cope with space either directly or indirectly nor is she attempting to do so (pre-efforts). Laban called movements which relate to weight and time (but not to space) earthy and rhythmic.

An educator or parent may want to distinguish between inattention (no attitude towards space) and indirect, free-floating attention. The former may indicate disinterest or inability to pay attention while the latter may indicate imaginative thinking.

In sum, the efforts direct and indirect involve an attitude towards space and serve the task of paying attention. They serve adaptation to external reality and make an impact in space. Ideally there should be a balance between the use of indirect and direct ways of paying attention.

## *Strength*

Using the effort of **strength**, one contends with gravity and weight. A person may use strength to deal with heavy objects and in determined exertion of pressure and authority. A toddler uses strength to push and pull heavy objects and enjoys fighting against the weight. A child will feel her own weight when rising. "A person must develop an attitude toward gravity as a condition for perceiving one's own weight and, secondarily, the weight and mass of objects" (Kestenberg, 1985, p. 34).

The use of strength enables one to make an impact on the environment (e.g., one can open a window, shove open a door, or issue a firm order). When one uses strength effectively to fight gravity, one gains a sense of one's own power and authority. A person who uses strength also conveys her power and authority to others.

Cognitively, strength is expressed in making serious determinations. People who use a lot of strength attack projects with determination and commitment; they are clear about what is important to them and they take their own intentions seriously.

---

### Exercise

Issue forth a command using strength and directness. Then try being authoritative using vehemence and straining. Which command carries "weight"? You can practice using strength, lifting or pushing objects, but you can also walk or speak with strength.

---

A person who uses an overabundance of strength tends to be ultra-authoritative, overly concerned with power and control. Such a person may be unable to defer to others. Conversely, one possessing very little strength has little authority, determination, or resolve.

### Vehemence and Straining Versus Strength

With strength a person can contend effectively with gravity. In contrast, using vehemence or straining the outer focus may be limited by the person's inner focus on how a task is performed. Watching someone use straining or vehemence, one is more impressed with the intensity of their passion (the high intensity bound or free flow, respectively) than with the effectiveness of the action or words. A parent may rave in a loud voice which carries "no weight;" in contrast, a low, but determined voice "carries weight" and instills obedience. Watching a person push a piano across the room with straining, what strikes the eye is the energy being exerted (straining) rather than the power of the mover (strength). If she uses strength, her energy will be more effectively harnessed.

### *Lightness*

The use of the effort of **lightness** creates springy motions and a buoyant attitude towards weight. A child may use lightness when tossing a ball or throwing up a feather. A dancer may soar with lightness, indulging in the sensation of "defying" gravity.

---

### Exercise

Try flicking crumbs off your lap. Note that you may use direct or indirect and lightness.

Conversing in a light-hearted manner, try saying "Who cares?" Do you have the sensation of escaping the pull of gravity? Try expressing enthusiasm about a beautiful painting. What gestures do you use?

---

Lightness is used in humor, tact, and expressions of happiness. Joking and laughing often promote a light attitude towards weight. People who use a lot of lightness are easily able to entertain and amuse us. They seem light-hearted and tend to "treat matters lightly." In other words, they take their own intentions and desires lightly. Someone who takes things too seriously may be advised to "lighten up" because lightness can be used to relieve and alleviate despondency or a somber mood.

Lightness is often used in the process of giving appreciation and admiration (see exercise above). In this way it also promotes inspiration. It is common to find lightness as a characteristic of those who are artistic, creative, and/or appreciative of things around them.

However, a person who uses an abundance of lightness may also be negatively evaluated in many cultures. One who skims lightly over knowledge may be deemed superficial. In American culture lightness is often associated with someone whose head is in the clouds (unrealistic), who is "air-headed," flaky, or superficial. In Iran, a person who is foolish is often labeled as "light" *(sabok)* whereas a person who is thoughtful is labeled "heavy" *(sangine)*. This is reversed in Morocco where lightness is associated with intelligence and heaviness with stupidity (Davis and Davis, 1993). There is some cross-cultural variance in movement qualities associated with intelligence.[3] Does this reflect different concepts of what intelligence is or the significance of movement qualities? In making interpretations one must be aware of cultural biases and perspectives.

## Lightness Versus Gentleness

With the use of lightness one can indulge in buoyancy. In contrast, when using gentleness one is only trying to be light by using low intensity tension flow. Gentleness includes the attitude of taking it easy while lightness encourages an upbeat, "I can escape the weight of the world" attitude. One can contrast the use of gentleness in stroking or caressing with the use of lightness in flicking or floating. One comforts a distressed friend with gentleness, but to use lightness would imply that one did not take his problem seriously.

In sum, a strong or light attitude toward weight is used in the service of weighing intentions and making determinations, either lightly or firmly. The attitude to weight denotes the nature or quality of intent.

### *Acceleration*

**Accelerating** actions fight time and are used to move things along more rapidly. One accelerates by increasing the pace of a movement. Acceleration is seen in the start of a race and in the swing of an arm. Some toddlers who still walk unsteadily will revert to crawling when they want to move faster.

A necessary acondition for perceiving motion in time, our own motion, and that of other objects is our attitude towards time. To achieve active control over motion in time, i.e., to resist the easy passage of time, the "wasting" of time, and the "spending" of time, we must be prepared to react aggressively with acceleration and to be decisive (Kestenberg, 1985, p. 74).

Acceleration is not necessarily fast, but rather refers to an increase in speed. This is an important point. Most activities which emphasize acceleration, such as car racing, skiing, skating, or living in the "fast lane" involve high speeds. However, the key factor is not speed, but a fighting attitude towards time. While maintaining a steady pace, even a very rapid one, one develops a sense of timelessness. It is the increase in pace which gives one a fighting attitude toward time.

## Exercise

Begin a conversation slowly. Then, realizing that your time is almost up, start speaking faster and faster. If you have a partner, you might both find yourselves speaking faster and faster together.

Note the use of acceleration on your way to work or an appointment when you are attempting to "beat" time. Note also the sense of timelessness when you maintain a steady speed, driving or even running.

People who accelerate often are seen in American society as effective people, good operators, doers. They make decisions and act upon them. They are uncomfortable with delays. The focus on fighting time is reflected in many aspects of society. Students are given limited time to complete an examination, encouraging speed. Leaders are expected to make decisions quickly. However, an overemphasis on acceleration may interfere with the proper pacing of tasks and use of careful deliberation.

Acceleration in the cognitive domain is seen in people whose thought processes build momentum. They often are able to grasp concepts with increasing speed once they begin to study.

## Suddenness Versus Acceleration

When told to hurry, toddlers may make a sudden move, but not necessarily continue because their sense of time is limited. To them, the sudden flash of movement is equivalent to speeding up, but it actually does little to time because it is based on an abrupt change of tension flow. Acceleration, in contrast, contends with time, preventing it from passing by easily. With acceleration one can build up speed, while with suddenness there is only a flash of movement or an almost instantaneous change.

## *Deceleration*

Using **decelerating** actions one can indulge and luxuriate in the passage of time. Deceleration is the process of slowing down. It can be seen in the two-year-old who drifts along or in the sightseer who indulges in the passage of time. Children and adults may decelerate in response to exhaustion or to conform to a speed limit. A person may slow down his pace, if he discovers that there is "plenty of time" or "extra time to kill" (Kestenberg, 1967). Deceleration offers a pleasurable sensation of indulging in time to those who are not caught up in the race against time.

## Exercise

Practice playing with time. Walk, accelerating faster and faster and then slow down. Experience the feeling of fighting and then indulging in time. Feel yourself slowing down at the end of a chore as one can stop fighting time.

Cognitively, deceleration leads to taking time in making decisions or coming to conclusions. Many people decelerate when dealing with difficult problems or decisions, preferring to proceed giving due time for deliberation. In some cultures slowing down is primarily associated with aging, weakness, or mental inadequacy. In many cultures (such as those in Sub-Saharan Africa) it is associated with wisdom as is old age.

Using deceleration in social contexts permits one to be gracious and hospitable. By slowing down one is expressing the attitude that one is ready to give up time in exchange for social goals. In contrast, when a person deals with machines, deceleration is generally devalued. One must be prepared to work at the machine's pace. In fact being "on time" gained importance during the Industrial Revolution when workers had to be ready when the machines were turned on. Particularly in the age of machines, those who frequently decelerate may find themselves left behind or may "miss the boat."

## Hesitation Versus Deceleration

Slowing down involves decreasing the pace, indulging in, and enjoying the passage of time. In contrast, when one hesitates, one pauses, holding back, generally in response to uncertainty or reluctance to proceed. It underlies procrastination. Rather than indulging in or fighting time, hesitation makes an interruption in its passage. One can compare the experienced driver who decelerates around a turn with the novice who brakes hesitatingly.

Some movements express no attitude toward time at all. Note that even when driving very fast, if a steady speed is maintained, a timeless quality emerges. It is the acceleration or deceleration that evokes and reflects an attitude towards time. Laban called movements which have weight and space but no time elements "stable" and "steady."

Coping with time by decelerating or accelerating is done in the service of making decisions. Deceleration and acceleration reflect on the nature and quality of decision-making processes.

## Effort Combinations

With maturation, children learn to cope with the environment by combining effort elements. Laban was fascinated with the way different effort elements can be combined. In a single action, a person may use one, two, or three effort elements. For example, there may be one element in a nod (direct), two in a step (direct and accelerated), and three in a punch (direct, accelerated, and strong). The choice of elements and combinations used varies with each individual mover and task.

A full effort as defined in the KMP system is composed of three effort elements and the flow factor (free or bound). In the Laban Movement Analysis system the flow factors free and bound are also considered efforts. This is not the case in the KMP, which does not recognize flow factors as efforts, but considers them in detail under tension flow. Table 5 shows examples of actions which are typically carried out using full efforts. Full efforts are used most often in sports and physical tasks. For example, one may hammer a nail with directness, strength, and acceleration. One may skate on ice using a glide which is direct, light, and decelerated.

Note, however, that most movements are not full efforts; they do not use all three possible effort elements relating to space, weight, and time. Laban called actions which combine just two effort elements "incomplete efforts" or "states." He suggested that they express inner attitudes such as those listed in Table 6.[4]

There are twenty-nine different possible actions using one, two, or three efforts, more of which are described by Penny Lewis in Chapter 16. People who often use combinations of effort elements have the ability to be more creative in their problem-solving than those

**Table 5**  Laban's Full Efforts.

| Full Effort | Elements | Examples |
|---|---|---|
| Punch | Direct, strong, accelerated | Punch down dough, shout an order, nod emphatically |
| Float | Indirect, light, decelerated | Walk dreamily, float down the stairs |
| Press | Direct, strong, decelerated | Press an idea upon another, press with an iron, bench press |
| Dab | Direct, light, accelerated | Dab paint on a canvas, tap a tempo |
| Slash | Indirect, strong, accelerated | Scything wheat, slashing with a sword |
| Flick | Indirect, light, accelerated | Flick mosquitos away from your head |
| Wring | Indirect, strong, decelerated | Wring clothes dry |
| Glide | Direct, light, decelerated | Glide smoothly directly through space |

**Table 6**  Laban's Incomplete Efforts: Inner Attitudes.

| Incomplete Efforts | Elements | Qualities | Discussion |
|---|---|---|---|
| Near attitudes | Weight and time, no space | Earthy, rhythmic, no attention | Evaluate and act without first having investigated, a person who just seems to know, an earth mother sage. Rhythmic dancing. |
| Awake | Space and time, no weight | Alertness, no intentionality | No evaluative process, collect information and act upon it without using one's judgement, taking things on faith, innocence. |
| Stable | Space and weight, no time | Steady, balanced, no decision | Creates ageless, unchanging quality, aware and thoughtful, but with inability to take action |

who use only one. They can cope with reality using space, weight, and time elements. These combinations support "creative intelligence."

Learning the names of the eight full effort combinations and incomplete efforts described by Laban aids in identifying efforts and remembering their qualities. It is also useful to practice looking for pre-efforts and efforts in the everyday movements of people. Kestenberg (1975) has suggested that frozen (or motionless) pre-efforts and efforts can be identified in paintings and photographs. Identification of movement qualities in paintings offers fascinating insights into the effect a painting has on its viewers.

## Rebounds in Efforts

A rebound in efforts is a diminishment of an effort quality. It offers a respite or time for recuperation and thus the ability to renew the quality with greater energy. For example, when hammering, the strength and acceleration used to drive a nail into a piece of wood would be exhausting if it were continuously sustained. However, the upswing offers a diminishment of the strength and acceleration and thus a respite for the increased strength and acceleration used for the next downswing. The use of rebounds is a sign of resiliency (Kestenberg and Sossin, 1979; see also Chapter 2).

Rebounds are also effective in social situations. For example, if an employer reprimands an employee using a direct and accelerating voice and gestures and sustains this mode, the employee may feel assaulted. If, on the other hand, the employer shifts from direct to indirect and then back to direct, e.g., "This task must be done today, hopefully this time limit is O.K. with you, but it must be done," the message can be confusing. One adaptive solution is to use a rebound in direct. This means that one does not veer into the opposite quality, indirect, but rather diminishes the direct element. The employer might say, "The job must be finished today. Pick whatever schedule is convenient for you as long as it is finished before the deadline." The message remains direct, but with a quality of easing up. Rebounds offer a breather without loss of momentum. In physical tasks, rebounds offer an opportunity to re-oxygenate tired muscles without losing the momentum of the action.

## Phrases

Particularly in work, efforts often occur in typical rhythmic phrases. These rhythms make work enjoyable rather than a chore (Lamb, 1961). A repeated sequence or theme of effort phrases gives "melody" to movement (Kestenberg, 1975). Phrases are not revealed in the diagram, but a profiler may go back to the raw data to discover characteristic phrasing of a mover.

## The Importance of a Balanced Movement Repertoire

Laban emphasized the importance of having a balance between fighting and indulging efforts. He pointed out that if strength is required for a particular job, a person who has a lot of strength but very little lightness is not necessarily a good person to hire. An ideal candidate is one who has "... the ability to produce efforts required for the job, and also simultaneously to call into play those balancing efforts which make his operations enduringly efficient" (Laban and Lawrence, 1974, p. 50). In many cultures of the world, fighting qualities are associated with masculinity and indulging qualities with femininity. These are not universal associations, however. Even in most circum-Mediterranean cultures where men are called upon to "prove" their masculinity, indulging efforts are culturally approved for men when they relate to babies, social superiors, and close male associates (Gilmore, 1990). However, women's use of fighting efforts is often strongly curtailed. For example, women are often expected to be indirect rather than direct in seeking their goals, and to be light-handed versus strong-willed. Changing cultural expectations in the United States has led to a number of re-evaluations of these gender roles. Sarah Bem (Bem and Bem, 1970), for example, suggested that the healthiest individuals are those who are androgynous or combine the so-called masculine and feminine qualities.[5] In the KMP framework it is similarly suggested that it is adaptive to have a balance of fighting and indulging efforts in the profiles of both men and women.

## Maturation and The Use of Efforts:

### *Key Features of Space, Weight, and Time in Early Childhood*

In the first year of life (represented by the top line of each diagram), babies are interested in the location of things. They investigate and search in space, attending indirectly or directly. We say that this first year is characterized by a focus on attention and interest in where things are.

In the second year of life, children become more interested in weight, pushing, pulling, and in weighing things lightly or with strength and developing evaluations about them. Based on these considerations, children formulate a concept of what they want. This leads to the development of intentionality and interest in what things are.

In the third year of life, children develop more interest in time. This leads to decision-making and action, either with deceleration or acceleration. The time elements of efforts are used for making decisions and being aware of when things happen.

## Gestures and Postures

Looking at the broader pattern of use of efforts in development leads to the study of gestures and postures. There are considerable differences in the way in which a person's body participates in an effort action in infancy, childhood, adolescence, and adulthood. One important difference has been the subject of considerable study and has been labeled, gestures and postures (Lamb, 1965; Ramsden, 1973; Kestenberg and Sossin, 1979).

**Gestures** are movements which occur in one or more parts of the body without involving the whole body in the same movement quality. If a person standing fairly still lightly waves an arm to a friend, this is an example of a gesture using the effort of lightness. The quality of lightness is only in her arm and the rest of her body does not participate in the lightness. Gesturing draws on the ability to functionally isolate body parts.

**Integrated Postures**[6]: In the KMP system, when a person moves her entire body in an integrated way using an effort quality, this is termed "an integrated posture in efforts." All parts of the body move in a sequential and continuous fashion, supporting and enhancing a movement. For example, one may stomp the ground in anger using the effort of strength in the torso, arms, and one leg while one's other leg supports the movement. Postures are generally asymmetrical because part of the body acts and another part, often the leg, supports.

Postures imply whole-hearted emotional and cognitive involvement. Kestenberg and Sossin (1979) believe that total commitment and lack of reservation in a postural movement is a reflection of the harmonious participation of all psychic agencies including the conscience (pp. 149–150). Thus, when a person waves a hand lightly to a friend using only a gesture, it suggests a partial commitment to the light-hearted greeting. If the lightness of the wave spreads to her whole body, she is expressing her whole-hearted commitment to the enthusiastic greeting. Her whole body and her wishes, desires, and conscience, are all actively participating in the action.

---

### Exercise

Compare the quality of gestural and postural movements. Refuse a child permission to go play in the street using a gesture of strength in your arm. Then try making the same statement with the effort of strength permeating your whole body.

Alternatively try a gestural effort of indirect with an indulging hand movement: "Okay, you may play outdoors." Then let the whole effort of indirect spread and give permission with a postural effort.

---

### *The Foundations of Gestures and Postures in Early Development*

Both gestural and postural movement provide important contributions to every day functioning. At times it is necessary to marshal one's whole body in service of a task and at other times it is equally necessary to be able to move part of one's body without the full participation of the rest. Early development provides the foundation for different levels of integration and differentiation of body parts in later life.

*Centralization*: When an infant is being nursed by her mother and attunes to her, the sucking rhythm may pervade her whole body. Through this process of centralization the movement quality spreads involving both the center and periphery of the body. This centralization of flow provides the foundation for postural movements later in development.

*Partial Stabilization*: A neonate is not readily able to purposefully move one part of his body in isolation from the rest. This ability develops gradually. For example, when an infant turns away from the person holding him, he learns to keep part of his body firm, in order to give support to the gesture of turning. This partial stabilization of the torso or central part of the body forms the foundation for movement in gestures.

Postures develop in latency, at about seven or eight years of age.[7] However, the latency child generally moves with a solid truck and a high level of differentiation of body parts. In other words, she typically isolates her torso and the peripheral parts of her body. Thus she is able to make clearly differentiated gestures. For example, she can mobilize her wrists and finger joints into defined gestures by inhibiting movement in her shoulder joints. These individual gestures may be well-coordinated, but they are separated from the central part of the body.

However, on occasion the latency child drops the typical inhibition, permits tension flow to spread throughout her body and bursts forth in a global posture.

**Global Postures** occur when an individual uses a movement quality which permeates his whole body. When his body is suffused with a single pattern, the separation of the periphery of the body and the center (necessary for creating gestures) breaks down. The spread of the movement quality throughout the whole body paves the way for unification of body parts into a postural effort (Kestenberg, 1975).

In global postures there is no separation of body parts which support or lead an action. The whole body participates in a relatively undifferentiated manner. Springing up with lightness like a cheerleader or leaping forward with the whole body accelerating are examples of global postures in efforts. Because there is little differentiation, global postures are usually symmetrical and lead to changes in position. They are often seen in exuberant teenagers who can be totally committed to something one second and then to something else the next (which makes them fun but impossible at times).

Global postures are striking because they emerge suddenly with almost no preparation. For example, a child standing still may, as if out of nowhere, break into a light and buoyant skip. She does not begin with an introductory gesture as an adult would. Global postures reflect total physical and mental involvement without pause for questioning, which is perhaps why a global posture makes such a great cheer. Global postures are forerunners of more mature integrated postures.

Integrated postures do not generally occur before late latency (10–11 years) or early adolescence. They also reflect a total psychological and physical commitment to a task or concept, but in a more mature manner. An integrated postural movement includes the full participation of one's body both to undertake an action and to support it on a firm base. Maturation is also seen in the development of gesture–posture–gesture phrasing.

### *Gesture–Posture–Gesture Phrase*[8]

Sometimes by latency we see children develop phrases of gestures and postures. However, the transitions are not smooth, but rather marked by pauses. For example, a child sitting and studying, upon hearing other children playing, may turn his head with acceleration (gesture), then pause. Next, he may leap away from the desk in a postural acceleration. The gesture was the trial movement undertaken before the superego or conscience fully endorses the act. The gesture reflects the wish to go. The pause reflects uncertainty. A follow-through with postural acceleration reflects the permission of the conscience: "It's OK. You've worked enough today."

By adolescence we see the development of more mature phrases. A mover may begin with a gesture in strength which leads smoothly into postural strength, and which then may end with a gesture in strength. This is a typical sequence seen in adults: **gesture–posture–gesture**. The first gesture is considered a trial action; the posture is the main theme supported by the conscience and the last gesture gives final closure to the theme. For example, a person may reach forward with her arms to begin to embrace a friend (gesture of deceleration and lightness). If the arm movement evolves into involvement of the whole body (posture) in deceleration and lightness, it becomes a gesture–posture phrase. The embrace may finish with a final gesture of lightness, creating a gesture–posture–gesture phrase. There is full commitment to the meaning involved in the effort quality use. In this case, the embrace completely embodies the attitude of lightness which may include admiration, pleasure, amusement, and light-heartedness.

Action Profilers and Movement Pattern Analysts focus on the conflict-free moment at which a gesture merges into a posture (called gesture–posture or posture–gesture merger). The gesture–posture phrase expresses the harmony of what someone may want and what one's conscience prescribes. If there is no merger, the notator does not score the movement.

Lamb (1965), a Movement Pattern Analyst, suggests that the more posture–gesture mergers occur, the more the individual is acting in accordance with his real self. In a careful study, Du Nann Winter and associates (1989) found that posture–gesture mergers are positively correlated with sincerity and occur most often when a person is relaxed, truthful, and "authentic." Lamb (1994) describes how ballroom dance teams trained in the use of gesture–posture mergers created movements so impressive that they won all competitions.

In the KMP we score gestures and postures individually because we are interested in their use in development and in areas of conflict as well as harmony.

**Gesture–posture clashing** occurs when the movement pattern of the posture clashes with the preceding gestural movement pattern. For example, one may bring a hand forward to grab someone with strength, but if the conscience does not give permission, no postural strength will develop. Instead the conscience may dictate that the greeting should be light-hearted. The person may commit to this and complete the greeting with postural lightness. A desire to demonstrate stronger dedication to the relationship may however re-emerge, leading to a final gesture which is strong. Thus, gesture–posture clashes reflect inner conflicts.

## Conclusion

The study of efforts reveals the way a mover copes with the environmental qualities of space, weight, and time both in a physical and cognitive manner. The profiler looks for a good balance and sufficient amounts of all elements which suggests that the individual has access to a variety of ways of coping with tasks and solving problems. The load factor, discussed in the chapters on interpretation, indicates the degree to which the mover tends to combine more than one effort element in an action. The frequent use of combinations is interpreted to indicate creative intelligence in the way one approaches and solves problems.

This chapter concludes the study of System I of the KMP which consists of four movement diagrams on the left side of the Profile. The movement qualities studied include patterns which reflect needs (rhythms), affect qualities (tension flow attributes), defenses against undesirable impulses and learning strategies (pre-efforts), and ways of coping with every day problems (efforts). The last section of this chapter examines the ways in which the various movement elements of System I combine in harmonious and clashing fashions and how these combinations can be interpreted. The chapter concludes with a discussion of the portrayal of development in the KMP system and examines the significance of the structure of diagrams.

## System I:  Tension Flow/Effort System

### *Clashing and Affinities in the Vertical Line of System I: Tension Flow, Pre-Efforts, and Efforts*

The study of how movements combine in harmonious or clashing ways offers valuable insights not only for understanding an individual mover, but also for unraveling interpersonal clashes and harmonies.

**A general affinity** exists between all fighting elements in System I, such as direct, vehemence, and acceleration. This simply means that when a person is using one fighting element, other fighting elements will combine into the movement in a harmonious or compatible manner. Likewise, there is also a general affinity between all indulging elements, such as indirect, gentleness, and deceleration. The use of affined movement qualities reflects intrapsychic harmony. In contrast, when disaffined or clashing combinations are used, it reflects a intrapsychic conflict. For example, if a person shakes his fist in anger using vehemence with acceleration, then two fighting elements blend to create an aggressive act. However, if one were to shake a fist using vehemence and hesitation, this would represent a clash. It would reflect an inner conflict between trying to do something in a fighting manner (or using a fighting type of defense, for example identifying with an aggressor) and avoiding engagement by pausing or hesitating. Likewise use of affined patterns such as graduality, flexibility, and lightness indicate a compatibility in feelings (tension flow attributes), defenses (pre-efforts), and coping mechanisms (efforts) (Kestenberg and Sossin, 1979).

One can add flow factors as well. An affinity exists between free flow and indulging elements and between bound flow and fighting elements (Laban, 1960; Lamb, 1961, 1965; Lamb and Turner, 1969). Table 7 displays examples of affined and clashing combinations within System I.

The following example illustrates a clash. Lamb (1992), observing American men and women hugging in public places, noticed that women often used free flow with directness,

**Table 7**   Examples of General Affinities and Clashes in System I.

*culture?*

| Affined Elements | Clashing Elements |
|---|---|
| Free flow and all indulging elements | Free flow and fighting elements |
| Bound flow and all fighting elements | Bound flow and indulging elements |
| Graduality, flexibility and deceleration | Graduality & channeling |
| Low intensity, gentle and indirect | High intensity and indirect |
| Abrupt, vehemence, and direct | Abrupt and indirect |

a clash between an indulging flow pattern and a fighting effort. This clash might have several different meanings depending on context. One interpretation could be that women, who are often taught not to use fighting elements, use free flow to ameliorate the impact of a fighting effort. In other words, they might act in an authoritative manner, direct and strong, yet use free flow, which gives a more carefree feeling, rather than the affined bound flow which is associated with control. This could reflect a conflict that many women might feel between being assertive and being indulging, particularly in public places. Such clashes might reflect the contradictory expectations of women in present-day North America.

Some adolescents use clashes so frequently that they feel more at ease using a clashing combination than using affined patterns. However, everyone uses clashes; in fact, many clashes are the basis of functional patterns of action. For example, it is affined to be indirect and gentle with someone, but in some circumstances it might be necessary to be direct and cushion it with gentleness. However, clashes bring together dissonant movement patterns and reflect the existence of some underlying conflicts. In the above example, one can recognize a conflict between wanting not to hurt someone and yet also getting directly to the point which has an aggressive component.

Clashes are not necessarily unpleasant, though some may feel awkward. For example, a strong parent may combine strength with gentleness to lift a small baby. Some clashes are difficult to do and evidently incompatible, for example, the combination of channeling and free flow, or being gentle and abrupt. Because of their discordant nature clashing combinations often make effective threat gestures, for example, strength and deceleration used in a slow glare can be extremely menacing.

---

### Exercise

Try combining affined elements such as flexibility, free flow, and lightness in a question to another person, such as "What would you like to do?" Then try using fighting elements strength and even bound flow to ask "What do you want to do?" When all elements are affined there is a harmonious quality to the movement and the underlying feelings.

Now try combining clashing elements such as low intensity, abruptness, and free flow to dart here and there. Or try gentleness with acceleration to pick up a fragile object quickly. Does it feel more harmonious to be abrupt with high intensity and gentle with deceleration?

---

### The Concept of Affinity and Clashing in Interpersonal Relationships

The positive or negative chemistry two people may feel when they first interact is often based on underlying clashes or affinities in their styles of movement. Dance/movement therapists draw on this concept by mirroring their clients' movements. Using the same movement quality as their client, they "start where the client is" and this helps develop rapport and a connection. However, it is not necessary nor always effective to use the same movement quality when attempting to connect or relate to another person. In some circumstances one may want to modify the other person's behavior or to connect using a movement quality more within one's own style. Use of an affined quality may be most appropriate. For example, how does a parent react to her child who is having a temper tantrum, kicking on the floor using suddenness and high intensity? Some parents would approach the child with graduality and gentleness. This clashing combination would probably not only be ineffective, but also unpleasant for the child. Instead, a parent could firmly (but not aggressively) pick up the child with steady even bound flow and strength to help contain the child's uncontrolled feelings. We will explore this topic further in the study of System II movement qualities in the following five chapters.

### Other Applications

Since Laban was interested in work productivity, he focused on the elements of movement which underlie adaptations to work (i.e., space, weight, and time). He recognized that certain movement qualities are affined and can be combined adaptively or may substitute for one another. For example, Laban pointed out that strength is an element of movement which can mobilize weight in the service of many tasks. However, individuals who do not have enough strength for a task may be able to complete it by using the allied movement of acceleration, e.g., using less strength, but more acceleration, as in swinging a tire onto a truck bed rather than lifting it. One can draw on the same concept in attempting to help a person overcome a learning difficulty. For example, a child who is constantly distracted (does not use sufficient channeling) and thus does not complete his work may not respond well to admonishments to concentrate more (i.e., channel). However, he may be able to overcome the problem to some extent by being given something about which he can feel great passion (vehemence). Eventually the use of vehemence may support the development of more channeling. To return to the dancer described earlier in this chapter, who was having problems achieving a lightness of feeling in her dance, she might be guided toward it through the use of indirect, an affined movement quality.

### Discussion of the Structure of the Profile: System I

The structure of the Profile has been developed over the course of more than twenty years by the Sands Point Movement Study Group. Basing their work on earlier theorists and practitioners and their own observation, experimentation, and clinical evaluation they have constructed a movement-based portrayal of development and psychic functioning. Now that the reader has gained some familiarity with the first section of the Profile, it may be appropriate to address some theoretical concerns about the degree to which the Profile reflects data or structures it.

Each of the four diagrams described in Chapters 1–4 are organized chronologically and developmentally along the vertical axis. In each case the top line of the diagram displays patterns which are prominent in the first year of life and continue for the second through third years of life in the same fashion. The diagrams are also structured to depict the polarities of indulging and fighting qualities. The reader may be pleased with the clear format, but may question the degree to which the form of representation reflects actual development.

Several points may be raised in regard to this question. First of all, the reader should recall that the lines of development do not reflect the emergence of a movement quality, but rather its tendency to rise to prominence in a specific phase of development. Ages given in association with specific subphases are averages which vary from individual to individual and to some extent from culture to culture.[9] While the actual ages or rates of development may be expected to vary considerably, the pattern and order of development appears to be consistent even cross-culturally (Konner, 1993).

The reader might also question whether the polarities described in the diagram's left and right sides (e.g., lightness and strength) are convenient categorizations or reflections of development. First it must be said that all categorizations are abstractions from data. Furthermore, the system of notation and the terminology used in diagrams 2–4 are qualitative and do not reflect degrees of differences. For example, the degree of strength or lightness used is not notated. Thus, the categories do impose a greater degree of polarity than actually exists. However, the study of development does seem to indicate that maturation moves in a spiral rather than linear form (Newman and Newman, 1991). Such oscillation from one polarity to the other in development may play an important role in extending the range of movement, thought, and feeling qualities which comprise our repertoire. Development seems to fluctuate between emphasizing indulging versus fighting movements and attitudes, both of which are needed for coping with the internal and external forces of life.

Thus there is no simple answer to the question posed here. To some extent any categorization does some injustice to observed behavior and raw data. However, the Profile is not stagnant. It has changed and will continue to change to reflect new insights and new data.

## Conclusion

Although culture may exert pressure on its members to be either aggressive or yielding, although each person may develop her own individual preferences, the processes of maturation and development offer a balanced and wide repertoire of movements to draw upon. Movement elements and their various combinations give us insight into individual preferences and proclivities of ourselves and those around us.

### Notes

1. The names of the six effort elements coined by Laban have been modified by Kestenberg and associates under the guidance of Lamb. Laban's original terms are: direct, flexible, strong and light, and quick and sustained (Laban and Lawrence, 1974, 1947).
2. A plane is a two-dimensional pathway in space. For example, reaching forward for an object on the floor, one's arm traverses the sagittal plane, incorporating the two dimensions forward and down. A movement which follows only one dimension (e.g., simply forward) creates only a line in space. It is suggested here that in creating lines, there is little attitude towards space. Rather, one uses lines (or directions) to pinpoint and locate items (see also Chapter 8).
3. There can also be various types of intelligence, which Howard Gardner has pointed out (1983).
4. Laban (1960) said that when three effort elements are active, the flow factor is dormant. However, in what he called "drives," a flow factor (bound or free) replaces one of the

effort elements. He described three combinations of two effort elements and one flow factor. They are:

*Passion Drive*, which consists of the effort elements of weight and time plus a flow factor. This combination is particularly expressive of emotions.

*Vision Drive*, which consists of a space and time effort plus a flow factor.

*Spell Drive*, which consists of a weight and time effort plus a flow factor. It radiates a quality of fascination (adapted from Kestenberg and Sossin, 1979). He also described the combinations of one effort element and one flow factor.

*Dreamlike* attitudes in actions composed of weight and flow elements. This combination creates bodily feelings and hazy fantasies.

*Mobile* attitudes in actions composed of time and flow elements, which create the qualities of mobilizing and progressing.

*Remote* attitudes in actions composed of space and flow elements, which create the qualities of pensiveness and visualizing outward (Laban, 1960).

5. Although Bem's work is dated and has been considerably revised by researchers including herself, the original concept of the benefits of balance is still valid.
6. This term was coined by Lamb (1965) who established the method of Action Profiling. However, today Action Profilers define the term differently. Note that the KMP usage is separate and distinct from the current Action Profile usage.
7. Global postures develop as early as five years of age but become more common in early latency.
8. This phrase, *gesture–posture–gesture*, should not be confused with *gesture–posture merging* (integrated movement), a movement pattern studied by Action Profilers. The KMP looks at dynamic patterns: phrases and changes. Action Profilers are interested in the moment a gesture merges into a posture.
9. On the average American babies can sit unsupported at eight months of age. In several African populations babies often sit earlier and spend more of their time in a vertical position. It may be predicted that cognitive and physical tasks associated with verticality will arise earlier in these populations. However, despite varied cultural influences on the rate of developmant, so far no differences in the order at which movement patterns mature has been found (Konner, 1991).

# CHAPTER 5

# Bipolar Shape Flow

The toddler is standing in the vertical plane and is using "bipolar widening" in her chest and throughout most of her body.

## An Introduction to System II Movement Diagrams

The movement qualities described in Chapters 5–9 are organized into diagrams similar to those for pre-efforts and efforts. However, there are some differences. In System I diagrams, the vitalizing force of the movement patterns described is tension flow.

All movement is based on combinations of bound and free flow and this gives the movement its dynamic quality and some emotional components. Free and bound are associated with pleasure and displeasure respectively. Through attunement to the tension flow pattern of other individuals one can achieve a sense of empathy for them, a feeling of how they feel.

In System II diagrams, the vitalizing force underlying the movement patterns described is **shape flow** in the form of growing or shrinking of bodily dimensions. Shape flow gives structure or form to tension flow by providing specific spatial components with which the dynamic qualities conform. Growing in shape flow tends to create open shapes associated with feelings of comfort. Shrinking in shape flow tends to create closed shapes associated with feelings of discomfort. Through adjustment to the shape flow pattern of other persons one can create a sense of trust, a feeling that there is a structure upon which one can rely (see Table 8).

There is a second important difference. In System I, the diagrams of movement qualities are organized to reflect the developmental progression of focus on space, weight, and time during the first three years of life. In System II, the diagrams are organized to reflect the developmental progression of focus on the spatial dimensions of horizontal, vertical, and sagittal during the first three years of life. In System II this means that we focus more on the movement of the body in space and the kinds of structures and shapes it creates. We use these movement qualities to help understand the relationship of the mover to self and to others.

In this chapter and in Chapters 6, 8, and 9, we also look at the matching and mismatching between System I and System II movement qualities or, in other words, the ways in which movement qualities from horizontally matched diagrams combine in harmonious or clashing ways. In Chapters 1–4 the reader was primarily offered interpretations for individual movement elements. Now in System II we begin to show how the different portions of the KMP may interrelate and how configurations of movement elements can be studied (see Table 8).

**Table 8**  Matching Diagrams of System I and System II.

| System I          Matches with | System II |
|---|---|
| **Tension Flow Attributes** | **Bipolar Shape Flow** |
| (Feelings) | (Self feelings) |
| Indulging elements | Open growing shapes |
| Fighting elements | Closed shrinking shapes |
|    Attunement in TFA |    Adjustment in shape flow |
|    creates empathy |    creates trust |
| **Tension Flow Attributes** | **Unipolar shape flow** |
| also match with | (attraction–repulsion) |
| **Pre-efforts** | **Shaping in Directions** |
| Indulging defenses | Open boundaries |
| Fighting defenses | Restricted boundaries |
| **Efforts** | **Shaping in Planes** |
| Indulging coping systems | Open relationships |
| Fighting coping systems | Closed relationships |

## Bipolar Shape Flow

At a social gathering one often encounters a person whose body shape grows outward, filling the space around her, while another shrinks inwardly contracting his body shape, as if willing himself to disappear. She exudes self-confidence. He appears to lack self-esteem. Although some individuals tend to maintain a shrunken or expanded body attitude, in everyday activities most people experience a range of growing and shrinking (Laban, 1950).[1]

"The rhythm of shape flow consists of alternations between growing and shrinking of body shape" (Kestenberg, 1967, p. 90) which underlie the plasticity of the body (Kestenberg and Sossin, 1979). The prototype of bipolar growing and shrinking is respiration. The body grows when air is inhaled and shrinks when air is exhaled. Similar processes of growing and shrinking form the basis for alimentation. We grow as we take in food and shrink in the process of expelling waste. The functioning of the heart and other body organs replicate this process. Growing and taking in allow the salutary environmental substances to enter our bodies in comfort, whereas shrinking enhances the process of expelling noxious substances (Kestenberg, 1984, p. 144). Growing and shrinking "… provide a structure for the organism's interaction with the environment" (Kestenberg, 1975, p. 197).

**Bipolar shape flow** refers specifically to symmetrical expansions and contractions.[2] Because the changes are symmetrical, bipolar shape flow encourages stability and an internal sense of balance. It also supports centering on the self and has been described as an expression of primary narcissism by psychoanalytic theorists.

This chapter begins with the development of emotional correlates of growing and shrinking. Some general concepts including dimensions, open and closed shapes, and an overview of matching and mismatching follow. The chapter continues with descriptions of the six elements of bipolar growing and shrinking with specific discussion of matching and mismatching included. The remainder of the chapter is devoted to discussion of related issues, such as the holding environment, body image and the sense of self, interpersonal relationships, and the communication of emotions.

### *Development of Emotional Correlates of Growing and Shrinking*

Bipolar growing and shrinking is closely related to the infant's global (or general) feelings of comfort and discomfort in the environment. Surrounded by warm, fresh air, the body grows symmetrically, taking in pleasant provisions from the environment. In contrast, surrounded by cold or polluted air, the body shrinks symmetrically to reduce exposure to an unpleasant environment. The infant's body shape will grow when placed in a warm bath and shrink when it is too cold.

---

### Exercise

From a sitting or reclining position, lengthen bipolarly (i.e., grow both upward and downward). Try growing in all three dimensions, lengthening, widening and bulging. Feel wide across your chest, tall and lengthened in your spine and legs, and full and bulging front to back. What feelings emerge?

Now try bipolar shrinking. Shrink into a narrow, shortened and hollowed shape. Remember that in bipolar hollowing you must hollow inward from both front and back. Use exhaling to facilitate bipolar shrinking. You may also try walking around the room narrowing bipolarly, i.e., contracting inward to create a closed-to-the-world shape. What feelings emerge?

---

The emotional associations of growing and shrinking develop through experiences in the global environment. Growing in response to physical comfort generalizes to growing in response to positive emotional sensations and moods. When one takes a deep breath, one may experience a feeling of exhilaration. Shrinking occurs in response to physical discomfort and this generalizes to shrinking in response to emotional pain. These are not invariable associations, however. Shrinking can be associated with sensations of comfort particularly when combined with free flow. For example, feelings of relief are often associated with expelling wastes, e.g., when exhaling after holding one's breath. Likewise growing too full (usually with bound flow) can create an uncomfortable sensation.

## The Diagram and System of Analysis of Bipolar Shape Flow

The six elements of bipolar shape flow (see Diagram 5) studied in the KMP reflect symmetrical ways of growing and shrinking in the horizontal, vertical, and sagittal dimensions.

### *The Dimensions*

Generalized patterns of growing and shrinking begin with the formation of life and continue to have a strong impact on development throughout the life span. As the infant matures, patterns of growing and shrinking become more differentiated and controlled. In the first year of life we see a preponderance of widening and narrowing in the horizontal dimension. The infant widens in a smile, narrows in a frown, and repeatedly widens and narrows as it learns to roll over. The second year brings an increase in the use of lengthening and shortening in the vertical dimension as the infant lengthens to stand up and shortens to squat down. The third year is dominated by an increase in bulging and hollowing in the

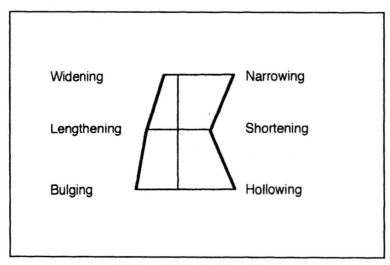

**Diagram 5.** Bipolar Shape Flow

sagittal dimension seen in the wistful contentment of the toddler who bulges out and in the hollowing associated with controlled urination.

### Open and Closed Shapes

Growing movements (widening, lengthening, or bulging) tend to create open shapes which expose the body to the environment. Shrinking movements (narrowing, shortening, or hollowing) tend to create closed shapes which reduce exposure of the body to outside contact.

### General Discussion of Matching and Mismatching:
### Bipolar Shape Flow and Tension Flow Attributes

There exists a wide array of potential movement pattern combinations available to the mover. Some combinations are "natural" or harmonious matches between various patterns while others are poor fits, mismatched, or clashing movement patterns. For example, the combination of the use of strength with a downward direction fits well or harmonizes. The movements work adaptively together with the support of gravity e.g. stomping down forcefully on grapes. In contrast, if a person uses strength to lift up a suitcase, this movement combination is a clash since it contends with the force of gravity and may feel awkward or difficult. The use of mismatched patterns may stem inherently from a task or it may reflect inner conflicts. For example, if a person smiles (an open inviting shape), adding free flow and flow adjustment (which relaxes boundaries), enhances the warmth of the expression. The message conveyed is open and pleasant. However, if one smiles with evenly held bound flow, the message is conflicted. It says, "I am opening up to you, but with constraint and firm boundaries." The smile appears artificial because the even flow clashes with the widening. Mismatched or clashing patterns can be used to convey conflicts, humor, or dramatic effect.

The term **match** is used very specifically to describe the combination of harmonious elements from horizontally aligned diagrams of System I and System II. Thus shape flow elements can match with tension flow elements, creating what is also termed a **horizontal affinity**. For example, widening in a smile is matched with free flow and flow adjustment. On the emotional level, feeling carefree and safe (expressed in free flow) is in harmony with open growing shapes which express comfort. Likewise, feelings of constraint and danger (expressed by bound flow) are in harmony with closed shrinking shapes which express discomfort. Mismatches or horizontal clashes reflect conflicts between these categories of feelings. For example, shrinking one's hand into a fist with free flow creates an ineffectual instrument for punching. Shape flow provides form or containment for tension flow, which provides the dynamic impact to these combinations.

Table 9 displays the affinities between tension flow attributes and bipolar shape flow, which the KMP analyst consults for evidence of matching and mismatching. Each element on the left side of the tension flow diagram is matched with a corresponding element on the left side of the shape flow diagram.

Thus, flow adjustment is matched with widening, and even flow matches with narrowing. "Rhythms of shape flow give structure to changes in tension, by providing patterns for interaction with need-satisfying or frustrating stimuli and objects" (Kestenberg, 1975, p. 197). This matching lays the foundation for harmony between feelings and self expression.

**Table 9** Matching of Tension Flow Attributes and Bipolar Shape Flow.

| System I | System II | System I | System II |
|---|---|---|---|
| Indulging with Open | | Fighting with Closed | |
| Flow adjustement | Widening | Even flow | Narrowing |
| Low intensity | Lengthening | High intensity | Shortening |
| Graduality | Bulging | Abruptness | Hollowing |
| Free flow | Growing | Bound flow | Shrinking |

## The Six Elements of Bipolar Shape Flow

### *The Horizontal Dimension*

The first two elements, **widening and narrowing**, create changes in the horizontal dimension (side to side). Bipolar shape flow movements in the horizontal dimension offer developmental precursors for first year of life skills, attention, exploration, and communication.

### *Widening*

When inhaling, the rib cage expands on both sides, providing the breath and torso support for the extension of the arms and legs. **Bipolar widening** can also occur in the face, hands, pelvis, and toes.

Widening in the horizontal dimension is associated with the first developmental phase of incorporation. Young infants widen to take in nourishment. Later they widen as they turn over and while smiling. When a well-cared-for infant sees the approach of a caregiver, he becomes suffused with good feelings and widens to take in the emotional or physical nourishment expected. In doing so, the infant displays trust in the other and enhances the infant/caregiver bond.

---

### Exercise

In a sitting position, try bipolar widening in different parts of your body. Widen in a facial gesture (a smile). Widen in your hand, letting it grow wider laterally from the palm through to the fingers; widen in the hips, spreading out in dancer's second position. Taking a deep breath supports widening in the chest which can expand to the arms.

Try offering something with your hand outstretched. Is your hand widened or narrowed? Can you give with narrowing?

---

Widening underlies good feelings about oneself, generosity, openness, and trust in the environment. These are interrelated feelings. Openness, for example, is associated with finding or seeking comfort in giving. Widening provides the foundation for generosity, the kind that gives comfort to the giver.

Widening also may reflect feelings of omnipotence. It creates a large body shape which, though not necessarily threatening, conveys a message that here is a person of significance. A widened frame also suggests the ability to support and thus be supportive. Wide shapes inspire trust. Sitting with a bipolarly widened frame is typical for men in many cultures.

In contrast, women are often encouraged to sit with their legs pressed together in a bipolarly narrowed frame (implying containment of their sexuality).

People who often widen enjoy attention, admiration, and activities centered on themselves. They derive comfort from taking in good things from the environment. As stated above, widening has a connection to the sucking stage (oral phase) of development, which focuses on incorporation.

Those who have an overabundance of widening (without a balanced amount of narrowing) may often feel unconsciously that everyone is "mother" and they expect love and praise unstintingly. Without narrowing, they are unable to return to themselves to seek comfort and draw on inner resources. They therefore can become overly dependent on others for their source of well-being and value. Their good feelings about themselves may attract positive attention, but they may be overly trusting and optimistic regarding the behavior of others. Furthermore, since widening communicates feelings of well-being, those who use a predominance of this movement element may find themselves receiving attention, but little care when they need it most (unless they learn to narrow more in order to express neediness).

### Matching and Mismatching

Widening provides the structure for and matches with flow adjustment and free flow.[3] To be trusting, accepting, and giving is aptly expressed with free flow and with adjustments to the situation or needs of self and others (i.e., flow adjustment). This combination expresses harmony between feelings of safety, adaptability, and feelings of oneself as an open, generous, trusting person.

Some combinations are clashes or mismatches. An example of a mismatch is widening with bound even flow in the chest area to receive an embrace. It is a clash to express evenly held feelings of caution or control with openness (widening). As discussed above, mismatched patterns are not necessarily maladaptive. They play an important role in expressing and dealing with conflicting feelings.

---

#### Exercise

Try smiling and note which tension flow attributes are involved. A natural smile generally widens with small flow adjustments and free flow. Try smiling with even bound flow. This clash creates a strained smile. Try widening with your arms using low intensity, flow adjustments, and free flow. What mood does this express? Then try a clash, using high intensity abrupt bound flow with widening. How welcoming is this gesture? Threatening gestures are often composed of clashing shape flow and tension flow patterns.

---

There is no as yet discovered one-to-one correspondence between particular movement combinations and specific emotions. However, certain clashes are ritualized or standardized forms for communication of emotionally laden messages.

### Narrowing

In exhalation the rib cage **narrows** and contracts, moving toward the body center. In the face, narrowing knits the brows and purses the lips. Other common areas of narrowing include the shoulders, hips, face, hands, and feet.

The biting rhythm of the six-month to one-year-old is not only associated with bound flow and firm boundaries of self, but also with a shrinking shape. Separation, increasingly initiated by the infant in the biting phase, is often accomplished by narrowing bipolarly with bound flow. Shrinking also contributes to a firmer and more defined body image typical of this phase. Narrowing into oneself may provide a feeling of self-containment which supports separation.

The infant expresses discomfort through narrowing. Narrowing in the face and torso may indicate that an infant is cold, hungry, or in pain (responding to global internal or external sources of discomfort). Persistent bipolar narrowing is associated with feelings of distrust in one's environment (i.e., the expectation that it will not give comfort or relief from pain). The contracted body created by narrowing reflects and expresses the feeling of being closed off from one's surroundings. It can create a restriction in the body associated with asthma or shallow breathing. On the other hand, because bipolar narrowing expresses feelings of depletion and deprivation, it can evoke pity and nurturing.

---

### Exercise

Try narrowing by contracting in the chest, hips, face, and hands. What feelings are associated with this shape? Conversely, begin with the feeling. Imagine being very cold and tired. What changes occur in your body shape?

Imagine feeling miserable and expecting that no one will come to comfort you. What body changes are associated with such feelings?

---

With an overabundance of narrowing, a person has difficulty entertaining and expressing feelings of generosity, openness, and receptivity. Furthermore, persistently narrowed shapes can have a discouraging effect on others, leading to neglect or avoidance. Normally a needy child evokes both feelings of wanting to nurture and feelings of wanting to escape from the neediness. Just as person with too little narrowing may fail to attract aid so may a person with too much narrowing. In impoverished northeast Brazil, for example, parents sometimes give up on babies who fail to thrive, saying that "this baby wants to die" (Scheper-Hughes, 1985). Having little expectation of finding comfort, such babies narrow into themselves and take no apparent interest in food. This, in turn, discourages caregiving. Adults in emotionally comparable states feel pessimistic about the outside world and communicate that they themselves are worthless and undeserving of care.

Most distressed children use a combination of narrowing and widening, which suggests both discomfort and distress (narrowing) and an openness to receive comfort (widening). For example, a crying child may narrow in the brow while widening in the mouth and torso, or may alternate widening and narrowing shapes. Narrowing balanced by widening serves important functions. Narrowing offers a time of coming into oneself which may give comfort (self-soothing) and convey distress and neediness to others. A balance of widening and narrowing allows for the expression of both comfort and discomfort. It offers the experience of trusting and distrusting, being open and being closed, all of which are necessary elements in our repertoire.

### Matching and Mismatching

Narrowing matches with even bound flow, providing an appropriate structure for expressing evenly controlled caution, discomfort or distrust. An embrace which is accomplished by narrowing with even bound flow firmly brings the embraced person inward toward oneself and creates a boundary separating both people from the outside world. This is a restrictive embrace. The clash or mismatch, narrowing with free flow, suggests a conflict between feeling safe and at ease and wanting to be closed off and separate.

---

**Exercise**

Imagine feeling distrustful and uncomfortable. What movement patterns evolve from these feelings? Did you narrow with even bound flow? If so, try narrowing with the clashing tension flow attributes of free flow and flow adjustment. Does using free flow and flow adjustment change the feeling tone of the movement? How?

---

### The Development of "Trust" in the First Year of Life

Both growing and shrinking in the horizontal dimension form the basis for the foundation of trust. To gain trust one has to feel comfortable focusing outward by growing as well as connecting to the self by shrinking. It is the dynamic, balanced process that creates the trust. If widening is too predominant, it usually indicates an outward search for trustworthy supplies without a sense of being centered in oneself as well.

Furthermore, in order to be able to make use of support from others, one has to be able to absorb it or take it in to oneself. For example, if a child widens to prepare to embrace mother, he must also narrow to bring mother in to himself. One often widens to take in the warmth of a spring day and then narrows to bring that pleasure closer to oneself.

### The Vertical Dimension

Lengthening and shortening create changes in the **vertical dimension** (the head–tail connection). Verticality is one of the earliest hallmarks of human evolution (Konner, 1977). As Sossin and Romer (1989) point out, the infant is vertical when held in an upright position by its caregiver long before it can stand (see also Konner, 1977). Verticality may act as a motor-perceptual base of infantile "omnipotence" as discussed by Winnicott (1965). Movements in the vertical dimension are related to qualities associated with the second year of life, such as intentionality, presentation, evaluation, and confrontation.

### Lengthening

**Bipolar lengthening** can be seen in the process of inhalation: the rib cage rises upward toward the head while the diaphragm moves downward into the abdominal cavity. Newborns lengthen and shorten bipolarly as they extend and flex the whole body in and out of the earlier intrauterine position. Toward the end of the first year and beginning of the second the infant uses bipolar lengthening and shortening movements for crawling, climbing, standing, and stooping. To rise to a standing position, the child may press downward while stretching upward, demonstrating bipolar lengthening. The sensation associated with this accomplishment is sometimes expressed by the child who proudly says, "I am so big."

---

**Exercise**

Bipolar lengthening occurs commonly in the spinal column, hands, feet, and face. A big yawn requires the lower jaw to stretch down while the upper jaw stretches up. Eyes may also lengthen bipolarly. Which emotion is expressed by this facial configuration?

Try to lengthen bipolarly in the torso, and evaluate associated feelings. (Remember: bipolar lengthening requires lengthening down as well as lengthening up. This may be accomplished by stretching down into the feet while lengthening up with one's head.)

---

Bipolar lengthening gives structure to feelings of comfort, elation, pride, and capability. Through bipolar lengthening, one grows big and feels capable of greatness.

### Matching and Mismatching

Low intensity matched with bipolar lengthening is conducive to feelings of pride, easy going humor, and optimism in free flow and mild concern in bound flow (Kestenberg, 1967). The mismatched combination of bipolar lengthening and high intensity bound flow is commonly used to express surprise (particularly with abruptness). In potentially dangerous contexts one may open oneself up (eyes, ears, mouth) to information in the surrounding environment while remaining guarded (bound flow). The clash reflects these contradictory tendencies.

---

#### Exercise

Try bipolar lengthening with low intensity free flow. The movement (a stretch or straightening up) exudes a feeling of comfort and perhaps pride. Try clashing combinations: what impression is given by a movement of lengthening with high intensity bound flow? Try also the combination of high intensity, abrupt, free flow with lengthening. The expression is transformed to joyful. Many other movement elements modify the movement and the associated emotions.

---

A person with an abundance of bipolar lengthening may appear perpetually elated, pleased with herself, or arrogant, depending on which combinations of tension flow attribute elements are used.

## Shortening

**Bipolar shortening** during exhalation and elimination consists of flexion or compression of the body toward the center in the vertical dimension. It is also used in climbing and stooping, pushing, expressing anger or pain or humility. A focus of the second year of life, bipolar shortening provides a center of stability. Bipolar shortening may be seen in the face, hands, feet or whole torso. It is often used in the demonstrations of anger and temper, such as making a fist, grinding the teeth and jaw, and pressing the lips together.

Bipolar shortening also may be seen in such gestures as shrugging (shortening up in the shoulders and shortening down with the head), which means, "I don't know" in North and South American and East African cultures (McNeill, 1985). In contrast, those who "know" tend to lengthen with pride.

---

#### Exercise

From a seated position, try shortening bipolarly into a shrunken ball shape. Note the feeling of making yourself small and coming into yourself. Try it with both bound and free flow. Note the difference in the associated feelings.

---

## *Matching and Mismatching*

Shortening matches with high intensity bound flow. High intensity bound flow expresses strong usually unpleasant feelings and shortening structures the body into a closed shape. Bipolar shortening serves as a protective gesture, or a mode of expression of deep emotions. Shortening up from the jaw and shortening down in the eyebrows (bipolar shortening of the face) with high intensity bound flow provides a facial structure for the expression of anger or intense pain. Bipolar shortening and becoming bound in the jaw may restrain a biting attack (verbal or physical). Restraint of or the preparation for aggression (bipolar shortening) seems to concentrate in those body parts most likely to participate in aggressive acts, such as the jaw or the fists. Use of bound flow with shortening in these areas serves also to communicate anger to others.[4] Shortening with high intensity bound flow may also be used in preparation for a lunge or leap forward, or a karate kick.

Persistent bipolar shortening with high intensity bound flow is associated with feeling tense and tied up inside. Stomach pains, constipation, difficulty in breathing, and feeling ill at ease are related both to the compression of organs and the emotional correlates of these movement patterns.

Shortening combined with low intensity (a mismatch) often reflects feeling small, ashamed, depressed, or withdrawn. Adding free flow introduces a pleasurable quality to the process of shrinking (coming into oneself). When young children combine shortening with low intensity, flow adjustments, and free flow they may be expressing feelings of pleasure and coyness (eliciting attention). Such movements may appear cute and appealing to an observer who may feel both dominant and protective toward "the child."[5]

---

### Exercise

Try expressing anger facially and verbally. Note that shortening with high intensity bound flow can be expressed in the voice as well as the face, making it possible to distinguish between an angry and a cheerful voice.

Try lying on your back, stretching out and then contracting. Note that it is natural to use free flow with lengthening and bound flow with shortening. Try the opposite. How does it influence your ability to stretch and contract?

---

### *The Development of "Stability" in the Second Year of Life*

Bipolar lengthening and shortening are both important elements in an individual's movement repertoire. The ability to express pride and importance needs to be balanced by the ability to express shame or insignificance. It is the dynamic interplay between lengthening and shortening that underlies stability. Children in the second year of life practice torso stability by stooping and standing up over and over. The creation of a stable torso through a balance of shortening and lengthening supports a solid connection between head and tail. Stability in the vertical dimension promotes a solid foundation for the child who will then begin to walk and run with an internal sense of balance. Children in the first year of life who were placed too often in "walkers" were prematurely propelled forward before they were able to develop torso stability. These children may have a poorer sense of balance when they learn to walk and run.

## The Sagittal Dimension

Bulging and hollowing create change in the **sagittal** dimension (forward and backward). Movements in the sagittal dimension are related to qualities associated with the third year of life, such as anticipation, decision, and operation.

## Bulging

**Bipolar bulging** is created by inhalation in the chest and belly as well as in the upper and lower back. It consists of growing in the sagittal dimension both frontally and in the back. Bipolar bulging also occurs if a person bulges forward with one anterior part of the body and concurrently bulges backward with another posterior part, e.g., bulging forward, with the chin and backward with the occipital skull, or forward with the chest and backward with the buttocks. Opera singers are able to bipolarly bulge as they breathe fully in the back as well as in the front in order to project their voices fully.

When two-year-olds begin to be more attuned to bladder functions and to feelings of fullness, they begin to move out of the vertical plane and more into the sagittal plane. Instead of focusing on the "I am so big" feeling of the earlier vertical stage, they now revel in new accomplishments. They discover a "filled up" sense of self who can accomplish things. This is closely related to Spitz's finding that the sense of self is at first an interoceptive or belly sense of self (Spitz, 1965). The earliest sense of fullness and satiation may first begin when the baby ingests milk in the context of the nurturing embrace of the caregiver.

Bulging is associated with feelings of fullness, satiation, gratification, and completion. A body attitude of bipolar bulging expresses a feeling of self-satisfaction, which in common parlance is sometimes negatively described as "feeling full of yourself." Bipolar bulging may also express feeling lucky that one has so much. Contented toddlers often listen to stories while bulging bipolarly, which signifies that they are feeling full as they absorb an interesting tale.

---

### Exercise

In order to achieve a sense of bipolar bulging, allow yourself to bulge forward with free flow in the abdomen and backward in the lower spine while inhaling. What feelings are associated with this use of bipolar shape flow and free flow?

Conversely, imagine it is a warm, glorious day and you have just had a great meal. What shape flow do you use? You might also try laughing heartily. Do you find yourself bulging and widening?

---

### *Matching and Mismatching*

Bulging gradually with free flow creates a harmonious feeling of good-natured self-confidence. One feels pleasure gradually building and comfort (growing) about taking in and thus enjoys the feeling of fullness. Combined with free flow, bulging indicates a satisfaction with what one has done; combined with bound flow it may create a defensive/aggressive stance suggesting, "Look what I could do to you."

Bulging with abruptness may create a disconcerting clash between comfortable self-confidence and alert caution. In the context of a sudden startle, an abrupt intake of air prepares one for action. Thus inhaling fully with bipolar bulging with abruptness is a case of a mismatch which can be functionally adaptive.

---

### Exercise

Try bulging gradually with bound flow. Does the bound flow undermine the feelings of comfort which usually accompany bulging? Try bulging with abruptness. What messages does this movement convey?

---

## Hollowing

In **hollowing** during exhalation, urination, and crying the torso shrinks inward. Both the back and the front hollow in toward the center of the body. This produces the "emaciated model" look or the appearance of anorexia or starvation. Hollowing supports the biological functions of moving food down the path of digestion (swallowing, processing, and then emptying the body of waste materials) by providing forward and backward shrinking. Hollowing is practiced frequently in the pelvic area in children in their third year of life as they gain control over urination.

The expressive role of hollowing is closely associated with its biological functions. Bipolar hollowing is seen in the face and torso of a person who has just smelled or eaten something distasteful. It conveys the emotion of disgust or the desire to rid oneself of something.[6] Hollowing may also express feelings of emptiness, hunger, and depletion.

---

### Exercise

Imagine being told that you have just eaten a worm. What is your bodily response? You may find that you shrink in more than one dimension, though hollowing is probably the predominant shape.

Imagine returning home to find that you have been robbed and nothing is left in your house. What bodily response accompanies those feelings?

---

An abundance of bipolar hollowing connotes feelings of dejection, emptiness, or loss. Depleted of energy and value, a person may feel needy and hungry for sources of comfort but lack the self-confidence and trust to seek them out.

### *Matching and Mismatching*

Expulsion of tears or cries of pain, coughing and sneezing, and related bodily functions are initiated by hollowing with bound flow and abruptness. These affined movement qualities are functionally adaptive to the goal of expulsion. Abrupt elimination of waste materials is a physiological response to stress in preparation for flight or fight. Hollowing with abrupt bound flow in response to a frightening situation typically takes place in the lower groin area. Hollowing with graduality and free flow is a mismatch which is used in a relaxed expulsion of waste materials. It is the physiological equivalent of giving up or letting go with a feeling of relief: "The battle is lost, but I'm glad it's over."

## Exercise

In response to an undefined threatening situation, hollow abruptly with bound flow (remember to hollow bipolarly in the front and back). Now try a clashing combination: hollow gradually with low intensity free flow. You may be able to capture this movement quality more easily by attempting to feel empty and dejected.

### *The Development of "Confidence" in the Third Year of Life*

Often alternating rhythmically, bulging and hollowing play important roles in biological functioning and emotional expressions. The alternation of hollowing and bulging in a crying child's distressed breathing offers the somewhat contradictory message of feeling distressed and depleted (hollowing) combined with the desire to be filled up (bulging).

The dynamic balance of bulging and hollowing support true self-confidence and the ability to inspire confidence. Self-confidence requires a coming into oneself as well as a going out to the world. Someone who primarily bulges looks puffed up, bloated, or full of himself. He may have much information, but it is hot air, because it has not been properly digested or processed. Incorporating, digesting, or understanding requires hollowing. Of course, with too much hollowing the information is too quickly expelled. The person looks depleted. The balance between bulging and hollowing affords the opportunity to go out into the world and yet return to find connections with self.

In sum, global comfort and comfort-seeking behaviors are generally associated with growing shape flow, and discomfort is often expressed with shrinking shape flow. In the horizontal dimension, a balance of widening and narrowing generates trust. In the vertical dimension, stability emerges from a balance of lengthening and shortening. In the sagittal dimension, when bulging and hollowing are balanced, a feeling of confidence develops.

### Neutral shape

In discussing tension flow, neutral flow refers to the minimal changes in free and bound flow which reflect reduced elasticity. However, **neutral shape** means "shapelessness," not minimal plasticity. When one encounters noxious stimuli, one shrinks to get away from it. When the situation is hopeless, however, a person may "dissolve," losing a sense of relationship to the environment and a coherent shape. Breathing (based on growing and shrinking) becomes shallow and irregular, with an emphasis on exhalation. Facial expression is devoid of meaning.

Neutral shape is commonly associated with a depressed sense of self; there is no internalized object, no internal feelings of comfort. Neutral shape is seen in very depressed babies. It is not typically seen in average development (as is neutral tension flow); it indicates a pathological condition.

### The Holding Environment

Growing and shrinking are integral aspects of the "holding environment of the infant" described by Winnicott (1965). One of the earliest experiences for most infants is the feeling of being supported and held in the uterus. While in the womb the fetus grows larger but continues to be held and contained; its needs are provided for. Even *in utero* the fetus has the capacity to grow (within the restricted space available) and shrink. After birth, infants usually continue to experience being held in the arms of a caregiver. The feelings of comfort and security get transmitted to infants by the predictability inherent in the regular breathing patterns of the caregiver in correspondence with the infants' own breathing rhythms. Supportive holding patterns and a predictable environment promote healthy development.

Kestenberg and Buelte (1977) describe different holding patterns: (a) a tight grasp, which may transmit feelings of anxiety and restriction, (b) a limp embrace which may engender fear of falling, and (c) a dynamic support, which incorporates mutual adjustment and breathing. Growing and shrinking, separating and becoming closer create a dynamic embrace which is characteristic of intimate relationships. The predictability in the rhythms of growing and shrinking as well as having received the appropriate response to expressions of discomfort encourage the infant to rely on the enviromnent as trustworthy. The infant learns that relief comes after expelling something noxious, that comfort follows discomfort, and togetherness follows separation (Kestenberg, 1985).

## Body Image Formation and Self Feelings[7]

The number of shape flow changes in a young infant is very high. Infants grow and shrink, flexing in the intrauterine position and then stretching out in facial expressions and in various early reflexes (e.g., startle). Shape flow movements decline as the infant develops a more defined body image. They continue to decline throughout life (Kestenberg, 1967).

The body image that has formed by adulthood to some extent reflects the holding environment experienced in early childhood. An infant who grows with inhalation toward a caregiver but finds no commensurate growth and support, feels disconnected and loses trust in the environment. Caregivers who themselves have not been held in mutually supportive ways tend to hold babies in similar ways that they were held, creating shrinking body images and feelings of self-doubt and distrust. Infants held with shrinking qualities begin to hold themselves with shrinking qualities and may learn to find a sense of self in shrinking and in disconnection.

"When a child is uncomfortable for too long, he or she loses trust in the environment and may assume a habitual shrunken body attitude" (Kestenberg, 1985, p. 44). Long-term physical illness can also lead to the adoption of bipolar shrinking as a body attitude (Sossin and Loman, 1992).

On the other hand

In the absence of parental responsiveness and mutuality of interaction, the child may show an excessive growing out into the world, [reflecting] an excessive degree of narcissistic neediness" (Sossin and Loman, 1992, p. 33).

An excessive growing without commensurate shrinking may reflect an inner insecurity or lack of self-trust. One must distinguish this excessive growing from a habitually expanded body attitude. Excessive growing has the disadvantages of exposure to dangerous elements in the environment, an overly trusting nature, and too much of an outward orientation. It is beneficial to be able to shrink into oneself (get in touch with one's own feelings) as well as to be able to grow outward, connecting with one's environment (Loman, 1994). A moderately expansive body attitude which encompasses balanced patterns of growing and shrinking reflects beneficial experiences and promotes adaptive responses. A balance of growing and shrinking offers the opportunity to develop reasonable feelings of trust, stability, and self-confidence and to experience a wide range of feelings. With a good balance, when the child feels comfortable and trusting she can be generous and expansive; where she feels uncomfortable and unsafe, she can be constricted and miserly. In varying contexts, rhythms of shape flow take her through feeling "...big and elated, small and subdued, full and proud, and empty and insignificant" (Kestenberg, 1967, p. 96).

### Interpersonal Relationships

There is a close relationship between growing and shrinking, feelings of comfort/discomfort, and the quality of being open or closed to the outside environment. When one feels comfortable and good about oneself and one's environment, one tends to grow and enlarge body boundaries, creating openness to the environment which increases relatedness. A person glowing with the feeling of being loved walks around with expanded body boundaries. A person with expanded body boundaries exudes self-confidence. In contrast, in response to feeling uncomfortable or unhappy one tends to shrink body boundaries, creating a contracted or closed self-image. Shrinking promotes greater centering on oneself and a decreasing relatedness to others.

Loman and Foley (1996) elaborate on the role of shape flow in the formation of interpersonal relationships. Through experiencing himself in relation to his caregiver, the infant develops a sense of self-in-relationship, or "being-in-relationship" (Miller, 1991). This is a relational sense of self which, until recently, has received much less attention than the individual sense of self. Relational Model theorist Jean Baker Miller suggests that:

(t)he infant experiences a sense of comfort only as the other is also comfortable ... only as they are both engaged in an emotional relationship that is moving toward greater well-being (Miller, 1991, p. 13; see also Jordan *et al.*, 1991).

According to Kestenberg and Buelte (1977) mutuality is a key element in the growing relationship between parent and child. As the infant and caregiver breathe together, both actively participate in the relationship. The infant mirrors the caregiver's shape and in turn influences the caregiver's shape flow. "Through attunement of tension flow and adjustment in shape flow in the near space between mother and child, they mirror each other's feelings in a reciprocal relationship ..." (Kestenberg, 1967, p. 105). Gradually, kinesthetic mirroring becomes supplemented by visually-induced mirroring of facial expressions and body movements which help the child to empathize and understand the emotions of others.

In most cases, children experience both instances of support and lack of support and develop an understanding of safe and dangerous situations; they learn to trust those who are trustworthy and distrust those who are not.

### Communication of Emotions: Can Specific Tension Flow and Shape Flow Qualities Define Specific Emotions?

While tension flow attributes regulate emotions (intense or low key, restrained or ebullient), shape flow structures their expression and thus participates in defining them. Through observation of changes in shape flow, emotions are most readily identified.[8] Shape flow thus serves as an early foundation for interpersonal communication.

However, research defining emotions according to patterns of shape flow and tension flow is in its initial stages. We do not yet know to what extent one can distinguish specific emotions using only the movement qualities of the KMP system. Nonetheless, the KMP has made contributions to our understanding of emotions. Kestenberg and Sossin (1994) studied KMP movement elements in the facial expression of emotions in infants. Their findings included the discovery that emotions are often expressed with clashing movement patterns. For example, anger often is expressed with a combination of bulging and shortening with bound flow, which would imply that elements of self-confidence, feeling small, and feeling constrained are all involved. It is also clear, however, that there is not only one movement configuration that expresses anger nor is anger a singular emotion. Emotion terms such as "anger" or "happiness" are generic labels for variously nuanced feelings. If there are no simple one-to-one correlations between what we call anger and movement qualities this is at least partly because of the inadequacy of linguistic terms for describing emotions and emotional expressions. Movement analysis broadens the scope of how we study emotions. It frees us from constraints of popular labels and allows for the meaningful study of emotions across linguistic and cultural boundaries.

As discussion of the various combinations of tension flow and shape flow illustrates, meaning is derived from configurations and combinations, not single elements. It is not enough to know that shortening is a preferred pattern of a mover; rather one needs to see with which qualities shortening is combined. Interpretations of specific movement qualities are given only to help the reader evaluate their contribution to larger movement configurations.

Unfortunately, some studies of expression of emotions focus exclusively on one element of shape flow or one body part, neglecting the complex mixtures that the study of shape flow and tension flow reveals. They therefore may erroneously find more cultural differences than actually exist. For example, one author reported that whereas Europeans stick out their chins when being aggressive or assertive, in Japanese to "stick out one's chin" means to be totally exhausted (Suzuki, 1978). However, a demonstration with Japanese subjects revealed that the posture of total exhaustion was initiated with a hollowing of the chest, shortening down in the neck, and a lapse into neutral flow. This posture bears little resemblance to bulging forward in bound flow as an aggressive stance. One cannot conclude that the same "gesture" expresses different emotions in Japan versus Europe. The difference is in the linguistic rather than nonverbal domain.

While there is little doubt that cultural environments affect both the experience and expression of emotion, the degree of universality and specificity cannot be assessed without a better study of the qualities of each gesture or posture described.

## Rhythms of Shape Flow

Rhythms of growing and shrinking in shape flow exist but they are not captured in our system of recording. Our system of notation uses paper (a two-dimensional surface) and cannot record the three dimensional properties of growing and shrinking. Another difficulty is that some growing and shrinking movement occurs within organs inside the body (e.g., the heart, lungs, stomach, and bowels) and cannot be observed outwardly. As these shape flow rhythms do exist, just as tension flow rhythms do, we hope that through new technology new methods of recording may evolve.

However, the study of shape flow in its present form still offers an important contribution to the understanding of self-feelings, body image, expressive modes, and development. The study of bipolar shape flow reveals ways in which forms of emotional expression are derived from and closely related to biological processes. Shape flow is also the foundation for relational development beginning with the self and expanding to others.

**Notes**

1. The terms "growing" and "shrinking" were coined by Laban (1950).
2. Laban first described the process of growing and shrinking and Warren Lamb coined the term "shape flow." Kestenberg found it necessary to distinguish between bipolar or symmetrical shape flow and unipolar or asymmetrical shape flow (the latter will be discussed in the following chapter).
3. "Affined with" can be defined as having a good fit with another movement pattern. A clash occurs when two movement patterns are disharmonious or disaffined.
4. It is interesting that in many animals such as the carnivores and primates, a yawn is used as a threat; it conveniently displays a set of sharp canines. Lengthening, graduality, and bound flow combine to form a yawn. Lengthening with bound flow says, "Look how big I am: beware." There is often a pleasurable gloating and feeling of pride in this gesture. In contrast, in anger and also in preparation for attack the jaw is clenched using shortening and bound flow. Shortening with bound flow serves to either temporarily restrain aggression or attack. There are also elements of being in touch with the earth and being stable associated with shortening.
5. Bipolar shortening with low intensity is often used as a submissive gesture. It implies, "I am so small like a child, don't hurt me." Bipolar lengthening may also be used in submission. It implies "I am open and vulnerable. Don't hurt me."
6. Note that this refers to general feelings of disgust rather than repulsion from a specific disgust evoking object. The latter stimulates unipolar hollowing back from a noxious stimulus.
7. The body image is a reflection of how a person imagines themselves to be. The body attitude is the way the body is held in motion and at rest.
8. However, as Ekman (1989) discovered, emotions can be miscued. A person may offer misleading shape flow, e.g., smiling when unhappy, or frowning when glad. Tension flow, less subject to conscious manipulation, is a more reliable, but less clearly defined indicator of emotional states. Bound flow, for example, suggests feelings of caution or restraint and free flow suggests care-free feelings. Roughly they can be associated with pleasure and displeasure. As previously stated, more specific emotions cannot be identified from tension flow patterns alone.

# CHAPTER 6

# Unipolar Shape Flow

Unipolar shape-flow factors in the faces of each individual convey feelings of approach or withdrawal. What other affects do you see?

In bipolar shape flow the body grows symmetrically, increasing exposure to the surrounding environment, and shrinks, diminishing exposure. Through the symmetrical process of growing and shrinking, bipolar shape flow gives the body stability. These biological rhythms (e.g., breathing rhythms) of growing and shrinking provide the prototype for growing unilaterally as an approach to attractive stimuli and shrinking unilaterally as a withdrawal from noxious stimuli (see also Mahler, 1971 in Kestenberg, 1975).[1] Asymmetrical growing and shrinking, termed **unipolar shape flow** (towards one direction or pole), provides the foundation for mobility.

Kestenberg (1967) offers the amoeba as a model for unipolar shape flow. The amoeba extends its body, approaching a source of nutrients in the environment, and then shrinks back toward itself. Unipolar movements are part of the system which extends bodily dimensions into space (Sossin and Loman, 1992) and then withdraws them. One can contrast sticking out a hand to pick up a cup[2] with stretching out toward the cup in order to reach it. Stretching toward the cup supported by the breathing apparatus (we inhale as we grow and exhale as we shrink) has a stronger affective component. According to Kestenberg (1967), "this 'flow of shape' is the apparatus of approach and withdrawal," attraction and repulsion (p. 86).

In the neonate, unipolar growing toward and shrinking from evolve from the bipolar system of global growing and shrinking (as in breathing) and from early tonic reflexes. For example, in the rooting reflex, the infant turns toward a touch on the cheek, and then towards the nipple. Widening with a breath unilaterally (unipolar) supports the infant's ability to successfully reach and grasp the nipple. When pricked by the doctor on the sole of her foot, an infant will **shorten up** her leg (withdrawing from the prick) demonstrating this shrinking unipolar pattern.

The neonate focuses on his own body and internal stimuli. In transition from moving from a fetal position *in utero* to stretching out after birth, the newborn still exhibits more shrinking than growing shape flow (Kestenberg, 1967). With maturation of visual and acoustic perception, the infant's tendency toward an inward body orientation becomes more balanced by an outward orientation. He begins growing unipolarly in order to make contact with attractive stimuli, and shrinks unipolarly in response to noxious stimuli.

Unipolar shape flow changes reflect and are closely associated with feelings of attraction or repulsion. When young children are attracted to an object, they will stretch out one part of their body (enlarging body boundaries) in order to reach for it. Growing toward the object demonstrates feelings of attraction to it. Likewise, in response to a painful stimulus, children will shrink away or contract their body boundaries, reflecting feelings of repulsion. Young children often show a high frequency of unipolar changes because they have a low threshold to stimuli (i.e., they are very responsive to stimuli) and have a high emotional investment in surrounding stimuli.

During a partner exercise in KMP training workshops, participants were instructed to give and to respond to an array of pleasant and mildly noxious stimuli (such as gently tapping the head or mildly poking the shoulder) using only unipolar shrinking and growing movements. The participants, who were adults, often reported that while moving in unipolar shape flow they felt childlike. Watching others engaged in unipolar shape flow changes, observers interpreted the movements as being expressive and feeling-laden (Goldman, 1992).

Because it expresses feelings of attraction and repulsion, unipolar shape flow plays an important role in the development of relationships. One of the earliest relationships which can be used as an example is the nursing infant–mother relationship. The infant grows towards her mother's nipple in order to take in nourishment and shrinks slightly away from the nipple while swallowing. The mother, in turn, breathes and grows into her breast, facilitating entry of the milk into the baby's mouth but shrinks slightly away from the baby as the baby swallows and the mother exhales. The baby and mother grow toward each other and shrink away from each other during nursing through unipolar shape flow. Using this unipolar shape flow rhythm of union and separation, the infant gains a rudimentary control over closeness and distance from the source of satisfaction. "This partial independence ... becomes the core of active initiation and termination of contact according to needs" (Kestenberg, 1967, p. 105).

Unipolar growing and shrinking is a characteristic mode of relating in many intimate relationships. Utilizing unipolar shape flow one grows toward need satisfying-stimuli and withdraws when satisfied, like the lover who turns over and falls asleep after lovemaking. The "love object" ceases to attract when it no longer offers need satisfaction or pleasant stimuli. The focus here is on the satisfaction of self.

Shrinking back into oneself can offer pleasurable contact; the interest often reserved for another person or thing may become invested in oneself. When pleasurable (with free flow) shrinking movements prevail over growing movements in adults, it may reflect a self centered personality (Kestenberg, 1967).

The infant's experience of receiving care, attention, and love through unipolar shape flow helps define the self image. For example, when a caregiver grows toward, picks up, and soothes a crying infant, meeting her need, the message of love is communicated: "You are a lovable, worthwhile person." If the infant is not properly responded to often enough, held limply without enough growing patterns, or given facial expressions of disgust through shrinking shape flow, she may feel unworthy of love.

Although unipolar movements are reflections of feelings underlying approach and withdrawal, in many functional acts, such as reaching for an object, the emotional component is reduced as the tasks are learned and become automatic. One can observe the large, expressive growing movement of a young child who stretches his arm and torso to indicate that he wants a special toy. In contrast, an older child who has mastered the skill of pointing, can simply use the arm alone, without overly stretching it with shape flow. The emotional aspect of unipolar shape flow becomes diminished for the older child who can show someone which toy he wants by a simple pointing gesture.

## The Diagram and Elements of Unipolar Shape Flow

In the study of unipolar shape flow we are interested not only in the polar opposite movements of growing and shrinking, but also in the role of unipolar movement as a bridge between bipolar shape flow and shaping in directions (discussed in Chapter 8). In order to reflect the developmental sequence, the unipolar shape flow diagram has been constructed in the manner shown in Diagram 6 (See Diagram 6). For example, both lengthening down and shortening down are placed on the right side of the diagram together, because they are both precursors of downward movements (see Chapter 8). Likewise both lengthening up and shortening up have been placed on the left side of the diagram as precursors to upward directional movements. This organization is based on maintaining the developmental sequence, and is discussed further later in the chapter.

**Lateral Widening** (widening to one side only) is seen primarily in the torso, shoulder, chest, pelvis, head, and hand, but may occur as a one-sided smile or a one-sided widening in the hand or foot. Widening is used in shifting towards a pleasant stimulus, such as a caregiver or an interesting object. Tango dancers, locked in a embrace side by side, widen unipolarly as they meet cheek to cheek. Widening initiated in the shoulder or pelvis is used

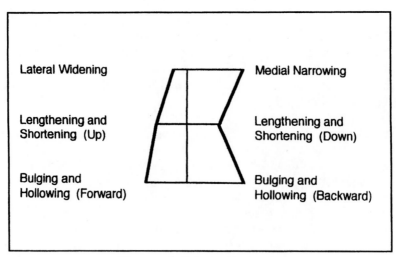

**Diagram 6.** Unipolar Shape Flow

in the process of turning over. An exhausted youngster may lean on and snuggle against her caregiver with unipolar widening.

---

### Exercise

Try widening to the side in the upper chest and shoulder toward a soft pillow. Feel the growing and extending of the body boundaries.

---

**Medial Narrowing** (narrowing toward the middle of the body) is seen primarily in the shoulder, torso, and pelvis, but may occur as a one-sided frown or a one-sided narrowing of the brow, hand, or foot. An infant may narrow on one side to initiate the turning over process, and then widen to complete the turn. Typically a person narrows away from an unpleasant person or object near her side by narrowing medially in the rib cage or shoulder area.

---

### Exercise

Try rolling over from a supine to a prone position. Where did widening and narrowing occur? Turning over generally requires narrowing in the shoulder to initiate the turn and then widening in the opposite shoulder to complete it. Alternatively, one can turn over using impetus from the pelvis.

If a partner is available, sit next to her on the floor. Stroke her shoulder to elicit a widening response and then gently poke her ribs for a narrowing response. Try widening towards each other and then narrowing away. This together/apart rhythm is one rhythm of relationships.

Now change the rhythm so that one person grows while the other shrinks. This can create a rocking side-to-side rhythm in which no separation from touching occurs. Do you have a preference for one pattern or the other?

---

Widening and narrowing are commonly used in the first year of life. Through unipolar widening and narrowing, the infant becomes acquainted with the two sides of the body and gains a sense of the midline which divides the right and left sides of the body.

### *Matching and Mismatching* (widening and narrowing unipolar shape flow with flow adjustment and even flow tension flow)

In his research, ethologist Schneirla (in Kestenberg, 1975) found that approach behavior (growing unipolarly) is correlated with smoothly running, continuous bodily processes (typically free flow) whereas withdrawal behavior (shrinking) is characterized by interruptive processes (typically bound flow). This corresponds to the patterns of matching and mismatching described in the previous chapter. Both bipolar and unipolar shape flow movement qualities provide the structure for tension flow attributes. Growing towards something or someone tends to be associated with feelings of safety and pleasure and thus involves the release of tension (free flow). More specifically, widening is matched with flow adjustment in free flow. Snuggling into someone's shoulder, one adjusts to his comforter's body and creates a pleasant contact. The mismatch (widening toward someone with evenly held bound flow) reflects a restraint against contact or a cautious approach. Widening with even flow has an aggressive quality. It is often used to shove or push someone next to you or to edge through a crowd.

Narrowing is affined with even bound flow. There is a harmony between feeling cautious or restrained (bound flow) and withdrawing or shrinking away from something. Narrowing with flow adjustment can be interpreted as the clash of withdrawing from unpleasant stimuli with accommodating feelings.[3] This combination may also convey ambivalence as in teasing or flirting, "I am sort of withdrawing from you, will you approach?" Mismatches are well-suited to the expression and communication of mixed messages.

---

### Exercise

Try narrowing away from an unpleasant person sitting next to you on a crowded bus. Do you use more free or more bound flow? Try the clash of narrowing with free flow and flow adjustment. Experiment changing this to bound flow with flow adjustment and note how the mood changes with bound flow.

Try widening toward someone with bound flow. Does this feel aggressive? You are inviting contact without pleasure. Remember that unipolar shape flow involves more than movement of a limb. The torso expands investing the movement with an emotional quality.

---

The matching of tension flow and unipolar shape flow patterns develops in the first year of life. The harmony between free flow and growing has an integrative effect on the development of self in relationship to objects. One learns to approach pleasant stimuli with pleasure and withdraw from noxious stimuli with caution. Mismatching patterns have a disorganizing effect; clashes distort the body image and the perception of objects. However, these distorted images can be rebuilt in a subsequent developmental phase in which harmony prevails (Kestenberg, 1967, 1975).

**Lengthening up** is seen in growing taller, reaching up to something, raising one's eyebrows, or in the upward turn of the mouth in a smile. As in bipolar lengthening there is often a sensation of elation associated with lengthening up. Eibl-Eibelsfeldt describes the "eyebrow flash," a raising of the eyebrows seen in expressions of surprise and in some cultures as a gesture of pleased greeting (1989).

---

### Exercise

Imagine a warm glow of sunshine above your head. Lengthen up toward it, feeling the stretch as body boundaries extend. Reach up for an object. Again, feel the reaching process create a stretch in the shoulder as the arm extends upward. Now try lengthening up in the torso, making yourself feel bigger than others.

The feeling of stretching upward contrasts with the sensation of bipolar lengthening where the body is stable and extended equally in both directions.

---

### *Matching and Mismatching* (lengthening up unipolar shape flow with low intensity and high intensity tension flow)

Lengthening up can be seen as one half of bipolar lengthening. It is horizontally matched with low intensity. When the eyebrow flash is done with bound rather than free flow it changes from a look of pleasure to one of fear or indignation (usually with abruptness also). When performed with narrowing, it suggests disapproval. Lengthening up with bound flow is typical of threat gestures, dominance behavior, and arrogance. There is a clash between feeling bigger than others and yet being displeased. As movement observers we must be careful to note whether a person who rises "politely" in greeting shortens down slightly (in the shoulders or head) to indicate deference or lengthens up with bound flow to indicate high status. There may be considerable variation in the way even a standardized movement is actually performed.

Lengthening up with high intensity is a mismatch seen in threat gestures, startle responses, and in preparation for attack. The high intensity invests the movement with a passionate quality. Lengthening up with high intensity free flow has a out-of-control quality which can be frightening. It reflects a conflict between pleasantly growing towards and expression of intense feelings.

**Lengthening down** is seen in reaching down for something, in stretching down into one's toes as when jumping down from a swing, and in the downward turn of the mouth and eyes in expressions of sadness. Children in their second year of life tend to enjoy games involving throwing and retrieving. Sitting in the high chair, the eighteen-month-old child throws down a piece of apple. Almost immediately, she stretches toward the apple, lengthening down to it. The most likely resolution to this part of the game is for the caregiver to return the apple to the high chair. The game may continue for awhile, depending on the caregiver's level of patience on that particular day.

---

### Exercise

Try reaching down to touch the floor. Feel the stretch going down into the fingers and the pull in the shoulder. Create a sad expression by lengthening down in the mouth.

---

### *Matching and Mismatching* (lengthening down unipolar shape flow with low intensity and high intensity tension flow)

Lengthening down does not match completely with low intensity. Contained within the combination of lengthening and downward in direction is an inherent clash. Lengthening is a growing movement normally associated with open shapes, and down is a direction associated with closed shapes (see Table 10). Lengthening down, however, is one of the precursors of the directional movement down and is placed on the right side of the diagram with closed shapes.[4] We resolve this problem by considering lengthening and down a **partial clash**. The mismatch with high intensity intensifies the clash and the **partial affinity** with low intensity ameliorates it.

One may lengthen down affectionately with low intensity to those who are smaller, such as children or pets. The lengthening aspect reflects feeling of attraction, the downward component implies that the attraction is to those who are smaller or below and the low intensity reflects mildly pleasant feelings. This is a relatively harmonious movement.

When lengthening down to an object which has emotional value, such as to a ring accidently dropped into a stream, one tends to utilize high intensity, which changes the quality of the movement. Now the movement of growing towards something invokes intense feelings of concern and is more conflicted.

Note that feelings of distress or sadness are expressed by a lengthening down in the mouth with low intensity, as in the expression, "She's really down in the mouth." This might be interpreted as reflecting an attraction toward low-key or down (sad) feelings.

---

### Exercise

Try lengthening down to pick up a small object. Did you use low intensity? What feelings are associated with this movement? If the object is large, do you turn to high intensity and lose the pleasurable feeling?

---

**Shortening down** is seen in shrinking down into oneself. It is frequently used in defecation and in response to gastrointestinal pain. Frequent shortening down into one's abdomen can predispose one to intestinal disorders. Shortening down is also used to express deference (as in shortening the head and neck down into the shoulders and thereby withdrawing from someone who is dominant or domineering). One shortens down to avoid dangerous stimuli from above, and shortens down in the brows to express consternation.

**Shortening up** is used in shrinking away from noxious stimuli from below and in many expressive gestures. While running barefoot across a cold floor, one may shorten up in order to have minimal contact with the ground. Upon touching a hot surface, a small child shortens up abruptly with her hand; one shortens up in the arms when holding onto a valued object (e.g., a toddler holding her baby doll) close to the body. Shortening up the upper lip in a gesture of anger or disgust is seen in many cultures. Shrugging involves the use of unipolar shortening up in the shoulders. Although the shortening is upward, it is still a gesture which makes one appear shorter and fits into the larger category of deference gestures (meaning "I have no knowledge" or "My opinion isn't important"). Of course, shortening up gestures may consist of many different movement combinations which subtly change the meaning.

---

### Exercise

Imagine walking along a trail and suddenly making head contact with a branch. How do you respond? Do you feel shortening down in the torso or turtle-like shrinking into your shoulders? Imagine being scolded and shortening down in response. Do you turn down the edges of your mouth? If you are offered a dish of unappetizing food, do you detect a short-ening up of your upper lip in your smile of "no thanks?"

---

### *Matching and Mismatching* (shortening down and shortening up unipolar shape flow with high intensity and low intensity tension flow)

Shortening down is matched with high intensity. Withdrawal from noxious stimuli is naturally affined with feelings of displeasure, anger, or fear. Shortening down with low intensity is a clash, reflecting the conflict of withdrawing from unpleasant stimuli with ease.

Shortening up, like lengthening down, in itself, is a partial clash. Withdrawing from nox-ious stimuli from below by shortening up with high intensity, such as shrinking away from a mouse, is a relatively harmonious response. Shortening up with low intensity suggests the conflict of moving away from an unpleasant stimuli in a polite way, such as grimacing only slightly in the mouth to react to stomach cramps while at a formal dinner.

---

### Exercise

Try shortening down in the torso with free flow and low intensity. Compare it with short-ening down with high intensity bound flow. The first is a collapse, the second more associ-ated with anger or pain.

---

Unipolar lengthening and shortening help the child become familiar with the upper and lower portions of her body. This familiarity helps the child climb and stand on tiptoe in the second year of life.

**Bulging forward** is typical of children who are entering the sagittal plane and evolving from toddlers into walkers. The forward bulge propels them out of the vertical dimension and into the sagittal. The early walker, instead of waddling from side to side using the vertical ("door plane") now is propelled forward into the sagittal ("wheel plane"). This more advanced type of walking is often initiated by a bulging forward in the torso. Sports fans often bulge forward in their chairs, and there is bulging forward of consenting partners during a kiss.

Bulging forward suggests an eagerness for contact. One of the earliest clues of a distur-bance in relationships described by parents of children with autism is that the child did not indicate a desire to be held, often demonstrated by bulging forward movements (Schwarz and Johnson, 1987).

**Bulging backward** is commonly used by a child in snuggling back into a caregiver's lap or a comfortable chair. One can also see it in pets, such as a cat arching its back to receive affection.

### *Matching and Mismatching* (bulging forward and bulging backward unipolar shape flow with gradual and abrupt tension flow)

Bulging forward toward something or someone implies a desire for contact and matches with a gradual patient approach. When one bulges forward with graduality and bound flow, the associated feelings are more cautious.

To bulge forward toward someone abruptly is a mismatch and appears as an aggressive, threatening gesture. When a person uses this mismatch, he may feel very impatient about making contact.

Bulging back with abruptness in bound flow is a partial clash. Backward, abrupt, and bound flow are affined,[5] but clash with the element of bulging, which is an open shape. This movement may be observed when a nervous child bulges back to his caregiver's lap after deciding it is not safe to join the older children. In contrast to bulging back with abruptness, one may see bulging back with graduality and bound flow as when an elderly person bulges backward to sit down into a chair. The bound flow is a reflection of the caution of the rearward approach.

---

### Exercise

While having a conversation with someone, bulge forward with graduality and bound flow. You will probably create an impression of being interested in the conversation. Alternatively, try the clash bulging forward with abrupt bound flow. What response does this yield?

Try sitting down, beginning with bulging back to find a place to sit, and then bulge back further into the chair or pillow. Note the shift between the use of bound flow in caution and free flow in finding pleasure.

---

**Hollowing backward** is used by a running child attempting to pull back and stop. Two-year-olds often sit hollow-bellied. Hollowing back is also used to withdraw or shrink back from unpleasant stimuli. It is commonly seen in someone who has a stomach ache or who associates a forward bulge with unattractiveness. In North American culture bulging forward in the chest is preferred over bulging forward in the belly (particularly in the case of women). When sucking in one's belly, one hollows away from the perceived protuberance.

Hollowing back is a typical response to surprise or fear. It can occur in the torso, pelvis, or face. After making an embarrassing comment, a person will often hollow back in shame.

**Hollowing forward** is used to withdraw from unpleasant stimuli from behind. One might arch his back to hollow forward in order to withdraw from an slap on the back or to make room for someone passing by from behind.

### *Matching and Mismatching* (hollowing back and hollowing forward unipolar shape flow with abrupt and gradual tension flow)

Hollowing back with abrupt bound flow is a matching combination which is functionally adaptive. It abruptly removes one from a potentially dangerous stimulus. The Martha Graham dance exercise which consists of an abrupt contraction (hollowing back) followed by a gradual bulging forward is based on affinities. However, one may also employ the mismatched use of hollowing back with gradual free flow in a pleasurable, catlike stretch.

---

### Exercise

Run toward something and then stop suddenly. Do you use hollowing back abruptly to stop? Walk into a closet or dark room and imagine a dark figure suddenly emerging. Did you hollow back abruptly? One may hollow back gradually in response to a slowly approaching unpleasant stimulus.

---

Unipolar bulging and hollowing acquaint the child with the front and the back of the body which is intrinsic to mastering walking forward and backward.

It is sometimes difficult to distinguish hollowing forward from bulging forward or hollowing back from bulging back. The observer must determine what is the main focus of the movement. For example, if a child grows forward to reach a toy, the attractive stimulus is forward and thus the movement is probably bulging forward, even though in the process a compensatory hollowing in the back takes place. One should also consider whether the movement was initiated in the front or the back of the body. For example, when a person leans back into a chair is the movement initiated by a bulging of the lower back or by a contraction and hollowing in the stomach? One must observe how each movement is stimulated and initiated in each case if possible.

---

### Exercise

Lean back into a comfortable chair while keeping your back straight. Now try leaning back first with bulging and then with hollowing. Are there different feelings associated with each type of shape flow?

---

## Conclusion

Growing toward others in unipolar shape flow builds relationships and shrinking away creates separation from others (but greater contact with self). Unipolar shape flow is thus used for approaching love objects and withdrawing from dangerous or noxious objects. Because these approaches and withdrawals involve the extension and contraction of body boundaries (an integral part of the self) they reflect and express the emotional component of our relationship to people and material objects in the environment.

People who use a large number of unipolar shape flow actions are very expressive of feelings of attraction and repulsion. They are highly reactive to stimuli in the environment (or perhaps are overstimulated).[6] Being keenly responsive to outer stimuli, they are particularly influenced by people and things around them. They may be dependent on others for their self concept, feeling worthy only when approached and unworthy when others withdraw from them (Lewis, 1996). In contrast, people with a greater amount of bipolar shape flow actions tend to be more stable and centered in their self concept.

Unipolar shape flow evolves from bipolar shape flow and serves as a precursor to directional shaping (Chapter 8). Directional movements are important in defenses against people and objects in space. Unipolar shape flow provides the foundation for defensive movements in several ways: (a) it identifies the feeling of attraction or repulsion toward stimuli (aiding in the determination of which stimuli are dangerous and which are safe), (b) it helps define the location (to the side, above, below, in front, or behind) of the thing against which one needs to defend, and (c) it helps define body parts and thus identify what needs to be protected.

## Notes

1. Mahler notes the parallels between Kestenberg's work and her own. Her research shows how letting go of the familiar is often a precondition for approaching new stimuli. Again we see the rhythm of growing and shrinking, though in KMP it is conceptualized as approach and withdrawal. (Mahler, 1971 in Kestenberg, 1975).

2. Reaching out to pick up a cup without stretching for it is usually accomplished with a directional movement (discussed in Chapter 8).
3. Often the process of withdrawal begins with free flow which supports mobility, but ends in bound flow which defines boundaries.
4. Part of the problem here is paradigmatic. The profile is constructed to reflect developmental patterns and patterns of affinity and clashing and it does so successfully in most cases. However, unipolar creates a difficulty since it bridges bipolar shape flow which is concerned with symmetrical changes in bodily dimensions and directional movements which are by nature asymmetrical. This issue is further discussed in the section on interpreting unipolar shape flow diagrams.
5. We use the word "affined" here because we are talking about several different movement elements, some of which are matched and some of which are general affinities.
6. See Appendix "Interpreting KMP Diagrams" for further discussion of this issue. A high number of unipolar actions may indicate that a child is often in an over-stimulating environment or that the child simply has difficulty in blocking out background "noise." It is likely that a high number of unipolar actions would be found among children with attention deficit disorders.

**CHAPTER 7**

# Shape Flow Design

The adults are stretching out into their reach space. Photocredit: Michael Moore.

The study of **shape flow design** is the study of the qualities of movements which individuals use to traverse the space around themselves known as the kinesphere. Three aspects of movement are considered in this diagram: (1) the mover's use of her surrounding personal space, i.e., near, intermediate, or reach space; (2) the basic design of spatial pathways of centrifugal (away from the body) or centripetal (toward the body) movement, and (3) the specific design factors or elements of the movement, i.e., **looping/linear**, **high/low amplitude**, and **rounded/angular reversals** (see Diagram 7). The preferred patterns reflect individual and cultural styles of relating to others.

Tracing pathways toward and away from the body are, like growing and shrinking and free and bound, fundamental aspects of movement. These and other shape flow design movements can be seen in all individuals from birth through old age. Infants exhibit a predominance of

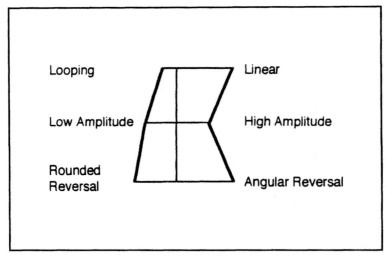

**Diagram 7.** Shape Flow Diagram

sharp reversals, linear movements, and use of near space (Kestenberg, 1967). Changes in centrifugal and centripetal patterns are common as infants fling their arms and legs outward and then draw them inward once more. Adolescents typically use more reach and intermediate space than do either infants or older adults. Further study of shape flow design is needed to develop more information on developmental and cultural norms.

Before beginning a description of the movement qualities which compose the shape flow design diagram, the reader must be cautioned. This category of movement has received the least amount of study. Collection of data on centripetal and centrifugal movement requires a three dimensional system of notation. Tracing these changes by hand two-dimensionally, offers a simplified and inadequate representation of a complex movement pattern. The inadequacy of this method of notation is revealed in a repeatedly low level of inter-observer reliability. As a result, profilers often describe information about shape flow design features in the body attitude, but do not attempt to construct a shape flow design frequency diagram. We include this shape flow design chapter because it is potentially valuable for future research. Due to the complexity of its notation and diagraming and the difficulty achieving reliability, we will not include a special section for diagraming or interpreting shape flow design in KMPs described in later chapters.

## Use of Space

There is a difference between the general use of the space around oneself and the use of space in interactions among people. In Edward T. Hall's study (1966) of proxemics he described cultures in which people prefer to interact with others who are in their own near space. He contrasted individuals in such cultures (e.g., Middle Easterners) with North Americans, whom he described as feeling uncomfortable when their near space is "invaded" by others.

In contrast to proxemics, which studies interpersonal space, shape flow design describes an individual mover's use of pathways through the space around oneself. Shape flow design can be notated based on observations of a person who moves alone. Even alone one can represent oneself as occupying a larger or smaller kinesphere. The process of notation resembles that of tension flow rhythm writing. Pathways of shape flow design movement are traced as they travel away from and toward the body traversing near, intermediate, and reach spaces. Within the various spaces (near, intermediate, and reach) specifie design factors (such as looping or linear) are drawn (see Figure 14).

**Near space** is defined as space which is close to the body. Gestures generally conducted in near space include hair twisting, thumb sucking, self touching, and hand wringing, all which occur without extension of the arms or legs. Such movements are often interpreted as indications of low self-confidence, restraint in social interactions, and personal reserve.

**Intermediate space** is that space which is reached with a moderate degree of extension of the extremities. It is between near and reach space. Many common gestures occupy this space. Everyday tasks, from typing on a computer to washing dishes, are conducted in intermediate space. In older age, people may restrict their movements to intermediate and near space, in response to joint restriction or physical limitations.

**Reach space** is the space used when one reaches out as far as one can. Strenuous physical tasks often require moving in reach space. Jumping jacks, window washing, ball throwing, karate kicks, and boxing punches require movers to stretch out into reach space. In fact, some people appear to transcend reach space and expand their kinesphere and body boundaries, seemingly filling a room with their energetic movements (Madden, 1993a). For example, an opera singer's use of reach space enlarges his movements, making it suitable to performance and reaching a large audience. Restricting a movement commonly done in reach space to intermediate or near space may signify that the mover's confidence or skill level has diminished. An over reliance on the use of gestures in reach space during everyday conversation may give the mover an exhibitionist or overly dramatic quality.

Of all the movement qualities studied in the KMP, shape flow design features are probably the most susceptible to cultural influence. One of the more readily apparent cross cultural variations is in the relative frequency or infrequency in the use of reach space. For example, Mitchell (1988) describes how his attempts to study a New York City Jewish community were hindered by his comparatively restrained "goyish" (non-Jewish) gesturing and use of space. His Jewish friends' advice to "interact in a more lively fashion and use more gestures," can be translated into "use more high amplitude centrifugal gestures which go out into reach space." Although cultural influences are important and interesting, within the study of one culture or subculture one can observe, notate, and evaluate individual differences.

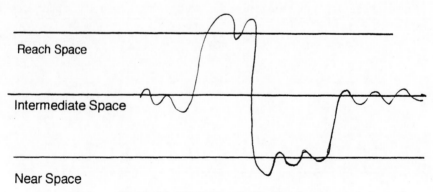

**Figure 14.** Shape Flow Design Notation.

## Centrifugal/Centripetal Pathways in Space

**Centripetal movements** are those directed toward one's own body. Hugging oneself, scratching oneself, and many self-touching gestures involve centripetal movement. Although a preliminary movement away from the body may occur, the primary impetus of the movement is towards oneself.

**Centrifugal movements** are those directed away from the body. Reaching out toward people or objects, stretching, or discarding something involves the use of centrifugal movements.

## Shape Flow Design Factors

Alan Lomax, Irmgard Bartieneff, and Forrestine Paulay (1967) studied the use of linear versus curvilinear dance movements cross-culturally. They found that movement patterns used in work were frequently replicated in folk dance patterns. For example, in cultures in which hoe agriculture was prevalent, such as in most of Africa and Native North America, dances typically used linear movements. Where scythes were used to reap crops (e.g., in the Middle East and Asia) loops and curves were more common in dances. One can also study the use of design qualities in styles of relating.

**Looping** movements follow circuitous pathways and may reflect agreeability and a likable style of relating in social interactions. **Linear** movements follow straight pathways and may reflect a remote style of interaction. They are commonly used for giving directions, discipline, and in self defense (see Chapter 8 for further discussion).

**High or low amplitudes** refer to the size of the excursion of the centripetal or centrifugal movement. High amplitudes are used in expansive gestures while low amplitudes are gestures which are restricted in size.

**Angular or rounded reversals** influence the way in which movements change direction. The change in direction may be sharp or angular or rounded and smooth. Angular reversals may create a jerky style of relating which appears curt or flippant. Rounded reversals harmonize and blend, inviting contact.

Kestenberg and Sossin (1979) suggest that linear, high amplitude, and angular movements convey a rude or forbidding attitude; looping, low amplitude, and rounded movements convey a friendly or permissive attitude.

Shape flow design is an area particularly in need of further study and it is hoped that people interested in cross-cultural differences and styles of relating will pursue this material. With the advent of more sophisticated computer technology which can capture three dimensional qualities of human movement this work will be more reliable and accessible.

# CHAPTER 8

# Shaping in Directions

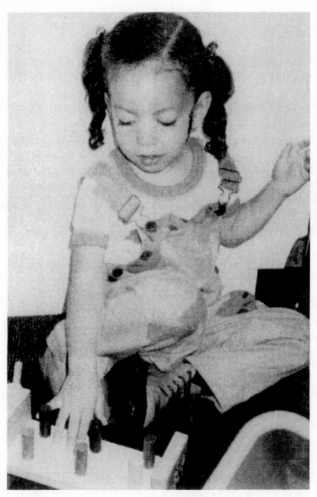

This girl is reaching down to the peg board using the Shaping in Directions of down and forward.

Using unipolar shape flow to shrink away from noxious stimuli and grow toward attractive stimuli offers an emotionally-laden mode of response to people and things in the environment. Unipolar shape flow also provides the foundation for a more mature pattern of movement, **shaping in directions**. While a very young child reaches toward something he wants in the distance, an older child can simply point towards the object. While a young child may shrink away from a bright light, an adult may cross an arm up over her eyes to shield them from the light.

Research in the field of psychology and nonverbal behavior supports the developmental progression described here (unipolar shape flow to shaping in directions). It is reported that reaching out (unipolar shape flow in KMP terms) is common in infants under six months of age and precedes pointing (shaping in directions) which was first seen at about fourteen months (Rime and Schiaratura, 1991; Zinober and Martlew, 1985; Masur, 1983). Reaching tends to decline in frequency after eleven months (Blake and Dolgoy, 1993).

This chapter describes the more mature movement patterns of shaping in directions (or directional movement). Directional movements appear to be very simple, such as pointing (with one's hand, foot, or head ) **sideways** or **across**, raising a hand **up** in the air or putting it **down**, taking a step **forward** or **backward**. However, observation and analysis have led to the discovery that such simple movements have varied and often complex meanings. The use of shaping in directions signifies the development of several new elements in interpersonal relationships and cognitive patterns. Directional movement provides the structure for localizing objects in space, defending against objects in the environment, labeling and defining, creating bridges for simple interpersonal relationships, developing abstract thought and language, and supporting learning processes. Each of these functions will be discussed briefly in this introduction to the chapter and then again with reference to each directional movement element. The chapter also considers the role of unipolar shape flow in providing the emotional component of directional movement and the matching and mismatching of pre-efforts with shaping in directions in learning and defenses.

Shaping in directions emerges when the child begins to project an arm or leg into space along linear or arc-like vectors. When a body part is aligned along a dimension, (horizontal, vertical, or sagittal) it traces a line in space, moving across, sideways, down, up, forward, and/or backward in relation to the torso of the body.

## Functions of Shaping in Directions

1. *Localizing Objects in Space*: Directional movements are used to locate people and things in space, as in finding mother by pointing to her: "There she is!" Children apparently first learn directions in relationship to their own bodies, as in "down below me" or "up above me."

2. *Defending Against Objects in the Environment*: Locating objects in space may also set the foundation for protecting oneself against them with closed shapes (across, down, and backward) or open shapes (sideways, up, and forward). Using unipolar shape flow a small child shrinks away from a noxious stimulus, but using directional movements, a person can offer several other defenses against a source of danger. She can raise an arm in a protective gesture to bar access to her body, she can knock away the noxious stimulus with a sideways movement (disarming the danger), she can step sideways eluding the danger, or can raise her hands in appeasement (showing that she is unarmed).

3. *Labeling and Defining*: When a person points to something straight ahead or gives directions ("It's over there"), a relationship between a person and a point in space is established (Goldman *et al.*, 1990). What is the nature of the relationship constructed by this linear projection? Drawing a line in space toward an object or person creates a focus on a specific point. A person is named, an object is labeled and defined: "That is Wayne." "This is a tree." The person or object is not comprehended in its three-dimensional entirety, but rather in a one-dimensional simplistic form. For example, at a party one may point to another person to give them a label or name. However, if one wants to offer a broader, more complex description of the person, one would not point but would use a three dimensional gesture to accompany one's speech instead.

4. *Creating Bridges to Interpersonal Relationships*: "To localize distant objects, we reach within the confines of our personal space and we point beyond our reach space into the general space, thus making it our own" (Kestenberg and Sossin, 1979, p. 155). In the process of locating and identifying people or things in space, directional movements trace a line from the self to the other, thus forming a connecting bridge between them. The bridge can be created by pointing, but also through a directional gaze or even by locating another person auditorally. Furthermore, for a child, seeing the parent or other caregiver or even hearing a familiar voice may at times substitute for the experience of touching, being held, or nursing. "Fixating an object by channeling one's attention and directing one's gaze towards it is often used in lieu of support" (Kestenberg, 1985, p. 54). Thus, when a child visually locates his mother in space, his gaze may replace a touch and can be used to soothe (Kestenberg, 1967). Locating someone in space with directional movements can come to replace reaching for them using unipolar shape flow.

This suggests that the use of directional movements is part of the process whereby visual contact and kinesthetic identification partially supplant tactile forms of communication. The visual image comes to be an abstraction which can represent the complex whole.

5. *Development of Abstract Thought and Language*: The use of shaping in directions represents a more abstract level of relating to others than does unipolar shape flow (reaching). McNeil (1987) describes pointing as the first gesture children use to represent an abstraction of an object.

Twenty years earlier Kestenberg pointed out that locating objects in space can serve as a precursor of verbal communication. Pointing to an object helps give it definition and paves the way for the labeling process of verbal language. "Aim-directed movements such as pointing precede language development, but continue to be the language of movement throughout life" (Kestenberg, 1967, p. 101). Later studies by psychologists and communication specialists supported and extended Kestenberg's thesis concerning the relationship of movement to cognition and speech. In a review of a number of studies Rime and Schiaratura (1991) concluded that "The data suggest that gestural behavior ... pave(s) the way for the later emergence of communicative abilities" (p. 252). Erllgring (1984) has found that gestures are not only developmental precursors to verbal communication, but also play an important role in facilitating speech and cognition throughout life.

How do gestures relate to and facilitate thought and speech? Many speakers who frequently gesticulate intuitively recognize that movement facilitates expression of thoughts. Kendon (1972), observing speakers, found that when a particular gesture could be definitely matched to a lexical item, the movement began before the lexical item.

These speech-associated gestures continued to be used with a similar frequency even when subjects could not see each other and thus the communicative value of the gestures was nil (Rime, 1983). This supports the conclusion that "speech-accompanying gestures" are involved in launching cognitive processes underlying speech (Rime and Schiaratura, 1991).[2] As Rime has written, gestures and bodily movement can be described as embodied thinking (Rime, 1983, p. 241). More specifically, Ekman and Friessen (1972) suggested that certain types of movements (ideographs) sketch the path or direction of thought. For example, as KMP observations reveal, there is a frequent association between a speaker's use of a backward gesture of the head (a directional movement) and the process of recalling the past.

Two studies also suggest that directional movements may be associated with only certain types of thought processes. In an experiment conducted by Goldman's study group (Goldman, 1990), speakers and listeners were asked to maintain continuous eye contact. The listeners were able to sustain eye contact (using a directional gaze) without any diffi-culty. The speakers, however, could not do so unless they were reciting by rote. In order to mentally access information for use in their speech, they apparently needed to be able to shift their gaze from place to place. A single directional gaze limited the speaker to a single train of thought (Goldman *et al.*, 1992). This result is supported by a study of Argyle and Cook (1976) which found that while listeners typically made eye contact 70% of the time, speakers did so only about 40% of the time.

Movement observation suggests that many of the speech-accompanying gestures are composed of shaping in directions and shaping in planes (discussed in Chapter 9). The examination of basic elements of movement in the KMP framework permits the discovery of more specific correlates between gestures and cognitive and speech processes.

6. *Learning Processes*: Based on observations, Kestenberg and associates concluded that particular learning styles and processes appear to be associated with particular directional movements. For example, making comparisons is associated with gestures which move sideways or across; evaluation is associated with up and down movements.

## Unipolar Shape Flow: The Emotional Component of Shaping in Directions

Notably absent from the above list of the many functions of shaping in directions is the expression of emotions. Like a toy soldier marching mechanically, most directional move-ments convey no feelings.[3] When a person looks upward or downward, this alone does not necessarily reflect feelings of elation or despair, although some non-KMP researchers have suggested otherwise (see discussion section below). However, it is clear that directional movements play an important role in defining emotions being expressed through the use of other movement qualities, especially unipolar shape flow and tension flow attributes.

Children often make shrinking or growing movements in combinations with directional gestures. The addition of a shape flow component gives emotional meaning to shaping in directions. For example, when an older child points to a toy using no shape flow, (no breath or torso involvement), this directional movement is dispassionate. It says, "There is the toy." When a one-year-old child reaches for a toy, bulging towards it, she is non-verbally expressing a felt need for that toy. The more the child bulges forward, the more her neediness or attraction to the toy is expressed.

The two movement qualities, bulging forward (unipolar shape flow) and pointing forward (shaping in directions) can be combined. A child can stretch forward as she points, communicating not only the object of her desire, but her feelings as well. The directional movement is a more developmentally mature response to external stimuli, but the shape flow element communicates emotional involvement.

Unipolar shape flow may initiate and give resilience to directional movements just as tension flow attributes give elasticity to pre-efforts. A significant difference is that every pre-effort is based on tension flow attributes, but directional movements may occur with or without an underlying unipolar shape flow change.

## Matching and Mismatching: Directions and Pre-efforts

Looking at the progression from early shape flow to more mature shaping in directions takes the analyst on a developmental journey. Looking vertically at the KMP (see Figure 1), we are able to follow the growing maturation of small children and to discover affined and clashing patterns.

However, as described in Chapters 5 and 6, KMP analysts also look at the KMP horizontally, comparing the patterns seen in System I and System II diagrams. In the case of shaping in directions, we look across to find matches and mismatches with pre-efforts. Pre-efforts, like directional movements, are used in both learning and in defenses. In the defensive mode, directional movements are used as defenses against external objects, while pre-efforts are oriented toward defending against one's own impulses. In practice, they are often used together. For example, when a person is fighting his way through a crowd, he may bring one arm across in front of himself for protection (directional movement across), but also his arm and his gaze may be channeling (pre-effort). He passes through the crowd without really seeing any faces. The channeling isolates him and his feelings from the crowd. When defending against an external object, one often must cope with one's inner feelings and impulses as well.

There is a more general match between directional movements which create open shapes, by moving sideways, up or forward and indulging pre-efforts. Likewise directional movements which create closed shapes match with fighting pre-efforts.

Shaping in directions provides a structure for the inner dynamics of pre-efforts. In the example above, a protective arm provides the structure for the process of isolating oneself not only from others but from one's feelings about others. The two movement categories, pre-efforts and directions, are linked together, just as are shape flow and tension flow attributes. For a list of the specific matching patterns see Table 10.

The pre-efforts and directional movements also combine to support various types of learning strategies. See Table 11.

The shaping in directions diagram consists of six directions or directional qualities (see Diagram 8). These directions are in relation to the body. Therefore, up is towards the head and down is towards the feet; likewise backward extends behind the body and forward extends sagittally from the front of the body. The diagram reflects the developmental continuity with unipolar shape flow. Closed shapes are on the right side of the diagram and open shapes are on the left. On the top line of the diagram are directions in the horizontal dimension; on the second line are directions in the vertical dimension, and on the third line are directions in the sagittal dimension.

Combining sideways, up, and forward (along a diagonal line) enlarges the limits of exposure. Combining across, down, and backward (in a diagonal line), closes off and bars access to the body (Kestenberg and Sossin, 1979).

**Table 10**   Matching Elements of Shaping in Directions and Pre-Efforts.

| Indulging Pre-Efforts and Extending Boundaries | Fighting Pre-Efforts and Restricting the Boundaries of Spatial Areas |
|---|---|
| Flexibility with moving sideways | Channeling with moving across the body |
| Gentleness with moving up | Vehemence/straining with moving down |
| Hesitation with moving forward | Suddenness with moving backward |

**Table 11**   Learning Table: Directions and Pre-Efforts.

| Pre-Efforts | Learning Patterns | Shaping in Directions |
|---|---|---|
| **Channeling** Isolating inner distractions | Learning to define issues preventing distractions | **Across** Preventing distractions |
| **Flexibility** Random associations, avoiding | Learning by association | **Sideways** Displacing, eluding |
| **Vehemence/Straining** Learning to conquer problems | Learning to attack problems through explanations | **Down** Learning to explain |
| **Gentleness** Learning without resistance or passion | Learning to seek explanations | **Up** Seeking guidance *spiritual?* |
| **Suddenness** Learning by sudden insight | Learning from the past | **Backward** Backtracking, remembering |
| **Hesitation** Pausing to consider | Learning to make step-by-step deductions | **Forward** Testing, moving sequentially |

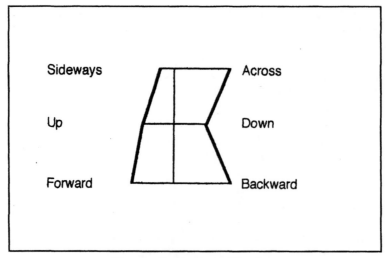

**Diagram 8.** Shaping in Directions

## The Six Elements of Shaping in Directions

### *Sideways*

**Sideways** is developmentally based on unipolar widening. It consists of a spoke-like (linear) or arc-like movement to the side in the horizontal dimension. Sideways includes linear movements of the arm from the shoulder straight out to the side (as when directing a motorist down the road) or from the side back to the chest (elbow out) in an arc-like movement (as when directing traffic to keep moving on). The eyes may move sideways, too, for example, when a child looks sideways toward its caregiver, locating him or her in space. A teacher may direct a student to go out of the room, tracing an outward arc with his hand. The movement locates or designates the direction in which the student should go. A sideways gesture used to locate someone in space is a precursor to exploration.

Sideways movements can serve several defensive functions. One moves sideways in order to side step or evade obstacles in one's path. In fencing, by staying in a sideways position the fencer offers only a small target and can more easily elude the opponent. A sideways arc-like movement (out from the chest) can defend by knocking a sword from an opponent's hand. An angry child in a high chair may sweep her hand outward knocking undesired food off to the side. One can stick an arm out sideways to create a barrier, impeding passersby.

Making a sideways movement with an arm or leg opens up access to one's body. This can mean an invitation to contact, as in the preparation for a formal hug[4] or can be a defensive gesture which shows that one is "unarmed." Opening up access to one's body expresses vulnerability which can disarm the aggression of an opponent. Looking sideways may combine locating something or someone in space and a defensive maneuver, such as cautiously checking for danger. Glancing to the right and to the left, one can check for ongoing traffic or look out for a predator. Frequent sideways movements may be indicative of a state of fearful anxiety and, if extreme, of paranoia.

The role of directional movements in learning and cognition can be seen most clearly in the movements associated with reading. In most writing systems of the world, the characters are arranged in horizontal rows requiring the use of sideways movements for reading and writing. On a very basic level, a disinclination to use sideways movements would contribute to reading problems. Preliminary observations of speakers indicates that sideways movements are associated with and support the cognitive process of making associations. A sideways look is also used to check up on someone else and thus is a precursor to the process of making comparisons. Combined with channeling, a sideways gesture is also used to separate concepts or objects. Sideways movements may also be used to divide and separate in a social context, as reflected in the sentence, "Take her aside and tell her privately."

---

### Exercise

Pretend that you are giving directions to a passing motorist. Point off to the side, locating the direction to be taken. Note that your arm moves in a linear fashion when you point to something.

Try the sideways arc, bringing your arm from your chest in an arc out to the side, and back as traffic police sometimes do when waving people on.

Try dividing or separating a group of objects into two piles. Do your hands first go forward and then make a sideways motion?

---

When sideways movements are used with unipolar widening, the movement takes on a more emotionally expressive quality. For example, using just the directional movement sideways one can cast a glance to check up on someone else. When the action includes unipolar widening, the gesture becomes an expression of real interest.

---

### Exercise

Try casting a glance with a sideways movement and then repeat, adding unipolar widening to the side with the glance. Can you feel the difference? You can also experience the affinity between widening and sideways when you use the two in combination.

---

### Specific Matches and Mismatches

Moving sideways gives structure to the pre-effort flexibility. They are affined movement qualities. In finding a pathway through a series of obstacles, one generally uses flexibility to avoid the obstacles, moving sideways in order to pass by with the least resistance. In disarming gestures, such as the sideways arc outward used in fencing, there is usually flexibility in the shoulder and/or wrist.

Combining flexibility and sideways movements in learning encourages patterns of associative thinking. One moves easily from one parallel idea to the next, creating the basis for comparison.

Channeling with a sideways movement is a mismatch between the aggressive quality of channeling and a directional movement which creates an open shape. Combined they can be used in barring access, creating boundaries, and in giving explicit orders.

---

### Exercise

Walk down a dark hallway, searching for the light switch. Reach out sideways as you step gingerly along. Note the use of flexibility as you fumble to find the light and elude obstacles.

Try moving both of your arms sideways outward with channeling like a policeman trying to hold back a crowd. Do you feel the clash between the vulnerable open shape and the definitiveness of channeling?

---

Use of a clashing pattern of movement as in the above example with the policeman can create an inner sense of conflict or may reflect conflicting styles of defending against one's urges and defending against outer threats. Channeling can serve to isolate oneself from inner distractions or to maintain focus. In contrast, a sideways movement involves opening oneself up to increased contact. Using both thus suggests a conflict or ambivalence.

### Across

**Across** is developmentally based on unipolar narrowing. It consists of movements which go across the body, passing the midline in the front or back of the body in the horizontal dimension. Across gestures include crossing the arms or legs, bringing an arm across the face, turning the head in order to look across (passing across the midline). All of these movements bar access to at least part of the body.

Across gestures are also used in many cultures to indicate refusal (Morris *et al.*, 1979). Long ago, Darwin suggested that shaking one's head to indicate "no" may derive from the gesture of the satiated infant turning away and refusing the breast (Darwin, 1872).[5]

An arc-like across gesture may be used to bring information or objects which are "out there" closer to oneself and thus more accessible and protected. The child may draw a toy back against his chest to protect it from rivals. (Note that this is a defensive gesture, not an embrace which would entail using a different quality of movement.)

One can use across movements to close oneself off from social contact and facilitate studying by barring outside distractions. If one draws an arm across one's body, this may serve to keep away unwanted sights or contacts with others, like the frightened child covering her face in a horror movie. Across/sideways is used in reading any horizontally written language.

---

### Exercise

While sitting at a desk, bring one arm across in front of you. Note that the movement must cross the midline of the body in the horizontal dimension. What effect does this move have? Then try a similar gesture but use an arc-like movement to bring an object, such as a pen, from a table across to your chest. This protects the object and bars access to other people. Add unipolar narrowing. What affect does this have? The words, "This is mine," may reflect the emotional quality of the movement.

---

### Matching and Mismatching

Across is matched with the pre-effort of channeling. One can use channeling to isolate one's distracting thoughts or feelings and across movements to shield oneself from outside distractions.

Using flexibility with across is a clash reflecting a conflict between closing oneself off from outside distractions and yet being open to distracting inner thoughts and ideas; one sets boundaries and at the same time the other subverts them. Perhaps some children who have an attention deficit disorder have a deficit in channeling off inner distractions while others have a deficit in barring outside distractions.

---

### Exercise

Try barring access to all the sights and sounds around you (arm across), but let your mind wander, facilitated by flexibility in the wrist. How well does this work to bar access to the body and prevent distractions or deviations?

---

Sideways and across movements are preferred movement patterns in the first year of life. They are used in locating objects and people in space and in maneuvers in the horizontal dimension such as feeding oneself (across), offering food to mother (sideways), and in gestures which refuse or seek food. Locating a person visually implies acceptance and looking away (across) implies rejection. Locating people and creating bridges to them is a precursor to establishing communication.

### *Up*

**Up** is developmentally based on unipolar lengthening up and shortening up. In the second year of life, the emphasis on standing up, reaching up, and looking up bring this pattern to the fore (along with downward movements).

Upward movements traverse the vertical dimension and include qualities associated with this dimension, such as presentation and confrontation. Standing up to show oneself is a form of presentation. If one intends to be confrontational or display a resolve to stand up for oneself, a simple upward directional movement would probably not be sufficient. One would need to also lengthen up (unipolar shape flow) to display an emotional involvement.

The directional movement up may be used as part of an appeasement gesture, for example, when one looks up to people in authority, trying to please them and/or fearing their power. However, the gesture is much stronger if accompanied by shortening downward which emphasizes that one feels smaller than and perhaps fears the other. Because they are smaller, children frequently look up to adults, admiring, pleasing, idealizing, or fearing them. The undefended open shape is "disarming" to others. Christian believers often direct the face, eyes, and hands in an upward gesture, appealing to God in a manner children use with their parents. Believers in Islam, Christianity, and Judaism at times bow down to God, offering deference and submission in a similar manner.

Upward movements generally have positive associations, and in fact, the word "up" is used in metaphoric phrases to connote rising up in the socio-economic scale or "climbing up the ladder of success." The rise to greatness is often represented architecturally, as in the throne of the king, which places him up higher than others, or in the long steps one has to climb up to reach an impressive government building.

The direction up is also involved in cognitive processes and learning. In learning, looking up is used in seeking guidance and asking questions. Looking up and down is a way of sizing someone up or taking their measure (seeing how big or worthy they are) and is a precursor of the process of evaluation.[6] In contrast, looking at a person sideways is a comparative process: checking to see if he is equal to oneself.

---

### Exercise

Try asking for something in a supplicating manner. Did you use an upward movement of the head? This appeasement gesture gives authority to the other person. Add lengthening up to the gesture to see how it changes the feeling tone.

Pretend you are taking an exam and are trying to think of the answer to a question. Did you raise your eyes or your head to seek the answer?

---

### *Specific Matches and Mismatches*

The directional movement upward is matched with the pre-effort of gentleness. Seeking to please, seeking explanations, and looking up to someone are all affined with a low key, gentle approach. The clash of an upward movement with the pre-effort of straining can be experienced by trying to lift a heavy object. The clash can be seen by observing the toddler or elderly person who struggles to stand up.

Moving upward with vehemence, also a clash, tends to be confrontational: raising one's hand to dispute an issue or at least to have a say, or "standing up to someone." Like many other threat gestures, rising with vehemence builds on clashing patterns and thus sends an impressive message.

---

### Exercise

Compare raising your hand with gentleness to raising it with vehemence. Try asking a question with an upward lilt in your voice and gentleness. How does the meaning change if a rising and vehement tone are used?

---

Moving upward is associated with achievement of a goal, whether it be a child who stands up for the first time and gains the vertical or an adult who climbs up the socio-economic hierarchy. If the affined pattern (lengthening up in unipolar shape flow) is added, the emotion of pride in the achievement can be expressed. For example, with an upward movement one may rise to receive a prize (humbly); with lengthening up one may look "puffed up with pride." Without the shape flow, the emotional component is minimized and the movement looks more mechanical.

---

### Exercise

Point upward without lengthening (extending) your torso. This is a directional movement. Now, as you point, extend your reach so that your body stretches upward. How does the stretching or extension influence the feeling?

You can also try standing up with or without lengthening your torso. When the body dimensions are extended, shape flow is involved.

---

### Down

**Down** is developmentally based on unipolar shortening down and lengthening down. Downward movements occur in the vertical dimension and may be used frequently in activities such as squatting, climbing down, reaching down, throwing down, and looking down, all common in the second year of life.

A downward movement, especially when combined with an across gesture and bound flow, can be used to put someone down, scold, criticize, or chastise. More positively, downward movements are associated with learning to explain and getting down to the heart of the matter. The combination of across and down helps in the process of defining.

---

### Exercise

Try various kinds of downward movements, including combinations with across and sideways. What movements do you use when setting limits with children? What gestures do you use when defining terms or rules?

---

In combination with shape flow, downward movements can play important expressive roles. A downward directional cast of the eyes is an integral part of the expression of emotions such as sadness, shyness, depression, shame, and embarrassment; these all involve breaking eye contact and barring access to the body. A downward-oriented facial expression used with bound flow and narrowing communicates a serious mood.

The shape flow enhances and helps define the expressive element. For example, bowing downward (without shrinking) is a formal gesture of deference. Bowing down with shortening down (shrinking) expresses a feeling of lowness or smallness relative to the other person. The combination of crouching down and looking up offers the message that one is inferior and small, yet seeking guidance from superiors. The combination of looking down and lengthening up (in the eyebrows) may express disdain, i.e., feeling superior and looking down at others.

---

**Exercise**

Try downward movements with and without changes in shape flow. For example, scolding a dog without shape flow may give an aura of objectivity, while use of shape flow reveals an emotional involvement.

---

### Specific Matches and Mismatches

Moving downward is matched with the pre-effort of vehemence or straining. If a person is vehement with a downward motion, the downward movement gives structure and definition to her passion. An individual may combine the two movements in the process of vigorously defining, clarifying, or demanding explanations. Often downward and across are paired with channeling and vehemence (or straining) in aggressive problem-solving and seeking to "get to the bottom" of the issue. The vertical dimension contributes to the confrontational aspect of "attacking problems."

Using downward with gentleness is a clash. A downward motion tends to close off access to one's body. This contrasts with the common use of gentleness in an attempt to be indulging or to "make nice." When someone attempts to "calm down" another person, there may be a subtle quality of condescension. One is trying to be nice and not hurt the other person who should really pull himself together. Likewise, although one is gentle, there may be a certain degree of keeping oneself closed off or distant. Calming someone down or even "putting one's foot down" gently, though comprised of clashing movements, can be very functional and effective responses. It may be adaptive in some circumstances to convey conflicting feelings, wishes, or thoughts.

---

**Exercise**

Compare attempting to express frustration using downward movements with vehemence: "No, that's enough now!" and the use of down with gentleness: "Please. Quiet down now." Typically one's voice becomes higher when using gentleness and screechy when using vehemence. Try using a high voice with vehemence and a screechy voice with gentleness.

---

In sum, up and down movements are prominent in the second year of life and are associated with making changes in the vertical dimension. They are used in sizing things up, which is a precursor to making evaluations.

## *Forward*

**Forward** is developmentally based on bulging or hollowing forward. Forward movements are seen in the walking or running movement of two-year-olds who are proficient walkers and in their pointing, staring, and/or reaching for objects in the sagittal dimension.

When a person steps forward or reaches forward, he initiates action and getting ahead, but also increases the exposure of his body to outside elements. This open shape can be a defense against aggressiveness of an opponent. An open (unarmed) hand moves forward in greeting. A similar openness is used in speech when one says, "I'll be open with you," which may mean, "I am exposing my thoughts to you, leaving myself vulnerable to a counterattack—don't take advantage." Open gestures may also be used in the process of defending oneself. For example, by bringing a hand forward and up one creates a boundary between oneself and others.

In learning, a person moves forward when progressing in a step-by-step manner. Each step forward involves the process of initiating and testing the procedure. Note that when following step-by-step procedures, one concentrates on moving forward from one step to the next (a linear perspective). This process is adaptive when one is learning a new task or new material. When used excessively the learner continually wants to know what is coming and is looking ahead rather than concentrating on the present problem. Forward movement acts as a precursor to the more complex process of anticipation which requires a broader perspective (non-linear), including consideration of goals and future consequences.

## Combining Directional Movements

When three directional movements are combined, a diagonal line is formed. For example, standing in the center of a room, if one points with one's right hand to the right upper corner of the room, one is combining the three directional movements up, sideways, and forward. This creates a diagonal movement which exposes the whole body. If one points to the ceiling straight ahead, one is only combining forward and up.

---

### Exercise

Ask a friend to walk toward you from across the room and then use a forward arm gesture to indicate when she should stop. Even open directional movement can be used to erect spatial boundaries. Explain to someone the step-by-step procedures necessary for accomplishing a task. Note the hand gestures which accompany the verbal instructions.

Try combining all three open directions, sideways, up, and forward, in a gesture with your arm. Now try all of the closed directions, across, down and backward.

---

### Directional Movement and Unipolar Shape Flow

Looking straight (forward) into someone's eyes can have a positive connotation of honesty, openness, or "being straight." It can also be deemed aggressive, particularly in cultures where little eye contact is preferred and looking down is seen as a sign of respect. Using a directional forward movement with bulging forward and bound flow creates a stare which is universally regarded as intrusive or threatening.

## *Specific Matches and Mismatches*

Moving forward is matched with the pre-effort of hesitation. When greeting someone in a disarming fashion one approaches openly and with hesitation, taking care not to startle. In contrast, combining a forward movement with suddenness is a clash which can threaten or frighten. When rushing forward to greet someone with enthusiasm, one generally moves one's arms out to the side to emphasize openness (and a desire to embrace) rather than attack.

In learning, moving forward combined with hesitation facilitates pausing to reconsider when one is unsure. Moving forward suddenly clashes with the process of step-by-step progress. It leads to jumping ahead without having necessarily mastered all the preceding material.

Rushing forward suddenly is a clashing defense often used to force oneself past fear and hesitation into action (i.e., counter-phobia).

---

### Exercise

Try approaching a friend by moving forward toward her with hesitation. Then try moving forward with suddenness. You can vary the effects by introducing free versus bound flow. An approach which uses forward, suddenness, and free flow can be overwhelming. Also try introducing other elements such as a sideways gesture with your arms.

---

### *Backward*

**Backward** is developmentally based on hollowing or bulging backward. One can step backward, point backward, move one's head or torso backward, or look backward. Moving backward is commonly used defensively as a protective gesture. One typically backs away from a source of danger or uncertainty. Stepping back helps close the body off and reduce its vulnerability. When all three closed shape directional movements (down, across, and backward) are combined, access to the whole body is barred.

In learning, using backward movements leads one to backtrack over material. Some students hate to go back over their work to check for mistakes and some teachers dread going over the same material repeatedly. There may be a certain monotony in retracing one's steps though it is often necessary. In going backward, one uses the past to provide secure footing. One also moves backward to check for mistakes and forward to correct them.

Looking back over the past or trying to recall something is often accompanied by a backward movement. People sometimes say, " ... yes, that takes me back," reaffirming an association between moving backward with the past and forward with the future. Recollections from the past can play a part in understanding the future, hence moving backward can be seen as a precursor of the process of anticipation.

---

### Exercise

Try to recollect some forgotten piece of information. What movement patterns did you use? The use of up and backward create the combination of seeking an explanation and deriving it from past memories. What movement do you use when you suddenly recall a piece of information or memory?

---

## Specific Matches and Mismatches

Backward is matched with suddenness. If one is withdrawing backward from danger, it is adaptive to do so suddenly rather than with hesitation. People often step back or move backward suddenly to indicate disbelief, shock, or dismay. This defensive response is probably related to the startle reflex. Webster's Dictionary defines "aback" as meaning dumbfounded, confused, or surprised (1976).

In learning, a flash of illumination from the past or a sudden recollection is often expressed by a sudden and backward movement of the upper torso and head, often accompanied by a gesture of the hand backward to the forehead.

The combination of a backward movement with hesitation is a clash. For example, withdrawing from danger hesitatingly indicates a conflict, perhaps between fear and curiosity. To recollect with hesitation may reflect a conflict between wanting to remember and being afraid to remember.

Backward and forward movements are related to the use of time, a focus of the third year of life. Forward and backward movements are precursors of the process of anticipation and initiation.

### Combining Directional Movements

When two or three closed shape directional movements are used in combination a diagonal line is produced. If one is standing in the center of a room and points with his right arm to the rear left bottom corner of the room, he is combining backward, across, and down. If one's right leg and head participate in the movement, this creates a very closed shape, protecting the most vulnerable parts of the body: the neck, chest, and groin.

---

### Exercise

Practice various combinations of directional movements. Imagine that you are standing inside a room. When you point to each of the eight corners on the ceiling and floor you are using eight different combinations of three directional movements.

---

### Review: Directional Movements and Unipolar Shape Flow

There is a basic connection between unipolar movements of attraction and repulsion and directional movements of defense. When one extends the body boundaries in order to approach an object, one opens and exposes one's body to outside contacts. When one shrinks away from a noxious stimulus, one contracts or closes off the body boundaries and protects the body. Directional movements are also involved in protection and exposure, but rather than changing the body boundaries, they protect or expose by creating linear barriers. This is a more mature form of defense. As described in the beginning of the chapter, a maturing child, rather than just shrinking away from a falling object, raises an arm to ward it off.

However, observations indicate that if one combines shape flow changes with directional movement, this gives a bodily investment to the movement, making it more expressive. Contrast pointing up with reaching or stretching upward. If one reaches upward it expresses feelings of attraction to an object or towards a mood, such as optimism (feeling "up" or "upbeat") because "things are looking up." Pointing to an object without using shape flow simply locates the object in space.

The degree to which directional movements in and of themselves can invest a gesture with emotional meaning is subject to further inquiry. Students of nonverbal behavior frequently describe downward movements as indicative of depression, shame, or despair. Meijer (1992) for example, suggests that one can infer surprise or amazement from a backward step when there is no non-emotional cause of the behavior. However, he also finds that no single movement quality is sufficient for the attribution of an emotion. He uses Laban effort terms such as "light", "direct" and "indirect" in combination with directional terminology, but he does not differentiate shape flow from directional movements or tension flow attributes from efforts. Does a "fast" backward step taken in surprise include hollowing back in his observations? Is it done with acceleration or abruptness? Does "strong pressure," which he associates with anger, reflect use of the effort of strength or the tension flow attribute of high intensity bound flow? In the KMP system we suggest that tension flow attributes and shape flow are more expressive of emotions than efforts and directional movements. Studies like that of Meijer and Waxer (1977) cited below suggest the benefit of closer collaboration of KMP followers with others engaged in nonverbal research.

## Discussion: Cultural Differences and Similarities

### A. Cross Cultural Differences in Cognition

Although the movement elements of the KMP system can be usefully applied to the study of any individuals with varied cultural backgrounds, the cross-cultural applicability of the interpretative framework has not been fully verified. There is some evidence to suggest that modifications of the standard interpretations may be necessary. For example, according to KMP theory, forward and backward movements which are focused in the sagittal dimension relate to time. The KMP formulation accords with the concept of time as something which moves forward to the future and backward into the past. We have observed that people attempting to recall information from the past often make a backward gesture. However the conception of the past as behind us and the future in front, though common, is not a cultural universal. People in some cultures understand the past as something which exists in front of a person (seen and known) while the future lies behind one (as yet unseen and unknown). Does this different conceptualization translate into different gesture-cognition correlations? Further study is required.

### B. Cultural Universals

In a study by Waxer (1977), raters successfully identified depression and anxiety in films of people from seven different cultures (unidentified). Anxiety was judged when observers saw a rigid torso, tremulous hand movements and sideways glances. This description might translate in KMP language into high intensity bound flow, abruptness, and sideways directional movements. Depression was consistently judged when observers saw a downward gaze, mouth down, and absence of hand movements. This might translate into directional down, shortening down in the mouth, and perhaps neutral flow in the hands.

The value of more precise observations and terminology for psychotherapists is clear. It is particularly important when working with people from diverse cultural backgrounds to understand sources of misunderstanding and misinterpretation.

## Notes

1. Kendon (1984) suggests that pointing (directional shaping) is derived from a ritualized form of reach (unipolar shape flow).
2. Kendon more recently found that if a transcript of a speech is plotted against the flow of speech-accompanying gestures, a close fit in phrasing of each is found (Kendon, 1984). However, Kendon generally believes that gestures offer an expressive element to speech. Others believe that gestures monitor speech and aid in the process of transforming meaning into words (Rime and Schiartura, 1991).
3. It is not accidental that soldiers are trained to march using clear directional motions: up, down, forward, back. They are made to appear like instruments of war, emotionless and inhuman. Their movements not only communicate this to onlookers, but to themselves as well.
4. A lateral extension of the arms in preparation for a hug creates a somewhat mechanical look. Adding bipolar widening and bulging forward would make the invitation more welcoming. One could also use "spreading," which is a movement pattern described in Chapter 9.
5. Darwin noticed that small children either turned their heads across or upward to refuse food. Both of these gestures, the upward head toss, and the head shake are commonly used by children and adults in numerous cultures to indicate refusal (Morris, 1979).
6. Various directional movements seem to be involved in the process of numerical evaluation. While Americans arrange numbers in vertical columns for the purpose of addition and subtraction, the Chinese abacus involves horizontal movements. However, in both cultures the horizontal (sideways) movement is used for counting with one's fingers and up and down and forward gestures are often used when counting out loud.

# CHAPTER 9

# Shaping in Planes

The girl on the right is "spreading" with her arms. What other patterns can you identify?

A hostess invites a guest in, not by pointing the way ("Go in there,") but rather with a spreading gesture that opens the way for the guest's entrance and promises hospitality. The hostess's arm sweeps through the horizontal plane, creating multi-dimensional spatial configurations. **Shaping in planes** creates the structure for complex relationships and meanings; shaping is about relationships, about how parts are interconnected (Madden, 1993b). Using a directional movement, one can point to another person; shaping in planes, one can enclose another in an embrace (Loman and Foley, 1996).

A directional movement is one-dimensional. In other words, with a directional movement one moves along a spoke-like (linear) or arc-like vector in one dimension in space. For example, if a person sitting at the head of a table pushes a plate forward and then brings it back, his hand moves forward and backward in the sagittal dimension of the table.

In contrast, the movement involved in shaping in planes traverses a plane. This means that the movement is at least two-dimensional. With shaping in planes one carves space in elliptical movements which traverse two or more dimensions or a plane (Kestenberg and Sossin, 1979). For example, if the person sitting at the head of the table begins wiping up a spilled drink, his hand moves not only forward and back, but also side to side in sweeping gestures. He is now shaping in the horizontal plane because his arm moves both along the width as well as the sagittal dimension of the table and thus includes at least two dimensions.

Every plane has two dimensions. The horizontal plane (sometimes called the "table" plane) is composed of the horizontal and sagittal dimensions (side to side and forward/backward). The vertical plane (sometimes called the "door" plane) consists of the two dimensions vertical and horizontal (up/down and side to side). Finally, the sagittal plane (or "wheel" plane) has the two dimensions sagittal and vertical (forward/backward and up/down). Thus a gesture which moves just up and down, e.g., painting the slats of a fence, is directional. A gesture which moves both up and down and side to side, e.g., polishing a brass door plate, is planal.

The meaning of a movement is affected both by the shape it traces and the plane it traverses.[1] Through observation and analysis of shaping movements, the KMP analyst gains understanding of the way the mover relates to others (object relations) as well as his styles of cognition. For example, movement patterns may reveal that a mover prefers one-to-one relationships or prefers multiple relationships. In the cognitive domain, a mover might tend to reach conclusions by looking ahead (advancing) or might favor reviewing the past (retreating) as a basis for making decisions.

This chapter discusses each of the six shaping elements and the three planes associated with them (see Diagram 9). After examining the meaning of movement elements of shaping in planes, the chapter covers the way shaping gives structure to and matches with effort elements.

Table 12 depicts the developmental progression from shaping in directions movement patterns to the more complex movement patterns of shaping in planes.

The only exception to the developmental sequence outlined below is that the two earliest shaping in planes qualities, enclosing and spreading, are actually seen in young babies before directional movements arise. However, the rest of the shaping elements tend to follow the developmental pattern suggested in the table. In general, shaping in planes is a more complex pattern of movement than directional movements both in movement terms and in the nature of the relationships and patterns of thinking which the movements support.

**Table 12**  Developmental Progression from Shaping in Directions to Shaping in Planes.

| Directions | Dimension | Shaping in Planes | Plane |
|---|---|---|---|
| Sideways | Horizontal | Spreading | Horizontal |
| Across | " | Enclosing | " |
| Up | Vertical | Ascending | Vertical |
| Down | " | Descending | " |
| Forward | Sagittal | Advancing | Sagittal |
| Backward | " | Retreating | " |

## The Diagram: Shaping in Planes

Diagram 9 displays the six shaping elements which will be discussed further below.

### *Enclosing*

**Enclosing** creates a closed shape and developmentally evolves from bipolar and unipolar narrowing and the directional movement across. With an enclosing gesture, one sweeps an arm across the horizontal plane to enclose space. The infant encloses the nursing mother in an embrace and may enclose a toy, bringing it close to herself, making it her own. In children, shaping gestures are often initiated by shape flow changes. For example, narrowing bipolarly in the chest and shoulders may initiate the enclosing gesture of an embrace. A young infant will also narrow unipolarly to initiate the enclosing gesture which facilitates turning over.

Enclosing facilitates taking in, bringing close together, gathering, and encompassing. Using enclosing, one relates to a select group or single person rather than a diverse number of people. Enclosing goes along with the feeling of possessiveness and exclusiveness, as in "This is my best friend." Enclosing compresses material into smaller spaces and thus facilitates unifying, consolidating, and reducing.

---

### Exercise

Try hugging yourself. Note that your arms do not make a simple arc, but rather an elliptical movement. They traverse the horizontal plane.

Try picking up an object from a table or desk in front of you. You probably used a linear directional movement going forward to the object and then backward toward yourself. If, however, you bring the object back with the attitude, "This is mine," you are more likely to use an enclosing gesture, evidencing a more complex relationship to the object. The emotional aspect of the movement is further enhanced by narrowing in shape flow.

---

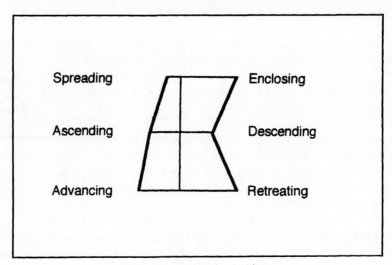

**Diagaram 9.** Shaping in Planes

People who prefer enclosing movements often enjoy the enclosed feeling of being in a valley or small, cozy nooks and crannies. They are likely to be more comfortable among a small circle of friends than being with large groups of people. If one has an overabundance of enclosing, one tends to become very possessive, to prefer exclusive relationships, and to have difficulty sharing.

### Specific Matches and Mismatches

Specific matching between effort and shaping develops only gradually and does not become a clear pattern until latency (Kestenberg, 1975). Matched efforts and shapes reflect harmony between ways of coping with space, weight, and time, and specific qualities of relationships. Enclosing is matched with direct. As described previously, using direct one can focus one's attention and engage in abstract thinking. Using enclosing structures the attention into a small, intimate space. For example, one encloses a friend with an arm and focuses attention on her or one encloses an object, bringing it close to oneself in order to pay direct attention to its specific qualities.

In combination, enclosing and direct support exploration and investigation within small spaces, consolidating, reducing, and abstracting issues, or in focused attention on a few close relationships.

If one encloses without paying attention to the person or object enclosed, the intimacy created will be superficial or devoid of meaning. A small child may bring a number of toys or friends close to him by enclosing them, but without direct attention, he will simply hold onto them as possessions. If one has the structure without the content or vice-versa, an imbalance exists.

Enclosing with indirect is a mismatch. The intimacy of enclosing clashes with free floating attention to a variety of things. One can imagine someone who gathers to herself an intimate group of people while simultaneously attending to others. This clash also typifies a small committee which tries to work together, but loses effectiveness because its members have too many different interests.

### Spreading

**Spreading** creates an open shape and is developmentally evolved from bipolar and unipolar widening and the directional movement sideways. A spreading gesture sweeps open like a hostess inviting in her friends. An infant may widen unipolarly in her shoulder and then spread with her arm in order to turn over from her stomach to her back. With an enclosing gesture an infant brings food to her mouth and with a spreading gesture she can offer the food to her parent. With a spreading gaze one can explore large spaces and scan the horizon.

Spreaders are the proverbial sowers of seed, giving, spreading, and distributing their ideas, feelings, and themselves to many people in many places.

People who have an abundance of spreading in their movement repertoire like to have a lot of space in which to scatter things. This arrangement may look messy to an "encloser" (who likes to keep things in condensed piles) but it may please a "spreader" to have access to a large array of information and possibilities.

A person who enjoys spreading movements tends to enjoy the broad vistas from a mountain top, wide open spaces, and relationships with an array of people. Spreading not only opens one's view, it also opens or exposes the person to her environment. Cognitively, spreading facilitates global perspectives, broad comparisons, and generalizations.

**Exercise**

Spread out an arm to invite someone in. Spread your gaze to explore a new place. Observe your desk. Do you prefer to spread material all over it or to keep papers in one place? Try spreading with different parts of the body such as the hand or hip.

Watch the kind of gestures used to accompany speech. Try saying, "All evergreens need spraying in the fall" using a spreading gesture. Then try it with an enclosing gesture. Does it work? How about saying, "This tree needs special attention." Did you use spreading or enclosing movements?

---

If one spreads to the near exclusion of enclosing, one gives and gives but does not take back to nourish oneself. One may "spread oneself too thin" like the proverbial "Jack of all trades, master of none." One becomes scattered, always reaching out to new people, places, and ideas.

A balance of spreading and enclosing creates relationships based on giving and taking, being able to accept and to refuse. It creates an explorer who spreads out to seek new ideas but then can consolidate the information or concepts. A good balance of spreading and enclosing supports experiencing diverse relationships while still maintaining special intimate ones.

### Specific Matches and Mismatches

Spreading is matched with the effort of indirect. When spreading with indirect or with floating attention one can attend to a variety of sights and sounds and can make generalizations about them. One creates group relationships attending to many people.

There is an imbalance if a person spreads often but rarely uses indirect. This suggests that the person spreads out to many different things or people but does not really pay attention to any of them. One can imagine an enthusiastic hostess spreading her arms out to greet many visitors, but not being able to remember anyone's names because she did not pay attention.

Spreading with direct attention is a clash. For example, a person might give a love object considerable direct attention, saying, "I am very interested in you." Nonetheless, the loved one feels unsupported, unembraced, and ultimately uncertain if the love is exclusive because the lover, instead of enclosing, is often spreading to include others. Although the attention may make the loved one feel very special in a crowd, the lovers are rarely alone together.

### Clashes Between Spreaders and Enclosers

While a person who emphasizes enclosing generally feels safe and comfortable with close intimate relationships, structured settings, tutoring, or teaching small groups, spreaders may feel trapped by exclusivity. They may prefer to include many people, many projects, and wide spaces in their lives. These differences affect styles of work, recreation, and relationships.

### Shaping in Planes and Shape Flow: Affinities and Clashes

Shaping in planes can occur without shape flow changes. For example, one may spread without widening. The spreading structures the exploration of large spaces, but does not contain a strong expressive component. If one spreads and uses the affined pattern of shape flow, widening, the widening supports and gives emotional meaning to the spreading. For example, if a hostess greets her guests with spreading only she will appear gracious, opening the way in for her guests. If she adds widening to the spreading, her greeting becomes a warm welcome.

Bipolar shape flow also adds the understructure and support for shaping in planes movements. For example, when spreading to prepare for a bear hug, bipolar widening in the torso provides stability for the action.

One may also use clashing patterns, for example, spreading with narrowing. This would suggest a restrained welcome, a conflicting message. Thus shape flow can support or conflict with the pattern of forming relationships suggested by shaping in planes (Loman and Foley, 1996).

*The Horizontal Plane*: Enclosing and spreading occur in the horizontal plane. The two dimensions used to create the horizontal plane's surface area are horizontal (primary dimension) and sagittal (secondary dimension). Movements in the "table" plane facilitate exploration of small and large spaces, and when used with spatial efforts, the give and take of communication.

During their first year, infants learn to move in all planes, but become adept in the horizontal. It fosters communication between infant and caregivers. We have seen that the horizontal is the feeding plane. Mirroring parents' movements, infants may begin to feed themselves and then to feed the caregiver. Spreading and enclosing form the basis for giving/taking and accepting/refusing within the horizontal plane. These early patterns form the basis of reciprocal types of communication.

Horizontal alignment in a group of people creates a circle formation. When people sit together in a circle aligned in the horizontal plane, they can easily discuss and explore issues and brainstorm new ideas. They can communicate in a reciprocal fashion, sharing a give and take of ideas. A teacher wanting to foster class discussion will arrange chairs in a circle. A parent and child can communicate more easily if they are sitting together sharing the horizontal plane rather than if one is standing and the other is sitting. When in a sitting position, a horizontal alignment usually involves a curved body shape creating a side-to-side and widened appearance (not necessarily symmetrical), such as sitting with arms and legs opening out in a rounded shape, arms on arm rests.

## Descending

**Descending** is a closed shape which is developmentally evolved from bipolar shortening, shortening down, and the directional movement down. Descending movements take place in the vertical plane. When the toddler throws a toy, the movement is most commonly done in the vertical plane, i.e., the object comes down on the side of the child, not in front of him. The throwing of the object may express the desire to create a confrontation with others. Descending movements challenge; with descending one can demand cooperation rather than ask for it. For example, a child demanding dessert may bang her fist downward in a sweeping gesture.

Descending is used for climbing down the face of a cliff or a ladder. Parents use descending to get to the level of their small children. Descending may be used toward subordinates in a way which may be condescending. When a dignitary nods her head to the crowds (dipping her head a little on one side and then the other), her descending gesture signals both her acknowledgment of them and her superiority. In contrast, bringing the head down (directionally) signals submission. This is because the use of the vertical plane (in the descending nod) is a presentational gesture, not a lowering of oneself.

Descending may express distress or despair, but is also used cognitively to get down to the heart of a matter, to get grounded. Searching for an answer to be found from within is frequently accompanied by a descending gesture of the head.

People with an abundance of descending movements may enjoy digging into the ground, gardening, being a "hands on" person, and delving deeply into things.

---

### Exercise

Stand against a wall or door with arms at shoulder height. Let your arms sweep in a descending movement. Note that they do not simply move downward (which would be a directional movement) but rather traverse the door plane in an elliptical shape. Standing away from the wall, but staying in the same plane, descend with one arm, using force. If you accompany the movement with the word, "No!" you will notice that your voice also tends to descend.

---

### *Specific Matches and Mismatches*

Descending is matched with the effort of strength. By slamming down one's fist with strength, one expresses serious or weighty (strong) intentions which are worthy of confrontation. Descending and strength are used in combination to offer explanations and definitions or to seek deep understanding. Descending gives the structure for making one's strong intentions or ideas clear. For example, if one has a lot of strength but little use of descending (an imbalance), the strength will not be given clear definition or focus. One may recognize that a person has serious intentions, but would not know what form they take. Strength with descending commands authority. Strength alone is simply strength.

Descending with lightness is a mismatch. This mismatch is used by ballet dancers taking their bows at the end of a performance, tactfully receiving appreciation. A tactful or light attitude towards one's intentions can conflict when being confrontational or demanding. Descending with lightness is often used in devaluing the seriousness of a demand or problem. Therefore, the combination can be useful in de-escalating a fight.

### *Ascending*

**Ascending** creates an open shape and is developmentally evolved from bipolar lengthening, unipolar lengthening up, and the directional movement up. When small children climb on jungle gym bars, ladders, stairs, and into adults' laps, they usually move in the vertical rather than the sagittal plane. Like salamanders, their arms and legs are spread out and ascend (and descend) in the vertical plane.

Ascending can be used for presenting, confronting, and inspiring. Upon finding a fascinating object such as a piece of lint or a feather, a small child will raise it (with an ascending gesture) to show it off or present it expectantly to an adult. This presentation confronts the adult with the child's aspirations to produce something great and worthwhile. Likewise, in ascending to a standing position, children attempt to meet the aspirations of their parents and prove themselves worthwhile. In reaching toward an adult with an ascending movement a child might say, "I want to be a fire fighter, just like you." With an ascending gesture or glance a child can express her admiration and idealization.

This boy is waving with his arms; note that each arm is using different patterns of Shaping in Planes.

People who use an abundance of ascending movements can "rise to any occasion" and inspire others with their own aspirations. They are often charismatic and help others confront their own aspirations as well. Pronounced aspiration facilitates ascending to higher goals, status, or levels of consciousness.

While those who prefer to descend tend to get deeply analytical about things and seek proof, ascenders are inspired and tend to take things more on faith. Descenders are more earthy, while ascenders may be more spiritual. The arm and head ascend to declare what we aspire to and descend to demand that it be done. Thus, with a balance, one may have high expectations (ascending) but can confront obstacles that arise when expectations are not met (descending).

## Exercise

Raise an object to display it to someone. You will probably do this in the vertical plane. Watch a lecturer. When does the person use ascending and when does the person use descending movements? Are most presentational movements in the vertical? Remember that an ascending gesture occurs in a door plane. It follows an ellipse having both an upward and sideways component.

---

## Specific Matches and Mismatches

Ascending is matched with the effort of lightness. One's aspirations are expressed best with buoyancy rather than with the weightiness of strength. A gay mood of joyfulness or good humor is often expressed with the combination of lightness of intention and aspiration to have a good time. Ascending without lightness is an imbalance. Without the buoyancy, ascending gestures are empty structures. Lightness without a structure of ascending is not clearly defined.

Ascending with strength is a clash; it expresses aspirations and hopes in a forceful manner. An example of this combination is the raised fist which ascends with strength, presenting a show of power and inspiring followers to battle. Descending with strength demonstrates authority; ascending with strength threatens to topple authority. The use of this clash suggests that there may be ambiguity behind such threatening gestures.

Clashes in the vertical plane offer an important introduction to the force of gravity. When toddlers combine ascending/strength or descending/lightness, they become acquainted with the weight of things. As they lift and lower objects they begin to assign values to them, which initiates the process of evaluation. Of course, children have begun to lift and lower themselves and objects using directional movements earlier, but these patterns give a very simple conceptualization of weight. With ascending and descending a more complex process of evaluation is possible.

---

### Exercise

Try lifting a heavy object straight up with a directional movement. Then try lifting it with a sweeping ascending gesture. Do you feel a more complex understanding of the weight of the object and its worth using ascending?

---

## Shaping and Shape Flow

The use of vertical shape flow introduces an expressive element to descending and ascending. The arm which is raised in an ascending gesture is invested with a strong emotion only if one also lengthens unipolarly upward as part of the action. As noted, bipolar vertical shape flow (lengthening and shortening) also introduces stability. When descending to pick up an object, bipolar shortening stabilizes the torso.

*The Vertical Plane*: Descending and ascending occur in the vertical plane. The vertical plane surface is created by combining the vertical dimension (primary dimension) with the horizontal dimension (secondary dimension). Movements in the "door" plane facilitate evaluation, presentation, and confrontation.

Standing in the vertical plane with one's head high and arms held on the hips or out to the side, the body replicates the shape of a door or wall. Standing or sitting aligned in the vertical creates a stable "I'm not going to budge" appearance typical of the "terrible twos." This alignment is used in "taking a firm stand," or "holding one's ground." It serves the purpose of confrontation.

A group which is vertically aligned stands (or sits) side by side, presenting themselves to others as in a panel. Communication among the group is not necessary nor readily possible; instead the group forms a unified structure, facing outsiders or adversaries, presenting themselves and/or confronting others. Football teams confront in a vertical alignment.

The vertical plane also serves the purpose of presentation. When information is presented in the vertical plane, it evokes interest and carries authority. If information is given in the horizontal plane, it has the quality of being offered for discussion. Thus a teacher can lecture more effectively standing up using the vertical plane and can carry on a seminar discussion more effectively sitting with a group in a circle. Members of a panel present (rather than discuss) when aligned in the vertical plane (Goldman, 1990).

As children learn to stand up, their bodies begin to take on a vertical alignment. They stand like little doors, widening to gain stability. As they get up and let themselves down, they become familiar with the principle dimension of the vertical plane.

In this phase, toddlers relate to adults as large people who may inspire them or threaten them, and to smaller children as people to threaten or to inspire. Children and parents may become sparring partners, contending with one another in the vertical plane (Kestenberg, 1967, p. 115).

### *Retreating*

**Retreating** creates a closed shape and is developmentally evolved from bipolar hollowing, unipolar hollowing back, and backward directional movement. An arm sweeping back, a bow, or a withdrawal are movements which typically traverse the sagittal plane in a retreat. A small child may retreat from an enclosing mother, terminating the contact. People may draw back from novel situations, new relationships, or seek refuge in the past, looking at the way things were as a model for how they should be. Retreating and enclosing, one can embrace the past nostalgically. People who understand through retreating tend to anticipate the future on the basis of what has happened in the past.

Through retreating from something or someone one terminates contact with it and may gain a new perspective, offering time for reflection. If she pulls back from a painting, she is able to see it with more depth of understanding. Likewise, she may withdraw from a relationship in order to understand it better. As it is often said, one "can't see the forest for the trees;" the big picture is lost if one is standing too close. In the process of drawing conclusions, one often must first withdraw intellectually in order to collect one's thoughts and construct a theme. One can move backward directionally or one can retreat; each movement is different and has different implications.

---

### Exercise

Take a step back, bending the knees and waist in a bow and letting your arm sweep back. If your movement had a sweeping quality, traversing the sagittal, then the movement was retreating. Try taking a linear step backward using a directional movement and note the difference. Does the latter feel more defensive?

---

A person who frequently retreats may withdraw socially from others or may withdraw into the past, dwelling on past achievements to the point where there is little progression to new accomplishments or pleasures. A person may draw so many lessons from the past that innovation becomes impossible.

## Retreating Versus the Directional Movement Backward

Directional movements are linear. In walking backward, one simply retraces one's steps. For example, in reviewing mathematics problems by going backward directionally one goes back over the same steps one took before. When one steps back from a painting it is only to focus more clearly on the outline of the figure drawn. Tourists taking photographs often step back to properly frame a scene.

Shaping in planes involves multidimensional movements. In retreating, a person sweeps backward, traversing the "wheel" plane. In retreating to review a problem one draws in all the ideas, reformulating and drawing conclusions. The review process offers the opportunity for a deeper understanding rather than a simple recapitulation of the material. A person who retreats from a painting does so seeking a deeper understanding and a change in the relationship between himself and the painting. The retreat facilitates a broader, deeper, and multi-dimensional perspective.

Through retreating one learns about the past by developing a relationship to it; through backward movements, one memorizes it.

## Specific Matches and Mismatches

Retreating is matched with the effort of acceleration. It is usually more adaptive to retreat from troubling relationships or dangerous situations with an accelerating rather than decelerating pace (remember that acceleration does not mean speed). A person who reminisces about the past will often sweep the listener into the earlier times with the increasing pace of an effective storyteller. A storyteller who decelerates loses her audience. Acceleration and retreating facilitate making decisions based on past experiences.

Retreating with deceleration does not facilitate escape; it expresses an ambivalence. There is a clash between wanting to leave and wanting to stay. However, retreating with deceleration is not necessarily dysfunctional. The clash or inner conflict may offer a socially appropriate message. For example, when saying goodbye to a friend, retreating with deceleration may appropriately express the regret about having to go. It is likely that someone recalling an unpleasant past will retreat with deceleration. "Oh yes, those were hard times" reflects a lack of desire to fully return to those times.

### *Advancing*

**Advancing** creates an open shape and is developmentally evolved from bipolar bulging, unipolar bulging forward, and the directional movement forward. Advancing movements are often used in throwing a ball, shaking hands, lifting a small child into the air, and moving ahead with enthusiasm. The child in the third year of life advances to meet new friends and new situations and to embark on adventures. In later childhood and in adulthood one attempts to advance by the merits of one's accomplishments. The gaze is to the future, plans are laid, and one is able to anticipate the consequences of actions taken.

People who advance frequently tend to be initiators, oriented toward starting things and proceeding with momentum. Advancers ambitiously establish agendas. They expect to be judged on the basis of what they have accomplished rather than who they are. In the extreme, the advancer becomes the overachiever.

Without a balance of retreating, the advancer makes decisions without looking back. Past experiences are not taken into consideration; only future contingencies are pondered. In social situations, those who advance more than they retreat may overwhelm others. They don't back off slightly to give the other person time to respond to the initiation. Instead they come right back with another advance, which may appear overeager or aggressive.

Advancing and retreating, however, are often in balance. In the wheel, advancing and retreating are inherently integrated. In throwing a ball, one's arm must first retreat to give momentum to the advance. In retreating one reviews the past and can then advance, applying past experience to the future.

---

### Exercise

Try advancing to meet a small child, sweeping her up into an embrace. Feel the full sweep of the sagittal plane. Go through the movements required to bowl or throw a ball.

Try discussing future plans and note what hand gestures you use. Watch others speaking.

---

### Advancing Versus the Directional Movement Forward

Moving forward, one moves ahead step by step. In advancing, one sweeps through the wheel plane in a multidimensional fashion which enhances the ability to anticipate and draw conclusions. In order to compare the two qualities, imagine an office manager who establishes routines well (using forward) but has no vision for the future (little advancing).

### *Shaping and Shape Flow*

Unipolar bulging and hollowing give an expressive component to advancing or retreating. Retreating with a backward sweep has a theatrical quality to it. Retreating with hollowing backward introduces the emotional quality of repulsion or fear. Bipolar bulging and hollowing give stability to shaping in the sagittal plane (advancing and retreating). In advancing with unipolar bulging one is in danger of tipping over. Bipolar bulging or hollowing centers the body even while it's in motion.

*The Sagittal Plane* is created by the sagittal (primary dimension) and vertical (secondary dimension) dimensions. Motor skills which are typically done in the sagittal plane include somersaulting, bicycling with the legs, tossing a ball, diving into a pool, and withdrawing backward. Alignment in the "wheel" plane facilitates anticipation and initiation of action or carrying out operations.

A person aligned in the sagittal plane looks poised to take off. Sitting, the body is narrow, one foot slightly in front of the other, one arm perhaps back and the other slightly forward, chest and head are oriented straight ahead. A group of people aligned in the sagittal form a "follow the leader" line, one behind the other. They are going somewhere, poised to accomplish something. They are doers.

Action-oriented people in the sagittal plane often find themselves in conflict with people who are debaters (vertical) or discussers (horizontal). While the doer is impatient with those who sit around discussing or debating issues, the debaters and discussers consider the doer rash and impetuous.

Children in the third year of life are often aligned in the sagittal plane. They run off from caregivers who may attempt to contain them. They advance toward and retreat from such systems of containment and security. They are adventurers, going off on expeditions and returning with tangible evidence of success. They enjoy pulling and pushing toys, making objects come to them or follow behind, all in the sagittal plane.

## Specific Matches and Mismatches

Advancing is matched with deceleration. It is adaptive to march forward and advance toward new ground with due deliberation. The clash, advancing with acceleration, implies little consideration of potential problems in new situations and new relationships. In most situations it is adaptive to retreat with acceleration to go over old material and advance with deceleration into new territory.

If one advances without much use of deceleration, this imbalance robs the movement of an inner dynamic sense of time. One may proceed without feeling time pass; one may make decisions and carry out operations with little variation in pace, doggedly moving onward (see Table 13).

Efforts and shaping in planes work together to support key functions as shown in Tables 14 and 15 below. An appropriate match of shaping and effort integrates the dynamic of efforts with the structure of relations created by shaping. If mismatches are used, it may lead to a conflict in communication (Lamb, 1961; Ramsden, 1973), relationships, or cognitive processing.

Table 15 displays types of cognitive processes which may be facilitated by the use of matched efforts and shaping elements. This material is a work in progress and is offered here to stimulate discussion and new ideas, not as a definitive conclusion.

**Table 13**  Matching Elements of Shaping in Planes and Efforts.

| Indulging Efforts with Open Shapes | Fighting Efforts with Closed Shapes |
| --- | --- |
| Indirect with spreading | Direct with enclosing |
| Light with ascending | Strength with descending |
| Deceleration with advancing | Acceleration with retreating |

**Table 14**  Behavior Patterns Formed by Shaping in Planes and Efforts.

| Efforts | Patterns | Shaping in Planes |
| --- | --- | --- |
| **Attention** (indirect/direct) | **Communication and Investigation** | **Exploration** (spreading/enclosing) |
| **Intention** (lightness/strength) | **Presentation and Evaluation** | **Confrontation** (ascending/descending |
| **Decision** (deceleration/acceleration | **Operation** | **Anticipation** (retreating/advancing) |

**Table 15**  Cognitive Process: Efforts and Shaping in Planes.

| Efforts | Process | Shaping in Planes |
|---------|---------|-------------------|
| *Direct*: abstract thinking | Consolidation and reduction | *Enclosing*: Exploring small areas |
| *Indirect*: multi-focused thinking, comparing | Generalizing, brain storming, comparing | *Spreading*: Exploring large areas |
| *Strength*: determination | Analytical, in depth thinking | *Descending*: seeking deep explanations |
| *Lightness*: skimming, glancing | Insightful | *Ascending*: seeking inspiration |
| *Acceleration*: rapid decisions | Drawing swift conclusions | *Retreating*: reviewing, anticipating on the basis of the past |
| *Deceleration*: deliberating | Drawing careful conclusions | *Advancing*: anticipating future consequences |

## Postures and Gestures in Shaping in Planes[2]

"**Postures** (a term coined by Lamb, 1961) do not pertain to static positions of the body, but rather to movement in which the whole body participates in one or more identical patterns" (Kestenberg and Sossin, 1979, p. 149). As described in Chapter 4, global postures are usually symmetrical and involve the whole body in the same movement pattern. For example, with a jump one can advance forward posturally. In integrated postures one part of the body supports the total involvement of the rest of the body.[3] Such postures are usually asymmetrical. In advancing to meet someone, one leg supports the advance of the rest of the body. This is deemed a postural movement because all body parts are either involved or supportive.

The involvement of the whole body in postural movements implies total psychological commitment to the action. In contrast, if even one part of the body does not participate, this indicates that the mover has some reservations.

Lamb originally focused on gesture–posture and posture–gesture mergers (gestures in one movement quality which merge into a postural movement or vice-versa) as an expression of authentic, healthy, conflict-free involvement (Lamb, 1965; Winter, 1992). In such integrated movement Goldman finds evidence of "... deeply held thoughts or feelings, even a statement of one's world view being expressed" (Goldman, 1994, p. 5). It may be that through frequent use of posture–gesture mergers speakers impress their audiences with their sincerity and are judged as effective.

The KMP system does not notate posture–gesture mergers, but focuses on the postures and gestures separately in order to reveal clashes or matches between the two. Kestenberg suggested that an initiating gesture is a trial movement which tests the waters, so to speak, before full commitment to the action. If there is a clash between the quality of the gesture and the quality of the postural movement, it indicates an inner conflict of the mover. For example, a person may begin an embrace with a gestural enclosing movement but instead of following through with a posture of enclosing, spreads posturally as he moves away. This gesture–posture clash may reflect a belief that it is not really proper to carry out the more enthusiastic, wholehearted embrace.

Kestenberg differentiates postures in efforts from postures in shaping. According to Kestenberg, postures in efforts express the full commitment of the mover to an action. This means that a person's conscience judges the desired action to be correct. Postures in shaping are seen as reflecting aspirations and ideals. Thus, for example, a postural use of strength suggests that it is both desirable and right to be forceful at that moment. Postural use of descending might be interpreted as reflecting an aspiration to be definitive and grounded. When postures in effort and its matching shape are used, a harmonious and convincing portrait emerges.

## Exercise

Advance forward to greet someone with heartfelt enthusiasm. Is your whole body involved in the process of advancing? Imagine advancing towards a lake during the summer time. Do you use a gesture to test out the water temperature or do you plunge in with postural advancing? Might you test out the water first with a gestural advance and then wholeheartedly dive in when you discover the temperature suits you?

### Discussion: Shaping in Planes and Complexity of Relationships

Shaping in planes carves space into multidimensional shapes (Kestenberg and Sossin, 1979). The multidimensional use of space facilitates the formation of complex relationships and complex cognitive patterns. If we use a two- or three-dimensional shaping movement to grasp a person's hand, give a hug, or pick up an object we have begun a complex relationship (Goldman, 1990). Madden (1993b) suggests that shaping creates context, meaning, structure, and organization.

One uses shaping in planes not only to represent the self-in-relationship but also to respond to and be moved by the other (Loman and Foley, 1996). Even someone in social isolation continues to exhibit personal styles of relational connectiveness through movement.

If an individual frequently combines shaping elements, e.g., ascending with advancing, this heightens the potential complexity and variability in modes of relating to others. The KMP uses the frequency of using combinations of shaping elements (the load factor) as a measure of social intelligence. This interpretation is in accord with the a growing recognition that varied types of intelligences exist and need to be recognized and developed (Goleman, 1995; Gardner, 1983).

It is likely that children who are raised in extended family and/or community-oriented settings develop complex ways of relating to others and the ability to enact varied roles. Holliday (1985) reported that the African-American school children she studied often exhibited a high social intelligence or social competence which stemmed from the highly social environment of their home lives. Hanna's (1984) description of "swing steps... bebopping... dancing" movements among low-income African-American children suggests a high usage of shaping in planes. She contrasts this with the greater use of "straight stiff arm" (or in KMP terms, directional movement) among middle-class white children she observed. These studies may lead us to hypothesize that children who have broad community relationships and/or intense and varied social experiences will exhibit complex and abundant shaping movements and will be likely to have a high social intelligence.

**Cognition and Shaping** In the KMP view, gestural shaping in planes also offers support for complex cognitive processes. It has been found that children who use sign language (presumably using many shaping gestures) create two-word sentences six to ten months earlier than children who communicate verbally (Stockoe, 1976). This suggests that complex gesturing stimulates complex cognitive formulations. Alternatively, Rime suggests that "the evolution of symbolic thinking...appears to elicit shifts...[that] lead to the progressive emergence of more complex...gestural speech-accompanying activities" (1991, p. 252). In either case, it is clear that gesture, speech, and cognition bear close and probably mutually reinforcing relationships.

We now conclude the discussion of the last diagram in the Kestenberg Movement Profile. However, before ending this chapter, we shall review the developmental progression of relationships from bipolar shape flow to shaping in planes.

### The Developmental Progression in System II: From Bipolar Shape Flow to Shaping in Planes

Growing and shrinking in bipolar shape flow, the infant learns about dimensions, volume, mass, and inside versus outside. The infant plays with his own body and that of his caregivers, and only then begins to experiment with other objects. Thus as the infant builds an image of his own body, he builds a more accurate image of things in his environment (Kestenberg, 1967).

Our body forms the basis for our understanding of shapes, spaces, and volume. The tongue explores the space of the mouth and discovers qualities of an enclosed shape. The hand reaches out to explore space around the body and the qualities of space in the kinesphere are learned. The child feels food in his mouth, air in his lungs, and feces in his abdomen; he experiences feelings of fullness and volume. When these substances are expelled (e.g., food is swallowed), the child senses the emptiness and loss of volume.

The transposition of shapes from the inside of the body to the outside is based on affinities between bipolar shape flow (feelings of internal fullness and emptiness) and shaping in planes (dealing with external space). Shrinking is affined with concave, closed forms of shaping such as enclosing, and growing is affined with convex, open forms such as spreading. Using such affinities the child experiences a harmonious joining of bodily feelings with spatial relationships which connect self to others.

Qualities of movement described in System II (right side of the KMP) portray the self and the self in relation to others. These movements provide the structure for the expression of self-feelings and relationships. The qualities of System I (left side of the KMP) provide the dynamics and breathe life into the structure provided by System II.

**Relational Stages of Development**   Loman and Foley (1996) have traced the development of relationships from early ones anchored in shape flow to more mature forms based on directional movement and shaping in planes.

In bipolar shape flow the infant grows and shrinks symmetrically, which has a stable and self-containing effect. Growing and shrinking in harmony with others encourages the development of a sense of trust. However, there is no way to reach out to another through bipolar changes, though growing can lead to contact and shrinking to separation.

Unipolar shape flow allows the individual to purposely shrink away from or grow toward another person. Growing toward implies feelings of comfort and trust, and shrinking away implies feelings of discomfort and distrust. Unipolar growing toward generally expresses desire for contact, but embracing is impossible using only unipolar shape flow movements.

The arc-like or spoke-like qualities of shaping in directions create a potential bridge for connecting personal space to general space. The relationship to others in the environment may be bridged by locating others in space or may be blocked by construction of barriers. However, directional movements tend to have a distancing effect because a line is created between people. It would be possible for movers using only directional movement to point to one another or to touch body parts (as in meeting elbows or fingers), but a true enclosing relationship cannot be formed. An open shape might invite contact, but the contact is simple rather than encompassing. One can imagine someone pointing to a loved one and even saying, "I love you. You are wonderful," expressing an abstract representation of the person, but doing nothing more. One can easily sense a defensiveness and a fear of real involvement when a person relates to another solely with directional movements.

With shaping in planes a more complex relationship can occur; an approach can turn into an embrace. The embrace creates a mutual relational space for intimate contact and the ability to explore multiple facets of the relationship. Similar results are reported by Aronoff, Woike, and Hyman (1987, p. 1050) who found that "... diagonal and angular body patterns convey threat, whereas round body patterns convey warmth".

### Development of Constant Relationships

When infants first relate to people and things they learn to recognize qualities experienced in near space where needs are satisfied. They identify the object by kinesthetic, visual, olfactory, and acoustic qualities familiar from the experience of close contact. Infants come to recognize people and objects by the sameness of their qualities and by the repetition of movements unique to each individual. An infant recognizes his primary caregiver because she belongs to his near space and retains those same qualities perceived in near space even when she is at a distance (Kestenberg, 1975).

An infant first relates to his primary caregiver as one who fulfills a need of the moment; she is milk, she is touch. He approaches her with unipolar growing to seek those comfort-giving qualities. But as these sensory experiences of her become integrated, as the sameness of her movement becomes learned, the child uses directional shaping to locate her in space and focus on her identity as a mother, grandmother, or other specific person. She becomes endowed with a singular identity, involving an abstraction from "she who satisfies basic needs" (hunger, thirst, protection). Shaping movements expand the nature of the relationship so that a parent or other caregiver is endowed with multi-dimensional facets (Kestenberg, 1967). With shaping, a caregiver can become a model of that to which a child aspires; she may become someone who defines and explains; one who shares in one's past and advances with one into the future.

These four movement patterns, bipolar, unipolar, directional movements, and shaping in planes are not mutually exclusive. In fact, the most emotionally connected embrace includes not only the enclosing element (shaping in the horizontal plane), but also growing toward the person (unipolar shape flow). Through the course of early development the child becomes more and more able to use a larger and larger range and variety of responses. The earliest patterns continue to play important adaptive functions later in childhood. It remains to be studied how this developmental sequence continues throughout the life span, perhaps becoming more limited in the later stages of adulthood.

### Overall Conclusions

The material in these nine chapters has been presented movement element by movement element in an attempt to familiarize the reader with some of the relationships between

movement, cognition, affect, and development as a whole. However it is extremely important to remember that there is no definitive one-to-one relationship between a movement
element and a psychological or cognitive pattern. Movement elements are combined in
many different configurations. These configurations exist within the larger context of
a movement repertoire which is expressed in multiple contexts of life. Looking at one
movement element is like looking at one piece of a jigsaw puzzle and attempting to
describe the whole picture. One piece gives information; it may even form the basis of an
hypothesis, but without the rest of the puzzle one should not draw definitive conclusions.

The Kestenberg Movement Profiler must attend to movement diagrams and then to the
profile as a whole. An interpretation should reference the setting or context. Referring back
to the raw data to look at phrasing and specific combinations is also helpful. In Chapter 14,
Mark Sossin will describe the way in which one approaches interpretation of the KMP as
a whole, using an adult as an illustrative case. In Chapter 15, Loman and Kestenberg-
Amighi offer an interpretation of a KMP of a child. In Chapter 16, Penny Lewis outlines
clinical interpretations of the various KMP movement qualities from her synthesis of theoretical perspectives.

There is so much information in a KMP that no analyst covers it all. Each develops a
focus based on the presenting problem, one's own personal theoretical perspectives, and/or
a research issue. Each of the three chapters on interpretation of KMPs offers the reader
a slightly different perspective.

The ability to interpret a KMP depends on understanding normative patterns and theoretical prescriptions (need for balance and for access to sufficient resources) as well as
understanding how each element fits into the whole.

Just as becoming an observer and notator requires training and time, so does the ability
to interpret profiles. Consider these chapters your introduction to understanding the meaning of movement as seen through the KMP framework.

## NOTES

1. A description of each plane can also be found in the overview section of the
   Introduction.
2. Gestures and postures in efforts were described in Chapter 4 of this text. Some of the
   general introductory material is repeated here as a review before the discussion of gestures and postures in shaping in planes.
3. Kestenberg adapted the term, "integrated postures" from Warren Lamb. However, present day Action Profilers and Movement Pattern Analysts do not necessarily use this
   term in the same way as Lamb did in the 1970's and Kestenberg does today.

# References

Abelin, E. (1975). Some further observations and comments on the earliest role of the father. *International Journal of Psycho-analysis, 56,* 293–302.

Ainsworth, M. (1967). *Infancy in Uganda.* Baltimore: John Hopkins University Press.

Ainsworth, M. (1969). Object relations, dependency and attachment. A theoretical review of the infant-mother relationship. *Child Development, 40,* 969–1027.

Ainsworth, M. (1973). The development of infant-mother attachment. In B. M. Caldwell and H. N. Riccuiti (Eds.), *Review of Child Development Research, Vol. 3.* Chicago: University of Chicago Press.

Allport, G. and Vernon, P. (1933). *Studies in expressive movement,* New York: The Macmillan Company.

Applegate, J. S. (1987). Beyond the dyad: Including the father in separation-individuation. *Child and Adolescent Social Work Journal, 4,* 92–105.

Applegate, J. S. (1990). Theory, culture and behavior: Object relations in context. *Child and Adolescent Social Work Journal, 7,* 85–100.

Argyle, M. and Cook, M. (1976). *Gaze and mutual gaze.* New York: Cambridge University Press.

Aronoff, J., Woike, B. and Hyman, L. (1992). Which are the stimuli in facial displays of anger and happiness? Configurational bases of emotion recognition. *Journal of Personality and Social psychology, 62*(6), 1050–1066.

Atley, S. H. (1991). *In search of a standard form of assessment: The Kestenberg Movement Profile as diagnostic tool and treatment guide integrated into the practice of dance therapy.* Unpublished master's thesis, Antioch New England Graduate School, Keene, NH.

Bainbridge Cohen, B. (1989). The alphabet of movement (Part I and II). *Contact Quarterly,* 20–38.

Bartenieff, I. (1962). Effort observation and effort assessment in rehabilitation. Lecture at the Dance Notation Bureau. National Notation Conference, New York.

Bartenieff, I. and Lewis, D. (1980). *Body movement: Coping with the environment.* Amsterdam: Gordon and Breach.

Bartenieff, I. and Davis, M. (1972). Effort-shape analysis of movement: The unity of expression and function. In *Body movement: Perspectives in research,* New York: Arno Press.

Bateson, G. and Mead, M. (1942). *Balinese character: A photographic essay.* A special publication of the New York Academy of Science. Vol. II. New York: Ballantine.

Beebe, B. and Stern, D. (1977). Engagement-disengagement and early object experiences. In M. Freedman and S. Grand (Eds.), *Communicative structures and psychic structures.* New York: Plenum Press.

Bem, D. and Bem, S. (1970). We're all nonconscious sexists. *Psychology Today, 4*(6).

Berlowe, J., Kestenberg, J. et al. (1995). *Training manual for the Kestenberg Movement Profile,* (rev. S. Loman). Keene, NH: Antioch New England Graduate School.

Binette, L. (1993). *A KMP analysis of moshing: The study of a communal ritual dance amongst adolescent males of the 1990s.* Unpublished master's thesis, Antioch New England Graduate School, Keene, NH.

Birdwhistell, R. (1970). *Kinesics and context: Essays on body motion communication.* Philadelphia: University of Pennsylvania Press.

Bowlby, J. (1977). The making and breaking of affectional bonds. *The British Journal of Psychiatry, 130,* 201–210.

Brazelton, T. (1977). Implications of infant development among the Mayan Indians of Mexico. In P. Eiderman, S. Tullin and A. Rosenfield (Eds.), *Culture and infancy* (pp. 151–188). New York: Academic Press.

Bridges, L. (1989). *Measuring the effect of dance/movement therapy on body image of institutionalized elderly using the KMP and projective drawings.* Unpublished master's thesis. Antioch New England Graduate School, Keene, NH.

Briggs, J. (1970). *Never in anger: Portrait of an eskimo family.* Cambridge, MA: Harvard University Press.

Bronfenbrenner, U. (1977). *Basic concepts. The ecology of human development.* Cambridge, MA: Harvard University Press.

Broude, G. (1988). Rethinking the couvade: Cross cultural evidence. *American Anthropologist, 90,* 902–911.

Burt, J. (1995). *Body, face, and voice: Nonverbal expressions of emotion in infancy.* Unpublished master's thesis. Allegheny University, Philadelphia, PA.

Caudill, W. and Weinstein, H. (1969). Maternal care and infant behavior in Japan and America. *Psychiatry, 32,* 12–43.

Chodorow, N. (1978). *The reproduction of mothering.* Berkeley, CA: University of California Press.

Condon, R. (1988). *Inuit youth: Growth and change in the Canadian arctic.* New Brunswick, NJ: Rutgers University Press.

Darwin, C. (1872/1895). *The expression of emotions in man and animals.* London: John Murray.

Davis, M. (1984). Nonverbal behavior and psychotherapy process research. In A. Wolfgang (Ed.), *Nonverbal behavior: Perspectives, applications, intercultural insights* (pp. 203–228). New York: C. J. Hogrefe, Inc.

Davis, M. (1985). Nonverbal behavior research and psychotherapy. In G. Streiker and R. H. Kiesner (Eds.), *From research to clinical practice,* New York: Plenum Press.

Davis, M. and Hadiks, D. (1990). Nonverbal behavior and client state changes during psychotherapy. *Journal of Clinical Psychology, 46,* 340–351.

Davis, M. and Hadiks, D. (1994). Nonverbal aspects of therapist attunement. *Journal of Clinical Psychology, 50,* 393–405.

Davis, S. (1993). Growing up in Morocco. In D. Bower and E. Early (Eds.), *Everyday life in the Muslim Middle East* (pp. 203–228). Bloomington, IN: Indiana University Press.

Davis, S. and Davis, D. (1993). Dilemmas of adolescence: Courtship, sex, and marriage in a Moroccan town. In D. Bower and E. Early (Eds.), *Everyday life in the Muslim Middle East* (pp. 84–90). Bloomington, IN: Indiana University Press.

Desjarlais, R. (1992). *Body and emotion*. Philadelphia: University of Pennsylvania Press.

Eckerman, C., Davis, O. and Didow, S. (1989). Toddlers' emerging ways of achieving social coordination with a peer. *Child Development, 60*, 440–453.

Eddy, M. (1992). Body mind dancing. In S. Loman and R. Brandt (Eds.), *The body-mind connection in human movement analysis* (pp. 203–227). Keene, NH: Antioch New England Graduate School.

Eible-Eibesfeldt, I. (1972). Similarities and differences between cultures in expressive movements. In R. A. Hinde (Ed.), *Nonverbal communication*. Cambridge: Cambridge University Press.

Eible-Eibesfeldt, I. (1975). *Ethology: The biology of behavior.* New York: Holt, Rinehart & Winston.

Ekman, P. (1977). Biological and cultural contributions to body and facial movement. In J. Blacking (Ed.), *The anthropology of the body*. London: Academic Press.

Ekman, P. (1984). Expression and the nature of emotion. In P. Ekman and K. Scherer (Eds.), *Approaches to emotion* (pp. 319–343). Hillsdale, NJ: Lawrence Erlbaum Associates.

Ekman, P. (1985). *Telling lies*. New York: Norton.

Ekman, P. (1989). The argument and evidence about universals in facial expression of emotion. In H. Wagner (Ed.), *Handbook of social psychophysiology*. London: John Wiley.

Ekman, T. and Friesen, W. (1972). Hand movements. *Journal of Communication, 22*, 353–374.

Ekman, P. and Friesen, W. (1975). *Unmasking the face*. Englewood Cliffs, NJ: Prentice-Hall.

Ekman, P. and Friesen, W. (1981). The repertoire of nonverbal behavior categories: Origins, usage and coding. In A. Kendon (Ed.), *Nonverbal communication, interaction and gesture* (pp. 67–105). The Hague: Mouton.

Ellgring, H. (1984). The study of nonverbal behavior and its applications: State of the art in Europe. In A. Wolfgang (Ed.), *Nonverbal behavior: Perspectives, applications and intercultural insights* (pp. 115–138). NewYork: C. J. Hogrefe, Inc.

Emde, R. (1981). Changing models of infancy and the nature of early development. *Journal of the American Psychoanalytic Association, 29*, 179–219.

Erikson, E. (1950/1963). *Childhood and society.* New York: Norton.

Erikson, E. (1959). *Identity and the life cycle*. New York: International Universities Press.

Erikson, E. (1975). *Life history and the historical moment*. New York: Norton.

Erikson, E. (1978). Reflections on Dr. Borg's life cycle. In E. Erikson (Ed.), *Adulthood*. (pp. 1–32). New York: Norton.

Erikson, E., Erikson, J. and Kivnick, H. (1986). *Vital involvement in old age*. New York: Nortorn.

Espenak, L. (1981). *Dance therapy: Theory and application*. Springfield, IL: Charles C. Thomas.

Faludi, S. (1991). *Backlash: The undeclared war against American women*, New York: Crown.

Freeman, D. and Fajardo, B. (1981). Maternal rhythmicity in three American cultures. In T. Field, A. Sostek, P. Vietze and P. Leiderman (Eds.), *Culture and early interaction* (pp. 133–148). Hillsdale, NJ: Lawrence Erlbaum Associates.

Freud, A. (1965). Normality and pathology in childhood: Assessments of development. In *The Writings of Anna Freud*, (*Vol. 6*). New York: International Universities Press.

Freud, S. (1933). Fragment of an analysis of a case of hysteria. In *Collected papers Vol. III*. London: Hogarth Press.

Fridlund, A. J. (1994). *Human facial expressions*. New York: Academic Press.

Fries, M. (1958). Some hypotheses on the role of the congenital activity type in personality and development. In *The Psychoanalytic Study of the Child, Vol. 8* (pp. 48–64). New York: International Universities Press.

Gardner, H. (1983). *Frames of mind: The theory of multiple intelligences*. New York: Basic Books.

Gedo, J. (1991). The biology of mind: A foreword. In F. M. Levin. (Ed.), *Mapping the mind*. Hillsdale, NJ: The Analytic Press.

Geertz, C. (1973). Person, time and conduct in Bali. In C. Geertz (Ed.), *The Interpretation of cultures*. (pp. 360–411). New York: Basic Books.

Gesell, A. (1940). *The first five years of life*. New York: Harper.

Gilmore, D. (1990). *Manhood in the making: Cultural concepts of masculinity*. New Haven, CT: Yale University Press.

Gilligan, C. (1979). A woman's place in a man's life cycle. *Harvard Educational Review, 40*(4), 431–446.

Goldman, E. (1990). Similarities and differences between the Kestenberg Movement Profile and the Action Profile. In P. Lewis and S. Loman (Eds.), *The Kestenberg Movement Profile: Its past, present applications and future directions*, (pp. 126–130). Keene, NH: Antioch New England Graduate School.

Goldman, E., Kestenberg, J. *et al.* (1992). *Study group report*. Unpublished manuscript.

Goleman, D. (1995). *Emotional intelligence*. New York: Bantam Books.

Greenspan, S. (1989). *Infancy and early childhood*, Madison CT: International Universities Press.

Hall, E. T. (1966). *The hidden dimension*. Garden City, NY: Doubleday.

Hall, E. T. (1977). *Beyond culture*. Garden City, NY: Anchor Books.

Hanna, J. (1984). Black/white differences, dance and dissonance. In A. Wolfgang (Ed.), *Nonverbal behavior: Perspectives, applications, and intercultural insights* (pp. 373–410). NY: C. J. Hogrefe Inc.

Hewlett, B. (1987). Intimate fathers: Patterns of paternal holding among Aka pygmies. In M. E. Lamb (Ed.), *The father's role: Cross cultural perspectives*, Hillsdale, NJ: Lawrence Erlbaum Associates.

Hewlett, B. (1992). Husband-wife reciprocitry and the father-infant relationship among Aka pygmies. In B. Hewlett (Ed.), *Father-child relations* (pp. 153–176). NY: Aldine De Gruyter.

Holliday, B. (1985). Developmental imperatives of social ecologies: Lessons learned from black children. In H. P. McAdoo and J. L. McAdoo (Eds.), *Black children: Social educational and parental environments* (pp. 53–70). Beverley Hills, CA: Sage.

Izard, C. (1977). *Human emotions*. New York: Plenum Press.

Izard, C. (1980). Cross cultural perspectives on emotion and emotion communication. In H. Triandis and W. Lonner (Eds.), *Handbook of Cross Cultural Psychology, Vol. 3*. Boston: Allyn and Bacon.

Izard, C. and Dougherty, I. (1982). Two complementary systems for measuring facial expressions in infants and children. In C. Izard (Ed.), *Measuring emotions in infants and children*. Cambridge: Cambridge University Press.

Jordan, J. V., Kalpan, A. G. Miller, J. B., Stiver, I. P. and Surrey, J. L. (Eds). (1991). *Women's growth in connection: Writings from the Stone center*. NY: Guilford Press.

Jordan, J. V., Surrey, J. L. and Kalpan, A. G. (1991). Women and empathy: Implications for psychological development and psychotherapy. In J. V. Jordan, A. G. Kalpan, J. B. Miller, I. P. Stiver and J. L. Surrey (Eds.), *Women's growth in connection: Writings from the Stone center* (pp. 27–50). NY: Guilford Press.

Kendon, A. (1972). Some relationships between body motion and speech. In A. W. Siegman and B. Pope (Eds.), *Studies in dyadic communication* (pp. 177–210). Elmsford, NY: Pergamon Press.

Kendon, A. (1984). Did gesture have the happiness to escape the curse at the confusion of Babel? In A. Wolfgang (Ed.), *Nonverbal behavior* (pp. 75–114). NY: C. J. Hogrefe, Inc.

Kestenberg, J. (1967). *The role of movement patterns in development, Vol. I.* NY: Dance Notation Bureau Press.

Kestenberg, J. S. (1975). *Children and parents: Psychoanalytic studies in development.* NY: Jason Aronson.

Kestenberg, J. S. (1976). Regression and reintegration in pregnancy. *Journal of the American Psychoanalytic Society, 24,* 213–250.

Kestenberg, J. S. (1978). Transsensus-outgoingness and Winnicott's intermediate zone. In S. A. Groinick and L. Barkin (Eds.), *Between reality and fantasy: Transitional objects and phenomena.* NY: Jason Aronson.

Kestenberg, J. S. (1985). The role of movement patterns in diagnosis and prevention. In D. A. Shaskan and W. L. Roller (Eds.), *Paul Schilder: Mind explorer* (pp. 97–160). NY: Human Sciences Press.

Kestenberg, J. S. (1992). The use of expressive arts in prevention: Facilitating the construction of objects. In S. Loman and R. Brandt (Eds.), *The body mind connection in human movement analysis.* Keene, NH: Antioch New England Graduate School.

Kestenberg, J. S. and Buelte, A. (1977). Prevention, infant therapy and the treatment of adults 1. Toward understanding mutuality, 2. Mutual holding and holding oneself up, *International Journal of Psychoanalytic Psychotherapy, 6,* 339–396.

Kestenberg, J. S. and Buelte, A. (1980). Prevention, infant therapy and the treatment of adults 3. Periods of vulnerability in transitions from stability to mobility and vice versa. In J. Call, E. Galenson and R. Tyson (Eds.), *Frontiers of infant psychiatry.* New York: Basic Books.

Kestenberg, J. S., Marcus, H., Robbins, E. Berlowe, J. and Buelte, A. (1975). Development of a young child as expressed through bodily movement: I. In *Children and parents: Psychoanalytic studies in development.* NY: Jason Aronson.

Kestenberg, J. S. and Kestenberg Amighi, J. (1991). *Kinder Zeigen, was sie bruchen: Wie eltem kindliche signale richtig deuten.* Salzburg, Austria: Veriag Anton Pustet.

Kestenberg, J. and Sossin, K. (1979). *The role of movement patterns in development.* NY: Dance Notation Bureau Press.

Kestenberg, J. and Sossin, K. (1994, April). Movement patterns in infant affect expression: Exploration of tension- and shape-flow features of the IFEEL pictures. Presented at the Fifth Kestenberg Movement Profile Conference, Antioch New England Graduate School, Keene, NH.

Kestenberg Amighi, J. (1990). The application of the KMP cross-culturally. In P. Lewis and S. Loman (Eds.), *The Kestenberg Movement Profile: Its past, present applications and future directions.* Keene, NH: Antioch New England Graduate School.

Kestenberg Amighi, J. and Loman, S. (in press) The Kestenberg Movement Profile. In N. Allison (Ed.), *The illustrated encyclopedia of body-mind.* NY: Rosen Publishing.

Kestenberg Amighi, J., Pinder, I. and Kestenberg, J. (1992). Nonverbal communication of affect in Bali: Movement in parenting and dance. In S. Loman and R. Brandt (Eds.),

*The body-mind connection in human movement analysis.* Keene, NH: Antioch New England Graduate School.

Koch, S. (1997). *The Kestenberg Movement Profile: A reliability study among student raters.* Unpublished master's thesis, Allegheny University of the Health Sciences, Philadelphia, PA.

Kohut, H. (1977). *The restoration of the self.* NY: International Universities Press.

Konner, M. (1977). Infancy among the Kalahari Desert San. In P. Leiderman, S. Tullein and A. Rosenfield (Eds.), *Culture and infancy* (pp. 287–328). NY: Academic Press.

Konner, M. (1991). *Childhood: A multicultural view.* Boston: Little, Brown and Co.

Laban, R. (1960). *The mastery of movement,* (2nd ed.). London: MacDonnald & Evans.

Laban, R. (1966). *The language of movement. A Guidebook to Choreutics.* Boston: Plays, Inc.

Laban, R. and Lawrence, F. C. (1974). *Effort.* London: MacDonald & Evans.

Lamb, M. E. (1981). *The role of the father in child development.* New York: John Wiley and Sons.

Lamb, W. (1961). *Movement assessment.* Unpublished manuscript.

Lamb, W. (1965). *Posture and gesture.* London: Gerald Duckworth.

Lamb, W. (1992). The essence of gender in movement. In S. Loman and R. Brandt (Eds.), *The body-mind connection in human movement analysis.* Keene, NH: Antioch New England Graduate School.

Lamb, W. (1994). Personal communication.

Lamb, W. and Turner, (1969). *Management behavior.* NY: International Universities Press.

Lamb, W. and Watson, E. (1987). *Body code: The meaning in movement,* (2nd ed.) London: Routledge and Kegan Paul.

Laughlin, C. (1993). *Brain, symbol and experience: Toward a neurophenomenology of human consciousness.* NY: Columbia University Press.

LeDoux, J. (1996). *The emotional brain.* NY: Simon & Schuster.

LeVine, R. (1977). Child rearing as a cultural adaptation. In P. Leiderman, S. Tullein and A. Rosenfield (Eds.), *Culture and infancy.* NY: Academic Press.

Levin, F. (1961) *Mapping the mind: The intersection of psychoanalysis and neuroscience.* Hillside, NJ: Analytic Press Inc.

Levinson, D. (1986). A conception of adult development. *American Psychologist, 41*(1).

Lewis, P. (1993). *Creative transformation: The healing power of the arts.* Willmette, Il: Chiron Publications.

Lizot, J. (1991). *Tales of the Yanomani* (trans. E. Simon). NY: Cambridge University Press.

Loman, S. (1990). Introduction to the Kestenberg Movement Profile. In P. Lewis and S. Loman (Eds.), *The Kestenberg Movement Profile: Its past, present applications and future directions* (pp. 52–64). Keene, NH: Antioch New England Graduate School.

Loman, S. (1992). Fetal movement notation: A method of attuning to the fetus. In S. Loman (Ed.), *The body-mind connection in human movement analysis.* Keene, NH: Antioch New England Graduate School.

Loman, S. (1994). Attuning to the fetus and young child: Approaches from dance/movement therapy. *ZERO TO THREE: Bulletin of the National Center for Clinical Infant Programs. 15*(1), 20–26.

Loman, S. (1997). Personal communication.

Loman, S. and Foley, L. (1996). Models for understanding the nonverbal process in relationships. *The Arts and Psychotherapy, 23*(4), 341–350.

Lomax, A., Bartenieff, I. and Paulay, F. (1967). Choreometrics. In A. Lomax (Ed.), *Folksong style and culture.* NY: American Association for the Advancement of Science.

Lotan, N. and Tziperman, E. (1996). KMP homepage. Http://www.weizmann.ac.il/ESER/ People/Eli/KMP/home.html.

Lowen, A. (1975). *Bioenergetics*, NY: Penguin Books.

Lutz, C. (1988). *Unnatural emotions: Every sentiments on a Micronesian Atoll and their challenge to Western theory*. Chicago: University of Chicago Press.

Madden, P. (1993a). *Kinesphere: Some thoughts on space*. Unpublished manuscript.

Madden, P. (1993b). *Shaping motion and movement*. Unpublished manuscript.

Mahler, M., Pine, F. and Bergman, A. (1975). *The psychological birth of the human infant: Symbiosis and individuation*. NY: Basic Books.

Masur, E. (1983). Gestural development, dual-directional signaling, and the transition to words. *Journal of Psycholinguistic Research, 12*(2), 93–109.

McCoubrey, C. (1984). *Effort observation in movement research: An interobserver reliability study*. Unpublished thesis. Allegheny University, Philadelphia, PA.

McCoubrey, C. (1987). Intersubjectivity versus objectivity: Implications for effort observations and training. *Movement Studies. A Journal of the Laban Bartenieff Institute for Movement Studies. Vol. 2: Observer Agreement* (pp. 3–6). NY: Laban/Bartenieff Institute for Movement Studies.

McNeill, D. (1985). So you think gestures are nonverbal! A reply to Feyereisen. *Psychological Review, 94*(4), 499–504.

Mehrabian, A. (1972). *Nonverbal communication*. Chicago: Aldine-Atherton.

Meijer, M. (1989). The contribution of general features of body movement to the attribution of emotions. *Journal of Nonverbal Behavior, 13*(4), 247–268.

Miller, J. B. (1991). The development of women's sense of self. In J. Jordan, A. G. Kaplan, J. B. Miller, L. P. Stiver and J. L. Surrey (Eds.), *Women's growth in connection: Writings from the Stone center* (pp. 11–26). NY: Guilford Press.

Mitchell, W. (1988). A Goy in the ghetto: Gentile-Jewish communication in fieldwork research. In J. Cole (Ed.), *Anthropology for the nineties* (pp. 59–72). NY: Free Press.

Morris, D., Collett, P., Marsh, P. and O'Shaughnessy, M. (1979). *Gestures*. NY: Stein and Day.

Muensterberger, W. (1968). Aspects of culture in psychoanalytic theory and practice. *Journal of the American Psychoanalytic Association, 16*, 651–670.

Murphy, Y. and Murphy, R. (1985). *Women of the forest*. NY: Columbia University Press.

Newman, B. and Newman P. (1991). *Development throughout life: A Psychosocial approach. pacific grove*, CA: Brooks/Cole Publishing Co.

North, M. (1971). *Body movement for children*. Boston: Plays, Inc.

North, M. (1972). *Personality assessment through movement*. London: MacDonald and Evans.

Parke, R. and Sawin, D. (1980). The family in early infancy: Social interactional and attitudinal analyses. In F. Pedersen (Ed.), *The father-infant relationship: Observational studies in a family context*. NY: Praeger.

Pruett, K. (1983). Infants of primary nurturing fathers. *The Psychoanalytic Study of the Child, 38*, 257–277.

Ramsden, P. (1973). *Top team planning*. New York: Halsted Wiley.

Ramsey, S. (1984). Double vision: Nonverbal behavior east and west. In A. Wolfgang (Ed.), *Nonverbal behavior* (pp. 139–153). NY: C. J. Hogrefe, Inc.

Reich, W. (1949). *Character analysis*, NY: Orgone Institute Press.

Ruttenberg, B., Kalish, B., Wenar, C. and Wolf, E. (1975). A description of the behavior rating instrument for autistic and other atypical children (BRIAAC). *Conference Proceedings of the American Dance Therapy Association, 9*, 139–142.

Rime, B. (1983). Nonverbal communication or nonverbal behavior: Towards a cognitive-motor theory of nonverbal behavior. In W. Doise and S. Moscovici (Eds.), *Current issues in European social psychology, Vol. 1.* Cambridge: Cambridge University Press.

Rime, B. and Schiaratura, L. (1991). Gesture and speech. In R. Feldman and B. Rime (Eds.), *Fundamentals of nonverbal behavior* (pp. 239–285). NY: Cambridge University Press.

Romer, G. and Sossin, K. M. (1989). Parent-infant holding patterns and their impact on infant perceptual and interactional experience. Paper presented at the Fourth International Congress on Pre- and Perinatal Psychology, University of Massachusetts, Amherst.

Scheflen, A., (1973). *Communicational structure: Analysis of a psychotherapy transaction.* Bloomington, IN: Indiana University Press.

Scheper-Hughes, N. (1985). Culture, scarcity, and maternal thinking, *Ethos, 13*(1).

Schilder, P. (1950). *Image and appearance of the human body.* NY: International Universities Press.

Schwartz, S. and Johnson, J. (1987). *Psychopathology of childhood.* NY: Pergamon Press.

Sossin, K. M. (1987). Reliability of the Kestenberg Movement Profile. In *Movement Studies. A Journal of the Laban Bartenieff Institute for Movement Studies. Vol. 2: Observer Agreement* (pp. 23–28). NY: Laban/Bartenieff Institute for Movement Studies.

Sossin, K. M. and Loman, S. (1992). Clinical applications of the Kestenberg Movement Profile. In S. Loman and R. Brandt (Eds.), *The body-mind connection in human movement analysis.* Keene, NH: Antioch New England Graduate School.

Spitz, R. (1965). *The first year of life: A psychoanalytic study of normal and deficient development of object relations.* NY: International Universities Press.

Stern, D. (1985). *The interpersonal world of the infant.* NY: Basic Books.

Stern, D. (1995). *The motherhood constellation.* NY: Basic Books.

Stiver, I. (1991). Beyond the Oedipus complex: Mothers and daughters. In J. Jordan, A. G. Kaplan, J. B. Miller, L. P. Stiver and J. L. Surrey (Eds.), *Women's growth in connection: Writings from the Stone center* (pp. 97–121). New York: Guilford Press.

Stockoe, W. (1980). Sign language and sign languages. *Annual Review of Anthropology, 9,* 365–390.

Surrey, J. (1991). The self-in relation: A theory of women's development. In J. Jordan, A. G. Kaplan, J. B. Miller, C. P. Stiver and J. L. Surrey (Eds.), *Women's growth in connection: Writings from the Stone center* (pp. 51–66). NY: Guilford Press.

Suzuki, E. (1978). *Japan and the Japanese: Words in culture,* (trans. Akira Miura). Tokyo: Kodsasha.

Tharp, R. G. (1994). Intergroup differences among Native Americans in socialization and child cognition: An ethnogenetic analysis. In P. Greenfield and R. Cocking (Eds.), *Cross/cultural roots of minority child development.* Hillsdale, NJ: Lawrence Erlbaum Associates.

Tomkins, S. S. (1962). *Affect, imagery, consciousness: The positive affects.* New York: Springer.

Tronick E. and Cohen, J. (1989). Infant-mother face-to-face interaction: Age and gender differences in coordination and the occurrence of miscoordination. *Child Development, 69,* 85–92.

Vaughn, B., Kipp, C. and Krakow, J. (1984). The emergence and consolidation of self-control from 18 to 30 months of age: Normative trends and individual differences. *Child Development, 55,* 990–1004.

Verney, T. (1981). *The secret life of the unborn child*. NY: Dell Publishing.

Waxer, P. (1984). Nonverbal aspects of psychotherapy: Discrete functions in the inter-cultural context. In A. Wolfgang (Ed.), *Nonverbal behavior* (pp. 229–252). NY: C. J. Hogrefe, Inc.

Webster's Third New International Dictionary (1976).

Whiting, B. B. (Ed.). (1963). *Six cultures: Studies of child rearing*, NY: John Wiley & Sons.

Wiken, U. (1991). *Managing turbulent hearts: A Balinese formula for living*, Chicago: University of Chicago Press.

Winnicott, (1965). *The maturational process and the facilitating environment*. Madison, CT: International Universities Press.

Winnicott, (1989). The mother-infant experience of mutuality. In *Psycho-analytic explorations*, Cambridge MA: Harvard University Press.

Winter, D. D. (1992). Body movement and cognitive style. In S. Loman and R. Brandt (Eds.), *The body-mind connection in human movement analysis* (pp. 153–202). Keene, NH: Antioch New England Graduate School.

Winter, D. D., Widell, C., Truitt, G., Shields, T. and George-Falvey, J. (1989). Empirical studies of posture-gesture mergers. *Journal of Nonverbal Behavior, 13*(4).

Zinober, B. and Martlew, M. (1985). Developmental changes in four types of gesture in relation to acts and vocalizations from 10 to 21 months. *British Journal of Developmental Psychology, 3*, 203–306.

# SECTION II

CHAPTER 10

# The KMP and Infant–Parent Psychotherapy

K. Mark Sossin

## Introduction

Designed and developed primarily within the context of making naturalistic observations of child and parent, the Kestenberg Movement Profile (KMP) offers special "windows" (Stern, 1985) or "ports of entry" (Stern, 1995) into the clinical infant–parent dyad. The KMP does so both as a methodologic instrument for classifying observations of nonverbal behavior and as a conceptual frame within which to address the nonverbal patterns of attunement, clashing, matching, and mismatching, along with patterns contributing to and reflective of reciprocity, mutuality, harmony, sensitivity, and attachment that have become elemental constructs for the infant–parent psychotherapist. The KMP offers a language of description that, in turn, promotes developmental appraisal and lends itself to the task of treatment planning by informing the therapist of the interactive repertoire of both parent and infant.

In this chapter, I will examine the KMP as a tool, and the Kestenberg formulations as establishing a foundation, for helping to appraise both primary and relationship disorders in infancy and early childhood (see Zero to Three, 1994), and for the development of therapeutic approaches in infant–parent psychotherapy (see Stern, 1995). Approaches derived from the KMP share their grounding in, and highlighting of, motor/nonverbal functioning. They are not singular in focus, but rather multifaceted; though aimed at change in the interactive behaviors in the infant–caregiver dyad, they also consider changes in the representational worlds of both infant and parent.

## Historical Roots of the KMP and Conceptualizations of the Dyad

Embodied in her development and application of primary prevention methods (exemplified for 30 years at the Center for Parents and Children), as well as in numerous writings dating even further, are observations and inferences reflecting Judith Kestenberg's anticipation of, and contribution toward, an appreciation of the infant as an active, thinking, knowing, feeling, and relating being. Employing an understanding of motor development, she also advanced the uncovering and refinement of assessment and intervention techniques for professionals to employ when early development and/or parent–infant relationships have gone awry. Conceptualizations of the infant that are currently the focus of much research and discussion in fields concerned with early childhood, e.g., pertaining to constitutional and maturational factors, regulatory processes, a range of available affects, mutual interactional patterns between infant and parent, and the nature of attunement in early development (some of which pose challenges to developmental psychoanalytic theory) were axiomatic in the fabric of Kestenberg's formulations. Kestenberg's framework for observing nonverbal behavior, reflected in the KMP, was both an outcome of her interest, and in turn, a perception-enhancing device that led to her proposed revisions of developmental phase theory, and to her insights regarding the infant–caregiver relationship.

Stern (1995) recently underscored the importance of the nonverbal content of clinical material with regard to both babies, for whom "…the nonverbal form carries most of the sense of events" (p. 200), and to adult individual or couples therapy, wherein characteristic interactive forms and patterns need to be delineated. Stern's comments parallel those of Kestenberg (1975) and colleagues; in fact, they reflect the motivations of the original Sands Point Movement Study Group in their attempts to find a language (both a research-facilitating coding system, and a professional jargon) to describe and differentiate movement patterns applicable across the life span. Primarily drawing upon analytic and therapeutic experiences, they were not trying to substitute the nonverbal for the verbal; rather, they sought to elevate the nonverbal to its status alongside verbal language, perceptions, and sensations for which useful descriptors and systems already existed. Moreover, the KMP systematizers moved away from the static and toward the movement process itself, and ventured to understand the relation between these processes and the individual's (including the infant's) representations.

In 1965, Kestenberg presented a lecture titled "Attunement and Clashing in Mother–Child Interaction." This lecture (published in Kestenberg, 1975) reflects her prescient dual appreciation of inborn maternal and infant characteristics interweaving with patterns of interaction and dynamic/representational features of the evolving relationship. She proffered a provisional set of classifications with which to describe the degree and nature of an observable skew in the mother–child relationship. These categories included: (1) complete attunement, (2) one-sided attunement, (3) functioning for the other, (4) partial attunement, (5) selective attunement, (6) generalized clashing, (7) partial clashing, and (8) selective clashing.

Collaborating with Arnhilt Buelte, who co-directed the Center for Parents and Children from its inception and contributed substantially to the strategic innovations of "retraining"/intervention techniques (Buelte, 1992), Kestenberg (Kestenberg and Buelte, 1977, 1983) wrote a series of three papers sharing the over-arching title "Prevention, Infant Therapy and the Treatment of Adults." In this series Kestenberg and Buelte followed selected developmental lines by extending the KMP-framework for discerning motor development to the understanding, in turn, of mutuality, holding patterns, and transitions from stability to mobility. In each, Kestenberg and Buelte carefully examined the analogs of qualitative motor expression, infant experience in the infant–caregiver context and processes identifiable in adult psychotherapeutic and psychoanalytic treatment. Kestenberg (1985b) continued the thesis forerun by the Kestenberg and Buelte papers in her delineation of the flow of empathy and trust in the infant–parent relationship, underscoring the distinctions between disturbances in empathy and breaches in trust, and through the description of a clinical case, she introduced methods anchored in an understanding of motor patterns aimed at re-attaining harmony in the relationship.

Kestenberg and colleagues continued to broaden the exploration of motor patterns to lend further insight into the psychological understanding of many developmentally relevant phenomena, such as the development of paternal attitudes (Kestenberg, Marcus, Sossin and Stevenson, 1982), pregnancy (Kestenberg, 1980), fetal experience (Kestenberg, 1987), early bonding (Kestenberg, 1990), holding (Romer and Sossin, 1990), narcissism and earliest experiences (Kestenberg and Borowitz, 1990), the impact of developmental disabilities on the evolving sense of self (Sossin, 1993), and aggression (Kestenberg, Sossin, Buelte, Schnee and Weinstein, 1993). Sossin and Loman (1992) outlined the clinical applications of the KMP, and this was furthered by Loman (1995) in her case study involving an application of the KMP to autism. This list is not at all exhaustive, but it is presented to illustrate the scope of applications of the movement profile. Despite the broad spectrum of these endeavors, the KMP work has largely remained unintegrated into other psychodynamically-informed and attachment-theory influenced models of infant–parent psychotherapy.[1]

## The Emergence of Infant–Parent Psychotherapy as a Modality

The value and efficacy of infant–parent psychotherapy, generally referring to joint intervention for parents and infants under 3 years of age, has become more widely appreciated since seminal papers began to emerge from Fraiberg's Infant Mental Health Program in the 70's (Fraiberg, Adelson and Shapiro, 1975; Fraiberg, Shapiro and Adelson, 1976). The variety of frames for the process has broadened across a spectrum of orientations, variously influenced by psychoanalytic theory, attachment theory, systems theory, and other branches of thought. A studied comparison of varied current approaches is offered by Stern (1995).

Deriving a great deal from her ingenious work with blind infants and their parents, Fraiberg (1977) was highly sensitive to the nonverbal transactional patterns she and her colleagues were observing, though these remained in descriptive narrative and not part of a classificatory scheme. Fraiberg *et al.* (1975) underscored the importance of keeping the parent's experience of his or her development, and memories of his or her primary relationships, within the frame of treatment. These "ghosts in the nursery" can lead to unfortunate repetitions of the past. Helping a parent consciously remember the problematic past can help a parent "identify with an injured child (the childhood self)" (p. 135), and then "the afflicted parents become the protectors of their children against the repetition of their own conflicted past" (p. 136). Bergman (1985) has considered the relationship between disturbances in early mothering and the mother's own developmental difficulties, especially in the mother's own early separation–individuation period. Research on "internal working models" of attachment relationships and reports of clinical work derived from attachment theory (Main, Kaplan and Cassidy, 1985; Bowlby, 1988; Zeanah, Benoit, Barton, Hirshberg, Regan and Lipsitt, 1994; Main and Solomon, 1990; Trad, 1993) have further extended our grasp of the nature of intergenerational transmission of early relational patterns and the manner in which they influence the thinking and feeling that correspond to the actual interaction patterns. The family systems model has also generated research work within developmental psychopathology confirming the nature of such intergenerational transmission, and also underscoring the relevance of ongoing factors such as marital satisfaction in influencing the child's security status (Cowan *et al.*, 1996). In the light of these considerations, it is notable that KMP notators have viewed the Body Attitude of an individual as likely reflecting some sustained quality that derives from early childhood. Hence, the body movement factors contributing to the Body Attitude bear influences upon the child, while simultaneously reflecting influences from the previous generation. It is presumed that there is some intergenerational transmission of movement qualities.

One framework for infant–parent psychotherapy, having evolved from the Fraiberg model, has been outlined by Lieberman and Pawl (1993). These authors offer perspectives upon many facets of such intricate treatment, which they characterize as frequently becoming a "bewildering endeavor" with magnified "dilemmas of focus and timing" (p. 436). Their considerations include: the mutative factor (i.e., the catalyst to change) in the quality of the therapist–parent relationship upon the infant–parent relationship; the complexities of countertransference, stress, and identifications within the treatment; the relevance of parental and infant diagnoses to clinical intervention planning; boundary issues; effectiveness; and, quite usefully, a review of common therapeutic mistakes. In doing so, Lieberman and Pawl described infant–parent therapists as finding "themselves daunted by the task of remaining constantly attuned to the unspoken signals of a baby in need, interpreting those signals, and incorporating this understanding into the work with the parents" (p. 437). It is especially in this regard that the KMP, amongst its many clinical applications (Sossin and Loman, 1992), offers the therapist a special means with which to identify the specific nature of the interactive-arenas of attunement and adjustment, or the lack of each, in the infant–parent relationship. Moreover, knowledge and use of the KMP assists the therapist in gleaning the signals of the baby, and from the position of the "potential space" (Winnicott, 1971) between parent and child, the therapist can identify the nonverbal tools the parent has with which to best meet the child's developmental needs.

## Mutuality and Reciprocity

Winnicott (1956) noted that during pregnancy and into infancy, a mother may usefully attain a state of "primary maternal preoccupation," a state Bergman (1985) describes as requiring an "ability to lose oneself in the other and emerge again" (p. 179). This serves as an underpinning to a stage in which the attainment of reciprocity is central. Many psychodynamic developmentalists agree, though their language may differ, that heightened reciprocity is significant for healthy passage through the first 5–6 months, followed by some degree of "letting go" by the mother (in the so-called differentiation subphase).[2]

From a descriptive standpoint, it is notable that in much literature the fact of reciprocity is discussed without detailing what it is that is being reciprocated. What behaviors are exchanged and sequenced? What factors are co-present in parent and infant? When can we really call them matching patterns? If synchronicity is attained, what are the specific qualities that maintain their connection? And could other patterns exist simultaneously that are not coordinated in this fashion?[3]

As is also reflected in the work of Greenspan (1992), this new perspective on infant–parent diagnostics and intervention has usefully drawn upon and integrated interdisciplinary knowledge bases; for example, it brings attention to "tactile sensitivities" and other sensory and organizational processing difficulties that have, over the years, been elaborated in pediatric occupational therapy (especially sensory-integrative therapy) and neuropsychology.[4] Hence, the neurologic language of "hypertonia," "hypotonia," "postural fixation," and the like has usefully entered the descriptive arena of mental health clinicians focused on early childhood. However, the literature most often still lacks a language anchored in the study of movement processes themselves for the highlighted patterns and qualities of the complex patterns and nonverbal behaviors themselves, and the KMP is very useful in this regard. For instance:

Anne, 6 months old, is sitting in her high chair awaiting feeding. Anne is a quiet and seemingly patient young girl who rarely fusses. Maria, Anne's mother, on the other hand, tends to be a hurried person, most often occupied with getting done what is in front of her so as to get to what is next. On this particular day, typically rushed Maria swiftly and tensely swoops the spoon toward Anne. Anne maintains her gaze upon mother and seems calmer than mother, but clearly she did not have the time to co-participate by reaching her mouth toward the spoon; such co-participation did not seem to be anticipated by either mother or daughter.

Such an example might simply be used to highlight a lack of reciprocity or attunement between mother and daughter. But, in KMP terms, based on observation and notation, we could note that there was a mismatch in timing, with Maria abrupt (and sudden or accelerated) and Anne gradual (and hesitating). Their tension levels were distinct, with Maria bound and Anne free or sometimes neutral. However, the KMP data indicate that both Maria and Anne were even in their flow and channeling and/or direct in their attention; i.e., there were indeed clashes in weight and time, but there was relative attunement and harmony in evenness and space.

Many such variations might be imagined. A mother and child could be attuned in intensity-level and timing, but not in degree of flow-adjustment or space, or a different child and mother (or Anne and Maria at a different time) might attune in one or more patterns while clashing in others. This is not limited to System I patterns (tension flow-effort) but also applies to System II patterns (shape flow-shaping), as well as to their intra-individual manners of matching or mismatching. If Maria moved forward and advanced quite often while they both enclosed and neither spread, then they would not match in the sagittal plane, however they would match in the horizontal plane (where enclosing and spreading take place). One can see that a more specific language stems from the KMP to describe behavioral arenas in which reciprocity or matching does or does not exist. In innumerable cases there is some attunement and some clashing, and some matching and some mismatching simultaneously occurring.

Diagnostically, dyadic parent–infant couples can usefully be subcategorized in terms of the manner in which they characteristically harmonize and in terms of the manner in which they tend to operate in disharmony. These "manners" are labeled in the KMP, and further grouped into developmentally meaningful clusters, represented as distinct KMP diagrams. We can then not only speak in general terms about a relative degree of mutuality, but we can more directly speak about the qualities of interaction that are mutual or reciprocated and the qualities that are not. Within a cluster, a parent and infant may show similarities of tension level, but differences in the way in which tension changes; or they may, for instance, share the way in which their shape flow alters in the vertical dimension, but not in the sagittal or horizontal dimensions.[5]

Many combinations of movement patterns are possible, and each lends itself to hypothesis generating interpretations. For example, a parent and infant sharing tension flow patterns may seem to have found the quintessence of empathy (Kestenberg, 1985a), while the same couple may differ in shape flow patterns (for example, the mother hollowing as the child bulges), such that they do not seem to have the building blocks of trust in place. Parent and infant partners may seem to share certain manners of defending but not certain manners of relating, and so forth.

Therapeutically, we can use the arenas of harmony as our clinical "ports of entry" (e.g., highlighting the attention-structure that Maria and Anne shared in their evenness of tension and spatial pre-efforts and efforts); through the focus on shared patterns, we can begin to seek repair in arenas of excessive clashing or mismatching. Consider the following example:

Bobby and his mom, Patricia, are struggling in their distress–comfort routines, which is affecting sleep patterns and leaving Patricia with a very diminished feeling about her capacity to soothe her son. Observation finds her to be very attentive and aware of Bobby's state, and they do fine when matched in indulging, low-intensity, gradual exchanges. When Bobby's pace quickens, so does Patricia's, when Bobby's intensity increases, Patricia's intensity increases too, but without concomitant adult patterns of strength. Bobby's flow adjustments, along with widening, are met by Patricia's highly bound-even flow and restrictive narrowing. His periodic growing includes bulging forward, but Patricia repeatedly shows bipolar hollowing and narrowing, feeling shrunken and helpless as she does.

We can see that there are both indulging and fighting (aggressive) patterns in which this mother and child can harmonize. In entering this scene clinically, we might point out to Patricia that she and Bobby seem to attune quite well when low-intensity, gradual tension flow qualities are primarily used. If this is a self-reflectively framed treatment, Patricia may recognize the developmental and relational importance of these patterns (e.g., she may associate the demonstrated patterns with meaningful and recognizable affects or attitudes, or she may even recognize these patterns as having been highly significant in her own early experience with caregivers) and such insight might greatly facilitate change. Memories of interactional rhythms and movement patterns often contribute substantially to therapeutic gains by paving a path for parental insight, and by facilitating parental empathy and adjustment. After all, the so called "ghosts in the nursery" exist in kinesthetic and movement modalities, too. But even in a more pragmatically-oriented treatment, identifying and demonstrating shared patterns can heighten feelings of competence and identification-with-the-baby on the part of the mother, setting the stage for addressing the way in which attunement breaks down. In this case, it appeared that Patricia was accurate in her identification of and (eager to respond to) some of Bobby's affective states and expressions (low-key states of satisfaction). She would enter into more intense states as well, but in a manner of contagion, rather than strength, she would exacerbate affects pertaining to fright or danger. Moreover, Patricia had difficulty supporting Bobby's growing into the world. Her shrinking, narrowing pattern in response to Bobby's growing, widening pattern fit with verbalizations reflecting her worries that Bobby wanted and felt "entitled" to too much. Pointing out their clash in movement and related feelings of comfort and discomfort led Patricia to describe her fantasized image of Bobby depleting her with his needs. The more she perceived him as laying claim upon her and the environmental provisions that she mediated, the more empty and deficient she felt. As these meanings became clear, the therapist suggested ways in which Patricia could exercise new patterns, e.g., in growing and widening with Bobby, in breathing together, in smiling in response to each other, and in a hand game they invented in a parent–infant therapy session. Patricia gained confidence in herself, and in her son and his own expression of confidence in the widening. At the same time, Patricia was encouraged to follow and join Bobby in flow adjustment and the manner of indirect attention that it fostered. Whereas Patricia had previously felt that she was "losing" Bobby in his flow adjustment, she came to find pleasure in his playful variations of flow level and her own anxiety and discomfort, previously expressed in her rigid, even, and narrow patterns. Patricia could now enjoy and better understand Bobby's manner, and their trust became enhanced.

In cases such as this, where a focus on movement patterns frames intervention in parent–infant psychotherapy, there is an interesting bi-directionality of influences. Psychological insight fosters a certain freedom with which to experience and explore alternative movement patterns, and experimenting with different movement patterns can both lead to psychological insight and to new and sustainable relational- and self-representations.

## Disorders of Attachment

As outlined by authors such as Zeanah, Mammen and Lieberman (1993) and Sroufe (1988), the ethological attachment theory introduced and developed over years by Bowlby (1988) has expanded upon the ways in which the infant's attachment behaviors promote proximity to and affinity with the caregiver, and the ways in which the caregiver promotes her or his role as a secure base. From the point of view of nonverbal behavior, we might ask what qualities of movement are involved, for both infant and parent, in attachment and related exploratory, affiliative, and fear/wariness systems. The well-known findings of Ainsworth (1973, Ainsworth *et al.*, 1978) and numerous others pertaining to patterns of reunion behavior have led to richer understandings of the ways in which the caregiver's sensitive care is linked to the infant's patterns of greater security, exploration, and overall greater anticipation that the caregiver will be available for comfort. Infant attachment classifications include "secure," "avoidant," "resistant," and "disorganized/disoriented" (Main, Kaplan and Cassidy, 1985; Main and Cassidy, 1988). These predominant patterns take shape as a function of the "internal working models" that the infant constructs during the latter part of the first year of life (and further evolve throughout life); these are memory structures that pertain to expectations one forms of "the other" in relationships.

Zeanah *et al.* (1993) proposed criteria for 5 types of attachment disorders: Nonattached, Indiscriminate, Inhibited, Aggressive, and Role-Reversed. One can draw a parallel to a classification scheme of Kestenberg (1975) described earlier in the chapter. In framing various manners in which infant and parent function with and for each other, Kestenberg suggested that problems in attunement and clashing experiences in mother–child interaction ranged "from mild developmental deviations to severe disturbances" (p. 160). In this early work, Kestenberg cited 3 principles:

1. The more complete the attunement between maternal and infantile characteristics (sensory thresholds, modes of perception, preferred motor rhythm, specific frustration tolerance, modes of tension rise, and preferred tension reduction modes), the more truly symbiotic the relationship.
2. The more disparate and desynchronized the maternal and infantile characteristics, the more we can expect early clashing and later conflict.
3. The road to normality is difficult to assess because it consists of both clashes and attunements in a complicated quantitative, qualitative, sequential relationship (Kestenberg, 1975, p. 160).

Integrating the attachment disorder classification with Kestenberg's framework regarding parent–child roles, the clinician gains insight into qualitative aspects of nonverbal patterns of responsiveness with regard to both positive and negative affective exchanges. For instance, Zeanah *et al.* (1993) use descriptive terms regarding the proposed types of attachment disorders that include relevant clinical categorizations such as "indiscriminately social," "shallow social responsiveness," "difficult to soothe," "actively avoids or withdraws too readily from social interaction ... ," as well as descriptors such as "excessively clinging," "compulsive compliance," and "anger" and "anxiety" (p. 339). However, these terms do not address the nature of the nonverbal expression and signaling evident in the interaction. The therapist doing dyadic treatment with a parent and child can observe and utilize the actual patterns employed by the partners. Recognizing the movement patterns that underlie and correspond to these clinical descriptors gives the infant–parent therapist a framework for the incorporation of movement-based interventions.

Twenty-two month old Carly showed an Aggressive Attachment Disorder with anxious-resistant features. She often got angry, and she bit and hit her mother, showing tension flow attributes bound flow, abruptness, high intensity even flow, along with, on the level of pre-efforts, alternating vehemence and straining. Her mother, Jean, experienced Carly as bossy, hostile, and overwhelming. Jean responded to Carly's temper by using a gentle voice and tone, and tried to soothe Carly by stroking her softly, with low intensity, graduality, and hesitation. Carly's mother appeared helpless, desperately hoping Carly would calm, feeling all the more deficient and weak when Carly would intensify her upset. Jean's discomfort was further accompanied by her hollowing shape flow as well as prominent retreating amongst her shaping patterns.

These features were evident in a KMP-informed infant–parent psychotherapy, and the therapist was able to demonstrate (in a nonjudgmental fashion) the movement patterns that embodied Jean's feelings of helplessness and ineffective manner. Moreover, the therapist modeled a manner of meeting Carly's intensity with firm strength and an enclosing manner along with some attuned tension flow patterns that allowed Carly to feel safely contained yet empathized with. Jean had been so fearful of being overly punitive that neither had she been adequately able to contain Carly, nor had she been able to help Carly develop the tools to contain herself.

### Framing the Foci of Infant–Parent Psychotherapy

The literature pertaining to early subjective states and the manner in which representations get formed in both infant and parent is broadening and deepening. Stern (1995) exemplifies this focus when he describes "moments- and schemas-of-being-with the self" (p. 109), paralleling "moments- and schemas-of-being-with others." In the series of papers referred to earlier super-titled "Prevention, Infant Therapy, and the Treatment of Adults," Kestenberg and Buelte (1977, 1983; Kestenberg, 1985a) formulated many of the perspectives the KMP brings to bear upon the parent–infant relationship, prevention, and intervention, though the framework of infant–parent psychotherapy is not specifically elaborated upon. The primary principles involve enhancing empathy and trust.

#### *Enhancing the Parent's Empathic Responsiveness to the Child's Signals*

Kestenberg (1985a) has defined "empathy" in kinesthetic terms as a "capacity to know another person's inner feelings, based on sensory experiences …. Empathy utilizes attunement in tension flow, which is based on kinesthetic identification with the tension changes of another person" (p. 162). To know how the child feels, the parent must attune to the child's patterns and resonate with them; the baby's feeling of "resonance" is what allows the baby to accept the parents' lead in altering the tension flow patterns.[6] In analyzing a comforting sequence, Kestenberg (1985a) clarified that attunement on the part of the caregiver is not sufficient; rather, clashing is an essential part of the interaction in which a mother may calm a baby, but through the selection of patterns by the mother and the experience of resonance, one partner follows the other, leading to the re-establishment of attunement: "A feeling of sameness is recreated that is an intrinsic aspect of empathy" (p. 141).

By identifying the importance of clashing and the reinstatement of harmony, Kestenberg's ideas are comparable with those of Tronick and Gianino (1986; cf. Beebe and

Lachmann, 1994), who highlight the process of "disruption and repair of expected interactions." They underscore the formative importance of the couple's ability to recoup from normally occurring breaches of attunement. These are conceptually akin to the emphasis in self-psychology on empathy and empathic ruptures. Such repairs are less available under certain circumstances, as when the mothering one is struggling with significant depression. Many less dramatic problems may also hinder attunement.

Kestenberg (1985a) identifies the role of "tension spots" (body parts remaining in high states of tension) and "dead spots" (body parts that have lost elasticity, that remain in neutral flow) in impeding the attainment of attunement by inhibiting transmission of tension flow. However, it is clear that the nature of the interchange in attunement is truly bi-directional, and Kestenberg indicates that sometimes within the mutual relationship of an "empathic alliance" babies can relax their mother's tension spots and animate their dead spots.

Attunement in tension flow also becomes the vehicle for recognition of affects in others. Such attunement can be both intra- and cross-modal; e.g., one partner's intensity factor may modulate in coordination with the prosodics of the other partner's voice.[7] Kestenberg notes that in the case of visual recognition of tension flow, shape flow often plays a mediating role. In the context of infant–parent psychotherapy, we attempt to identify those factors contributing to the enhancement of the attunement as well as those factors hindering the transmission of and ability to react to tension flow changes in others.

A mother, Sharon, and 6 month-old son, Jimmy, were seen in consultation. The baby, diagnosed by current standards, has a Regulatory Disorder Type I: Hypersensitive Type (cf. Zero to Three, 1994; Greenspan and Wieder, 1992), evident in poor self-soothing abilities, excessive fearfulness, over-reactivity to routine sensory experiences, and frequent night wakings. It was very apparent that the mother was fatigued from sleeplessness and struggling with anger; both the fatigue and the anger impeded the transmission of tension flow, making for diminished attunement overall. This also exacerbated some difficulties associated with selective attunement. It appeared that this mother, influenced by inherent proclivities and her own history of attunement experiences, more readily attuned to the intensity factors (in the pre-weight dimension) without a corresponding attunement to the flow adjustment/even (pre-spatial) or graduality/abruptness (pre-time) dimensions of the tension flow attributes.

In this case, the infant–parent therapist focused on the well-being of both the child and the mother, and upon the dyadic exchange between them. Sharon required help to re-establish hope, both for herself and for the child. Empathy for the mother's state, modeled by the therapist through attunement with the mother, contributed greatly to the mother's ability to attune to her son. This mother needed help in re-establishing her own equilibrium. Fortunately, the father agreed to assist with more of the night wakings and with those soothing efforts that did not involve nursing. In addition to exploring the relevant aspects of the mother's own history of attachments, and assisting her in usefully identifying with her child again, the therapist specifically used the KMP to purposefully attune to the mother in the dimensions that she was least able to attune to her child in. For example, the therapist used harmonic flow adjustment and even flow as well as graduality and abruptness, both in tension and in intonation. For this mother, it was also helpful to verbally identify tension flow changes as they were occurring in the baby that she did not seem to respond to. The therapist made comments like, "Jimmy is holding the way he's feeling," (even flow); "then he wiggled into another state of being, let's see how he does that (flow adjustment);" "my goodness, his feeling seemed to change so abruptly ... how does that feel to you? ... I wonder how that feels to him?"

In this case, profiles of both mother and infant informed the therapist of a gamut of similar and dissimilar patterns in the pair. The mother's profiled pre-efforts pointed to her own defenses against certain 'drives' evident in tension flow rhythms and manifested in feelings in tension flow attributes. The KMP illuminated the mutually-influenced disjunctions between Sharon and Jimmy, and equipped the therapist to first focus on attunement regarding those patterns substantially within the repertoire of each before focusing on patterns largely lacking in either partner.

### Enhancing the Development of Trust Between Parent and Child

According to Kestenberg (1985a), "the apparatus of shape flow is the conveyor of trust in the environment. It is the foremost vehicle of relatedness to others … (it) has many functions that all are programmed for interaction" (p. 143). In reference to the coordination of tension flow and shape flow in breathing, for instance, Kestenberg notes "the transmission of tension flow helps us to experience the feeling tones that go with respiration; the transmission of shape flow allows us to interpret these feelings and develop trust in ourselves and others" (p. 144). Within the KMP model, the infant's capacity for trust evolves from his or her expectation that discomfort will be followed by assuagement and comfort. Discomfort that is too impinging for too long without relief leads to a loss of trust. The bipolar shape flow attributes reflect dimensional factors modulating intake, output, and expressiveness in relation to the environment. The unipolar shape flow attributes serve attraction/approach to agreeable and repulsion/withdrawal from noxious stimuli (see Chapters 5 and 6). Problems of inhibited cuing and miscuing arise in shape flow that contribute to difficulties in the development of trust between child and parent.

A two-and-a-half-year-old girl, Sophie, had been having severe abdominal pains of undetermined origin for nearly a year. They were marked by periods of notable displeasure and discomfort, evident in exceedingly high tension flow, but also by bipolar hollowing, shortening and narrowing; Sophie would press into her lower abdominal and genital region with her fisted hand, and use unipolar shape flow to generally shrink away from her approaching mother, Jane. For months Sophie had undergone numerous medical tests, exploring gastrointestinal, urological, allergy, metabolic, and neurologic possibilities, many of which involved heightened negative affective experiences for Sophie, though the parents were quite thoughtful in their attempts to prevent trauma. Sophie and Jane were seen in dyadic treatment only secondarily to explore psychogenic aspects of what was dubbed the "posturing," which was then assumed to be of organic origin. They were seen primarily because of marked features of insecurity, characteristic of anxious-resistant attachment difficulties, magnified by the mother's work and travel schedule that limited their time together. In addition to making the time they had together more predictable on the macro level, the micro level of their interaction was addressed. Jane was prone to laugh and smile excessively, even in the face of Sophie's shrinking gestures and facial grimacing. In this fashion, Jane was not adjusting her shape flow to Sophie's in a manner that could engender trust.

It appeared that Sophie's experience of episodic attunement in tension flow, along with frequent clashes in shape flow contributed to increasing degrees of mistrust, and an increase in her anxious-resistant patterns of seeking, clinging to, and screaming at her mother, whose very presence could elicit a temper tantrum. The therapist became very aware of Jane's tension and shape flow changes, and became alert to the disruption–repair sequences in shape flow, especially those that did not seem readily repairable because of Jane's proclivity for smiling and lengthening (mismatched with her own even and high-intensity tension flow attributes). To a certain degree, the therapists' own adjustments in shape flow seemed to modulate Jane's more extreme patterns. The therapist also verbalized regarding the mismatches (as the laughing so often accompanied sad and/or angry reports) in their relationship, and then commented, as it occurred, regarding Sophie's shrinking patterns, asking Jane what Sophie might be feeling. This simple co-observational stance with the mother was not threatening, but brought up a great deal of historical material which was helpful in explaining why Jane was so intolerant and avoidant of the negative affects Sophie was expressing. The therapist then commented about how Jane herself did not show these feelings in her facial gestures even when the content of what she said was distressing.

This relatively simple exchange promoted the mother's ability to match Sophie's shape flow, to more clearly receive and express cues, and to repair disruptions (which, in turn, contributed greatly to improved trust and reduced frequency of "posturing" and reduced evidence of an attachment disorder), and opened the door for further exploration of other aspects of their relationship.

## Nonverbal Systems and Understandings of Clinically Meaningful Affects

As we appraise disharmony or mismatching between parent and child, we take into consideration the consonance/dissonance and matching/mismatching that each partner brings to the interaction. If a child is prone to substantial even flow and widening, by repertoire, and her mother is prone to similarly large degrees of flow adjustment and narrowing, and process observation finds that these mismatches occur frequently in the movement of each, then our focus is not only on the lack of harmony in both tension and shape flow between mother and child, but also the intrapersonal mismatching within each of them. The intersystemic conflict reflected by the mismatching evident in each individual's KMP heightens the vulnerability of the couple to enter into interactive mismatching.

How we observe, what we observe, and the manner in which we classify what we observe varies according to the clinical or research question and the theory and bias of the researcher. There have been several different schemes developed for the purpose of addressing different research questions. At one end of the spectrum, exemplified by Birdwhistell (1970), the relationship between a movement and its deciphered meaning is assumed to be arbitrary, i.e., the meaning is assigned by culture. In contrast, research utilizing the IFEEL pictures (Emde, Osofsky and Butterfield, 1993), has relied primarily upon a tradition anchored in Darwin's (1895) meticulous observations of evolutionary patterns in animals, and was later followed by Tomkins (1962), Ekman (1989; Ekman and Friesen, 1979), and Izard (1977). The Darwin–Ekman tradition conceives of more iconic associations as well as more intrinsic relationships between movement patterns and their meanings (cf. Davis, 1973). Observations of infant behavior and parent–infant interaction often imply more intrinsic relationships that allow for developmental, evolutionary and clinical significance.[8]

Commenting on those systems of movement analysis that recognize built-in connections between pattern and meaning, Davis (1973) notes, "... the intrinsic relationship is more consonant with the notion that movement patterns are reflections or inherent parts of central organizing processes ... " (p. 93). Whereas most descriptive systems applied in developmental research draw upon methods denoting the attainment of a still-frame characteristic, based upon either ethologically-anchored universals or upon culturally defined characteristics (e.g., a smile, a raised brow, a fisted hand), the KMP identifies elementary movement processes that change the body's elasticity, plasticity, attitude to space, weight, or time and/or its linear or curvilinear relationship to its own kinesphere. It is along these lines that Labananalytic approaches in general (Laban, 1966; Bartenieff and Lewis, 1980) and the Kestenberg Movement Profile (KMP) specifically (Kestenberg, 1975; Kestenberg and Sossin, 1979; Loman and Sossin, 1992) differ in a significant way from more widely applied systems. Laban (1966) considered the perception of one's own movements and of the movements of others to be "basic experiences." He described movement as "living architecture—living in the sense of changing emplacements as well as changing cohesion" (p. 5). It is in this sense that the KMP deals with intrinsic resemblances between movement and meaning in its coding system by, in Labananalytic fashion, identifying pure motion factors, features, and their combinations in terms of dimensions and qualities of movement themselves; furthermore, it relates these patterns to aspects of emotion and personality as well as to intrapsychic processes.

Kestenberg's system resonates with Stern's (1995) emphasis on actual interactive experience and on "the self-experience of being with another" (p. 81) as fundamental in the construction of representations. It is not simply a coincidence that both Kestenberg and Stern, in their separate considerations of affects (or feelings), turned to the flow of music as bearing a key resemblance, and that they both stress the fact that affects are experienced temporally. This insight has led Stern to describe the "temporal feeling shape" (p. 84), highlighting the contours of hedonics, arousal, and motivation. In their approach to affects, Kestenberg and Sossin (1994) distinguish three broad classes of affect, each expressed in further differentiated styles through patterns of movement and their combinations. Primary modes of kinesthetic self-regulation—bound and free tension flow, bipolar, and also unipolar growing and shrinking shape flow—are the conveyers of feelings on both intrapersonal and interpersonal levels.

Stern (1993, 1995) elaborates upon his idea of temporal feeling shapes by focusing on "protonarrative envelopes"—periods of time holding discrete feeling shapes and motives, which are inferred to be experienced by the infant as distinct global units of subjective experience. Kestenberg and Sossin (1979) similarly schematized inner experience when they described the parallel processes of tension flow and shape flow design over time. The KMP framework emphasizes the importance of "phrasing" as a time structure, incorporating rhythm- and action-sequences into uniphasic or multiphasic orderings of movement patterns. The infant–parent psychotherapist can usefully examine the characteristic phrasing of both child and adult to find out when (e.g., in the introduction, main theme, transition, or ending of characteristic phrases) various harmonies or clashes are more likely to occur.

For example, the interactive phrasing of one parent and child may typically achieve a reasonable degree of harmony in the main themes of phrases, yet just as typically get derailed in a manner of disjunction (or disengagement) accompanying transitions. Alternatively, a different parent–infant couple may transit well into co-action, but too rarely match in their main theme patterns. Note, however, that too much matching would not be desirable beyond the height of so-called "symbiotic" functioning, and some parents need help tolerating the degrees of clashing and mismatching that are necessary to healthy development. Such observations may lend clues to the manner of difficulty encountered in specific contexts, such as in nursing/feeding, comforting, changing, etc., and these impressions can further inform and equip the therapist to assist parent and child not only with specific patterns (that are used too much or too little) but with the manner in which these patterns function within typical phrases.

## Intervention Within Infant–Parent Psychotherapy

Utilizing the KMP, the raw data of movement patterns of infant and parent inform the therapist about patterns and phrasing that go awry. At the level of profile analysis, the compatibility of repertoires between partners is indicated. The therapeutic approach that is then employed may operate on several levels at once.

Stern (1995) describes the infant of a depressed mother as entering into a way-of-being-with that may involve being with through identification and imitation, or by trying to reanimate the mother and the self in relation to the mother; this fits the observations of many who have looked at depressed mother–infant couplings, and parallels Kestenberg's (1975) description of the infant who is functioning for the mother in a one-sided attunement. Either model predicts that later development may replay such schemata in choices and styles regarding relationships. What the KMP equips us to do is to knowingly attend to various patterns of animation and responsivity, and to identify which ones might be more relevant to a particular clinical situation. In broad outline, the mother who adjusts to the infant with corresponding shape flow may engender the development of a certain predictability and trust, yet this may be in the absence of attunement in tension flow, conveying (via this model) a lack of empathy. Similarly, resonating tension flow may communicate corresponding feeling states in the absence of matching adjustments of shape flow, hence producing an interactive state with empathy but without trust. Tension and shape flow are distinct modalities channeling affectively meaningful exchange, and the attributes of each, and their combinations and clusters, allow for clinically useful mapping of arenas of matching and mismatching, which can then frame the therapeutic agenda.

Overtly, the target of the therapy employing the KMP is the interaction or relationship, specifically defined in terms of the patterns of movement. The behavior of each partner may function as a port of entry. In this fashion, especially as the approach may pertain to "interaction guidance" for the parent, the KMP may be employed to inform a therapy (see also McDonough, 1993) by providing a tool with which to point out the process—means by which the parent attunes, supports, and/or otherwise heightens sensitivity to the baby. The therapist who is informed by the KMP may look at raw data to clarify the nature of patterned phrases of movement. A mother may be shown a facilitative manner of holding the child (cf. Romer and Sossin, 1990), or perhaps how to use shape flow, tension flow, and effort factors in breathing with and lending support to the baby.

There are advantages to video-taping ongoing behavior between parent and child in the early phases of assessment and/or intervention. As other authors have found (e.g., Stern, 1995), there may sometimes be utility in sharing the video material with the parent for evocative or educative purposes (though one must be cautious in appraising the appropriateness of such use in light of the quality of the alliance with the parent and the state of ongoing transferences). This practice is also useful because it allows the KMP notator to complete whole profiles on each partner (possibly one parent and one child, but other family members may be notated as well). The overlapping of a child's profile upon the parent's profile allows for direct comparison of overall repertoires; this tells a great deal about the resources each partner brings to the interaction, and generates hypotheses about the realms in which either might experience and feel relative degrees of reciprocity and mutuality, attunement, adjustment, matching, and mismatching.

Use of the KMP in dyadic assessment and treatment invites the use of "dual profiling," in which one KMP is directly compared to another. This can be done both statistically and graphically, as one profile (shaded, perhaps, in one color) is overlain upon another profile (shaded in another color). Areas of harmony and clashing and interpersonal matching and mismatching of repertoires become readily apparent. Note that the comparison of profiles as generally applied does not lend itself to direct examination of ongoing interaction. Looking at two profiles, we infer co-action by the dyadic partners (e.g., mother and baby).

However, we can return to a more microanalytic study to more closely examine the particular parts of phrases, combinations of patterns, and their sequences that might pertain to the predicament that finds the partners seeking consultation. Employing the KMP, it is only at the raw data level that we see actual patterns of interaction, and it is at the Profile level that we see constellations of movement repertoires.

However, while short-term, pragmatic interventions within the context of parent-guidance may follow this approach (amplified by KMP observations), the therapist may also attempt to intervene directly with the infant to alter the infant's patterns. The therapist can use his or her knowledge of the infant's movements to demonstrate the infant's motoric, regulatory and interactive capacities, helping the parent to know her or his infant better, thereby educatively helping to alter the parent's representation of the child. The movement therapist may want to guide and/or facilitate movements of the parent and/or infant that foster developmental stage progression for the child, and more optimal intrapersonal and interactive patterns.

Moreover, the dynamic infant–parent therapist can use the interpretive value of the KMP, in addition to more usual verbal techniques, to enter through the parent's representations. In fact, the fullest use of the KMP allows the therapist to work on multiple therapeutic targets, helping the parent to see herself as a better–able parent (her own self-representation) and, simultaneously, to help her see her child's resources more clearly. Such methods can take full advantage of insight and historically-relevant verbal modalities in addition to the focus on nonverbal behavior. The goal in a particular case, wherein the infant may be showing an insecure or perhaps disorganized attachment style, may include helping the mother, for instance, to come to terms with harm and disappointments from her past. Her movement patterns can be very valuable to the therapist because they might provide clues to the nature of contributing factors that may pertain to both the manner in which the parent treats the child and the manner in which the child's behavior elicits complicating identificatory or conflictual responses from the parent.

## Discussion

To date, impressions of the interaction drawn from KMP analyses have been made by extrapolation, i.e., through a deductive process that rests on the inference that the distribution of movement patterns evident in each profile (most reflective of a repertoire) are, in fact, reflective of the patterns used in co-action that are the constituent factors in attunement and clashing, matching, and mismatching. The KMP has not been formally applied in dual-screen microanalytic frame-by-frame research that has led to so many rich contributions to our understanding of early development (e.g., by Beebe, Jaffe and Feldstein (1992); Stern (1991); Tronick and Cohn, 1989). Though KMP notators have looked at parallel movement processes within certain time-frames in video-analysis of dual movement processes, there has been no substantial research into such application. Future research employing the KMP needs to look directly at co-action by the dyadic partners (e.g., mother and baby). Such movement behavior can be notated and compared within concordant time to more closely examine the particular parts of phrases, combinations of patterns, and their sequences that allow for more direct examination of moments in which the partners are using affined or non-affined patterns. Clinically, these might pertain even more directly to the predicament that finds the partners seeking consultation. Moreover, such research is needed to clarify the validity of the more inferential KMP analyses.

In the text above, examples were cited wherein the KMP classificatory scheme was variously used as a tool for the therapist to assess the affect exchange and other manners of interaction that may go awry. As a tool anchored in a developmental model, the KMP further offers the infant–parent psychotherapist conduits to amelioration and repair by alerting the therapist to essential aspects of developmental phase progression and to the nature of movement resources that each partner enters the therapy with. The therapist may help equip the infant to more successfully attune to and/or elicit favorable responses from the parent; and the KMP offers a unique and valuable approach to aiding the therapist in helping the parent alter problematic aspects of self-representation as a parent and problematic aspects of representations of their own infant. Hence, the KMP approach is not wedded to one therapeutic goal, but rather informs the therapist about the confluent commingling of dynamics entailed in the lives of infant and parent. The body of preventative work published by Kestenberg and colleagues lends a valuable springboard to future research and to methods of efficient and effective clinical interventions.

### Notes

1. A possible factor in the lack of more widespread use and recognition of the Profile is the perceived complexity of the KMP (a factor that this book will hopefully attenuate). A related factor is that just as movement specialists often don't share Kestenberg's background in psychiatry and psychoanalytic psychology, so too is it that many of those in the psychoanalytic and therapeutic communities to whom Kestenberg and colleagues have addressed their ideas about primary prevention and early intervention methods don't have movement backgrounds; they find the Laban-derived KMP system too labor-intensive and conceptually inaccessible. It can also be argued that those utilizing the KMP have failed to produce enough well-designed research, and to elucidate their theory and perspectives persuasively enough to garner more acknowledgment.
2. "Selective cuing" becomes more prominent at this time in development: Further differentiation and autonomy will follow alongside the explorations of the environment and more independent locomotion characteristic of what has been called the practicing subphase (Mahler, Pine and Bergman, 1975).
3. A new diagnostic classification and nomenclature has fortunately evolved (Zero to Three, 1994) that appropriately highlights the significance of motor activity, rhythmicity, and affective tone, as in the Axis I primary diagnoses of Regulatory Disorders ("400.") and Disorders of Relating and Communicating ("700."), and, furthermore, highlights the behavioral qualities of interaction and the nature of fit in the Axis II diagnoses of Relationship Disorders ("900."). Within this classification scheme, many diagnostic descriptors pertain to qualities of "motor tension," "facial expressions," "physical handling" (e.g., as "awkward" or "tense"), "reactivity" to stimuli ("over-" or "under"), "muscle stability," qualitative aspects of "movement quality" and so forth.
4. Akin to new diagnostic approaches to disorders in early childhood is an appreciation of the need to assess behavioral regulation and sensori-motor organization. To adequately attend to excessive fear in a young child, one needs to appraise whether the child has problems with sensory processing. The apparent fears may be a function of over-sensitivity to touch, sound, or visual stimuli—input for which the child may not adequately feel prepared to cope with. Such a sensory-integrative approach was originally articulated by Ayers (1979), and more recently by many others, such as DeGangi (1996). Greenspan

(1992) has succeeded in incorporating this perspective in assessment and treatment, while still attending to the psychodynamics and interactional processes evident. Greenspan underscores the necessity of becoming equipped to appraise motor functioning. He wrote:

> The motor system, both fine and gross, is the main tool a child has for communicating his own intentions and both his intellectual and emotional signals. To the degree that learning occurs through two-way communication, the giving and taking of information, the motor system is critical for the child's intellectual and emotional development. For example, before words become important, the child communicates through his motor gestures (i.e., the ability to put his hands up to ask to be picked up in a clear way is the child's way of communicating dependency). If the child has a motor planning or motor tone problem and hits father in the nose instead of reaching out when the child wants to be picked up, emotional signaling and a sense of cause-and-effect logic are undermined … equally important is the sense the child gets of his body doing what he intends it to do … the child's confidence in his ability to deal with aggression will be influenced by his confidence in his motor system. If his body seems to be out of control and does not do what he wants it to do, he becomes more fearful that his aggressive feelings can get out of control. Also, he becomes less confident that he can protect himself or escape from danger" (Greenspan, 1992, pp. 702–703).

Here, Greenspan nicely synthesizes aspects of motor and psychological functioning. It also brings to mind the relationship between the underlying regulatory processes of tension flow and shape flow, and the manner in which they influence defensive coping efforts evident in precursors of effort and shaping of space in directions, which in turn will impact feelings of confidence and mastery that will also be reflected in the KMP.

5.  Risk factors for breaches of attunement and adjustment in the flow of interaction, and for the compromised psychological development that may follow, may derive from multiple sources, both biological and psychological. For example, early bodily experiences of an infant with neuro-developmental deficit, alongside the repercussions for the parent, may lead to impediments along the path of the narcissistic line of development (Sossin, 1993).

6.  Kestenberg (1985a) drew upon the concept of resonance as it exists in music and voice to extend it to the parent–infant context of mutual processes. As the vehicle for empathy and attunement in ongoing interaction, Kestenberg introduced the concept of resonance to address the process of change (such as increasing or decreasing intensity) in the ongoing interaction. Resonance captured the process by which, for example, a mother would step away from (or out of) sameness with the baby's flow, leading the baby to follow suit, which reestablishes harmony at a slightly different level.

7.  Perhaps amodal representations, which have been established in early cognitive development (Meltzoff and Borton, 1979; Bahrick, 1988) also pertain to affects and their multiple sensory components. Moreover, within the domain of visual recognition, perhaps there is a kind of hard-wired "preparedness" for tension flow and shape flow inputs.

8.  However, the patterns are generally coded as per attributional labeling, and this is then handled reductionistically to fit with the model of a finite set of affects, and also because it makes it more manageable.

## References

Ainsworth, M. D. S. (1973). The development of infant-mother attachment. In B. M. Caldwell and H. N. Ricciuti (Eds.), *Review of child development research, Vol. 3.* Chicago: University of Chicago Press.

Ainsworth, M. D. S., Blehar, M. C., Waters, E. and Wall, S. (1978). *Patterns of attachment: Assessed in the strange situation and at home.* Hillsdale, NJ: Lawrence Erlbaum.

Ayers, A. J. (1979). *Sensory integration and the child.* Los Angeles: Western Psychological Services.

Bahrick, L. E. (1988). Intermodal learning in infancy: Learning on the basis of two kinds of invariant relations in audible and visible events. *Child Development, 59,* 197–209.

Bartenieff, L. and Lewis, D. (1980). *Body movement: Coping with the environment.* New York: Gordon & Breach.

Beebe, B., Jaffe, J. and Feldstein, S. (1992). Mother-infant vocal dialogues. *Infant Behavior and Development: Abstracts.*

Beebe, B. and Lachmann, F. M. (1994). Representation and internalization in infancy: Three principles of salience. *Psychoanalytic Psychology, 11,* 127–165.

Bergman, A. (1985). The mother's experience during the earliest phases of infant development. In E. J. Anthony and G. H. Pollock (Eds.), *Parental influences in health and disease.* Boston: Little, Brown.

Birdwhistell, R. L. (1970). *Kinesics and context: Essays in body motion.* Philadelphia: University of Pennsylvania.

Bowlby, J. (1988). *A secure base.* New York: Basic Books.

Buelte, A. (1992). Movement retraining. In S. Loman (Ed.), *The body-mind connection in human movement analysis.* Keene, NH: Antioch New England Graduate School.

Cowan, P. A., Cohn, D. A., Cowan, C. P. and Pearson, J. L. (1996). Parents' attachment histories and children's externalizing and internalizing behaviors: Exploring family systems models of linkage. *Journal of Consulting and Clinical Psychology, 64,* 53–63.

Darwin, C. (1895). *The expression of the emotions in man and animals.* Chicago: The University of Chicago Press, 1965.

Davis, M. (1973). *Towards understanding the intrinsic in body movement.* New York: Arno.

DeGangi, G. A. (1996). Sensory integration in infants and young children. In: S. I. Greenspan, H. Osofsky and K. Pruett (Eds.), *Handbook of child and adolescent psychiatry.* New York: Basic Books.

Ekman, P. (1989). The argument and evidence about universals in facial expressions of emotion. In H. Wagner and A. Manstead (Eds.), *Handbook of social psychophysiology.* Chichester, England: Wiley.

Ekman, P. and Friesen, W. C. (1979). *Unmasking the face.* Englewood Cliffs, NJ: Prentice-Hall.

Emde, R. N., Osofsky, J. and Butterfield, P. M. (1993). *The IFEEL pictures: A new instrument for interpreting emotions.* Clinical Infant Reports. Madison, CT: International Universities Press.

Fraiberg, S. (1977). *Insights from the blind: Comparative studies of blind and sighted infants.* New York: Basic Books.

Fraiberg, S., Adelson, E. and Shapiro, V. (1975). Ghosts in the nursery: A psychoanalytic approach to the problems of impaired infant-mother relationships. *Journal of the American Academy of Child Psychiatry, 14,* 387–421.

Fraiberg, S., Shapiro, V. and Adelson, E. (1976). Infant-parent psychotherapy on behalf of a child in a critical nutritional state. *Psychoanalytic Study of the Child, 31,* 461–491.

Greenspan, S. (1992). *Infancy and early childhood.* Madison, CT: International Universities Press.

Izard, C. E. (1977). *Human emotions.* New York: Plenum Press.

Kestenberg, J. S. (1975). *Children and parents.* New York: Aronson.

Kestenberg, J. S. (1980). Pregnancy as a developmental phase. *Journal of Biological Experience, 3,* 58–66.

Kestenberg, J. S. (1985a). The flow of empathy and trust between mother and child. In E. J. Anthony and G. H. Pollock (Eds.), *Parental influences in health and disease.* Boston: Little, Brown.

Kestenberg, J. S. (1985b). The role of movement patterns in diagnosis and prevention. In D. A. Shaskan and W. L. Roller (Eds.), *Paul Schilder: Mind explorer.* New York: Human Sciences Press.

Kestenberg, J. S. (1987). Empathy for the fetus. In T. Verny (Ed.), *Pre- and Perinatal psychology: An introduction.* New York: Human Sciences Press.

Kestenberg, J. S. (1990). What are the ingredients of bonding prenatally? *International Journal of Prenatal & Perinatal Studies, 1,* 119–124.

Kestenberg, J. S. and Borowitz, E. (1990). On narcissism and masochism in the fetus and the neonate. *Pre- and Perinatal Psychology Journal, 8.*

Kestenberg, J. S. and Buelte, A. (1977). Prevention, infant therapy and the treatment of adults, I: Toward understanding mutuality; II: Mutual holding and holding oneself up. *International Journal of Psychoanalytic Psychotherapy, 6,* 339–396.

Kestenberg, J. S. and Buelte, A. (1983). Prevention, infant therapy and the treatment of adults, III: Periods of vulnerability and transition from stability to mobility and vice versa. In J. S. Call, E. Galenson and R. L. Tyson (Eds.), *Frontiers of infant psychiatry.* New York: Basic Books.

Kestenberg, J. S., Marcus, H., Sossin, K. M. and Stevenson, R. (1982). The development of paternal attitudes. In S. H. Cath, A. R. Gurwitt and J. M. Ross (Eds.), *Father and child: Developmental and clinical perspectives.* Boston: Little, Brown.

Kestenberg, J. S. and Sossin, K. M. (1979). *The role of movement patterns in development, 2.* New York: Dance Notation Bureau Press.

Kestenberg, J. S. and Sossin, K. M. (1994). Movement patterns in infant affect expression: Exploration of tension- and shape-flow features of the IFEEL pictures. Presented at the Fifth Kestenberg Movement Profile Conference, Sponsored by Antioch New England Graduate School, April, 1994.

Kestenberg, J. S., Sossin, K. M., Buelte, A., Schnee, E. and Weinstein, J. (1993). Manifestations of aggression: An exploration of movement patterns. In T. B. Cohen, M. H. Etezady and B. L. Pacella (Eds.), *The vulnerable child, Vol. 1.* Madison, CT: International Universities Press.

Laban, R. (1966). *The language of movement: A guidebook to choreutics.* Boston: Plays, Inc.

Lieberman, A.F. and Pawl, J.H. (1993). Infant-parent psychotherapy. In C. Zeanah (Ed.) *Handbook of infant mental health.* New York: Guilford.

Loman, S. (1995). The case of Warren: A KMP approach to autism. In F. Levy (Ed.), *Dance and other expressive arts therapies.* New York: Routledge.

Mahler, M. S., Pine, F. and Bergman, A. (1975). *The psychological birth of the human infant.* New York: Basic Books.

Main, M. and Cassidy, J. (1988). Categories of response to reunion with the parent at age six: Predictable from in fant attachment classifications and stable over a one-month period. *Developmental Psychology, 24,* 415–426.

Main, M. and Solomon, J. (1986). Discovery of an insecure-disorganized/disoriented attachment pattern. In T. B. Brazelton and M. W. Yogman (Eds.), *Affective Development in Infancy* (pp. 95–124). Norwood, N.J: Ablex.

Main, M., Kaplan, N. and Cassidy, J. (1985). Security in infancy, childhood and adulthood: A move to the level of representation. In I. Bretherton and E. Waters (Eds.), *Growing point in attachment: Theory and research. Monographs of the Society for Research in child Development, 209*, 66–104. Chicago: University of Chicago Press.

McDonough, S. (1993). Interaction guidance: Understanding and treating early infant-caregiver relationship disturbances. In C. H. Zeanah (Ed.), *Handbook of infant mental health.* New York: Guilford.

Meltzoff, A. N. and Borton, R. W. (1979). Intermodal matching by human neonates. *Nature, 282,* 470–476.

Romer, G. and Sossin, K. M. (1990). Parent-infant holding patterns and their impact on infant perceptual and interactional experience. *Pre- and Peri-Natal Psychology, 5,* 60–85.

Sossin, K. M. (1993). Pre- and postnatal repercussions of handicapping conditions upon the narcissistic line of development. *Pre- and Perinatal Psychology Journal, 7,* 195–213.

Sossin, K.M. and Loman, S. (1992). Clinical applications of the KMP. In S. Loman (Ed.), *The body-mind connection in human movement analysis.* Keene, NH: Antioch New England Graduate School.

Sroufe, L. (1988). The role of infant-caregiver attachment in development. In J. Belsky and T. Nezworksi (Eds.), *Clinical implications of attachment.* Hillsdale, NJ: Lawrence Earlbaum.

Stern, D. N. (1985). *The interpersonal world of the infant.* New York: Basic Books.

Stern, D. N. (1991). Maternal representations: A clinical and subjective phenomenological view. *Infant Mental Health Journal, 12 (3),* 174–186.

Stern, D. N. (1993). Acting versus remembering in transference love and infantile love. In E. S. Person, A. Hagelin and P. Fonagy (Eds.), *On Freud's observations on transference-love.* International Psychoanalytic Association. New Haven: Yale.

Stern, D. N. (1995). *The motherhood constellation.* New York: Basic Books.

Tomkins, S. S. (1962). *Affect, imagery, consciousness.* New York: Springer.

Trad, P. V. (1993). *Short-term parent-infant psychotherapy.* New York: Basic Books.

Tronick, E. and Cohn, J. (1989). Infant-mother face-to-face interaction: Age and gender differences in coordination and miscoordination. *Child Development, 59,* 85–92.

Tronick, E. and Gianino, A. (1986). Interactive mismatch and repair: challenges to the coping infant. *Zero to Three: Bulletin of the National Center Clinical Infant Programs, 5,* 1–6.

Winnicott, D. W. (1956). Primary maternal preoccupation. In *D. W. Winnicott collected papers: Through paediatrics to Psychoanalysis.* New York: Basic books, 1958.

Winnicott, D. W. (1971). *Playing and reality.* New York: Basic Books.

Zeanah, C. H., Benoit, D., Hirshberg, L., Barton, M. L. and Regan, C. (1994). Mothers' representations of their infants are concordant with infant attachment classifications. *Developmental Issues in Psychiatry and Psychology, 1,* 1–14.

Zeanah, C. H., Mammen, O. K. and Lieberman, A. F. (1993). Disorders of attachment. In C. H. Zeanah (Ed.), *Handbook of infant mental health.* New York: Guilford.

Zero to Three (1994). *Diagnostic classification: 0–3: Diagnostic classification of mental health and developmental disorders of infancy and early childhood.* Arlington, VA: Zero to Three/National Center for Clinical Infant Programs.

CHAPTER 11

# The KMP as a Tool for Dance/Movement Therapy[1]

## Susan Loman and Hillary Merman

The aim of this chapter is to demonstrate how the KMP can be utilized by dance/movement therapists who use movement as a language and a medium for diagnosis, treatment planning, intervention, and interaction. The KMP lends itself naturally to dance/movement therapy, synthesizing nonverbal behavior with psychological theory and interpretation (Merman, 1990). Both authors are dance/movement therapists who have benefited from the Kestenberg Movement Profile and its concepts in their clinical work. Vignettes from our work with a variety of child and adult clients are used to help illustrate the value in using this system. After a brief introduction to dance/movement therapy and its historic relationship to the KMP, relevant KMP concepts are described. Finally, we offer case material to exemplify clinical applications in each category of the KMP.

### Basic Description of Dance/Movement Therapy

Dance/movement therapy is a form of psychotherapy which utilizes movement as the medium of interaction and personality change. Grounded in the healing processes of dance (Schmais, 1985), dance/movement therapy bridges creative expression with psychological theory. Chace, the founder of dance/movement therapy, states:

Dance therapy is the specific use of rhythmic bodily action employed as a tool in the rehabilitation of patients ... The Dance Therapist combines verbal and non-verbal communication to enable a patient to express feeling, to participate in human relationships, to increase personal self-esteem, to develop a more realistic concept of his body image, and through all these to achieve some feeling of relaxation and enjoyment (Chace, 1975b, p. 144).

The main method in initiating trusting and meaningful contact with patients is mirroring, or joining them in movement. Levy (1988) describes this powerful concept which Marian Chace developed as a way of

... reflecting a deep emotional acceptance and communication ... By taking the patient's nonverbal and symbolic communications seriously, and helping to broaden, expand and clarify them, Chace demonstrated her immediate desire and ability to meet the patient "where he/she is" emotionally and thus to understand and accept the patient on a deep and genuine level ... In this sense she helped to validate the patient's immediate experience of him/herself (pp. 25, 26).

Moving with patients in this way provides a basis for relating and effecting change on a movement level. Principles of dance/movement therapy are: that personality is reflected in movement and that this behavior is communicative; changes in an individual's movement life will bring about personality change; and that the larger one's movement repertoire, the more options the individual will have for coping with her own needs and the demands of the environment (Lewis, 1972; Schmais, 1974).

## The KMP and Dance/Movement Therapy

Dance/movement therapists have been quite successful in their ability to establish relationships with clients, empathize, and provide a vehicle for transformation and healing through the use of the body. The therapeutic process, however, may appear mysterious to those not trained in dance/movement therapy. The language and psychological implications of body movement are difficult to describe clearly and communicate to others. To bridge this gap, a comprehensive system of movement analysis, using its own vocabulary, is of great value. Laban Movement Analysis (LMA) has been helpful to many dance/movement therapists in this regard (Laban and Lawrence, 1947; Laban, 1960). The KMP is a Laban-influenced system which expands on Laban Movement Analysis, adding refinements, new categories, and a developmental framework.

Because the KMP observes natural movement processes and doesn't require the client to follow any specific instructions, it can be used with populations of any age and level, verbal or nonverbal. The KMP outlines an individual's level of developmental functioning, movement preferences (including strengths, potentialities, deficits, and weaknesses), areas of psychological harmony and conflict, and ways of relating to others (historically and in the present).

Movement patterns evolve and change as the individual matures. The KMP outlines a predictable sequence of movement development which parallels psychological development. The following brief description of Chace's work with a child with autism provides us with a glimpse of her use of a developmental orientation:

... you go back through the developmental pattern in a rhythmic movement session ... you go back completely to the infantile developmental stages, working through them as the child is ready and capable of doing so ... (Chace, 1975a, p. 224).

Dance/movement therapists working with families can use the KMP to compare the profiles of two (or more) family members, identifying and measuring interpersonal harmony and clashing. When traumatic events impede the normal maturation process, reactions get stored in the body and are reflected in movement. Through movement observation and intervention techniques, the dance/movement therapist can assess developmental–relational issues which may be troubling individuals and the family as a whole. In this way use of the KMP informs the therapeutic process.

The KMP can be used for pre- and post-testing to determine whether or not treatment has promoted change. The KMP framework can be used to guide therapeutic choices within a session, and to track progress in the session over time. For example, it can be used to analyze the effect of specific movement interventions on subsequent interactions. The KMP supports the therapist's intuition by providing a rationale and means of measuring the success or failure of interventions.

The process of notating the client's movement and putting this information into a diagram makes the therapist's observations of movement behavior tangible.

After notating and tallying up the data ... the dance therapist will get a sense for the ratio or percentage of these qualities in a client's movement repertoire, which will represent in more concrete terms just how inhibited, cautious, carefree or de-animated one is ... Secondly, it gives concrete form (a percentage value) to a hard to quantify area (a movement quality), facilitating diagnosis and writing and speaking about clients (Atley, 1991, pp. 97–98).

The KMP can be used for assessment and as a research tool (using the entire system) or it can be adapted to the clinician's particular needs. The concepts can be used even if the KMP is not formally constructed. For instance, Hillary Merman created an assessment form and research tool based on the KMP and drawing on LMA (Merman, 1986, 1990).

Although Kestenberg framed her interpretation of movement in terms compatible with Anna Freud's (1965) developmental assessment theory, Atley points out that:

... the profile can be used and interpreted in movement terms alone; its use does not require the integration of a psychoanalytic perspective. Learning the profile is a grounding experience, helping one to identify and understand more about ... nonverbal communication ... (pp. 228–229).

For example, Janet Lemon (1990) wrote her master's thesis on the application of the KMP in professional sports and profiled American football player Joe Montana. In order to appeal to an audience interested in sports, she modified the KMP language to fit her specific application of the work. None of the terminology she adopted was linked to any particular theory.

However, many dance/movement therapists, as psychotherapists, do seek a clear theoretical orientation to their work and a bridge between psychodynamic psychotherapy and body movement. Dance/movement therapists have several options to best fit the KMP into their own therapeutic styles and theoretical orientations. If they choose to use psychoanalytic language and theory, the KMP (which traces ego development and object relationships through movement) can provide the link between psychoanalytic theory and movement. Other theoretical orientations can and have been integrated compatibly with the KMP. These include Laban Movement Analysis, Gestalt therapy, self psychology, and family therapy models, to name a few.

Although the outcome of treatment may be just as effective for those therapists not trained in KMP, the KMP-trained therapist can utilize a more comprehensive vocabulary to aid in communication and in creating a developmental metapsychological framework. The KMP framework provides a system with which to validate intuitive knowledge, plan, implement, and monitor change. Observational skills become fine-tuned, the therapist's ability to empathize becomes heightened, and work becomes more focused. The KMP provides dance/movement therapists with an in-depth tool for observing, assessing, and working with the nonverbal language of clients.

In regards to movement analysis, the KMP helps the dance/movement therapist find meaning and make sense of a wide range of behaviors: what is developmental, skill-building, relational, or maladaptive? Movement concepts embedded in the KMP offer a range of intervention possibilities which are based on theoretical understanding. Some of these key concepts are attunement, adjustment, empathy, clashing, holding patterns, body alignment, and the sequence and meaning of movement phases of development.

### *Attunement in Tension Flow and Adjustment in Shape Flow:*
### *The Basis for Empathy and Trust*

One of the basic tools for nonverbal intervention utilized by dance/movement therapists is mirroring, a global term referring to the therapeutic movement relationship between therapist and client. The Kestenberg Movement Profile is especially useful to dance/movement therapists in providing guidelines which enable the therapist to refine ways to mirror through kinesthetic attunement in tension flow and adjustment in shape flow (Kestenberg, 1985a). According to Kestenberg, tension flow is defined as

a succession of changes in the tension of the body. The basic rhythm of tension flow is an alternation of free and bound flow of tension, which reflects the facilitation and inhibition of nervous impulses ... Attunement in tension flow occurs when tension flow changes in one person lead to similar changes in the other person. Empathy is based on the perception of tension changes (p. 163).

Kestenberg's definition of shape flow is:

... a succession of changes in the shape of the body. The basic rhythm of shape flow is an alternation of growing (as in inhalation and smiling) and shrinking (as in exhalation or frowning). The respiratory rhythm is the core mechanism that gives shape to the body ... Expressive movements are based on derivatives or direct expressions of changes in breathing ... The range of trust and mistrust is based on taking in what is good and ejecting what is bad. The proper balance between the two engenders the feeling of trustworthiness in the self and others (p. 162).

Tension flow rhythms reflect early needs, drives, feelings, and specific developmental issues and achievements; attributes of tension flow reflect affective states and temperament. Shape flow serves early sensations of comfort and discomfort, attraction and repulsion, and creates a structure for feelings of safety and support.

Attunement, the process of responsively duplicating changes in muscle tension, is based on mutual empathy. As it only involves internal muscle movement, the body shape may not change significantly. Even though the degree of muscle tension is matched, the shape of the body does not need to be matched (Loman, 1991). For example, to attune to a child who is jumping, the attuner only needs to bounce slightly up and down and not jump with full body action. Adjustment, the process of responsively duplicating movement patterns regulating the breathing rhythm, is based on mutual trust. Here, the tension changes do not need to be matched, but the overall shape of the body is matched. Applying the concept of adjustment to the jumping example would require the adjuster to actually stretch up and shorten in body length with the mover. Distinguishing these qualities can enhance the therapeutic process. Ideally, the therapist can attune to the client's movements, provide empathic support through shared muscle tension, and adjust to the shape of the client's body. Adjusting to the client in this way symbolizes the actual physical support of the original caregiver and enhances the trustworthy and predictable relationship that allows the client to engage more comfortably in the therapeutic process.

During attunement, the therapist (attuner) responds to the mover's physical needs and feelings. "Visual attunement" is accomplished while looking at, but not touching, the mover. For example, if an infant kicks his legs vigorously, the therapist can identify how this movement feels by simultaneously moving a body part of her own such as her hand. The attuner would not have to kick her own legs nor necessarily completely duplicate the rhythm (Loman, 1990). "Touch attunement" is similar to visual attunement but includes the component of touch. In touch attunement, the attuner might place her hand on the mover and match the tension changes felt in that hand, while moving with the mover in the same rhythm and degree of tension exerted. There may be little movement at all, apart from small changes in the contraction or stretch in the muscles. While attuning, movement may be felt in the hand alone or throughout the whole body. The numerous variables and sensory combinations inherent in empathic attunement are described by Stern (1985) as "intermodal attunement." As he states:

There are some qualities or properties that are held in common by most or all of the modalities of perception. These include intensity, shape, time, and number. Such qualities of perception can be abstracted by any sensory mode from the invariant properties of the stimulus world and then translated into other modalities of perception. For example a rhythm such as "long short" (——— –), can be delivered in or abstracted from sight, audition, smell, touch, or taste (p. 152).

Responding with visual, tactile, or auditory/vocal/verbal attunement can soothe an upset child or adult and lead to mutual understanding. The degree of tension exhibited by the mover can be matched initially and then developed into less intense, more soothing patterns (Loman, 1980). Crying infants respond well if their rhythm and intensity level is matched, rather than met with the polar opposite quality of gentleness.

The matching of intensity created through the engagement in "intermodal attunement" conveys a kinesthetic experience of mutuality to both therapist and client. As Jordan (1991) emphasizes:

Mutual relationships in which one feels heard, seen, understood, and known, as well as listening, seeing, understanding, and emotionally available, are vitally important to most people's psychological well-being. In many ways we know ourselves through relationship (p. 96).

## Case Example with a Children's Group

Attunement concepts can be applied in both individual and group sessions. The following session takes place in a primary prevention setting with children and caregivers. In this group, children and their caregivers are exposed to a variety of art forms to encourage creative communication and expression as well as to support the children's developmental movement experiences.

During an art session using clay, the therapist attuned with Laura who was squeezing and pressing the clay. The therapist matched the pressing quality of the child's movement by feeling it in her own body. The movement was not "copied" identically. As the therapist attuned to the child's pressing, she communicated to Laura that she wanted to join in her activity as well as understand her enjoyment of this creative expression. Other children in the group were invited to join, and a feeling of community spirit developed around the embodied action of pressing.

A dance/movement therapist familiar with her own shape flow and tension flow movement preferences is able to enter into the therapeutic relational process with greater clarity. Ideally, he or she could match whatever feeling state the client presents (Lewis and Loman, 1992). Therapists have their own movement preferences, however, which may enhance, but also may clash with the movement patterns of those with whom they work. At times it can be very difficult to attune to certain clients.

Especially challenging to therapists is working with clients who demonstrate an excess of neutral flow. Attuning to clients who lack animation and move with limpness, woodenness, or blankness may involve the therapist entering into neutral flow with the client.

While this approach may be appropriate for a period of time, prolonged periods in neutral flow may ultimately serve disconnection. As it remains the "therapist's major responsibility and task to help move the relationship back into connection from periods of disconnection" (Stiver, 1992, p. 6), it is of benefit for the therapist to have an in-depth understanding of her personal movement preferences as well as inhibitions. This conscious awareness towards self-empathy and an embodied relationship serves as the vessel for both the creation and expression of often ambiguous and conflictual feeling states (Lewis, 1993).

### Sidney: Case Example with a Client Using Neutral Flow

In this example the therapist leads a dance/movement therapy group on an short-term adult inpatient unit where dance/movement therapy was part of the regular activities therapy program. Grouped by level of functioning, these patients were generally psychotic or severely depressed and had difficulty expressing themselves verbally or interacting with others:

I stood next to Sidney, a pale, lanky young man in a hospital gown. He stood with his shoulders narrowed, arms dangled at his sides, feet close together in an unstable stance. Respecting his fragile boundaries, I held his hand with low intensity free flow, or sometimes with gentleness or lightness. These tension flow, pre-effort, and effort qualities were affinities with his neutral free flow which looked and felt like limpness. We all held hands, which Sidney allowed. Using indulgent movement qualities like his own, I was not only able to connect with Sidney but also to form a bridge between him and the other livelier group members. Sidney moved very slowly and carefully as the group became more animated and closer; the group evolved into a small circle doing balancing exercises which required individuals to find their own center and also allowed for holding onto neighbors for support. Sidney cooperated passively by walking or standing still. At one point everyone but Sidney had one knee up while balancing on the other leg. The group stood in this way for some time, waiting for Sidney. Finally, I turned to him with adjustment in tension flow and said softly, smiling, "Come on, Sidney, we can't wait much longer." He suppressed a giggle, smiled, and, with hesitation, lifted his leg. He remained in relationship with other people after that, and began first to draw expressively and then to speak with me (Merman, 1982).

As Stiver (1992) points out, "When patient and therapist can move with the rhythm of connection and disconnection and come to understand together what triggers disconnection and how these problems can be resolved, the therapeutic alliance becomes strengthened" (p. 6). Empathy can be created by the therapist's attention to and engagement with the numerous "holding" vessels available within the therapeutic partnership (Lewis, 1993).

### Case Example Working with an Individual Child

The therapist describes the following case vignette to illustrate attunement concepts while working with a three-year-old boy who was diagnosed with autism:

I attuned to the child's movements, which provided him empathic support through shared muscle tension. I also adjusted to the shape of his body, promoting trustworthy and reliable interactions that allowed him to develop a nonverbal relationship at his own pace. He began this particular session by marching around an exercise mat in the middle of the therapy room. His shoulders were tense and raised; his body appeared rigid. He lifted his knees up high, while making thumping sounds with his feet. He vocalized a short "e" sound every time he stepped down. I duplicated his marching rhythm by patting my hands on the mat in time with the rhythm of his feet. I also joined him in the "e" sounds.

He noticed my patting sounds, smiled, and changed his march to quick, short runs. I matched these changes by quickening and slowing down the beat in response to the child. Maintaining eye contact with me while repeatedly switching from running to marching, he watched to make sure that

I followed his variations. He looked away, turned away, squinted, and laughed playfully. When he looked away, I looked away; when he squinted at me, I squinted back at him.

The child then changed the pattern of circling around me to running away from the circle and returning to a spot behind me. He turned around, squinted, laughed, and ran back to me. As he left the circle, I began to lean my body back to look at him, which made him laugh. This developed further as I lay back every time the child left the circle, and returned to a sitting position when he re-entered the circle. Through my action, I responded to the child's change in pattern with a similar, although not identical, change. I decided to remain lying down once, in order to see how he would react. He approached, and when I didn't get up, he put his hand on my knee in a gesture that seemed to indicate that he wanted me to sit up. When I responded by sitting up, he smiled, laughed, and maintained eye contact with me.

A pattern developed between us. When the child ran to the corner, I lay down, and then when he ran back, he touched my knee to get me to sit up. Later, he used more strength to push my head up. When it was time for the session to end, I offered him my hand. We marched hand in hand back to the classroom making "e" sounds and smiling (Loman, 1995).

This was the first time the child showed some continued awareness of the therapist through maintained eye contact, smiling, vocalizing, and touch. A new trust seemed to develop which allowed him to take initiative and exert some control over the environment, exhibited by his touching the therapist's knee and head to lift her up. Responding to him by duplicating his rhythm via "intermodal attunement" (Stern, 1985) instead of imitating his march seemed to enable the child to respond to the therapist more creatively.

The development of a movement ritual helped establish a predictable form for structuring the relationship. A consistent "holding environment" (Winnicott, 1965) and sense of continuity can be created in therapy by providing sameness over time both in the physical layout of the therapy space and in the consistent presence of the dance/movement therapist. Predictability in a relationship provides the form from which trust can emerge and flourish. Creativity, spontaneity, and emotional dynamics can all be contained within a consistent structure.

This child was able to relate to the therapist, within the safety of the ritual, until he was ready to try new and spontaneous patterns. The ritual was created initially when the therapist matched rhythmic sounds (movement empathy) to the beat of his marching movements. It became more elaborate as the sessions progressed, and then began to diminish as he was able to establish the beginning stages of a genuine interaction. It is evident in this interaction that attunement on an embodied level helped lay the foundation for the development of a mutually empathic relationship.

The KMP concepts of attunement, adjustment, affinity, and clashing can be very useful to the dance/movement therapy process. They help the therapist identify when the client is moving with harmonious or dissonant movement patterns as well as when movement interaction reflects empathy and trust. The following matching and mismatching of tension flow and shape flow patterns exemplify relevant concepts which the KMP-trained dance/movement therapist can identify and use in treatment:

*Attunement without adjustment*—the sharing of tension flow patterns with another person without the corresponding shape flow patterns, illustrating internal feelings without outward expression. Attunement alone is not sufficient in the therapist–client relationship. The therapist wishes to communicate not only empathy and understanding, but also support, structure, and confidence (Sossin and Loman, 1992).

*Adjustment without attunement*—the sharing of shape flow patterns with another person without the corresponding tension flow patterns, demonstrating the appearance of emotion without the internal sensation. For example, even though the client shows a shape of anger, such as shortening down, there would be no accompanying dynamic of feeling or high intensity. The therapist would match only the client's shape of the body, not the dynamics of emotions. The structure for feelings is matched but not the feelings themselves.

*Clashing*—interacting with the opposite extreme movement qualities, such as one person using high intensity bound flow while the other uses low intensity free flow. For example, an enraged client in high intensity even flow who hears a response in low intensity flow adjustment such as "don't worry, it's all right," is unlikely to feel understood (Sossin and Loman, 1992). Clashing patterns during early feeding experiences are particularly important, as this is when children learn to regulate their intake; the clashes may lead to eating disorders later (Charone, 1982). For instance, a 13-month-old boy is sitting face-to-face with his mother, who is feeding him with a spoon. His attention wanders around the room, characterized by the tension flow attributes of graduality, low intensity, and flow adjustment. His mother abruptly narrows her brow and shoulders, and raises her level of intensity. From her perspective, he is disinterested, unenthusiastic; from his perspective, she is disturbing and insistent. His indulgent movement pattern, and her fighting one, clash. These differences in tension flow attributes often reflect different temperaments; the clashing pattern is continually repeated in various interactions. Dissatisfaction, conflict, and possible long-term problems may result.

A certain degree of clashing is expected in the developmental process. It is helpful in the process of differentiating oneself from others and in learning to adapt to those with a variety of temperaments. Excessive clashing can be problematic when the child is working on specific developmental tasks.

*Using affined rather than matched movement qualities*—interacting with another person using related or similar qualities (not identical movement qualities) promotes a supportive, but nonsynchronous interaction. An example of using affined qualities is when the therapist responds to a client's hesitant approach to the dance/movement therapy session by using accommodating and slightly flexible movements. Hesitation and flexibility are both indulgent precursors of effort in the KMP (Merman, 1990).

Generally, dance/movement therapists have successfully responded to their clients through mirroring (the global term). There is a magical quality to this work which many therapists have identified as intuition. Dance/movement therapists can begin to demystify their methods and discover the reason why their interventions are effective or not, both theoretically and practically, by learning KMP concepts of tension flow attunement and shape flow adjustment which help to refine the more general concept of "mirroring."

### Clinical Examples Within Specific KMP Categories

The following sections in this chapter provide clinical examples within KMP categories. The reader who is unfamiliar with KMP terminology is referred to earlier chapters in the text which define all terms.

### Tension Flow Rhythms

Kestenberg (1985b) believes that each of the rhythms is derived from primary biological functioning. The development of the rhythms is associated with both physiological and psychological maturation. The sucking rhythm, for example, is used not only for nutritive sucking, but also may be used for self-soothing, affectionate patting, nodding, and rocking. The strain/release rhythm is the prototypical rhythm for defecation, but it is used for climbing, crawling, pushing, and marching activities, too. Because these rhythms derive from basic biological needs, knowledge of an individual's tension flow rhythms gives information about needs and drives, developmental stage attained, level of fixation or regression, and the ratio of indulging to fighting qualities. Comparing two or more tension flow rhythm diagrams (e.g., those of mother and child) cues one to the relative attunement and/or clashing likely to appear in interaction on the level of needs.

## Identifying Developmental Themes

Rhythms originate in a specific body zone to serve primary biological functions but continue to develop and spread to other parts of the body. They may be visible in movement patterns which cover a wide range of activities. To demonstrate how these rhythms reveal themselves in creative expression in young children, the therapist describes work with children during the ages when particular rhythms are dominant. The examples come from a creative movement group for parents and children between the ages of six months to four years old:

A popular theme for three-year-olds is the creation of big and small ocean waves with the parachute. The children can swim in the ocean on top of the waves, or go underneath the parachute and swim underwater. Images of fish swimming, finding their houses, and avoiding monsters help to keep the activity interesting. These suggestions reflect inner genital (swaying) themes typical of the three- to four-year-old: feeling vague inner bodily sensations, wishing to be soothed by the mother, wanting to know where babies come from and to have a baby, wanting to remember one's babyhood, and feeling maternal (Kestenberg, 1975). Embodying and exploring creatively on this developmental level contribute to the group's cohesion and to the children's growth.

A group of four-year-olds enjoys the activity of pretending to be popcorn, choosing to grow small as kernels prior to popping, and becoming big and jumping when ready to be "popped." Finally, they decide when the popcorn is ready and if they will have a party. The themes of growing large and more powerful, shooting through space and enjoyment of strong motor activity all reflect outer genital (jumping) phase-specific issues and the age-appropriate movement needs of these children.

A KMP-trained dance/movement therapist can identify the patient's developmental issues through movement observation and can help the patient appropriately express these themes:

In one dance/movement therapy group I led on an acute psychiatric unit, a woman with schizophrenia was pacing back and forth during the session as she often did. I was able to incorporate her pacing into a group movement interaction utilizing her abrupt, stop-start, pacing rhythm. The patient was encouraged to lead the group in a movement interaction which two-and-a-half-year-old children in the starting/stopping phase enjoy. The session included her rhythm which consisted of starting and stopping suddenly. The patient responded well to initiating and terminating the group's actions by saying "stop," then "go." One reason she responded so favorably to this structure was that it fit into her level of movement development. During the dance/movement therapy group, I was able to engage her by incorporating her developmental theme into the group; her self-involved pacing was transformed into a sense of mastery and interaction (Loman, 1990).

## Developmental Sequencing

The KMP approach can further an understanding of the sequence of movement phases typical in development and enable the therapist to provide a suitable environment in which the developmental process can evolve. The dance/movement therapist can adapt to a child's needs, which is especially important when the child is making the transition to a more mature phase of development. With a background of knowing how to help a child channel and express age-appropriate movement into creative outlets, the therapist can help the child express intense movement qualities within the safety of the therapeutic container.

Warren was referred to dance/movement therapy by his teacher to promote communication and socialization. He attended a nonresidential school for children with special needs as he was diagnosed with autism. When I began working with Warren, aged four, he was functioning primarily in the anal strain/release phase of development, typical of an eighteen-month-old child. In this phase the child is working on bowel control, climbing skills, stability, autonomy, verticality, organization, confrontation, intentionality, and presentation of the self. I was able to determine that Warren was functioning in this phase by observation of the following movement patterns: anal strain/release rhythms; the use of vertical (upwards and downwards) movement patterns; use of high intensity; use of straining (which attempts to control gravity by binding muscle tension); of vehemence and of strength; holding his body in one solid piece with his upper and lower body firmly connected; and interest in climbing activities. These movement qualities dominated his activities and vocalizations.

In the course of treatment, Warren began to make a transition to the next phase of development, the urethral phase. He became more fluid and mobile in his movements (time-conscious) rather than being stable and weight-conscious. He began to experiment with moving his hands and arms with continuous flowing and floating motions, and to initiate running and chasing interactions with a sagittal (forward and backward) plane orientation. Rather than working on issues of confrontation and assertion, the new tasks were initiating and terminating relationships, operating in the world, and understanding fast and slow pacing.

During such a vulnerable transition period to a new phase of development, it was essential that I support the child's practice of newly emerging movement patterns. Although a complete Kestenberg Movement Profile was not constructed on this child, I was able to make my assessments based on movement observations in the dance/movement therapy sessions. I relied on observations, interaction, and interventions based on the KMP system. A main goal was to facilitate his mastery of developmental phases which he had not yet worked through (Loman, 1995).

## Tension Flow Attributes

The tension flow attributes category of movement patterns relates to emotional expression. Being aware of the nonverbal aspects of affect can assist the dance/movement therapist in assessing the specifics of a client's repertoire of feelings (Lewis and Loman, 1992).

The dance/movement therapist's own tension flow attribute preferences are brought into the therapeutic process; they may influence which clients the therapist can attune with more easily. A great breach of attunement, especially in the early trust-building phase of treatment, interferes with the ability to make contact, foster understanding, and empathize with clients. Ideally, the dance/movement therapist would have awareness of and access to all of the attributes so that she could relate to whatever feeling state the client presents.

The therapist describes a session with a group of geriatric patients attending dance/movement therapy for the first time. These patients were from the nursing home component of a local psychiatric hospital and had been brought to this community center to be assessed for their ability to participate in and benefit from dance/movement therapy:

In order to establish a comfortable structure and rapport, the chairs were arranged in a circle formation and familiar swing music was playing. I began by mirroring small, spontaneous gestures made in response to the rhythm of the music and most members became more involved physically; a sense of group cohesiveness began to develop. One woman showed much resistance from the beginning. The ability to identify her primary expression of feelings through tension flow attributes helped me both gain an understanding and build trust with her. Her body attitude was colored by the predominant tension flow attribute of high intensity bound flow; her feet were firmly planted and spaced widely apart; her arms were folded over a protuberant stomach; there was widening to the sides in shape flow; and her face was set (bound flow). Her stance and expression were reminiscent of a stubborn two-year-old. In response to her self-presentation, I interacted politely but distantly with her while more actively joining other group members. Without a confrontation with "authority" her interest increased and she eventually began to participate with her peers. Interestingly, she later initiated gentle upward reaches while sharing that she liked church. This indicated her use of reaction formation (gentleness, in pre-effort), confirming my earlier hypothesis of anger and the need for control. Her nonverbal behavior, highlighted by tension flow attributes, had been a powerful signal for identifying unresolved developmental issues and her style of relating with others. Beginning with tension flow attributes paved the way for more group involvement and meaningful interactions (Merman, 1976).

Goals for treatment can be based on the assessment of the client's repertoire of tension flow attributes. The ratio of free to bound movements a person uses gives information about how unconstrained or careless or how restrained and anxious he or she is. Too much restraint inhibits functioning; too much free movement signals a deficiency in control. Healthy functioning strikes a dynamic balance between bound and free flow, so that most movement alternates rhythmically on a continuum between the two polarities.

Other relevant diagnostic features include measures of complexity or simplicity of affect expression, the ratio between controlling and spontaneously expressing feelings, and information about animated versus de-animated movement qualities.

## Precursors of Effort (Pre-efforts)

The KMP framework can make "unpleasant" affects, passivity, and the seeming absence of movement tolerable and understandable to the therapist (and so, to the patients). The dance/movement therapist can then make informed choices based on observed and felt clues as to where and how to join, structure, and effect change with extremely regressed patients. In the following case example the therapist begins with tension flow and shape flow, uses indulgent attributes, and moves up the developmental ladder to more mature qualities in pre-effort and directional movement:

This group was with middle-aged and older adults hospitalized in the adult short-term inpatient unit. This was their first dance/movement therapy group and one of their early groups together. Movement assessment information was shared with unit staff to aid in treatment planning.

I noted the dominant group mood of depression and withdrawal expressed in the predominance of neutral tension flow and channeling, and in the lack of eye contact, speech, and relatedness. Where to start? How to mobilize?

In this group the members sat in chairs in a circle; I put on rhythmic, non-intrusive music. I sat quietly with the patients, and then invited them to feel how heavy (neutral bound flow) they felt, to become aware of the support of the chairs behind their backs and under their seats, to feel where their bodies felt comfortable or uncomfortable that day. I asked them to become aware of their breathing, and how their backs grew wider on the inhales, and a bit more narrow on the exhales (this was based on a predominant stance of bipolar widening in shape flow in body attitude). I then asked the patients to rub their backs gently against the back of the chair, thus introducing some flow adjustment, and to try lifting and dropping an arm to the side (low intensity bound to free flow with graduality). These affined attribute qualities helped them move from neutral flow, reflecting feelings of depression, caution, and helplessness, to indulgent attribute qualities expressive of calmness, patience, and adaptability. By using their "heaviness" they began to move side to side in the horizontal dimension (a developmental prelude to communicating in the horizontal plane).

I noted the clash of bound tension flow with bipolar widening, which indicates caution while growing into the environment (Kestenberg and Sossin, 1979). Bipolar shape flow, which occurs very early in life, expresses global feelings of comfort/discomfort. Recognizing the level of regression of these patients, their need to be given to and to take (Erikson, 1950), I used the space, chairs, my voice, and directions to provide support and structure, to "feed" them, and to go with the resistance at the same time. As they felt supported and accepted, they were able to get in touch with themselves on a body level.

Soothing rocking movements, reflective of the early oral stage of development, ensued followed by rhythmic opening and closing of the hands in the same quality. Active patting and massaging of body parts helped to increase self-awareness and self-nurturance. More energetic tapping of hands and feet followed in a biting type of rhythm, serving heightened alertness, definition of body parts and boundaries, and differentiation (Kestenberg, 1975). The group was able to synchronize while moving in these rhythms. As individual mobility and group energy increased patients began to become aware of each other, to look, speak, and interact; pre-effort began to appear in their repertoires.

Hesitation and then gentleness (precursors of deceleration and lightness in effort) were used for reaching across to shake hands and for patting a neighbor's hand, shoulder, knee, or foot. Participants no longer relied solely on my suggestions but spontaneously offered their own. The group mood changed from isolation and depression to one of tentative and then pleasant greeting, discovery, and sharing (Merman, 1983).

Psychiatric patients often show extreme exaggerations or restrictions in movement (Bartenieff and Davis, 1972). From a KMP perspective, patients often use a small range of more mature qualities (effort and shaping) and rely on overuse of one or two precursors. There may be a predominance of tension flow rhythms and the use of space may be severely restricted. Expanding the range of pre-effort promotes new ways of learning. In the above example, patients made contact slowly and carefully using hesitation and gentleness in pre-effort. They were not ready to delve more deeply but had the positive experience of meeting each other because it felt safe and under their control. Learning in this context could mean that total withdrawal from others may not be necessary; the alternatives of protecting oneself and going at one's own pace exist.

The use of precursors of effort can also introduce new movements which expand the range of defenses available to the individual. An example of this might be working with gentleness to foster reaction–formation in overly aggressive individuals. The therapist can also strive to develop available precursors into efforts, such as developing channeling into directness.

The following dance/movement therapy group took place in an adult partial hospitalization program. A core group of patients had been together for some months, with new members gradually added. The therapist describes working with an individual within the group format. Issues being addressed at that time were inclusion and exclusion, dominance, assertiveness, and self-esteem:

Robert had a frenetic, impulsive style and seemed to be responding to internal stimuli. The task at one point in the group was for individual group members to take turns breaking into the circle which consisted of patients tightly holding hands. Robert was able to engage in the group when I matched his channeling in pre-effort or when I used similar qualities such as directness or symmetrical directional movement. Whenever other qualities predominated, such as flexibility or indirectness, he consistently withdrew. When using his preferred qualities, he was able to pay attention and become more direct for brief periods of time. At one of those times after pacing around the outside of the circle, he took charge, used directness and suddenness to enter the center with clear intentionality, postural movement, and affect. This was an integrated movement accompanied by both anger and elation, and gained him much positive attention. Channeling in movement can serve separating affect from thought. Supporting this defense in movement may have helped him control unmanageable feelings and impulses. At the same time, developing from channeling to directness in effort assisted him in more outer-directed, adaptive movement, where he had the experience of being effective in the group (Merman, 1989).

Whenever one tries very hard to do something new or uncomfortable, the focus is more on one's own body and how it is going to function than on coping with space, weight, or time. As a result, pre-efforts are used and are helpful in the learning stage; once an activity is learned, however, efforts will emerge and movement will occur more efficiently. To exemplify the lack of impact precursors of effort have on the external environment, the therapist describes the following case scenario:

This group of three children and three dance/movement therapists took place at a school for special needs children. The children were referred by their teacher to work on social skills and movement development. During this small group session with three developmentally delayed boys, one child, Eli (age 4) arrived late to the session. Michael and Kenny, the other children in the session, were already involved. Eli stamped on the mat angrily with the precursor of effort, vehemence. I duplicated these qualities in muscle tension and in the shape of my body. Michael seemed pleased to see Eli and immediately went over to him. In response to a perceived intrusion into his personal space, Eli opened his mouth to bare his teeth. He resisted Michael's advances by standing still and using the precursor of effort, channeling (maintaining an even level of muscle tension). These immature forms of aggression had minimal effect on Michael, who continued play (Loman, 1977).

Assessing a patient's defensive make-up and learning style in movement gives invaluable clues to inner dynamics, developmental level, diagnosis, expectable behavior, and potential for improved coping. Knowledge of and use of pre-efforts can be especially useful in short-term treatment where, due to the nature of the setting, assessment and intervention must occur quite rapidly. In addition, use of precursors over time enables the therapist to see, monitor, and work with these movement qualities which bridge unconscious and conscious processes.

The dance/movement therapist must be able to observe very small movement, as seen in seemingly inert, regressed, or depressed patients; join at that level; and assist the patient in expanding his or her range of movement. Less mature movement qualities, in tension flow and precursors of effort, provide information and can be developed to more sophisticated, adaptive qualities in effort. Shape flow, directions, and shaping then provide the "container" for these modes of expression, learning, and adaptation (Merman, 1990, p. 86).

## Efforts

Individuals gradually develop their own characteristic distribution of effort elements. The line of development of an effort element may be traced back to a specific precursor of effort and, even further, to a specific tension flow attribute pattern. A mature constellation of effort elements shows an individual's preferences in terms of attention, intention, and decision-making (Laban, 1960).

## Case Example with a Child

Maturation of movement patterns enables individuals to have an impact on the environment. The therapist describes her work with Eli, who is making progress in maturing towards effort qualities:

Initially, Eli, the developmentally delayed four-year-old, expressed his anger by showing his teeth in an aggressive manner, which had little or no effect on the other children in the setting. As the therapy continued, he was able to use more adaptive movement qualities and to show his feelings more overtly, as in tantrum-like behavior. Towards the end of treatment, he was able to use patterns for self-defense, such as holding tightly onto his toys when other children tried to grab them. He was also able to interact more appropriately with the two other boys present in the sessions. Interventions were initiated to encourage Eli to stand up for himself. It was also important to be able to set clear limits and to help Eli structure and channel the onset of aggression, which was typical of his phase of development. It was necessary for me to be able to match the child's intensity and to model mature forms of strength (Loman, 1977).

## Case Example with Adults

A value in dance/movement therapy with adults is to achieve dynamic movement as seen in the use of efforts. The therapist describes a dance/movement therapy group with developmentally delayed/emotionally disturbed adults in a day treatment setting. These clients with limited verbal abilities were referred to dance/movement therapy to improve socialization skills:

The group members came in upset and agitated, shoving furniture, cursing; some were standing and rocking violently, others kicked a large therapy ball with vehemence, abruptness, or strength. The potential for the acting out of aggression was great. I invited members to use their hands (rather than feet) to hit the ball across the floor to someone in the room. After modeling this activity to introduce attention in space, I directed group members to smack the ball right in front of themselves before passing it to the person next to them. My modeling that action with affect gave group members permission to express symbolized anger at the ball. As this reflected their moods (anger, frustration, and fear) and their preferred movements, I was able to ameliorate their fighting patterns by introducing direct focus, bound flow, and containment in space, creating a safer structure for the emotional expression.

Continuing with the theme of containment, the anal strain/release rhythm was incorporated into the movement expression. Because the anal strain/release rhythm is of relatively long duration, it has an organizing influence on other rhythms and can have an organizing influence on fragmented, volatile patients. It also provides a more appropriate way to assert oneself without endangering others. Observing and responding to a group member's pushing action, I asked each person to give the ball a push right in front of themselves, long enough to "really press as hard as you can," "see how strong you can be." The directive was suggested to assist the patients in transforming their unrestrained free flow to more containment and caution in bound flow. The pushing motion was accompanied by grunts, exhalations, and other vocalizations. The activity led to several variations on the pressing theme including: picking up and squeezing the ball, trying to crush it by sitting on it, and pushing a knee into it. The precursor of effort quality of straining was often used. Spontaneous verbalizations proclaimed "bad ball," "go away," "I hate you," etc., and the mood shifted from one of helplessness to enjoyment in shared self-expression and skill development. As the high intensity decreased and self-control increased, group members could throw the ball through space to each other with intentionality and mastery in effort. The less mature temper-tantrum movements reflective of aggression and control issues typical in the second year of life (anal phase) had been transformed to the more mature qualities of the phase: assertiveness, representation, and presentation. Qualities of directness and strength were matched with harmonious directional and shaping movements. Tired, they sat in chairs, able to engage in a "cool down" of recuperative, indulgent movements, and to verbalize briefly about their earlier feelings of anger (Merman, 1992).

Once boundaries and safety were established in the group, the initial movement qualities of tension flow and attributes could be developed to more adaptive ones (bound flow, graduality), then to precursors (straining, channeling) serving missing but needed defenses, and finally to effort (direct, strength). These individuals had suffered much abuse in the past. The group members tended to lack indulgent patterns and showed an excess of fighting ones. Prone to identify with their aggressors and to disorganize readily, they could be quite dangerous to themselves and to others. Developmental dance/movement therapy was the treatment of choice for these patients with poor cognitive skills and language ability. This session is an example of providing patients with the opportunity to develop immature qualities into more mature patterns with the goals of improving impulse control, coping, and social skills.

### Relational Development

The developmental progression inherent in the framework of the KMP can provide the nonverbal foundations of relational development. The KMP offers movement descriptions beginning with early infant–caregiver interactions, evolving into more multidimensional and complex interactions. For the purposes of exploring relational development, the right side of the KMP, which documents a line of development dealing with relationships to people and things (Loman, 1990), is focused upon. The progression of relational developmental movement patterns (bipolar shape flow, unipolar shape flow, shaping in directions, and shaping in planes) are briefly summarized below in order to lay the groundwork for further discussion.

### Shape Flow

Shape flow patterns provide a means to express and structure internal feelings about relationships. When people feel safe in an environment, for example, they tend to "grow," enlarging their body boundaries. Growing while in a fear-provoking environment may produce a clash between internal feelings (fear) and their outward expression (growing movement). When there is a disturbance in the balance between feeling and expression, individuals may move in conflicting movement patterns and have difficulty communicating their needs and feelings effectively in relationships.

The infant's formation of positive self-feelings depends upon a trustworthy environment. As self-trust is built, the foundation for interaction with others is provided.

Some dance/movement therapists have looked at movement qualities underlying the development of trust, or shape flow adjustment. Lewis (1984) refers to harmonizing in shape flow breathing rhythms to facilitate the development of trust between the patient and the therapist. In describing her technique of "breathing together," Siegel (1984) relates:

I place my hand on the chest of the client and he or she reciprocates ... I try to pick up the other's breathing rhythm ... After many sessions, a steady rhythmic rocking emerges that expresses our breathing together comfortably and easily. This is another step toward the formation of a true transference relationship (p. 107).

Although other dance/movement therapists (Skove, 1986) have written about various movement responses used to develop trust and rapport, Kestenberg's ideas of shape flow provide a developmentally-based grounding for an in-depth analysis of the trust level of individual or group functioning.

## Bipolar Shape Flow

From birth, bipolar shape flow serves the expression of self-feelings, providing the non-verbal medium for demonstrating feelings and moods related to pleasure (comfort) and displeasure (discomfort). The body responds to the global environment through expanding (growing) and contracting (shrinking) movements in horizontal, vertical, and sagittal dimensions. The infant and caregiver, through shared shape flow patterns, may develop a relationship based on mutual support through interactions such as adjusting to each other's breathing and holding patterns. Trust develops out of the predictability inherent in compatible breathing rhythms and supportive holding patterns.

## Unipolar Shape Flow

Unipolar shape flow, which exists *in utero* and throughout the lifespan, provides the source for approaching people and pleasant stimuli and withdrawing from unpleasant stimuli or noxious contact. It serves as a basis for communication, interactional rhythms, and the core of attraction and repulsion. The body grows toward and shrinks from real or imaginary stimuli that can be attractive or repelling. People grow when they feel comfortable and express satisfaction, increasing contact with others. Shrinking reduces relatedness as the body responds to pain and unpleasant feelings. A rhythm of growing and shrinking helps to form nonverbal interaction styles. Through unipolar shape flow patterns, the infant can grow and shrink asymmetrically in response to specific stimuli and people in the environment. The infant can now reveal, through expanding and contracting shapes, which interactions are attracting (by growing) and which are repelling (by shrinking). The unipolar shape flow patterns provide the structure for discriminating between and responding to feelings of safety and danger.

## Shaping in Directions

Extending body boundaries between oneself and another can be articulated through shaping in directions. These spoke-like and arc-like movements are used to locate people and things in space (such as pointing to someone) and to form protective boundaries used in defending oneself (such as crossing the arm in front of the body). The ability to erect clear boundaries for self-protection is considered a more developmentally advanced step than unipolar shape flow. In unipolar shrinking, for example, the individual can only become smaller and shrink away from a dangerous environment or an attacker. When using shaping in directions, however, the individual is able to protect the body by creating linear vectors in space that can shield the body from an attacker (i.e., raising the arm to ward off a blow from above).

## Shaping in Planes

The most advanced level of interpersonal relationships can be expressed with shaping in planes. The mover creates concave and convex multidimensional forms that carve space in combinations of horizontal, vertical, and sagittal planes. Unlike spoke-like and arc-like movements, shaping in planes involves elliptical movements which create trace forms, outlining a volume of space. They can represent three dimensional aspects of interaction and are often seen in animated conversation where the participants are fully engaged.

These planes also reflect developmental maturation. In the first year of life, the child is learning to explore large and small spatial areas in the horizontal plane. As the child begins the second year of life, he or she is utilizing the vertical plane to climb, stoop, stand, and confront the world. During the third year of life, toddlers are off and running in the sagittal plane. They have no time to discuss nor will they listen to confrontations; they are gone before the speech is over.

The implication of the use of movement patterns involving shaping parallels the Relational Model's criteria for mutually enhancing relationships (Loman and Foley, 1996). Not unlike Jordan's (1991) description of the "intersubjective, mutual quality of sexual involvement" (p. 89), shaping allows for the full expression of oneself. Movements which encourage the formation and holding of space imply a sense of creativity and potential. The movers are engaged in the freedom of fully representing themselves in relationship, while responding to and being moved by each other. The developmental capacity for shaping affords ever deepening levels of relational connectedness, with its foundation in authentic self-representation. As Jordan (1991) has stated:

In the interplay of bodies and heightened feelings, in finding interest in the response of the other, in coming to know the impact of one's own action on the other and opening to the other's affecting us, there is opportunity for such intensity, pleasure, and growth (p. 90).

The ability to shape, create, and contain the embodied environment through affective engagement with oneself, another, and the bi-personal space generates feelings of connectedness and empathy (Lewis, 1993).

## Case Example

This example involves a dance/movement therapy group with higher functioning patients in an adult partial hospital program. These patients live at home and attend therapy groups in an intensive eight-week program aimed at a rapid return to school or work. This session illustrates a progression leading to shaping in planes:

The group begins with a movement warm-up in a circle. These clients have been together for awhile and share leadership. They move in a linear fashion using directional shaping, reflecting simplicity or defensiveness in their object relationships.

In order to work with their preferred patterns and address relational ability, I structure a section of the session drawing on the defense scale of Laban (Bartenieff and Lewis, 1980): "Reach up, down, across, to the side, back, forwards, now add words: I feel up, down, etc." The patients begin to verbalize feeling words for the directions on their own. The forward movement brings them close together, and some begin to move in a more effortful way, sharing dynamics and emotions.

Moving sideways and across (horizontal dimension), they say playfully, "get away from me," "leave me alone," and "get over here," etc.; in the vertical dimension (up and down) they offer "no" and "yes" while mock arguing, asserting, and presenting themselves. As they become more involved, the linear movements become fuller and shaping begins to emerge. By the end of the session they are holding hands and performing intricate bows while retreating, and offering courtly greetings while advancing in the sagittal plane, ascending with lightness and descending with strength in the vertical, and spreading to and enclosing each other for hugs in the horizontal plane.

Defensiveness has given way to exploration of relationships. The patients then discuss their preferences for the different directions and planes, connecting those feelings which stood out for them to people in their "real" lives. Some state that they have had a new experience: having fun with all their feelings (even the "unacceptable" ones) while others mirrored, echoed, accepted, and enjoyed all they offered (Miller, 1981; Merman, 1989).

To further illustrate the development of more mature movement qualities, the therapist describes her work with an individual client seen in private practice over time:

The client began treatment to address her eating disorder and the loneliness and fatigue she experienced following the break-up of a relationship five years earlier. In order that I might evaluate the client's movement qualities, I asked her to improvise. In response to an invitation to move, the client ran around the room in large circles, using the effort quality of acceleration and the direction of forward. While her body demonstrated the effort of direct, her head frequently moved around with flexibility (in pre-effort), which often serves the defense of avoidance. The clashing of movement qualities within her body indicated an internal conflict. While talking, she encroached on my space as she used small continuous finger motions on her own body. These motions had both the soothing quality of the sucking rhythm and the impatient quality of the starting/stopping rhythm.

My impression of the client was that she was a motivated, goal-directed but possibly driven woman who, while expending much energy, lacked an ability to recuperate. Her movements suggested conflicts such as a contrast between her ability to function independently (her use of coping skills such as efforts) and her expression of neediness (her use of self-soothing rhythms, self-touch, and the inappropriate proximity she created between us). Informed by placing her movement themes within the KMP framework, I expected to observe urethral phase (third year) coping skills for oral phase (first year) issues of deprivation.

As the course of treatment progressed, it became clear that this client preferred to use large movements through space. During one session, I suggested that she try something different—to improvise staying in one place. Standing still, she shortened down with bent knees, her chest hollowing back in unipolar shape flow and her head drooped forward and down. Throughout her body there was a preponderance of neutral free flow, indicating de-animation. Limply and gradually she sank to the floor, ending in a small heap. When asked what she was feeling, she noted with surprise, "Depression."

During the verbal processing of this session, the conflicts expressed in her movement were discussed. Her use of fast-paced movement was connected to her fast-paced achievement-oriented lifestyle. Her use of acceleration with the direction of forward in the sagittal dimension helped her run away from feelings of dependency, deprivation, and possible rage. The price she paid for not facing her feelings was exhaustion, loneliness, and depression. We related her movement patterns to her lifestyle and supported the current discovery of an inner feeling (which also helped her to feel when she is hungry and full) now that she was able to slow down. She said she felt seen and understood through the movement interactions and the verbal processing.

The therapy progressed from structured movement with the therapist to increasingly unstructured, improvised movement of the client on her own. Subsequent treatment dealt with working through issues of depression and rage relating to her unstable, often absent mother and her verbally and physically abusive father. She repeatedly created patterns in relationships and jobs which led to rejection. It took a period of time for her anger to surface and find tolerable expression through movement and words, and finally, in relationship to me.

During the middle phase of treatment she would stamp downwards with straining while expressing anger and frustration (a match in pre-effort and direction); later she could verbalize anger towards idealized parents and towards me. During the end of treatment, she punched forward and ran and leapt with strength or lightness, expressing exuberance as well as anger. The quality of deceleration (in the sagittal plane) entered her repertoire, adding more coping skills. As seen in these examples, use of affined effort and shaping patterns came to outnumber clashes. Matches, such as strength with descending, emerged. Another sign of improvement was the increase in the number of "postural movements." More postural movement (the use of the whole body) is an indication of increased emotional and physical involvement. Although the client's proclivity remained "being on the move," recuperative phrases allowed her to rest in movement, and to take vacations and begin a serious relationship. During the termination session, she sat calmly and comfortably at an appropriate distance from me, spoke softly, and was able to share silence. Because this highly verbal client had been prone to the defenses of intellectualization, rationalization, and isolation, the movement work enabled her to access previously cut-off bodily and emotional feeling states. She was then able to work through and transform intrapsychic and relational issues on both movement and verbal levels (Merman, 1993).

This case has been used to illustrate the application of KMP concepts within dance/ movement therapy work. The KMP framework aided in assessment, evaluation, treatment planning, and implementation. The client's movement repertoire evolved over the course of treatment, building more mature, harmonious movement patterns and reflecting emotional growth and integration.

## Stages in Relational Development

There is a wide variety of individual movement using bipolar shape flow, unipolar shape flow, shaping in directions, and shaping in planes. Movement repertoires are influenced by the following factors: individual preference, stage of development, genetic inheritance, family and culture (Amighi, 1990), gender (Lamb, 1992; Kestenberg and Marcus, 1979) and the environment. The following example (Loman and Foley, 1996) illustrates the evolution of relational stages in development. The act of hugging (or embracing) will be traced through the developmental sequence inherent in the KMP:

In the earliest stage of development (bipolar shape flow) the individual can only grow and shrink symmetrically, which has a stable and self-contained effect. There is no way to reach outward towards another while using only bipolar shape flow. While already in an embrace, the movers can share breathing rhythms by inhaling and exhaling in coordination with one another. Using the next category, unipolar shape flow, the individual can grow towards another person through snuggling into the chest or other comfortable body part. This approach might signal the desire for a hug or contact with the other, but there would be no actual embrace possible using only unipolar shape flow movements.

The arc-like or spoke-like qualities available in shaping in directions tend to have a distancing effect, creating a line between people. It would be possible for movers to point to one another or to touch body parts (as in meeting elbows or fingers), but a true enclosing relationship could not be formed. Only when the individual can use the arm/s to encircle another with shaping in the horizontal plane can the most effective approach for hugging occur. In shaping in planes, the movers can actually embrace fully by creating a mutual relational space for intimate contact.

If breath support (through shape flow) is used during hugging, the interaction is even more connected. The embracers can breathe into each other while inhaling and breathe away from each other on the exhale (Kestenberg, 1978). Unlike reciprocal breathing, this breathing rhythm provides the model for a healthy relational balance between coming together and coming apart (personal space). This pattern of synchronous yet individual breathing allows for the embracers to experience connectedness without losing their unique experiences of self (Stiver, 1992). In reciprocal breathing, the breathers are always in contact (one inhales into the other's exhale). There is no possibility of space between people, the movers become enmeshed.

Certain shape flow qualities (growing and shrinking) can have a conflicting rather than supporting effect on relational connection. A gesture of invitation, such as spreading out the arm, can give a mixed signal when the shoulder shrinks up at the same time. The arm suggests a welcoming motion, but the shoulder gives the impression of holding back. Such conflicting movement patterns portray the "paradox," as defined within the Relational Model. As Miller and Stiver (1991) outline:

In the face of repeated experiences of disconnection, we believe people yearn even more for relationships to help with the confused mixture of feelings. However, they also become so afraid of engaging with others about their experience, that they keep important parts of themselves out of relationship, i.e., they develop techniques for staying out of connection... Precisely in the face of so needing connection, we develop a repertoire of methods, which we believe we must maintain, to keep us out of real engagement (p. 2).

A gesture of spreading toward connection may well be combined with that of shrinking from the object of one's desire. Patterns of growing towards and shrinking away from others, the formation of trustworthy and untrustworthy relationships, and early patterns of physical support and holding have a lasting impact on relationships. The development of response patterns to childhood abuse and/or trauma, illness, unpredictable caretakers and environments, and over- or under-stimulation also affect relationships. Nonverbal therapeutic interventions are especially effective when trauma has occurred on a bodily level or when a child was pre-verbal.

### Summary and Discussion

As all of the diagrams of the KMP fit together to create a comprehensive tool for movement analysis. The KMP captures the multiplicity of movements and their diverse forms of interaction in a way that is both complex and exceedingly organized. The KMP does take time to master. Unlike rating scales, the KMP is a complex instrument, requiring skilled and experienced notators.

Dance/movement therapists are currently using the KMP for research and to enhance their skills at observation, diagnosis, treatment planning, and intervention. KMP graduates have applied the KMP in a variety of ways. Some have used the whole profile to obtain diagnostic information and treatment ideas for clinical populations (Atley, 1991; Lewis, 1990; Loman and Kasovac, 1997). Others have measured the client's progress over time by profiling before and after treatment (Daigle, 1993; Schulz, 1998). One innovative graduate profiled a group of adolescents in a club doing a dance called "moshing" (Binette, 1993). She was able to gain insights into the social implications of this popular dance form. Some graduate students used the medium of video to create their master's theses, incorporating the KMP in a multimedia form (Berger, 1994; Korn, 1990). Anthropologists (Amighi, 1992) have profiled Balinese babies and clinical psychologists (Sossin, 1983) have profiled various clinical populations. The Center for Parents and Children used the KMP as the basis for understanding family dynamics, movement development, and for developing techniques for primary prevention interventions (Loman, 1994).

Many areas of research and clinical application have yet to be pursued. Future studies can produce norms for healthy and clinical populations across culture, age, and gender from which a statistical outline of diagnostic indicators can be drawn (Sossin and Loman, 1992). Longitudinal research with the KMP can advance developmental issues from early infancy. Detailed studies of specific diagnostic populations are needed to establish the range of individual variation within groups. Other subjects for study could include premature infants and individuals with physical illnesses. More research can also increase our understanding of risk factors, prevention, and early intervention approaches with vulnerable infants and children (Romer and Sossin, 1990; Kestenberg, 1989; Kestenberg and Buelte, 1980).

Methodological research can examine the reliability of the current notation (Sossin, 1987) and develop amended profiling procedures as needed for specific applications. Computer programs (Lotan, 1994) are being developed to facilitate scoring and correlation of profiles (Sossin, 1994). The validity of the current interpretive schema can be examined, and specific distributions can be related to variables such as IQ, depression, neurological impairment, defense mechanisms, and various conflicts.

The Kestenberg Movement Profile can provide dance/movement therapists with a tool for enhancing the understanding of the subtle and intricate possibilities for nonverbal relationship. It provides a vocabulary and a well-developed system of notation to clearly describe the nonverbal aspects continually occurring within relationships. An increased knowledge of the complexities involved in nonverbal communication serves to enhance clinical understanding and intervention methods. Movement observation and interaction encourage empathy and relational embodiedness, both of self and other.

The KMP has much to offer as an assessment and clinical tool, and for enhancing skills of observing, describing, and analyzing nonverbal behavior. We encourage its widespread use within the dance/movement therapy profession.

## Note

1. This is an expanded version of a previously published article under the title, "The KMP: A Tool for Dance/Movement Therapy" which appeared in the *American Journal of Dance Therapy, Vol. 18, No. 1, Spring/Summer* 1996. This chapter is reprinted with permission from the publisher.

## References

Amighi, J. K. (1990). The application of the KMP cross-culturally. In P. Lewis and S. Loman (Eds.), *The Kestenberg Movement Profile: Its past, present applications, and future directions*. Keene, NH: Antioch New England Graduate School.

Amighi, J. K. (1992). Nonverbal communication of affect in Bali: Movement in parenting and dance. In S. Loman and R. Brandt (Eds.), *The body mind connection in human movement analysis*. Keene, NH: Antioch New England Graduate School.

Atley, S. H. (1991). *In search of a standard form of assessment: The Kestenberg Movement Profile as diagnostic tool and treatment guide integrated into the practice of dance therapy*. Unpublished master's thesis, Antioch New England Graduate School, Keene, NH.

Bartenieff, I. and Davis, M. (1972). Effort-shape analysis of movement: The unity of expression and function. In *Body movement: perspectives in research*. New York: Arno Press.

Bartenieff, I. and Lewis, D. (1980). *Body movement: Coping with the environment*. New York: Gordon and Breach Publishers.

Berger, K. J. (1994). *Language of motion: An introduction to the Kestenberg Movement Profile*. Unpublished master's thesis, Antioch New England Graduate School, Keene, NH.

Binette, L. (1993). *A KMP analysis of moshing: The study of a communal ritual dance amongst adolescent males of the 1990's*. Unpublished master's thesis, Antioch New England Graduate School, Keene, NH.

Charone, J. K. (1982). Eating disorders: Their genesis in the mother-infant relationship. *International Journal of Eating Disorders*, 1, 15–42.

Chace, M. (1975a) Audio-taped discussion—Body image. In H. Chaiklin (Ed.) *Marian Chace: Her papers.* Columbia, MD: American Dance Therapy Association.

Chace, M. (1975b) Dance alone is not enough ... In H. Chaiklin (Ed.) *Marian Chace: Her papers.* Columbia, MD: American Dance Therapy Association.

Daigle, R. (1993). *Application of the Kestenberg Movement Profile to the clinical assessment of the mother-autistic child dyad.* Unpublished master's thesis, Antioch New England Graduate School, Keene, NH.

Erikson, E. (1950). *Childhood & society.* New York: W. W. Norton & Co.

Freud, A. (1965). Normality and pathology in childhood: Assessments of development. In *The writings of Anna Freud (Vol. 6).* New York: International Universities Press.

Jordan, J. V. (1991). The meaning of mutuality. In Jordan, J. V., Kaplan, A. G., Miller, J. B., Stiver, I. P. and Surrey, J. L. (1991). *Women's growth in connection: Writings from the Stone Center* (pp. 81–96). New York: The Guilford Press.

Kestenberg, J. S. (1975). *Children and parents.* New York: Jason Aronson.

Kestenberg, J. S. (1978). Transsensus-outgoingness and Winnicott's intermediate zone. In S. A. Grolnick and L. Barkin (Eds.), *Between reality and fantasy: Transitional objects and phenomena.* New York: Jason Aronson.

Kestenberg, J. S. (1985a). The flow of empathy and trust between mother and child. In E. J. Anthony and G. H. Pollack (Eds.), *Parental influences: In health and disease* (pp. 137–163). Boston: Little Brown.

Kestenberg, J. S. (1985b). The role of movement patterns in diagnosis and prevention. In D. A. Shaskan and W. L. Roller (Eds.), *Paul Schilder: Mind explorer* (pp. 97–160). New York: Human Sciences Press.

Kestenberg, J. S. (1989, March). What are the ingredients of bonding prenatally and postnatally? Paper presented at the International Congress on Pre- and Perinatal Psychology and Medicine, Jerusalem, Israel.

Kestenberg, J. S. and Buelte, A. (1980). Prevention, infant therapy and the treatment of adults: 3. Periods of vulnerability in transitions from stability to mobility and vice versa. In J. Call, E. Galenson and R. Tyson (Eds.), *Frontiers of infant psychiatry.* New York: Basic Books.

Kestenberg, J. S. and Marcus, H. (1979). Hypothetical monosex and bisexuality. In M.C. Nelson and J. Ikenberry (Eds.), *Frontiers of infant psychiatry.* New York: Human Sciences Press.

Kestenberg, J. S. and Sossin, K. (1979). *The role of movement patterns in development. Volume II.* New York: Dance Notation Bureau.

Korn, S. (1990). *Rhythms of life: The Kestenberg Movement Profile and dance therapy.* Video master's thesis. Lesley College, Cambridge, MA.

Laban, R. and Lawrence, F. C. (1947). *Effort. London:* MacDonald & Evans.

Laban, R. (1960) *The mastery of movement.* (2nd ed.). London: MacDonald & Evans.

Lamb, W. (1992). The essence of gender in movement. In S. Loman and R. Brandt (Eds.), *The body mind connection in human movement analysis.* Keene, NH: Antioch New England Graduate School.

Lemon, J. (1990). *The use of dance/movement therapy in professional sport: A Kestenberg Movement Profile of Joe Montana.* Unpublished master's thesis, Antioch New England Graduate School, Keene, NH.

Levy, F. (1988). *Dance/movement therapy: A healing art.* Reston, Virginia: American Alliance for Health, Physical Education, Recreation, and Dance.

Lewis, P. (1972). *Theory and methods in dance/movement therapy.* Dubuque, IA: Kendal/Hunt Publishing Co.

Lewis, P. (Ed.) (1984). *Theoretical approaches in dance-movement therapy, Vol. II.* (2nd ed.). Dubuque, IA: W.C. Brown-Kendal/Hunt Publishing Co.

Lewis, P. (1990). The Kestenberg Movement Profile in the psychotherapeutic process with borderline disorders. In P. Lewis and S. Loman (Eds.), *The Kestenberg Movement Profile: Its past, present applications, and future directions.* Keene, NH: Antioch New England Graduate School.

Lewis, P. (1993). *Creative transformation: The healing power of the arts.* Wilmette, IL: Chiron Publications.

Lewis, P. and Loman, S. (1992). Movement components of affect: Tension flow attributes within the Kestenberg Movement Profile (KMP). *American Dance Therapy Association 27th Annual Conference Proceedings.* Columbia, MD: American Dance Therapy Association.

Loman, S. (1977). Case notes.

Loman, S. (1990). Introduction to the Kestenberg Movement Profile. In P. Lewis and S. Loman (Eds.), *The Kestenberg Movement Profile: Its past, present applications and future directions.* Keene, NH: Antioch New England Graduate School.

Loman, S. (1991). Refining movement interventions in dance/movement therapy: A model of nonverbal interaction utilizing the Kestenberg Movement Profile (KMP) system of movement analysis. In *Shadow & light: Moving toward wholeness.* Columbia, MD: American Dance Therapy Association.

Loman, S. (1994). Attuning to the fetus and the young child: Approaches from Dance/movement therapy. *ZERO TO THREE Bulletin of National Center for Clincal Infant Programs. Vol. 15.* No. 1 August/September.

Loman, S. (1995). In F. Levy, (Ed.). The case of Warren: A KMP approach to autism. *Dance and other expressive art therapies: When words are not enough.* New York: Routledge Publications.

Loman, S. and Foley, L. (1996). Models for understanding the nonverbal process in relationships. *The Arts in Psychotherapy, 23 (4),* 341–350.

Loman, S. and Kasovac, N. (1997). The Kestenberg Movement Profile of an infant with non-progressive myopathy post heart transplant. In *Resilience in changing times: Shaping the future and extending our reach.* Columbia, MD: American Dance Therapy Association.

Lotan, N. (1994). Personal communication.

Merman, H. (1976). Case notes.

Merman, H. (1982). Case notes.

Merman, H. (1983). Case notes.

Merman, H. (1986). The development of a dance/movement therapy assessment tool. Certification Project. New York: Laban Institute of Movement Studies.

Merman, H. (1989). Case notes.

Merman, H. (1990). The use of precursors of effort in dance/movement therapy. In P. Lewis and S. Loman (Eds.), *The Kestenberg Movement Profile: Its past, present applications and future directions.* Keene, NH: Antioch New England Graduate School.

Merman, H. (1992). Case notes.

Merman, H. (1993). Case notes.

Miller, A. (1981). *The drama of the gifted child.* New York: Basic Books, Inc.

Miller, J. B. and Stiver, I. P. (1991). *A relational reframing of therapy. Work in Progress, (No. 52).* Wellesley, MA: Stone Center Working Paper Series.

Romer, G. and Sossin, M. K. (1990). Parent-infant holding patterns and their impact on infant perceptual and interactional experience. *Journal of Pre- and Peri-Natal Psychology, 5(1),* 69–85.

Schmais, C. (1985). Healing process in group dance therapy. *American Journal of Dance Therapy* (8).

Schmais, C. (1974). Dance therapy in perspective. *Focus on Dance VII-Dance Therapy.* Reston, Virginia: American Alliance for Health, Physical Education, Recreation, and Dance.

Schulz, M. (1998). *Psycho-educational therapy with the horse as a medium and its influence on children with autistic attitudes: Evaluation of a long term psychomotor project through different means of movement analysis.* Pending doctoral dissertation. University of Dortmund, Germany.

Siegel, E. (1984). *Dance-movement therapy. Mirror of our selves.* New York: Human Sciences Press.

Skove, E. (1986). The psychophysical effects on the dance/movement therapist working with a schizophrenic population. *American Journal of Dance Therapy,* (9), 6.

Sossin, K. M. (1983). Movement patterns of infant and mother and the ontogenesis of aggression. *Dissertation Abstracts International 45.* (University Microfilm No. 8405489).

Sossin, K. M. (1987). Reliability of the Kestenberg Movement Profile. *Movement Studies: Observer Agreement, Vol. 2,* 23–28. New York: Laban Institute of Movement Studies.

Sossin, K. M. (1993). Pre- and postnatal repercussions of handicapping conditions upon the narcissistic line of development. *Journal of Pre- and Peri-Natal Psychology, 7(3),* 195–213.

Sossin, K. M. (1994). Personal communication.

Sossin, K. and Loman, S. (1992). Clinical applications of the Kestenberg Movement Profile. In S. Loman and R. Brandt (Eds.), *The body mind connection in human movement analysis .* Keene, NH: Antioch New England Graduate School.

Stern, D. N. (1985). *The interpersonal world of the infant; A view from psychoanalysis and developmental psychology.* New York: Basic Books.

Stiver, I. P. (1992). *A relational approach to therapeutic impasses. Work in Progress, (No. 58).* Wellesley, MA: Stone Center Working Paper Series.

Winnicott, D. W. (1965). *The maturational processes and the facilitating environment.* New York: International Universities Press.

CHAPTER 12

# Healing Early Child Abuse: The Application of the Kestenberg Movement Profile and Its Concepts

Penny Lewis

## Introduction: Child Abuse Model

Much of psychotherapy has shifted from a medical model in which non-organic patients are viewed as sick to one in which they are seen as having been abused by improper parenting, gender stereotyping, and/or cultural values and stigma. Post Traumatic Stress Disorder is becoming a more frequent diagnosis. The concept of child abuse has expanded from physical beatings and sexual perpetrations to include various forms of emotional, verbal, and spiritual assaults. Symptoms of these forms of abuse have been hidden in our culture for some time. For example, Western society has considered it appropriate for white males to feel better-than, invulnerable, perfectionistic, angry, anti-dependent, and hierarchically competitive (Mellody, 1989, p. 27) while women were to feel less-than, have no boundaries, be codependent caregivers and carry the more vulnerable feelings of hurt, fear, and sadness for the male.

Addictions often go hand-in-hand with improper parenting. Like the definition of child abuse, the concept of addiction has expanded as well. The list enlarges from alcohol and substance abuse to include eating disorders such as bulimia, anorexia and obesity, smoking, gambling, retail shopping, sex, love, money, power, work, etc. These dysfunctional patterns are learned from families or peer cultures or represent personal intrapsychic adaptations whose motivation is based on childhood survival. These patterns continue into adulthood and outlive their appropriateness. These individuals may experience present reality as if it was a carbon copy of their past. They may act and react in significant relationships based upon their abusive relationships with their primary caregivers, and recreate their relationship to their family or prior peer culture in current social and work groups.

If they had non-nurturing and devaluing parents, they may be unable to experience a realistic sense of self. This lack of self-esteem results in a person feeling empty, less than or reactively better than others. Their abusive primary care givers are then internalized and become inner critics and shamers, abandoning or traumatizing the inner self (sometimes referred to as the inner child). Occasionally the abusive parent wants to live off the child's greatness and so never relativizes the natural grandiosity of normal infancy. When internalized, this inner object never allows the ego-self to live a regular, normal life. Their capacity to work is atrophied because they are somehow supposed to reach the pinnacle of greatness without ever having to exert any time or attention.

If separation and autonomy are traumatized through personal space violation, as with physical abuse or denial of privacy, individuals may have inadequate boundaries. With inadequate boundaries they can become perpetual victims to others' perpetrations or they may have wall-like boundaries and isolate themselves or have faulty boundaries in certain areas and continue to receive the type of abuse they incurred in childhood.

If too much separation is given through abandonment, or over-stressed (as with males in our culture), individuals may become "needless and wantless" and employ addictions as false mothers to avoid the reality of having needs. If individuals are encouraged to remain dependent, as many women are, or those whose parents cannot let them go, they may become overly dependent or codependent, resulting in their not being able to meet their own needs.

If the home environment is unstable, children will not have the needed consistent, emotionally present parenting. This results in immature, emotionally labile adults. If children become parentified or spousified within the nuclear family, they will tend to be over-controlling and hyper-responsible as adults.

These individuals enter therapy because their lives are not working for them. For example, they cannot sustain relationships and/or jobs, or they have begun to move from denial into accountability regarding their addictions. They may have flashbacks of abuse, or have become distressed because of all the implicit promises of their childhood survival patterns (such as, "if I am a perfect giver, then I will get what I need") are not panning out.

## The Application of the KMP in Evaluation and Healing Child Abuse

The Kestenberg Movement Profile, with its rich developmentally-based conceptual resources, is a powerful tool in the assessment and healing of child abuse. When these movement patterns are analyzed, they offer insight into object relations, psychodynamic, abuse, and addiction theories. A rich observational window opens for the dance/movement therapist through which to hypothesize the type of trauma and the developmentally-based dysfunctional parenting which may have occurred. Clearly not all imbalances in a profile are the result of child abuse, but those discussed here must raise a red flag of concern to be further explored.

## The KMP and Assessment of Child Abuse

### Sense of Self, Self-Esteem, Inner Child

Indications of a sense of self are reflective in an individual's use of bipolar and unipolar shape flow, which is expressive of self-feelings and responses to the internalized object. If an individual moves comfortably between growing and shrinking in three dimensions stimulated by natural breath flow, the KMP analyst can assess that there is a realistic sense of self inside which can experience a sense of trust (widening and narrowing), balance and pride (lengthening), stability (shortening), confidence (bulging), and appropriate reduction of confidence (hollowing). Individuals with a shape flow body attitude of unipolarly hollowing backward give the message that their sense of self is inadequate. This is, because the sense of self forms from a sense of belly-fullness which develops gradually through the developmental stage of symbiosis and separation and individuation (Mahler, 1968; Lewis, 1983, 1984, 1986, 1987, 1990, 1993b). Individuals may convey the message that their belly is empty regardless of the amount of food which has been eaten. Frequently this hollowing backward is accompanied by bipolar narrowing in the horizontal dimension, which can be interpreted to mean that they do not reach out to others frequently due to a feeling that they aren't worth giving to. They may also shorten downward in unipolar shape flow which may translate into a feeling of being shorter, or in abuse theory, an experience of feeling "less-than." Those individuals who were raised by their primary caregivers to be better than others so that parents could live off their offspring's greatness will tend to have the opposite shape flow body attitude. They will remain in an expansive bulging, lengthening, and widening position, taking up as much room as they can.

### Vulnerability and Boundary Formation

Indications of whether or not internal and external boundaries are present can be discovered in patterns of tension flow rhythms, directional shape, and pre-efforts. Internal boundaries address ego boundary (the capacity to discriminate inner reality from outer reality) and skin body boundary (the capacity to discriminate what is "me" from "not me"). This first boundary develops with the presence of the oral sadistic (fighting) biting and snapping teething phase which heralds a child's separation from his mother. If there is an inadequate or an over-dominance of *os* rhythms in a person's movement, abuse may have occurred at this phase. Incessant patting, tapping, and held jaws [e.g., nocturnal teeth grinding or tempro mandibular joint syndrome (TMJ)] all indicate a difficulty either expressing what is inside out or not wanting what is outside to enter. If there is a low frequency of the oral biting and snapping rhythm, individuals often compensate by maintaining a high level of bound flow throughout their external muscles which Reich called "body armoring" (1949) and abuse theory calls "wall-like boundaries."

Pre-efforts and directional shape address ego defenses and defenses against objects, respectively. The presence of pre-efforts can suggest that there is some measure of discrimination which is occurring with reference to maintaining an ego boundary. Directional shape addresses body protection by barring access or expanding personal space.

External boundaries, or what effort/shape trained dance therapists have called the "kinesphere," is the personal space around an individual within which they feel comfortable in relation to another. These boundaries are violated with physical abuse. Boundaries can be identified when the anal sadistic (fighting) strain/release or defecatory rhythm is present and localized in the lower torso of the individual. The use of directional downwards and the pre-effort of vehemence contribute to the definition of boundaries. If individuals have few of these assertive movements in their repertoire, they may find themselves continuously victimized and violated. The key here is to have access to libidinal (indulging) efforts and tension flow demonstrating one's capacity to be vulnerable, but also have sadistic (fighting) efforts and tension flow rhythms demonstrating that one also has the capacity to have boundaries and protect oneself.

### Inner Parent/Internalized Object: Inner Shamer, Critic, Judge or Good Parent

Children not only internalize a sense of self, but they internalize their primary caregivers as well, and their reactions to them. If children have been abused it will leave an imprint on their bodies' reactions to others (shape flow-shape system) and their feelings and adaptations (tension flow-effort system). For example, if a person exhibits a predominance of unipolar shrinking, the KMP analyst may hypothesize that the primary caregiver was noxious, i.e., abusive to the individual as a child. Bipolar narrowing may suggest that it was unsafe to reach out to the parents because they weren't there or because they would have attacked the child physically or emotionally. Directional shape can be used for self-protection against objects typically by erecting barriers. Clinically-oriented KMP analysts are interested in observing if any of these movement factors are employed inappropriately in a present situation. When this occurs, it can be proposed that the individuals are acting not out of present reality cues but out of a childhood survival pattern triggered by an unrealistic fear of abuse. For example, inappropriate use of across can suggest a desire to isolate and close off the body surface through the crossing of arms or legs. Moving upwards can suggest a desire to perhaps float up and away, often part of anorexics' desire to avoid confronting the devouring mother. Moving backward can suggest a person's childhood pattern of attempting to escape the abuse, while moving forward with suddenness can suggest a counterphobic childhood pattern of survival in relation to an abusive parent.

Tension flow attributes address the control of expression of affects. They specifically reflect feeling responses to safety and danger. Free flow generally expresses playful ease and carefree feelings and, in extreme, loss of control; while bound flow provides the basis for caution, or in extreme, repression and anxiety-indicators of childhood abuse. For example, if an individual employs a dominance of even level of intensity and free flow this gives a feeling of poise and calm. Even level of intensity with bound flow may indicate a wary hypervigilance. The over-use of high intensity of tension flow demonstrates an excitability which often suggests early abuse which has left the individual over-reactive in adult life. Some individuals react to explosive parents by maintaining a pattern of low intensity so as not to stimulate any outbursts from them. This is true also of individuals who persistently employ gradual changes in flow, especially when in bound. The message with this tension flow action is that one should not rock the boat by acting too spontaneously. Individuals who develop patterns of persistent abrupt changes of flow tend to be impulsive, irritable, and jumpy. This may be a reaction to parents with volatile mood swings.

Where there is very little tension flow alteration, the message may be that it wasn't safe or okay to feel in the family. Perhaps a parent felt too much or perhaps it was considered base, unladylike, or unacceptable in a given culture (such as in many East Asian societies) to demonstrate strong feelings. In this case more neutral flow may be used. One may see gradual de-animation or a more severely disassociative, depersonalized, needless and wantless response. In these extreme cases, severe physical abuse may have been present.

The presence of shaping in planes suggests that individuals are capable of more complex ways of relating to others. This could point to richer relationships with primary caregivers. However, it is also important to take into consideration gender and cultural factors. Women in the West have been encouraged to be in relation to others, while white men have been raised to separate and be in competition. Typically women demonstrate a greater use of shaping in planes than men. Some Native American cultures raise their children to employ more directional shape than shaping.

The above reflects a few of the KMP elements which have been found in this author's clinical practice which may indicate child abuse. The following addresses the use of KMP in the recovery process.

## The KMP in the Healing of Child Abuse

The healing of child abuse requires the individual to return imaginally to each abuse setting and occasion; take the inner child to a safe place; and, as an adult, confront the perpetrator(s). When addictions are used as false mothers in attempts to fill the void of the absence of self and object, they too need to be confronted as the abusers they really are. Once the inner child is freed from the abuse, re- or co-parenting can occur in the choreography of object relations (Lewis, 1983, 1987, 1990, 1993b). Reparenting is a technique in which the therapist, as a role model, responds like a good parent might to the client's inner child. This is done not to reinforce dependency needs, but rather for the purpose of the client viewing proper parenting and, if time allows, internalizing a "good enough parent". This technique is utilized when the client is unable to co-parent with the therapist because there are no previous healthy internal objects upon which to draw.

With a healed, loved inner child and a supportive, positive internalized parent who ensures and encourages healthy boundaries and expression of needs and wants, the individual is freed to respond appropriately in the moment and continue to unfold in her life.

The Kestenberg Movement Profile can not only assist in the identification of abuse, but KMP concepts can help aid in the therapeutic process of recovery (Lewis, 1993b). This is particularly true in the phase of confrontation of parental abusers and/or addictions and in the subtle reparenting that is often needed.

The choreography of object relations may need to start from the beginning relationship with the mother if abuse occurred right from birth. The developmentally-based Kestenberg concepts of tension flow rhythms and bipolar and unipolar shape flow provide a movement map of the progression from infancy to pre-schooler (Kestenberg, 1956; Kestenberg and Buelte, 1977; Kestenberg and Sossin, 1979; Sossin, 1990).

The patient identifies the developmental point to begin reparenting through his movement. If oral libidinal (indulging) rhythms and the horizontal plane dominate then the therapist knows to mirror in the horizontal plane, attune to the oral rhythm, and perhaps hold the individual or at least sit in an open position representing the symbiotic phase.

If oral sadistic (fighting) rhythms, glaring, devouring eyes, and tense jaw are dominant, then the therapist knows to maintain an opened horizontal position and be aware of skin boundaries and the concept of "me/not me" with a differentiating transference. Looking at and looking away, engaging in movements which pat/tap the person in a biting rhythms or gently massaging in a chewing rhythm, and encouraging embodiment of snarling and growling creatures help reinforce this phase.

If the anal libidinal (indulging) rhythm is dominant with a whiny, ambivalent vocal tone, the therapist knows that the practicing subphase of separation and individuation is present. Switching now to the vertical plane, the therapist focuses on the patient's spatial distancing and returning as a means of choreographing trial separation from the good mother. Pushing away and pulling towards, being hugged and leaving then returning for refueling are all appropriate themes.

If anal sadistic (fighting) defecatory rhythms are present, the therapist knows to maintain the vertical plane, sit vis-a-vis the client, and imagine clear external boundaries in a rapprochement transference. Movement themes of power and assertion, independence and presentation are encouraged.

If urethral libidinal (indulging) and sadistic (fighting) rhythms of a liquid, flowing quality and starting/stopping running, respectively, are present, then the therapist can assume the individual has achieved the beginning of self and object internalization and constancy.

The therapist then can diminish her involvement and become more a witness in the individual's unfolding in improvisational or authentic movement or dream or art embodiment (Lewis, 1982, 1985, 1988, 1990, 1993a).

## Clinical Example of the Application of KMP Concepts in the Healing of Child Abuse in Group Therapy

Three examples from an authentic sound, movement, and drama group will be offered to illustrate a variety of recovery processes. Authentic movement is an unstructured dance therapy technique of active imagination in which clients experience being moved by their unconscious (Lewis, 1980, 1982, 1985, 1988, 1990, 1993a, 1993b, 1994). Some individuals feel various sensations and are moved in response to them. Most, however, create imagistic environments and move within them. These can be recreations of the past that emerge from the unconscious realm to be consciously known or reclaimed by the mover, or they may be new symbolic experiences that are unfolding for the individual to embody and integrate into their personality. This therapist has added sound and dramatic improvisation to this model (Lewis, 1993a).

### Role of Therapist

Although many who teach authentic movement encourage the therapist to remain an uninvolved witness, this therapist has found this to be unnecessarily limiting. In this model therapists (like the mover/client/patient) shift their minds away from ego-based thoughts. But instead of receiving from their own unconscious, they create an inner vessel and wait to receive from the mover's unconscious through the use of the somatic countertransference (Lewis, 1984, 1992, 1993a).

### *Mary*

Mary, a woman in her fifties, has been a member of this group for three years for the purpose of working on early child abuse in which she was emotionally not seen, heard, or valued. In the past group work she had begun to "have her own voice," as she phrased it, and to allow very early felt experiences to enter into her authentic sound-movement therapy process. Initially her voice tone employed only low intensity in tension flow with a full range of spatial and temporal attributes. Now in authentic sound, she was beginning to employ high intensity, which, with matching sounds on my part, began to progress into the pre-effort of vehemence. She then added words to the tone, and speaking to her imagined family yelled, "Shut up! I don't want to hear it anymore!" In later groups she tested this in relation to other members. During processing she stated she felt we were all "jabbering" and she preferred to "say nothing." I responded by shifting my horizontal communicating posture to vertical and affirmed her right to choose not to speak, employing even flow and high intensity of tone. It was after this phase in her work that she began to have body-felt memories. Lying on the floor, she would feel strapped in. She reported that she found it difficult to breathe and move. Over several authentic movement groups the sensation recurred until the image came into full figure: she had been harnessed in her crib as an infant. Her mother had wanted to keep her down. In processing she began to talk about how her mother never allowed her to do what she wanted and that she was never allowed to stand up to her and disagree. The ability to assume verticality and to claim all the vertical affinities of tension flow [high intensity, anal sadistic (fighting) rhythms, the pre-effort of vehemence, and the effort of strength] became crucial. In one authentic movement group she again found herself harnessed in the horizontal. She began to crawl on the floor. She cried, "I can't feel my legs! They're numb." She dragged herself like a paraplegic to the futon sofa and began to struggle in vain to stand. I moved over to her to be a good mother advocate. I said, "We must take your mother's harness off you, so you will be free. Your child self can't do it; she is too small, but the adult in you can do it. Can you take the harness off the little one? I will help, too, if you like." With that, she and I imaginally tugged and ripped this shackle off her torso and hurled it away. I began quietly saying (using neutral high intensity) "No more." She then joined the chant, enlarging the range into high intensity and using her recently claimed vehemence. She then pulled herself up and stood in the vertical, breathing fully for the first time.

### John

John, a man in his thirties, had joined the group during this time. After a few sessions he began to talk about how he had difficulty sustaining relationships with women and (not so surprisingly) how controlling and invasive his mother was. I would always respond with expressions of disgust toward his mother and support for his right to have his own life.

It was about the time that Mary was re-experiencing her toddler self in a harness that John, in an authentic movement process, experienced himself to be in his boyhood room. He began rolling from side to side. I was aware that he was getting close to Mary who I knew was in a very vulnerable position. Mary was vocally weepy. John heard her and transferred his mother onto her. "Get out of my room!" he yelled vehemently. Mary was in no position to respond, as she herself was re-experiencing her own abuse. I quickly came over and placed my body in between him and Mary. Hoping to capture the transference I responded, "What do you mean? Your room is my room." "Get out!" he yelled. In as witchy a voice as I could conjure up, I retorted, "I need to live off you. I'm empty inside. I want your life force." With that he turned and began employing strength and directness, shoving me out of his space. Sliding along the floor I begged in a diminishing voice, "Don't send me away. I need you. I'll find a way to manipulate myself back into your life." With a final shove he yelled, "Never!"

Week after week he moved and vocalized in a choking, regurgitating manner. This sound movement process employed the tension flow rhythms in service to separation and elimination: oral sadistic (fighting) spitting and anal sadistic (fighting) deep, intense defecatory sounds. In processing he would report that his mother was like so much phlegm in his chest, keeping him from feeling "inspired." In one group, after engaging in this release, he began to sing/chant in a different way. Prior to this, his voice had originated from his throat. Now it sounded like it came from his chest and diaphragm and had a flowing urethral and feminine-identified inner genital wave-like rhythmic quality. Both these rhythms demonstrated a developmental progression from the anal sadistic (fighting) independence phase to one of moving into the world. He had a powerful baritone voice with rich resonance. After a few minutes I felt intuitively called to sing although it was clear to me it wasn't my voice. I feel now it may have been the voice of his own feminine side, perhaps freed for the first time from the shadow of the mother. The improvisational duet flowed with the harmonic ease of a practiced piece. He later reported being able to more easily experience closeness with a woman.

### Susan

Susan, a woman in her late twenties, had been a member of this group for a number of years. During that time she had worked diligently in authentic sound and movement to free herself from her childhood history with an engulfing mother and a molesting father. She frequently found herself embodying various animals from which she would begin to claim instinctual elements. She explored the spirited nature of a bird and the sleek, powerful quality of a panther. In one group she returned to her "fetal self." During processing time she described feeling like she was "just skin over bone." She had placed herself close to where I was seated and piled pillows up around her. "I was trying to get out of my mother's womb. She was empty and wanting to keep me in." During this time she was engaging in an inner genital sadistic (fighting) surging/birthing rhythm. Her intensity was so powerful that I could easily experience it without actually visually attending. I began to imagine myself as a midwife. During processing Susan reported that she had the distinct feeling that I was trying to soothe her mother so that she would let Susan go.

After Susan had birthed herself she began to rock in an oral rhythm just as an infant might. At this time I mirrored her rock vocally with a lullaby. She then began to slither around the floor (she reported feeling snake-like) and gradually began to employ more pre-efforts and then efforts. She later stated that she had evolved into what felt to be a witch. Upon further processing it became clear that this witch represented the split-off of a powerful part of herself which was never allowed to develop in her parent's home.

## Clinical Example of the Application of KMP Concepts in Healing of Child Abuse in Individual Therapy

Individual depth work allows for the subtle nuances of the movements associated with early object related trauma to be monitored from moment to moment by the therapist and responded to through her subtle tension and shape flow changes, co-creating within the bipersonal field, a transitional space of healing. The role of the therapist is paramount in healing early stages of development; for just as no infant could evolve a sense of self without the attentive ministerings of the attuned mother, no adult can do so either. Additionally, just as children know if their parents truly love and know them deeply, clients as well are not fooled by therapists "going though the motions" of acting like they care. Thus the tension and shape flow of the therapist originates not from the cognitive left hemisphere, but from the core of the body allowing the shape flow to emerge from the solar plexus and heart and the tension flow to develop spontaneously from the maternal zones associated with the infant's gratification and well being.

Because self formation and the internalization of the object is accomplished in and with the body, embodied techniques which employ the imaginal-transitional play space are utilized. Hence movement and drama focusing on enacted personification of the developing inner child self, intrapsychic survival mechanisms, addictions, and other split off aspects of the psyche as well as the internalized parents can be embodied by both client and therapist in service to healing and the healthy choreography of object relations.

### Laura

Laura, a bright woman in her early thirties with a strong ego, was referred by a former client. She entered the room gracefully and quickly smiled with a widened grin and intense eyes reflecting to me a riveting quality of total positive regard. I felt immediately moved into a state of idealization. I then began to receive the full transference of a mother that needed to be pedestaled or there would be no chance of receiving any attention let alone love. I pondered internally as to whether she unconsciously felt she needed to heal me, the mother-therapist, first i.e. to fill me with narcissistic supplies in hopes there would be enough to send back to her. I immediately began to send support, care, and valuing back to her through the imaginal realm of the somatic countertransference (Lewis, 1984, 1992, 1993). I learned from her that her mother was empty and enmeshed and her father narcissistic. She was ignored or engulfed by the mother and spousified by the father. Neither parent could instill in her a sense of self. I wrote in my notes from this first hour, "must have very good boundaries with her. She needs to have her new sense of self encouraged and supported as she claims more of herself".

## Orality

The only one who noticed her was her father, but only in relation to what she looked like and what she did that he could use for his own aggrandizement. He had sexualized her and now her sexuality was split from her inner substance and used to seduce in order to be seen. As she role played her mother while I interviewed her, I noticed her upper torso lengthen upward and bulge forward. I began feeling as if I were in the presence of an ice queen who consisted solely of an outer shell. It became exceedingly difficult to make sure I did not get caught in her excellently trained ability to mirror what the other wanted and give it to them. Much of my response to her was on a nonverbal level. I would sit in an opened horizontal posturing and attune to her breath and trace oral rhythms. In this type of transference, however, who is mirroring whom can be a very subtle, and at times, a confusing pas de deux.

In five sessions her trust was sufficient enough to begin the work of self formation. During this hour she realized that she had given up her soul's manifestation in return for the hopes of parental love. I asked her if she would be willing to let me in i.e. for my soul to find her soul. Would she let me look inside her? She was intrigued; and looking into my eyes, she allowed me to look into hers. This suggestion brought us into the transpersonal. I connected to my soul and began looking inside her for a spark of "I"ness. Eventually she allowed me to find her. She said after, "I feel like we weren't the only beings in this room. I felt someone saying 'wake Up'". I responded, "Let those words be your Koan."

The next week she brought in a dream in which she was lead by a psychopomp figure into "seeing the light in the darkness, like the light that shines at the bottom of the sea." I encouraged her to embody this experience. She began by kneeling with her head downward. Her lower torso began to move in an inner genital sadistic (fighting)-birthing rhythm. She then said, "I need to do this with someone." I then moved toward her and I supported her as we both moved in this birthing rhythm which resulted in her capacity to see the light of her soul in the darkness of her childhood. We finished the movement sequence by her indulging in eye to eye contact. I felt her beginning to absorb my genuine care. She questioned, "Will you receive my anger too." I smiled back and imagined her whole and sent the image back to her.

In this next hour she reported dreaming that she was "deep in liquid-like a womb, and I feel my center". I suggested that she embody the dream. She lay on the floor. I sat next to her and supported her back with my hand gently following the flow of her breath with synchronized oral-sucking rhythms. Embodying her fetal self, she began to speak, "I feel empty." I respond in an inner genital-oral soothing rhythm, "Yes little one, that is because there was no one to feed you, but we will fill you with love and care and you will feel full."

"I need to see myself" was Laura's first comment at the beginning of the next session. I brought her a mirror and encouraged her to look into her own eyes. "I am worried. I need space; I am empty." She continued to use the mirror off and on as she moved into the movement space in the room. She was aware of her inner judge that we had explored in earlier sessions. She was able tell it to leave her alone. Her inner mother then appeared in this imaginal process and her rhythms changed from libidnal to oral sadistic-biting. She growled and snapped and clawed the rug as she struggled to claim the needed differentiation from her. In the next hour her persona charming false self was personified by her telling her to stop expressing anger, that no on would like her, that it's not safe. Feeling that this survival mechanism needed to be externalized so that she could more fully claim her nascent self, I took over role playing it while she embodied her angry self.

Throughout the next few months she continued to embody the growing infant-toddler self. She often would begin the session connecting to the early infant. In one hour she said she imagined an egg that was between us; I then created a nest of pillows around her. She became concerned that the pillows barred access to me. So I moved next to her and extended my arm into the nest like an umbilical chord which I gestured in an oral rhythm in synchrony to her nodding head. In the nest she began to posit the concept of whole parents: "I have hated both my parents and stayed away to separate from them, but I now think that they are neither all good nor all bad."

The next session she employed the oral sadistic (fighting) biting rhythm as she crawled everywhere in the movement space. Embodying this differentiating self she related that she felt more energy, and that she wanted to "rip at the veils that keep me from being more here". She then related this to her mother and became angry once again at her mother's lack of connection. I elected to receive the negative transference and veiling myself in a parachute, I began to role play her mother, "If you become real, I will leave you; or make you go; or make you wrong or bad." Laura responded with more differentiating and assertive tension flow.

With each session she continued to embody the differentiating toddler creeping and crawling while separating and discriminating her thoughts and feelings from her mother's. In one session she repeatedly reached out and grabbed in an oral sadistic (fighting) rhythm. Once again she became contaminated by the negativity of her inner mother. "My mother is surrounding me with her disgust. I shouldn't grab or want or need!" I mirrored her sounds of exclamation while placing the parachute around her to externalize and objectify her experience of her invoked mother surrounding her with disgust. Additionally I placed a pillow between her and me. Laura continued to moan. I caressed the pillow in an oral inner genital rhythm and supported her back while she lay on the floor. As the shamed child she said, "I am yucky; my mother said I was disgusting." "It's a good thing," I responded keeping in the orality of the stage; "because otherwise she would have devoured you." "yeah," she returned; "It was safest to hide." Gradually she removed the parachute and risked being present in the room with me. For several minutes she looked into my eyes and received my good will toward her "a drop at a time" while I reassured her that her needs were not yucky but normal.

## Anality

She began to crawl and roll about the room smearing the rug with anal libidinal (indulging) and anal libidinal (indulging) sadistic (fighting) mixed rhythms. "I can be yucky and you won't push me away." I meanwhile sat some distance away in a vertical body attitude reflecting her transition into the anal phases. In processing I suggested she needed to sort her mother's and father's yuckiness from her own good shit. As the power to have pleasure in one's own bodily products paves the way for creativity.

It was four months from the first sign of anality before she stood. She brought in a powerful dream. "I am at my mother's childhood home. The sky gets dark, ominous. The wind comes. The house collapses. It's snowing and icing. I only have time to grab one thing-my sturdy walking shoes. I leave and fall into the ice flows. I call for help, but a friend of mine (who has gone through a lot of recovery) says, 'You can stand.' And I do." I suggested that she embody the dream. She was able to stand but tried to move into the sagittal prematurely. Her arms were unable to move in a reciprocal manner to her gait. In the next session she again moved to a vertical standing position and this time asserted herself utilizing anal sadistic (fighting) rhythms as she invoked her mother in the room. "I hate you! You couldn't see me. I wasn't allowed to get angry or say you weren't mothering me. You told me I was mean. I felt I couldn't leave you because I would never get your love!" I again maintain a vertical position and imagine her whole with pride. Following this session she arrived wearing a pair of red slacks and exclaimed, "My life has been about standing up."

In the past her former confrontative Mastersonian therapist had been the only powerful voice. She had internalized as her inner judge. This last therapy appeared incomplete as it focused on external boundary formation without the needed early rechoreography and evolving self formation. The split self had never healed into a whole realistic sense of self and other.

### Creativity, Sexuality and Self formation

Subsequently she had several dreams that she was pregnant. Her creativity began to expand at work as she was given new projects. Her sexuality that had been split off in service to gaining her father's and subsequent men of authority's value and approval, began to be reclaimed. In one session she gathered several figures from the sand play shelves and arranged them on the rug. Her libidinal needy self, her boundaried rapprochement self, her ego, and two Aphrodite statutes: one white, one brown. As the white goddess, she addressed her inner psyche's personifications, "I will seduce men and give them what ever they want." As the brown Aphrodite, "All men just want sex; they don't ever see me or want to. So I'll give it to them and have power over them." Her libidinal child self responded to the split off sexuality, "Oh take me with you; maybe I'll be loved too." But the new rapprochement self said to the needy child, "Wait! Just Wait! I am the one to help and protect you, not the sex vamp. She can't take care of you she can't take care of herself."

It was only a matter of time before these split Aphrodites transformed and shifted away from the father complex and joined the adult ego. Additionally the libidinal (indulging) "good self" and the sadistic, (fighting) "angry self" integrated such that she was able to be fully present, vulnerable and protected. She became more and more spiritually connected as well, and her focus gradually shifted away from the past, toward the "bigger picture" and her role in it.

### Summary

Therapists now understand that much of the work in therapy requires an expanded understanding of early child abuse and the resultant survival patterns and addictions.

The Kestenberg Movement Profile provides a rich developmentally-based window into identification of this abuse. In addition, the KMP concepts offer an understanding of key elements which are crucial in the recovery and healing process in the patient/therapist relationship.

## References

Kestenberg, J. (1956). On the development of maternal feelings in early childhood. In *The Psychoanalytic Study of the Child XI*. New York: International Universities Press, pp. 275–291.

Kestenberg, J. and Buelte, A. (1977). Prevention, infant therapy and the treatment of adults, I. Toward understanding mutuality, and II. Mutual holding and holding oneself up. *International Journal of Psychoanalytic Psychotherapy*. 1977: VI: pp. 339–366, 367–396.

Kestenberg, J. and Sossin, M. (1979). *The role of movement patterns in development II*. New York: Dance Notation Bureau.

Lewis Bernstein, P. (1980). The union of the gestalt concept of experiment and Jungian active imagination. *The Gestalt Journal, III*: 2, pp. 36–45.

Lewis Bernstein, P. (1982). Authentic movement as active imagination. In *The compendium of psychotherapeutic techniques*, Harriman, J. ed., Springfield, IL: Charles C. Thomas.

Lewis Bernstein, P. (1985). Embodied transformational images in movement therapy. *Journal of Mental Imagery*, 9/4.

Lewis Bernstein, P. and Singer, (1983). *The choreography of object relations*. Keene: Antioch New England Graduate School.

Lewis, P. (1984). *Theoretical approaches in dance movement therapy*, Vol. II. Dubuque: Kendall Hunt Pub.

Lewis, P. (1986). *Theoretical approaches in dance movement therapy*, Vol. I. Dubuque: Kendall/Hunt Pub.

Lewis, P. (1987). The expressive arts therapies in the choreography of object relations. *The Arts in Psychotherapy Journal*, 1987, Vol. 14.

Lewis, P. (1988). The transformative process in the imaginal realm. *The Arts in Psychotherapy Journal*, 1985, Vol. 15.

Lewis, P. (1990). The Kestenberg Movement Profile in the psychotherapeutic process with borderlines. In P. Lewis and S. Loman (Eds.) *The Kestenberg Movement Profile: Its past, present applications and future directions*. Keene: Antioch New England Graduate School., pp. 65–84.

Lewis, P. (1992). The use of the creative arts in transference/countertransference relationships. *The Arts in Psychotherapy Journal*. Vol. 19.

Lewis, P. (1993a). *Creative transformation: The healing power of the arts*. Wilmette: Chiron Publishing Co.

Lewis, P. (1993b). Kestenberg Movement Profile interpretation: Clinical, cultural and organizational application; In *Following our dreams: dynamics of motivation*. Columbia: American Dance Therapy Association.

Lewis, P. (1994). *The clinical interpretation of the Kestenberg Movement Profile-work in progress*. (Available through Dr. Penny Lewis 978-388-3035)

Mahler, M. (1968). *On human symbiosis and the vicissitudes of individuation*. New York: International Universities Press.

Melody, P. and Miller, A. W. (1989). *Recovery from codependency*, San Francisco: Harper & Row.

Reich, W. (1949). *Character analysis*. New York: Farbar, Straus, and Giroux.

Sossin, M. (1990). Metapsychological considerations of the psychologies incorporated in the KMP system. In Lewis, P. and Loman, S. (Eds.). *The Kestenberg Movement Profile, Its past, present applications and future directions*. Keene: Antioch New England Graduate School.

# CHAPTER 13

# The Interface Between the Kestenberg Movement Profile and Body–Mind Centering

Susan Loman, Amelia Ender and Kim Burden

## Introduction

The focus of this chapter is to present the relevant portions of the BMC which support and enhance understanding of the five phases of development inherent in the KMP: oral, anal, urethral, inner genital and outer genital. The authors consider this paper a work in progress and a beginning step towards developing a more comprehensive study of the similarities and differences between the two systems.

The first three KMP phases are affined with the development of space, weight and time and occur in the horizontal, vertical and sagittal planes, respectively. It was in the first three KMP phases that the most observable BMC patterns were found, offering insight into perceptual-motor and nervous system patterning. In the inner and outer genital phases, organ and endocrine supports of the BMC patterns come into play which involve cross-planal, diagonal and elliptical movement. Since most of our experience has focused on the first three phases, we have chosen to place greater emphasis on them and to present the inner and outer genital phases in a slightly more condensed manner.

## Introduction to Body–Mind Centering (BMC)

We will begin with a brief introduction to Body–Mind Centering for those readers who may not be familiar with it. Bonnie Bainbridge Cohen's background in movement and Occupational therapy led her to a lifetime exploration of how the body moves and how the mind is expressed by the body through movement.

The two primary streams through the extensive Body–Mind Centering body of material are the cognitive and experiential study of the body systems: skeletal, muscular, nervous, endocrine, fluid, organ, ligament and fascia, and human developmental movement, based upon phylogenetic and ontogenetic evolutionary progressions. For the purposes of this chapter, we will focus primarily on the developmental movement system, which examines movement patterns experienced roughly during the first year of life, from in utero through walking. This is an elaborate system which includes primitive reflexes, righting reactions, equilibrium responses and the Basic Neurological Patterns (BNP) (see Figure 15) developed by Bonnie Bainbridge Cohen.

The approach is elaborate and unique because it utilizes and incorporates language and concepts, both conventional and original, to create a unified and multi-dimensional theory of development. Although a traditionally defined reflex may be part of BMC vocabulary, it will be explored in a non-traditional manner, i.e., it is never looked at in isolation. It is considered in relationship to body tissues and systems, to other movement patterns and problems, and within the context of the individual's overall expression and behavior. Bainbridge Cohen feels (1993b) these "automatic movement responses" are not extinguished after their early expressed period. As all volitional movements, they are available to examine and repattern throughout our lives.

Bainbridge Cohen states (1993a) that fundamental to a BMC approach is discovering the "relationship between the smallest level of activity in the body and the largest movement of the body." In doing so, the individual focuses on neurological and perceptual organization occurring during the first year in an attempt to awaken and reawaken early body pathways and relationships which may have been suppressed or repressed for a variety of reasons; these pathways are ancient evolutionary guideposts hardwired into our species,

**Prevertebrate Patterns** include:

> **Cellular breathing** is the internal breathing and movement present in all the cells of the body. It underlies postural tone and all other patterns of movement.

> In **naval radiation,** movement of all parts of the body relate to each other via the naval.

> **Mouthing** is movement initiated by the mouth reaching into space.

> **Pre-spinal movement** is soft sequential movement initiated by the digestive tract and spinal cord and brain.

**Vertebrate Patterns** are based on:

> **Spinal movement** (head to tail).

> **Homologous movement** (the two upper limbs &/or the two lower limbs moving together and symmetrically).

> **Homolateral movement** (movement of the limbs on the same side of the body).

> **Contralateral movement** (movement of the upper limb on one side and the opposite lower limb).

**Figure 15.** Sequence of Basic Neurological Patterns: Prevertebrate and Vertebrate.

which may be "resurrected" with the proper stimulation. In exploring the inherent intelligence and sequencing beneath our movement choices, we are invariably led back to the cellular level of expression. Movement and choice originate with the cell, the smallest unit of "awareness and intelligence" which still embodies our individuality.

…cells move and nerves register and store the pattern of the movement. Once stored in the nervous system, the nervous system can then initiate or control the movement of the cells. The cellular initiation of movement is original experience; the nervous system initiation of movement is controlled experience based on the pathways laid down by past experience (ibid, p. 1).

Bainbridge Cohen (1993a) describes,

…the innate genetic or evolutionary memories that are contained in each cell and in the nervous system. These are potential patterns of movement that when appropriately stimulated become manifested as experience. These potential pathways are passed to each person, as are other human characteristics, through the egg and sperm. While one is born with these potential patterns, one does not experience them until they are stimulated into existence (p. 1).

A propos the above, Bainbridge Cohen feels the developmental territory explored during the first year is crucial in laying the foundation for perceptual-motor activity throughout life. While it is ideal to work with infants with developmental challenges during the first year, as stated, the material is available to work with at any stage of development.

The developmental overlaps between BMC and KMP reveal that movement patterns which occur during the first year of life according to BMC are recapitulated in an increasingly complex and sophisticated manner in the KMP phases from birth through six years. The antecedents and body-based relationships underlying the KMP are visible through Bainbridge Cohen's developmental movement system. The detail and focus with which BMC examines the patterns of the first year of life may provide an important support for the phases of the KMP (see Table 16).

Bainbridge Cohen (1993b), when asked what made her feel that the first year of life is crucial in the perceptual-motor development of the child, answered:

This is when the relation of the perceptual process (the way one perceives) and the motor process (the way one moves or acts in the world) is established. This is the baseline for how you will be processing activity, either in receiving or perceiving, throughout your life. The importance of working with babies during the first year is that I feel it sets up a broader baseline, offering more choices in not only how to see events or problems, but how to act on them; it gives them the most multiplicity of direction (p. 99).

The remainder of this chapter will take each KMP phase in turn and relate it to supporting BMC patterns and reflexes. The following information will be included in each phase: developmental task, plane, region of body, body attitude, drive, object constancy, BMC patterns and BMC reflexes. The developmental tasks of each phase are particularly pertinent to this discussion since both systems emphasize the importance of the perceptual-motor development of the child.

## Oral Phase

Kestenberg (1975) describes the task of the oral phase as the establishment of a primary system of communication, the focus being on the infants' needs for nourishment, bonding, and then separation in the second (biting) portion of the phase. During this phase, infants are establishing themselves in space, relating to the mother or primary caregiver primarily

**Table 16** Developmental Sequencing.

| BMC Pattern | Plane | KMP Phase |
| --- | --- | --- |
| Cellular Breathing | | |
| Navel Radiation | | |
| Mouthing | Horizontal | Oral sucking and snapping |
| Prespinal | Horizontal | Oral sucking and anal twisting |
| Spinal Yield and Push (Head) | All planes | |
| Spinal Yield and Push (Tail) | All planes | |
| Spinal Reach/Pull (Head) | All planes | |
| Spinal Reach/Pull (Tail) | All planes | |
| Homologous Yield and Push Upper Extremity | Vertical/Sagittal | Anal strain/release |
| Homologous Yield and Push Lower Extremity | Vertical/Sagittal | Anal strain/release |
| Homologous Reach and Pull Upper Extremity | Vertical/Sagittal | Anal strain/release |
| Homologous Reach and Pull Lower Extremity | Vertical/Sagittal | Anal strain/release |
| Homolateral Yield and Push Upper Extremity | Vertical | Anal strain/release |
| Homolateral Yield and Push Lower Extremity | Vertical/Sagittal | Anal strain/release |
| Contralateral Reach and Pull Upper Extremity | Sagittal/Cross planal | Anal twisting, Urethral running/drifting and starting/stopping |
| Contralateral Reach and Pull Lower Extremity | Sagittal/Cross planal | Anal twisting, Urethral running/drifting and starting/stopping |
| | Diagonal/Cross planal | Inner genital swaying and surging/birthing |
| | Diagonal/Cross planal | Outer genital jumping and spurting/ramming |

through the act of feeding. The mouth is of supreme importance and the horizontal plane is the plane in which feeding takes place. The child here is developing constancy in space through regular, close contact with the caregiver. The body is horizontally aligned and the oral body ego is "functionally prehensile" (Kestenberg, 1975), with subsequent movements evolving around attention and exploring such as: scanning, comprehending, and communicating. Infants shape toward the mother in the horizontal plane during feeding. The interplay of "growing and shrinking, of reaching and scooping, scattering and gathering" (p. 201) form the basis of the care giver/infant relationship.

Similarly, BMC regards the horizontal plane as the plane of attention, receptivity, searching and communication (Bainbridge Cohen, 1990). It is in the horizontal plane that we gain the ability to attend both to our own internal sensations and to external stimuli; we gain the flexibility to make transitions between singular focus and multi-focus. The reflexes and developmental activities of early infancy revolve around turning towards and away from mother, and are initially primarily motivated by oral sensation. Bonding is engendered by nursing, sucking–swallowing and rooting reflexes. These oral activities, as well as the smell, feel, and taste of the mother while the child is nursing promote pleasurable sensation throughout the digestive tube and organ system, and enhance the development of the parasympathetic nervous system. The parasympathetic nervous system is that part of the nervous system that directs attention inward and blood flow to organs to facilitate digestive and organic processes.

During the first three months of life, the infant's focus ideally, is primarily parasympathetic, i.e., turning inward, inner focus, attention to nourishment and the oral cavity. This encourages subsequent interest in the environment and development of the sympathetic nervous system (that part of the nervous system that directs the tension outward and blood flow to the muscles and bones to facilitate acting in the world). Early parasympathetic expression supports organic transitions, motivated by interest, curiosity and desire, between inner and outer focus. The mouth (supported by the nose) is the first extremity to reach out, grasp, accept, reject, explore space and organize sensory information; this activity of the mouth will be generalized to the eyes and hands, thereby expanding the infant's capacity to communicate, relate and explore. There is a clear parallel here with the KMP in that both systems are acknowledging the oral zone, as crucial in establishing the baseline for communication and relationship.

This continuum from parasympathetic focus to sympathetic focus occurs as the hands and eyes move from exploring the mother's breast and face to exploring the larger world, and back again. It continues as the infant is able to venture further away from the mother/caregiver and returns for nursing, snuggling and/or reassurance. This theme provides a baseline for transitions between inner and outer focus throughout one's life.

### Basic Neurological Patterns

The two earliest Basic Neurological Patterns (BNP)s (Cellular Breathing and Naval Radiation) are central to all subsequent organization, and correlate with the movements of simple contraction and expansion, or shape flow in the KMP. These very early patterns, which globally encourage flow of breath and fluids throughout the body, tend to enhance the later experience of localizing sensation and organization of movement.

Cellular Breathing is the basic pattern of one-celled animals, ovum and sperm, and each cell within us. Cellular Breathing establishes internal respiration (like bipolar shape flow), the intake and excretion of oxygen and carbon dioxide and other nutrients between the cell and its surroundings, providing the cell with a self-regulating mechanism for survival. Individual cells organize into specialized groups (tissues) which in turn form larger systems (organs). It is at the cellular level that relationship with self and other is established.

Navel Radiation is the pattern of "radial symmetry with the center of control in the middle of the body" (Bainbridge Cohen, 1990, p. 8). All limbs are connected to the navel center and have equal importance in movement and perception. It is through navel radiation that the infant differentiates between body parts as in unipolar shape flow, and it is through the equal connection of all limbs to the navel that each limb is able to "know" the other limbs. It is a very important pattern, for "If any of the extremities fail to integrate at this stage, Mouthing and the future vertebrate patterns will be weakened or absent." (p. 9)

The horizontal plane is established through rolling, turning, and rotating around a central, vertical axis. Initially this axis is soft and flexible, reaching from mouth to anus through the digestive tube, as well as from head to tail through the soft tissue of the Central Nervous System. The next two Basic Neurological Patterns which we explore to experience this sensation are Mouthing and Prespinal. Mouthing develops in utero, is the pattern of the nursing newborn, and is central to facilitating movement of the head and whole body of the fetus and newborn. As stated, the mouth functions as the first extremity to explore the environment and underlies patterns of development of all the other limbs. Perceptions and sensation of the mouth and nose precede those of the other special senses of the head; they pattern our perceptual process and continue to play an important supportive function in perception and movement of the head. "One can observe this underlying, supportive motor planning of the mouth in movements of the tongue and mouths of young children and the verbalization of adults when they are engaged in learning new tasks." (Bainbridge Cohen, 1993c, p. 16).

As we explore sensation and initiation of movement from the mouth and nose, we find the impulses generated travel through the digestive tube to the anus and produce the soft, squirming movements characteristic of the Prespinal Pattern. This is the pattern of the squirming newborn and is initiated from the soft tissue of the digestive system as well as the soft tissue of the Central Nervous System. "This organic, serpentine movement appears as a continuation of the infant's control of the mouth as it develops skill in nursing. Adults manifest the Prespinal Pattern in the softness and flexibility of their bodies ... . This "soft spinal" ... pattern underlies and establishes a base of sequential mobility for the later development of the "hard spine" movements initiated in the bony vertebral column ... (Bainbridge Cohen, 1993c, p. 23). The focus is soft, organic, internally directed and the rhythm of the movement similar to the KMP sucking rhythm. This pattern is also significant in facilitating the twisting rhythm of the anal indulging stage.

As our bony vertebral column solidifies, the soft, digestive and Central Nervous System axis assumes more supportive roles and we move into the Spinal Patterns. The strong central axis between our head and tail allows us to begin to lever our bones in opposition to gravity, experience our own body boundaries and extend further into the world. As we become structurally more capable of controlling our movements, our perceptual and relational world grows; conversely, our growing interest supports our structural integrity.

Spinal Patterns are evidenced in the "fetus developing the strength required for birthing and the newborn infant beginning to overcome the force of gravity." (Bainbridge Cohen, 1993c, p. 30). Sequential movement of the spine initiated at the head and/or tail "develops the strength of centrally initiated movement." (p. 32). It begins to define the parameters of one's personal kinesphere and provides a base for all other vertebrate patterns. The vertical axis is established at this time, as is the horizontal plane through rotation around the axis.

## BMC Reflexes

At this point we would like to focus on Bainbridge Cohen's unique and innovative approach to understanding the significance of reflexes, righting reactions and equilibrium responses. Bainbridge Cohen states,

I became frustrated and dissatisfied with the traditional approach which views these patterns as static, isolated reaction ... . I am utilizing the traditional approach where I can, but I want to come upon it in a different way: to thread the patterns together, to rename some so their names better express their movement, to fill in the gaps with new reflexes, to show how each pattern leads into the next, how each reflex has an opposite reflex for mutual modulation, and how the earlier patterns are present in the later ones. ... Underneath all successful, effortless movement are integrated reflexes, righting reactions and equilibrium responses. (1993b, p. 122).

She continues:

Reflexes create the pathways that allow the Mind to express itself in movement. They establish basic gross patterns of function that utilize and underlie all movements. They are the alphabet of movement and combine together to create more varied patterns of movement (p. 124).

A comprehensive or in depth discussion of the Reflexes, Righting Reactions and Equilibrium Responses is beyond the scope of the chapter, nor were they the primary focus of our course experience. However, it was inevitable that they come into the classroom, since BMC looks at these reflexive components as building blocks of developmental movement. Several were presented to the students to facilitate teaching the patterns. They are early and primary pathways that underlie our basic body attitudes and relational choices with respect to self, other, gravity and space. For example, the Tonic Labyrinthine Reflex, named for the balance function of the labyrinths of the inner ear, draws the infant towards the ground, while the Head Righting Reactions, utilizing receptors which are located in the neck, enables the infant to lift away from gravity.

In observing movement using the KMP, for instance during the second year of life, we may notice some children's tendency to be drawn towards the ground (straining rhythm and shortening), while others seem to "bounce" away from the earth (lightness and lengthening). Children who appear to be drawn to the ground would be expressing an affinity with the Tonic Lab Reflex; children who rise away from the earth would be more affined with Head Righting. Although there are many ways to describe this phenomenon from a BMC standpoint, one useful avenue to explore is reflexive vocabulary with regard to Tonic Lab and Head Righting. This would give us information about why they are making their choices, and would provide a repatterning tool, if necessary, to help them find balance between "gravity" and "space." Where children or adults are on this continuum, will influence all subsequent movement choices and is therefore important to bring into an understanding of movement constellations and preferences.

Following are some reflexes we explore to support the themes of the oral phase. The Tonic Labyrinthine Reflex (or "Tonic Lab") is one of the first to develop and underlies bonding with Earth, drawing us toward gravity by "increasing postural tone (a sense of aliveness ...) of the muscles on the underside of the body" (p. 127). Tonic Lab supports the ability to bond and establishes the horizontal plane in low space, which allows one to then establish the vertical plane as an outgrowth. In other words, infants first establish their internal horizontal sense through rolling in relation to gravity, and then are able to rise up from this relationship with gravity in order to establish themselves vertically.

Several reflexes support the ability to explore this rolling in the horizontal plane. The Oral Rooting Reflex, which is initially stimulated by touch on the cheek or lips, allows the infant to search and reach for its mothers nipple, and underlies oral tracking, tracking of the special senses of the head, and development of the tongue, which is needed for eating and speaking. The Sucking–Swallowing Reflex is an early reflex closely related to oral rooting which is stimulated by receptors on the lips and mouth. It involves the rhythmic taking hold and releasing that characterizes the nursing rhythm. It is this reflex that may match the KMP oral sucking rhythm the most closely with its particular pattern of flow changes.

Head Righting Reactions "are automatic reactions which bring the head and torso into mutual alignment to each other and into vertical orientation in space in relation to gravity" (Bainbridge Cohen, 1990, p. 99). They facilitate "identification with the upward anti-gravitational force. As the head guides the movement of the rest of the body, this reaction underlies our ability to lift our head, rise to vertical and move away from the Earth" (Bainbridge Cohen, 1993b, p. 127). They begin at birth, modulate development throughout the first year, and remain active throughout our lives. These mid brain reactions support the transition from horizontal to vertical and from the centrally initiated movement of the spinal patterns to the peripherally initiated movements of the homologous patterns.

## The Anal Phase

The anal phase, occurring at the end of the first year and into the second year of life, is concerned with the developmental task of self presentation occurring most visibly when children can stabilize themselves and confront the world by pulling or pushing themselves up into a vertical stance. The transition before becoming vertical involves being able to locomote on all fours and master anal twisting rhythms at the waist and in the pelvis while crawling. Earlier locomotion was accomplished when twisting rhythms were used in turning and rolling over. Anal twisting rhythms are subtle, smooth adjustments in tension flow used to change body positions and to use fine motor skills such as picking up small objects with pincer movement. These indulging rhythms can also be seen in playful snuggling and in squirming.

As the child matures, anal straining rhythms of evenly held high intensity of tension emerge which assist children's interest in pulling and/or pushing themselves into a standing position. The vertical plane is the plane of confrontation, and the child is concerned with establishing object constancy in regard to weight. Children are clearly able to show what they want. Their bodies begin to become solid units of resistance as they become internally strong, able to control their bowels, and externally strong, able to pull up to standing and lift heavy objects. As the child "holds himself up and he holds what is inside of him... aligned in the vertical plane, he becomes part of the adult world .... A harmonious mother–child couple develops a system of stabilizing–releasing (mobilizing)..." (Kestenberg, 1975, p. 205). At this point, children begin to establish their beings, saying "I am here" and are able to determine what they want—the development of clear intentionality.

### Basic Neurological Patterns

The antecedents and foundations for the anal phase, as well as for the characteristics of the vertical plane, are expressed well before the child's second birthday. Kestenberg and Bainbridge Cohen agree that these somatic expressions in the vertical plane include "determination, intention, stability and presentation." In BMC, both the Homologous and Homolateral BNPs establish the development of the vertical plane. The infant of around three to five months, lying prone and pushing up onto its forearms, is demonstrating the Homologous Push Pattern. This is a symmetrical pattern involving simultaneous movement of both arms or both legs together. One is struck by the effort and intensity involved in the transition from predominantly spinal movement to bearing weight in the limbs to lift away from the earth. This pattern, pushing first from the hands and forearms and then from the feet, enhances the stable, straining aspects of the anal phase. Many of the themes that characterize the anal phase are seen at this time: the power of the push and the effort involved in opposing gravity; the increase in strength and harnessing of intention to control one's body weight and gain access to a greater perceptual and functional range; the determination to move towards a desired goal, and concomitant use of the lower part of the body to facilitate locomotion (although minimal at this time).

In *Physical Therapy for Children*, Campbell (1994) articulates a key developmental principle characteristic of both BMC and KMP. Growth is viewed "not as a linear process but a spiral one where structure and function jointly mature leading to regression, asymmetries and reorganization." (p. 16). The spiraling and overlapping nature of the progression of the BNP is evidenced in the transition from centrally initiated movement to peripherally initiated movement; we see the earlier patterns, Naval Radiation, Mouthing, Prespinal and Spinal, enlisted in support of the Homologous and Homolateral Push Patterns. We would particularly like to focus on the area around the coccyx/anus which is predominant in both the Prespinal and Spinal Patterns, and provides crucial support for the anal and urethral KMP rhythms.

While bones of the vertebral column are adding more density and Head Righting is enabling movement away from gravity, the underlying Prespinal Pattern (discussed above) continues to provide support for the bony spine and brings attention to the end of the digestive tube and the end of the spinal cord. Heightened sensation and curiosity in the lower part of the body facilitates activation of the pelvic floor, thereby helping infants to find their feet and connection to the ground.[1] BMC refers to the area around the coccyx, where the end of the cauda equina of the spinal cord and the end of the digestive tube meet as the tail. Because the infant (and adult) demonstrates increased perceptivity and sensation around this cluster of sensitive tissue, we often speak of a "tail brain" that reaches and searches.

The ability to actively engage the tail is crucial for support, locomotion and propulsion, as well as the ability to come to vertical and assert oneself. It is interesting to note the key role that the "soft spine," composed of both digestive and nervous system tissue, assumes as communicator and modulator for the musculo-skeletal system. The flexibility, fluidity and delicate sensitivity of the soft spine and particularly the tail, is called upon for all weight shifts, level changes, transitions and overall articulation through the lower body. In watching children's mobility we see that the foundations built in the anal twisting phase carry through to other mobilizing phases such as the running and starting/stopping phases.

The Homolateral Pattern and related reflexes are also significant in establishing the vertical plane. "This is the pattern of reptiles and of the human infant crawling on its belly. It differentiates the right side of the body from the left side and establishes shifts of weight asymmetrically through the limbs in the vertical plane through patterns of lateral flexion and abduction and adduction" (Bainbridge Cohen, 1993c, p. 58). The lateral movement in combination with spinal attention, allows the infant to be attentive in all directions, greatly expanding their perceptual choices, and more mobile, enhancing their possibilities of reaching what they want. The Homolateral Push from the lower is a propulsive movement providing the infant with its first experience of covering distance through space. This is a transitional pattern between the anal and urethral phases, between the Homologous and Contralateral Patterns. The Homolateral Pattern "... is the foundation for how we reach out towards our goals—objects, people, ideas—uniting our attention with the force of intention." (Bainbridge Cohen, 1993b, p. 149). We see again the influence of the earlier patterns, i.e., the desire, interest and curiosity initiated at the oral cavity, and the locomotive and propulsive interest generated at the tail. This will lead us to the sagittal plane and mastery of locomotion, characteristic of the Contralateral Pattern in the quadruped position, and characteristic of the urethral phase in the upright position.

### BMC Reflexes

The Asymmetrical Tonic Neck Reflex (ATNR) and Hand-to-Mouth Reflex, which underlie the crawling of the Homolateral Pattern, are further examples of Bainbridge Cohen's approach to reflexes. The ATNR is defined as follows:

... when the infant is lying prone or supine and the head is turned to the side, there is an increase in extensor tone in the arm and leg on the face side, and an increase in flexor tone in the arm and leg on the skill side ... (p. 86).

Bainbridge Cohen, (1993b) defines the Hand-to-Mouth Reflex below:

The opposite response takes place in the Hand-to-Mouth Reflex—the arm and leg on the face side flex, the arm and leg on the skill side extend, and the neck flexes forward (p. 149).

The ATNR, which underlies eye-hand coordination and reaching (Bainbridge Cohen, 1993b), directs attention out to the environment; the Hand-to-Mouth (named by Bainbridge Cohen), which underlies mouth-hand coordination and gathering, directs attention back to oneself. We observe that these reflexes are on a continuum in which they modulate each other. Once again we explore the relationship between the two and the implications of an individual's preference along this continuum.

The Spinal Lateral Curve, the Gallant, Abdominal Reflex, and Neck Mobility Reflex involve lateral movements and differentiate between right and left halves of the body. They are stimulated by tactile receptors in the stimulated area. For example, when the infant is prone (on its belly) and is stimulated on its back on either side of the navel under the ribs, the infant will laterally flex its lumbar spine on the stimulated side (Gallant Reflex). The Abdominal Reflex is similar, except that it occurs when the infant is supine (on its back) and is stimulated on its belly. The Neck Mobility Reflex occurs in response to stimulation of the neck and results in lateral movement of the neck toward the stimulated side. It should be noted that these reflexes become integrated quite early in development and occur without outside stimulation by around two months of age. They stimulate lateral mobility along the length of the spine, which allows for freedom of homolateral movement and differentiation between body halves. This greater sense of differentiation and the strength and stability of the Homologous Pattern allow children to approach the anal phase of "Here I am" and to begin to establish a sense of self in the world.

### The Urethral Phase

In the urethral phase, the developmental task is to establish object constancy in time and increase the capacity for operation. Children can now sequence actions, make choices, anticipate, and say "when." The predominant plane is sagittal and the body attitude is fluid, agile, and elastic. Children are in constant motion, "bubbling over with fluids" (Kestenberg, 1975, p. 208), as they gain control over bladder, kidney, and urethral functions.

### Basic Neurological Patterns

Here the BMC patterns of Contralateral creeping and all the previous patterns support the urethral phase, although the BMC patterns are already in place and the child is no longer actively engaged in creeping on hands and knees. The patterns have become integrated and are able to support locomotion forward into the world. To move out in the sagittal plane, gain control of changes in flow (urination and stopping and starting), and to gain more awareness and concept of time, the BNPs and their associated reflexes need to be assimilated in the child's movement vocabulary. Spinal Patterns establish a central core and vertical axis necessary for movement in the horizontal plane and for opposing gravity in the vertical plane. Homologous Patterns differentiate the upper and lower parts of the body and provide strength and weight-bearing skills needed for stopping and starting. Homolateral Push Patterns establish strength and articulation in the vertical plane required for steady upright movement, and for reaching out for the objects that the child "intends" to reach.

Contralateral creeping is "classic crawling" in which children are able to move rapidly and skillfully on all fours. Integrated walking is also contralateral movement. While primarily sagittal in orientation, the Contralateral Pattern integrates the three planes, initiates spirallic movement and facilitates smooth transitions and level changes. This pattern moves infants into a higher brain level and integrates the halves of the brain as well as emphasizing diagonal relationships in the body and crossing of the midline. Consequently, it promotes the ability to assimilate more complex ideas including the concept of time sequence and predictability. Perceptions and the special senses of the head are engaged in increasingly sophisticated ways, enhancing infants' abilities to identify and pursue their desires.

### BMC Reflexes

Underlying contralateral movement and the sagittal plane in general are: the Tonic Lumbar and Lumbar Reach Reflexes. The Tonic Lumbar and Lumbar Reach Reflexes are based upon the relationship of the pelvis and thorax and are complimentary patterns. The Tonic Lumbar Reflex underlies "rolling from supine to hands and knees and contralateral movements of the limbs" (1990, p. 93), while Lumbar Reach underlies "rolling from prone to supine when initiated from rotation of the chest and contralateral movements of the limbs" (p. 95). Both reflexes are very clearly seen in patterns of throwing and hitting in sports and involve the response of the pelvis to changes in position of the thorax and of the thorax in relation to the pelvis. It is interesting to note that the above reflexes emphasize rotation at the waist (supporting movement in the sagittal plane), while the ATNR and Hand-to-Mouth Reflexes emphasize the relationship of the head to the thorax at the neck (supporting movement in the vertical plane). Tonic Lumbar and Lumbar Reach Reflexes facilitate the ability to move out of a given position into sagittal locomotion or action and are vital for coordinated contralateral bipedal movement. If these reflexes are not fully experienced or integrated, children may be frustrated in their efforts to explore space freely.

Because the nervous system is the system that receives and relays information to the rest of the body and establishes the "perceptual base from which we view and interact with our internal and external worlds" (Bainbridge Cohen, 1993b, p. 3), the progression through the

BNPs is essential in order to access the widest possible range of choices. It is important to once again remind the reader that these patterns, as well as the primitive reflexes, the righting reactions, and most of the equilibrium responses are in place by approximately the end of the first year of life. This has meaning for us as we look at how BMC can support the subsequent phases of the KMP.

## Inner Genital and Outer Genital Phases

In addition to looking at the BNPs and reflexes, the authors are also beginning to examine the expression of various body systems in the KMP. Preliminary experiential data suggests that the inner genital phase reveals itself in more internal, organic shapes and movements while the outer genital movements are ballistic and explosive and parallel the "sudden burst" actions of the endocrine glands. BMC research indicates that specific endocrine glands, organs and fluids act to support each BNP, and these systems determine the dynamic qualities of the patterns; similarly a body systems exploration of all the KMP patterns may prove interesting in further understanding connections between KMP and BMC.

Kestenberg describes the task of the inner genital phase as a time for the child to "combine what he has learned and practiced into complex behavioral entities and phrases" (1975, p. 248). This is a time for integration, development of multidimensional characteristics, both physically and psychologically, and divergent body attitudes. It coincides with the development of the inner genitalia and is a time of confusion, questioning (the "why?" stage), and periods of regression to earlier, more "babyish" behaviors. This confusion and "nagging" is due to the feeling of fullness inside that does not result in a "product" as did the fullness of the earlier anal and urethral phases (Kestenberg, 1980). Such feelings of fullness are characteristic of the movements of the organs, which have proprioceptive qualities. The organs may be sensed and felt even though we may not be fully aware of their processes.

The outer genital phase occurring between the age of four and six years, is an incredibly energetic phase. It manifests in ballistic, jumping rhythms, externalized expression, and heightened intensity of drive (Kestenberg and Kestenberg Amighi, 1991). The power of the child's body posture, now a unified working system with limbs acting as an extension of the trunk, gives the child the strength and intention to propel into space, delighting in jumping games and seemingly rough, unbridled energy (Kestenberg, 1975). Such intense, bursting movements are characteristic of endocrine-quality movements, which involve external expression and chemical balance and communication through the body.

Having covered the phases and the respective BMC supporting patterns, it is clear that we are barely beginning to scratch the surface of the interface between the two systems. KMP and BMC are both vast studies full of information about the human form and psyche. We hope this preliminary comparison of these two systems is just the beginning of future fruitful dialogues about the human developmental process.

## Notes

1. In the very young infant lying on its back, we see the rolling and rocking motions initiated at the pelvic floor and anus extend into kicking motions of the legs. In the infant learning to sit, the reach of the tail initiates lowering to the ground from a quadruped position, and push from the tail precipitates rising. This is seen again when

children are starting to rise to vertical, raising and lowering their weight in standing and squatting.

## References

Bainbridge Cohen, B. (1990). *The Evolutionary origins of movement.* Amherst, MA: The School for Body-Mind Centering™.

Bainbridge Cohen, B. (1993a). *Cellular and nervous system learning and control.* Unpublished class notes.

Bainbridge Cohen, B. (1993b). *Sensing, feeling, and action: The experiential anatomy of Body Mind Centering.* Northampton, MA: Contact Editions.

Bainbridge Cohen, B. (1993c). *The Evolutionary origins of movement (Updated version).* Amherst, MA: The School for Body-Mind Centering™.

Campbell, S. (Ed.) (1994). *Physical therapy for children.* Philadelphia: W. B. Saunders Company.

Eddy, M. (1992). Body mind dancing. In S. Loman and R. Brandt (Eds.), *The body mind connection in human movement analysis.* Keene, NH.: Antioch New England Graduate School.

Kestenberg, J. S. (1975). *Children and parents: Psychoanalytic studies in development.* New York: Jason Aronson.

Kestenberg, J. S. (1980). The inner-genital phase—pre phallic and pre oedipal. In D. Mendel (Ed.), *Early feminine development: Contemporary psychoanalytic views.* New York: Spectrum Publications.

Kestenberg, J. S. and Kestenberg Amighi, J. (1991). *Kinder Zeigen, was sie bruchen: Wie eltern kindliche signale richtig deuten.* Salzburg, Austria: Verlag Anton Pustet.

Loman, S., Ender, A. and Burden, K. (1994, April). The interface between the Kestenberg Movement Profile and Body Mind Centering. Presentation at the Fourth Kestenberg Movement Profile Conference. Antioch New England Graduate School. Keene, NH.

# SECTION III

CHAPTER 14

# Interpretation of an Adult Profile: Observations in a Parent-Child Setting

K. Mark Sossin

## Introduction

In this chapter the reader is taken through the process of KMP interpretation using the case of an adult woman named Bess. In this KMP analysis, the author illustrates how to apply psychodynamic theory as a framework for assessment. The reader may note that diagraming and diagram interpretation are summarized in the Appendix.

Before the case of Bess is presented, the chapter begins with the KMP's origins and historical relationship with psychodynamic and developmental principles. The KMP as a nonverbal tool is compared with other classical developmental systems of appraisal. The chapter goes on to explain the inferential nature of the KMP and how it compares with the Rorschach test in its evolution as a psychodynamic diagnostic assessment tool. The final section of the chapter provides a detailed KMP interpretation of Bess in keeping with a psychodynamic framework.

## The KMP as a Key to the Nonverbal in Appraisal

The Kestenberg Movement Profile, as developed and elaborated over the last 30 years, is a diagnostic tool, focusing on nonverbal aspects of behavior, and applicable across the developmental spectrum. What results is a sophisticated instrument which can be used for assessment. It provides information about an individual's intra- and inter-systemic functioning, and about inner harmonies and conflicts. In addition, the KMP enables us to speak in operationalized and relative terms about the nature of attunement and adjustment in dyads. To date, the diagnostic application of the KMP has been extended by those of us who have applied the KMP in clinical as well as primary prevention settings, pertaining to infants, children and adults.

In the author's opinion, there is a disparity between the significant utility of the KMP in appraisal and intervention planning and its relatively uncommon use in clinical settings. This discrepancy may be a function of a number of factors, including the KMP's current complexity—to learn and to apply—and the lack of more broad-based developmental and clinical research aimed at the establishment of greater normative data, and toward the establishment of further support for an agreed-upon interpretive schema.

Several different theoretical models are compatible with the observational system encoded in the KMP methodology (Sossin, 1990), and, hence, different strategies for interpretation have evolved, and many more might be imagined. The meanings of movement patterns and of profile interpretation have been previously described (Kestenberg, 1965, 1967, 1985; Kestenberg and Sossin, 1979; Sossin and Loman, 1992; Loman, 1990, 1995; Loman and Merman, 1996), and these have been linked with applications in diagnosis, prevention, and varied therapeutic modalities. In general, these interpretive approaches have been framed in terms of diagnostic/developmental assessments, and they have emphasized the relationship between specific patterns of movement and conceptually correlated psychic functions. These ideas correspond in considerable measure with the information outlined in the preceding chapters.

Movement patterns are understood to develop in an epigenetic sequence. KMP analysis of the individual assesses the movement repertoire in terms of indications of psychic harmony and conflict along with the resources for conflict resolution. Interpersonal applications of the KMP have largely pertained to dyadic parent–child patterns, utilizing the profile to study areas of mutual influence, harmony, and clashing.

Kestenberg's finding of correspondence between KMPs and clinical Diagnostic Developmental Profiles (A. Freud, 1965) of children treated at the Hampstead Clinic laid a foundation for substantiation of the psychoanalytic and developmental interpretive scheme that has historically been most closely associated with the KMP (cf. Kestenberg, 1975; Kestenberg and Sossin, 1979). Anna Freud had contributed a model for the "comprehensive metapsychological profile of the child, i.e. a picture which contains dynamic, genetic, economic, structural and adaptive data" (A. Freud, 1965, p. 139). Kestenberg (1975, 1985) paralleled this model in addressing development in terms of drives, phase developmental dominance, libido distribution, defenses employed, ego development, superego formation, and the level and quality of object relationships. Early KMP researchers found clinical evidence demonstrating that some aspects of aggression could be discovered by noting the distribution between indulging and fighting/aggressive System I patterns. Adaptive ego development, reflected in part by effort gestures could be compared to superego development, as reflected in postures. The nature of the individual's defensive organization could also be examined, as reflected in the precursors of effort (defenses against drives) or shaping in directions (defenses against objects). Developmental regressions and/or fixations could be identified, and study of harmonies and clashes could elucidate important details about the nature of conflict experienced. Hence, the KMP was deemed able to offer a complex picture of an individual, pertinent to a dynamic diagnosis.

Theoretical developments in both psychoanalysis and KMP evolution have created shifts in language and emphasis. Moreover, a reliance on direct observation for appraisal of infants and preverbal children, along with a nonverbal avenue of understanding, has led the KMP well beyond theoretically constructed views of development or psychodynamics. Kestenberg (1985) herself, used movement observation to base reformulations of psychosexual phase theory, leading to new developmental insights. This focus on observation as a method, and movement patterns as the focus of such observation, has meant that the KMP is not wedded to any one theoretical school of thought (Sossin, 1990). Further case-study and anecdotal confirmation of the KMP's utility as an assessment tool has accumulated over the years, but exacting correlative studies of the KMP and established psychological tests, and alternatively derived diagnoses, have yet to be completed (cf. Kestenberg and Sossin, 1994). Such studies are necessary, alongside the establishment of statistical norms, to confirm the interpretive validity of the KMP.

Psychodiagnostic concerns should lead to the development of coherent and careful methods of applying interpretive strategies to the KMP. My regard for Kestenberg's work reflects my view that it offers a rich and developmentally intelligible way of interpreting the nonverbal. Mahler, 1971 described Kestenberg's notational system as a "new key." Mahler went on:

It will probably take time for work of the kind the author has done to be adequately understood, learned, appreciated and finally integrated. But I am convinced that the day will come when [Kestenberg's] "new key" will be adopted, her alphabet and grammar will be learned and will be more generally appreciated and utilized" (pp. 213).

As has been reviewed, the KMP framework took shape as an observational and cataloging tool as an extension of Laban's (1960; Bartenieff and Lewis, 1980) systematic approach to movement. Interpretively, the KMP has psychodynamic roots in Freud, several psychoanalytic developmental theorists, and clearly draws upon the work of Schilder (1935; Kestenberg, 1985). Its origins lay in the need for analysts to appraise the infant and preverbal child from an analytic perspective, yet is particularly notable in that it stands as an interpretive tool across the age spectrum. What distinguishes the KMP body of work is the fact that the movement patterns described are part of a coherent system of movement analysis anchored in neurodevelopmental and somatopsychic functioning.

In many ways, the KMP is comparable to the Diagnostic Developmental Profile (A. Freud, 1965) in the spheres of psychic and object-relational processes it classifies. Although we posit different frequency levels at different ages, most elementary movement qualities are available from early infancy. This fact leads to another important aspect of the profile: the ability to compare profiles of parent and child. Hence, representing co-action, or at least the idea of matching/mismatching repertoires, was built in from the start. However, in the KMP assessment of child and parent, the same scale can be applied to each partner in the dyad, unlike an A. Freud Developmental Profile, or even Ernst Freud's Baby Profile (W. E. Freud, 1971).

It is recognized that infants have many competencies in interactive and state regulation (Brazelton, 1992). The KMP highlights two such modes of regulation: the ability of the child to modulate her own tension level, and the ability of the child to adjust her body in shape. Both of these modes of regulation follow along developmental lines, elaborated into specific nonverbal behaviors. Analogous to how we see the inner-psychic-world phenomena of child and adult patients (in terms of needs, wishes, self- and object-relations) that are revealed to us in their words, the KMP work suggests (as did Schilder, 1951) that elements of these inner feelings and experiences are encoded in the body attitude and movement processes.

## The Inferential Nature of KMP Analysis

KMP analysis is always inferential, i.e., it remains a step removed from an analysis of process data. For instance, if an individual demonstrates a high degree of the effort strength and a similarly high degree of the shaping pattern descending, we may infer that the individual provides the matched structure for the dynamic effort. However, we truly don't know if weight efforts are accompanied by vertical shaping patterns unless we look at the actions moment to moment.

The KMP represents frequency data laid out in a manner that readily represents, in graphic form, relative frequencies in meaningful clusters and across defined continua. We are not assured, in such analysis, that the individual actually used the matching patterns, or mismatching patterns for that matter, together. In the case of two individuals, such as a mother and baby, we may find comparable repertoires, leading us to infer the indicated degree of harmony of patterns, but, again, we cannot say for sure whether the individuals shared those patterns within a temporal frame. Though profilers tend to assume that the temporal features are properly reflected in the data, the more exacting probabilities (of deducing process from KMP frequencies) have yet to be determined satisfactorily by research.

In this fashion, the KMP is analogous to the Rorschach test (Exner, 1993), which pertains to perceptual processes; in the use of both measures, significant interpretive value lies in the summary of frequencies, ratios, and applied equations. In the case of the KMP, the current interpretations of such summary numeric details are anchored in the clinical impressions formed from several KMP profilers across several hundred profiles, and is anchored in the developmental theory detailed by Kestenberg (e.g., 1975) and colleagues in numerous writings.

### The Need for Further Validity Studies

We still need normative data (for age, gender, diagnosis, etc.) in order to answer basic questions such as: how much unipolar shortening is expected in a two-year-old boy?; or, what is the mean (and associated standard deviation) for the effort load factor in a thirty-year-old man? Answers to such questions have yet to be published. Normative data is being compiled, and will hopefully be available to assist KMP profilers. Hopefully, such data will also emerge for dyads, such as parents and children at different stages and ages of development. At this time, the "normal limits" of harmonizing, clashing, matching, and mismatching patterns between partners remains impressionistic, understandably giving rise to misgivings by other researchers and clinicians, and making it more difficult for novice notators to apply because they lack the normative sense developed by more experienced evaluators (who, no doubt, would also benefit from these referenced norms).

A basic premise of the KMP is that movement patterns, as operationalized within this system, are direct reflections of states, feelings, impulses, dispositions, masteries, and conflicts. More research is needed to further substantiate these postulates, though a body of literature exploring the psychological meaning of movement as cataloged utilizing Laban-derived systems has grown substantially (cf. Bartenieff and Lewis, 1980; Davis, 1985; Lamb and Watson, 1987; Kestenberg, 1980; Winter, 1992). In an initial investigation of reliability, Sossin (1987) found support for inter-rater reliability. However, further reliability studies are recommended to explore reliability across rater, subject and movement patterns. Another KMP premise refers to the general temporal stability of movement patterns for a given individual. Here, too, extensive longitudinal data will be required to validate predictions stemming from KMP analyses. It is likely that different patterns of movement attain temporal stability at different points in development, and some patterns are probably much more inclined toward stability than others.

### *Comparison with the Rorschach Test*

At first glance, the Rorschach Ink Blot Test shares little with the KMP. The Rorschach is administered in a very specific manner, according to a standardized methodology, with a finite number of stimulus cards, eliciting verbalized perceptual, problem-solving, and sometimes projective responses that are then scored and analyzed. In comparison, the KMP draws upon relatively naturally occurring behaviors, with minimal control over influencing stimuli, and the behavior that is observed is nonverbal.

However, there are similarities evidenced in a few features: interpretive approaches to both techniques grew out of psychodynamic theory, and in both cases, the calculation and derivation of frequencies, percentages, ratios, and specified equations lend themselves to interpretation about presumably stable dispositions, traits, and personality characteristics that go well beyond the assessment situation. In both cases, theory is required to posit and explore the nature of the connection between the observed phenomena and the feature interpreted. Both the Rorschach and KMP, without directly examining these features, can examine clusters of data related to features such as affect, capacity for control, degree of stress, and sense of self. Both the Rorschach and KMP share "global" approaches to interpretation; data is not interpreted in isolation, but rather with the configuration of all the data (Exner, 1993; Kestenberg and Sossin, 1979). It is essential that the KMP analyst use the data to generate hypotheses, and then synthesize an understanding from these hypotheses in a manner that brings out a coherent and meaningful story about the observed individual. Although it is tempting to interpret and draw conclusions from specific frequencies of data, it is prudent to take a complete view of the KMP.

Historically, the Rorschach evolved in accordance with different systematizers and experts over time, until at one point there were five separate systems, with significant distinctions amongst them, training and guiding Rorschach evaluators. Eventually, Exner (1993) synthesized the systems, and prompted extensive normative data collection that provides reference data for age, psychopathology, and other factors that pertain to predictable differences. In some ways, the KMP parallels the earlier period of Rorschach development in which a rich and complex interpretive tool lacked the necessary normative data to more unequivocally lend validation to some interpretive methods, and to guide the interpreter in determining the distinctiveness of particular profile features.

## Introduction to KMP Interpretation

When involved in KMP interpretation, it is important to keep in mind that psychological interpretation is a process. As Levy (1963) suggested without considering movement in particular, the first stage in interpretation is propositional, and then there must be integration. The third stage uses the integration of findings to develop conclusions that pertain to the questions that prompted the assessment in the first place. In a manner that again parallels the Rorschach, we approach interpretation of the KMP by first reviewing the variables (movement factors) by clusters, then looking at the clusters as part of a larger whole and relating the data to the therapeutic or research questions.

The primary approach to interpretation of a KMP of an individual of any age involves identifying the correspondences between frequency measures (high or low, balanced or skewed movement qualities) and the developmental and psychological processes linked to that specific pattern and to the cluster of patterns of which it is a part. The basis for such interpretation was detailed in the preceding chapters. In overly condensed fashion (elaborated from Kestenberg, 1985), psychodynamic concepts correspond to movement patterns in the following fashion:

| | |
|---|---|
| (1) Drives: | > Tension Flow Rhythms |
| (2) Safety-Danger Affects | > Tension Flow Attributes |
| (3) Defenses against Drives | > Precursors of Effort |
| (4) Coping Reactions | > Efforts |
| (5) Comfort–Discomfort Affects and Relations Between Moods and States | > Bipolar Shape Flow |
| (6) Attraction–Repulsion Affects and Reactions to Stimuli | > Unipolar Shape Flow |
| (7) [Styles of Relating and Manners] | > [Shape Flow Design] |
| (8) Simple Relationships with Objects and Defenses Against Objects | > Shaping in Directions |
| (9) Complex Relationships with Objects | > Shaping in Planes |

## KMP Interpretation of Bess

In order to illustrate how to interpret a KMP of an adult, we will use the case of Bess. In this KMP analysis, the author illustrates how to apply psychodynamic theory as a framework for assessment.

### *Context*

A thirty-two-year-old woman, Bess, was observed and video-recorded in the context of a weekly-attended university-based playgroup. The primarily parent-driven playgroup, involving only six families, was designed as a primary prevention/research setting within a university doctoral program in school/clinical child psychology. In this setting, graduate students regularly gain observational experience involving infancy and early childhood. Observational research is carried out pertaining to styles of parenting, attachment processes and affect development. Parents voluntarily bring their children from birth to 3 years to develop a sense of community with other families and to have the opportunity to seek information and advice from the co-directing faculty psychologists on issues related to child development and parenting. Bess joined the center when her child was two-months old. She wished to meet with other parents and to provide her daughter an opportunity to be with other children.

On the day of the videotaping used for this profiling, there were a few other mothers, children, and staff also in attendance. This mother was with her then six-month-old child. She had attended the nursery by this point for 4 months, and was used to the regular routine of ongoing video-recording, student note-taking and such. During the course of the twenty-five-minute video clip, she was variously engaged with her daughter, other children, and mothers; and, for at least half of the time was seated, sometimes with her daughter on her lap. For a few minutes, while feeding her daughter by spoon, she became engaged in an animated conversation with one of the faculty psychologists, describing recent motherhood experiences.

*Body Attitude*  A tall woman, Bess maintained a fairly vertical alignment, making notable sagittal adjustments when holding her daughter. A few habitual movements were noted, such as flipping her hair back away from her face, and, with various degrees of bound tension, mechanically manipulating one of a few small objects with her hand. When socially engaged, she smiled frequently.

*Diagrams*  All diagrams are simply graphical ways of representing frequency data. Each movement pattern is plotted across from its polar opposite pattern, within the cluster of other patterns it relates to. Following procedures outlined in the KMP Manual

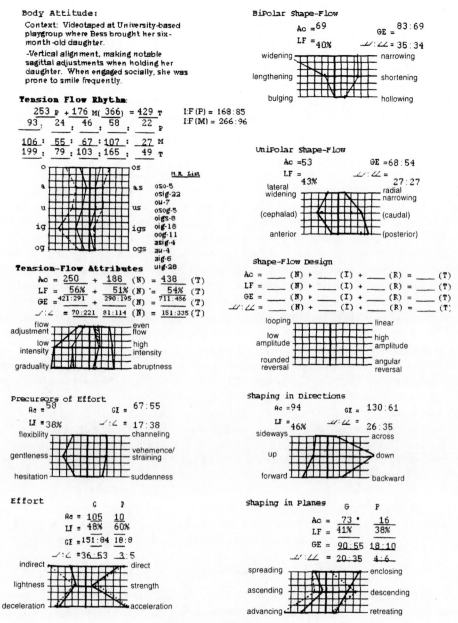

**Figure 16.** KMP of Bess.

(Berlowe, Kestenberg *et al.*, 1995), the frequency of each movement factor is transposed to a plot-point, so that within a cluster, the greater the frequency of occurrence of a given behavior, the larger that specified part of the diagram will be. A plot point of 3.2 would represent twice as many occurrences of that pattern as a plot point of 1.6. For precursors of effort and effort, the order of placement corresponds to the developmental sequence of space, weight, and time. For all of the shape flow-shaping patterns, the order of placement corresponds to the developmental sequence of horizontal–vertical-sagittal.

As previously reviewed, the layout of the diagrams corresponds to developmental, dynamic, structural, and relational levels of analysis which may be applied in interpretation. For example, Kestenberg (1985) states that "the left side of the profile represents motions related to the state of needs and to responses to inner and outer pressures, while the right side represents reaction to stimuli and to objects" (p. 115). In addition, there is a developmental progression from diagrams on the top of the page to those lower on the page, and from upper to lower lines within diagrams; lower diagrams (and lower lines) represent more advanced patterns which evolve from patterns that emerge earlier.

### Sequential Strategies in Profile Interpretation

When we go about a KMP assessment, we can choose various strategies of interpretation. We are not likely to discuss each and every element, but rather to focus on balances, imbalances, matches, mismatches, and cluster comparisons. While we usually begin with rhythms and attributes, we may continue to examine the remaining diagrams in various sequential order. In a clinical situation, the sequence of analysis is often determined by the diagnostic questions. For instance, if failure to master some adaptation was our concern, or if some symptom appeared to stem from inadequate defenses against impulses (e.g., a child referred for excessive temper tantrums, or if there was a question of anxiety interfering with learning), we might proceed from a look at tension flow attributes (TFA) directly to precursors of effort (PE) and then efforts (E). If someone's distress lies very much in the quality of relationships, we might start with the shape flow-shaping side of the profile.[1]

In general, when an individual does not present a problem clinically, the evaluator usually begins with TFRs and continues down "vertically" through System I and then from bipolar shape flow "vertically" down through System II to shaping in planes, to be followed by an examination of matching and mismatching between patterns that bear relation to one another across systems. However, as imbalances or mismatches are discovered, or other hypotheses are generated, the evaluator is guided along a more specific path of interpretation.[2]

For now, strategies have not been delineated in categorical terms (though this might be attempted in the future). Certainly, one guidepost would be that, no matter what the order, the complete profile must be considered in its entirety when using the KMP clinically. Interpretation of the profile is a process of hypothesis generation and hypothesis appraisal. The sequential strategy chosen pertains to the deductive process the evaluator follows, and determines the sequential manner in which hypotheses are considered. The strategic choices may follow either from diagnostic questions or from initial findings from the KMP.

### I. Tension-Flow Rhythms Diagram

The TFR diagram differs conceptually and procedurally from the other eight diagrams. One might say that the others are Effort-Shape driven, and the TFR diagram is developmentally and theoretically driven. The ten recognized tension flow rhythms are formatted across 5 polar continua, corresponding to Kestenberg's model of developmental sequence: oral, anal, urethral, inner-genital, and outer-genital phases; the patterns represented on the left are of the indulgent or libidinal variety, and on the right they are of the more fighting/aggressive (or "sadistic")[3] variety.

*Format of TFR Diagram*    In fact, the TFR diagram is graphically two distinct diagrams traced in overlapping fashion. The inside diagram reflects the relative frequencies of ten "pure" rhythms, and the outer diagram reflects the relative frequencies of "mixed" rhythms. On the notational level, pure rhythms look just like the paradigmatic forms that are linked to each labeled rhythm (see Chapter 1, Figures 3–12). Since each developmental phase in Kestenberg's system is anchored in bodily zone functions, each pure rhythm, though it can occur in any part of the body, bears a likeness to the pattern serving the zone-specific function. Hence, conceived on a somatopsychic level, the "pure" rhythm is deemed to be particularly adapted for the achievement of indulging or fighting satisfaction by that zone, and in the service of needs associated with the developmental phase linked to and organized through that zone. Developmentally, we expect rhythms to become more differentiated (pure) in phases in which they are dominant.

"Mixed" rhythms are created by two or more rhythms modifying one another. The "mixed" rhythm does not look just like the paradigmatic form; either it generally holds its general form while incorporating other identifiable rhythms within it (this is a "leading" rhythm, and, technically is counted as both mixed and pure), or its form seems to be cast by the confluence of two or more pure rhythmic qualities, none of which are remarkably predominant (this type is counted only as "mixed"). Interpretively, it has been generally held that mixed rhythms reflect congenital and early-determined preferences. The highest frequencies within the mixed rhythms are indicative of the preferred style the individual has of meeting his or her needs. Kestenberg (1985) suggested that these preferred rhythms may be predictive of where along the developmental path fixations and regressions might most likely occur.

Plot points are counted out from the center line and connected to the center line to aid visualization. As indicated, the "inner" diagram, marked by plot points that are connected by a solid line, is indicative of pure rhythms. The frequency of the same pattern occurring as elements within mixed rhythms is then added to the pure TFR plot-point and connected with a dashed line. For example, below we see that the plot point for Bess's mixed oral (sucking) rhythm is 2.2; this is added to the 1.6 plot point for pure oral (sucking), so the outside diagram represents a "total" oral (sucking) rhythm of 3.8.

*Equations and Ratios*   The very top equation, $253P + 176\ (366)M = 429$ tells us that there were, in total, 253 pure rhythms in addition to 176 mixed rhythms. The components (366) are derived as the sum of all the elements contributing to all the mixed rhythms (e.g., "oig" has 2 components and "oigog" has 3). If 176 mixed rhythms have 366 components, this indicates that most mixed rhythms consisted of 2 components, but that some had more. The mixed rhythms are actually listed next to the diagram. The most frequently occurring combinations are generally highlighted for emphasis, and as a cue for interpretation.

We then see several ratios. The three 5-part ratios on the left show the number of each phase-related rhythm (for each phase, indulging and fighting subphase types are combined). Here we see the greatest number of rhythms were oral (in pure, mixed, and total), and the second most frequent was the inner-genital pattern (this was the most in mixed). Then the left side and right side of the diagram and ratios are compared across phase-levels in two L:S equations (standing for libidinal:sadistic, now more often referred to as I:F—indulging: fighting); one is for the pure rhythm patterns and the other is for mixed rhythm patterns. In the case of Bess, she showed a notable inclination toward more indulging patterns, having almost a 2:1 ratio in pure (168:85), increasing to a 2.8:1 ratio in mixed (266:96). Looking at the listed mixed rhythms, we note that the most common mixed rhythms include "osig" (osf) (22), "oig" (of) (18) and "oog" (op) (11).

*Interpretive Strategies for TFR, Pure and Mixed*   Pure rhythms indicate the manner of satisfying specific needs. Pure rhythms are more differentiated than mixed rhythms, and it appears that pure rhythms are less influenced than the mixed by attunement to others or by contextual factors. A high ratio of pure to mixed rhythms suggests an individual with a high degree of organization, and a low ratio suggests a lower degree of organization and structure. Individuals with relatively low ratios of pure to mixed may be quite (or overly) prone to accommodate their needs to other people or to outside influences.

*Normative Considerations Regarding TFRs*　While we await the outcome of more definitive normative research, we can offer these general findings that most KMP specialists con-
cur with and employ in their interpretive work. (1) Oral rhythms (of both "o" and "os" types)
tend to be the most prevalent across all ages. (2) "igs," the inner genital surging/ birthing
rhythm, is the least frequent, especially in its pure form, partly because it is so large. (3)
Similarly, because it is large, "as" is not a common pure rhythm. (4) Specific rhythms tend to
be prevalent in accordance with developmental phases in children 0–6 years as discussed in
Chapter 1. (5) A higher level of fighting rhythms (especially "og" and "ogs") is often
found in the transition from one phase to another (Kestenberg, Sossin, Buelte, Schnee and
Weinstein, 1993). They seem to promote change. (6) We expect approximately a $2:1$ ratio
of $L:S$ ($I:F$) in mixed rhythms, but we expect almost equal numbers in pure rhythms
($1:1.2$ ratio). Some KMP analysts expect more "s" in pure rhythms because they are
deemed to be more differentiating rhythms, but due to a lack of normative research, more
study is needed on this statistic before the norm is clarified.

*Interpretations of Bess's Tension Flow Rhythm Diagram*　The theory presented thus far
suggests that tension flow rhythms convey to us the state of the mover's needs and drives
(Kestenberg, 1985). In examining Bess's KMP, we see that in pure rhythms, Bess shows
a balance between "o" (oral sucking) and "os" (oral snapping), both of which are prevalent,
as might be expected. However, pure inner genital indulgent patterns appeared as most frequent, suggesting an agreeable, organizing, and nurturing presence, which may be her
style, but may also be amplified by her current caregiving role. The $L:S$ ($I:F$)(P) ratio of
$168:85$ (this $2:1$ appears unusually skewed toward the indulging side), suggests an especially accommodating nature, and raises the question of whether there are sufficient fighting (aggressive) qualities for her to define and differentiate her needs as well as aim toward
need satisfaction. However, it has been our observation that this skew may be partly a function of her mothering role at this time in her life, and that her own differentiation of needs,
characterologically, may not be as inadequate as it might appear. Thus, to draw that kind of
conclusion, one would have to see her at a different point in time, when she is not so
directly involved in the caregiving of her baby.

We generally expect indulging to increase, relative to fighting in the mixed rhythms, and
in fact this is the case with Bess, but here it went form a high ratio of $2:1$ to an even higher
one of $2.8:1$, suggesting that Bess is using her resources to adapt and modify her needs
(possibly for the sake of others). She may be over-adapting.[4]

In general, the literature on the KMP followed the premise that tension flow rhythms
were drive-laden, id-anchored patterns which were not readily modified by context.
However, Kestenberg's own works on pregnancy, and the developmental phases of childhood, adolescence, and later phases, demonstrated that there were major changes in organization of needs, drives, and aspirations that could be expected in early parenthood. This
may have been the case with Bess. In later observations of a period of difficulties for her,
and even later periods of direction and determination, we saw a shift towards assertion
manifested in movement terms, especially by a decrease in inner genital movement patterns and an increase in outer genital rhythms and in each of the fighting rhythms.

## II. Tension Flow Attributes

*Reading the Tension Flow Attribute (TFA) Diagram*　Above the tension flow attribute
diagram are four rows (3 columns) of numbers, put in the form of equations. The pattern
seen here is consistent with the other diagrams in the KMP, however, there are

certain complexities that pertain specifically to tension flow attributes. The TFA diagram is really a composite of three separate diagrams. We identify in the top row the number of actions that are neutral, the number that are animate, and the number of total actions. Similarly, we identify the load factors for those actions in animated flow, neutral flow, and for the total. Two primary ratios, the gain : expense[5] and free : bound ratios, are identified for those elements and/or actions that are in animated flow, neutral flow, and the total.

Another complexity is the manner in which tension flow attributes incorporate something we call "rebounds." These actions pertain to that portion of a movement phrase in which there was a diminished quality in the service of its regeneration. Rebounds thus reflect one's ability to be resilient (Kestenberg and Sossin, 1979). When one is getting more abrupt, one might need to get less abrupt to again get more abrupt. The mover may never have gotten into graduality; the person may have just diminished abruptness.

*Description of Tension flow Attributes* Tension flow attributes reflect temperamental qualities and affects that pertain to safety and danger (hence, they can convey feelings of intactness and anxiety). Tension flow attributes are not themselves affects, rather they are the medium of expression of affects of pleasure and displeasure. Shades and complexities of these affects are related to the varied combinations, sequences and intervals between changes that characterize the flow (in time). For example, contrast an abruptly adopted stare, evenly held in high intensity bound flow (as when stern or frightened) with a gradual easing of tension, mildly adjusting the brow (as when indulging in a pleasant thought) (Sossin, 1983; Kestenberg, 1985).

"Basic affects" (fear, sadness, anger, etc.) would actually be expressed by combinations of tension flow and shape flow attributes (Kestenberg and Sossin, 1994). In fact, tension flow and shape flow tend to co-occur, creating complex emotional responses. Shape flow gives structure to tension flow as plasticity gives structure to elasticity, just as the latter two groupings of affective qualities—born in relationships—give structure to affective experiences of pleasure/displeasure that are not intrinsically tied to relationships.

Neutral flow, represented at the center of the tension flow attribute diagram, reflects those movement patterns which employ changes in tension-flow within the narrow "neutral zone." These movements appear de-animated or numb. As indicated in Chapter 2, free neutral flow may be represented as something like the flowing of water, while bound neutral flow is more like the flow of molasses. More intense-bound neutral flow becomes stone-like. Neutral flow pertains to inanimate qualities, whereas tension-flow that is animated pertains to qualities that we would refer to as vitalized.

*Expectations of Data* In the absence of more definitive normative data, we might share some expectations and general rules that KMP analysts generally employ. It is common to find that approximately 18–30% of all tension flow attributes are in neutral flow. If an individual has substantially more than 30%, we would wonder why they are numbing themselves so often.[6] It would not be unusual to see a high proportion of neutral flow in someone who was ill, in a very young baby, or in a very elderly person. However, if those characteristics didn't pertain, we might wonder why neutral flow and de-animation were so in evidence. We might think of neutral flow, through its de-animation and numbing, as contributing to a primitive, early defensive process (or, parallel to developmental considerations of Stolorow and Lachmann (1980), we might term these "pre-stages of defense"). If someone had substantially less than 18% neutral flow, we might hypothesize that they are not using a sufficient amount of "down time."

Next, we look at the load factor (LF). To oversimplify somewhat, the load factor could tell us about the complexity of these safety–danger affects. A LF of about 35% suggests that affective shifts are occurring on quite a simple level. We might wonder whether the individual has sufficient affective resources. If the LF gets over 50%, we might wonder whether affects are overly complex, and we might become concerned that the individual could be overwhelmed by the affects; hence, affects could be a burden rather than a resource. We would be interested in comparing what the complexity of affects is in neutral flow versus animated flow. Individuals who have higher load factors in neutral flow allow themselves to combine feelings more often while they are in a dazed or dulled state.

Another ratio considered is the relationship between the number of attributes/elements and flow changes, called the gain: expense ratio (GE). The number of elements is associated with the gain, and the number of flow changes is associated with the expense. A lot of free-bound changes without changes in attributes is associated with spontaneity, but also with less control in affective processes and shifts. The use of more elements relative to flow is indicative of a more mature and controlled way of regulating affects.

We also compare the number of tension flow rhythms to the total number of tension flow attribute-actions. When there are substantially more rhythms than attributes it indicates that an individual is strongly driven to fulfill his or her needs with limited modulation. If the disparity goes in the other direction, then it is indicative that there is a great deal of affect regulation going on, and, in fact, a diminished impetus to satisfy needs. We like to see a fairly even balance between TFA and TFR totals. Until such time that future normative data refines our guidelines for interpretation, a review of data suggests that we might use 10% as a criterion for treating the numbers as significantly different.

The last ratio pertaining to tension flow attributes that is listed above the diagram is the free:bound ratio. If an individual has more free than bound, it suggests a capacity for relaxation and feelings of safety, though in more extreme cases, it could also mean losing control. If the ratio falls in the other direction, i.e., if the individual uses bound flow significantly more than free flow, then we would hypothesize that there is anxiety and/or excessive constraint.

*Interpreting the Tension flow Attribute Diagram*    Looking at the KMP of Bess, we see that, overall, 5 of the 6 patterns appear to be amply represented. However, Bess shows fairly little flow adjustment. Her greater proclivity for even flow relative to flow adjustment, along with her propensity for bound flow, suggests that she was feeling more serious, steady-state, and cautious than carefree and modulating.

If one takes a clinical perspective, a picture begins to emerge that lends itself to explication. Here is a woman who experiences little differentiation of need expression. She uses few rebounds; hence, she has little resilience. She is very low in terms of flow adjustment; hence, we see Bess as a person with few differentiated needs, without the resilience or coping abilities that rebounds and flow adjustment would offer her in handling everyday stressors.

We notice the high load factor (56% animated, 54% total). This raises a concern that the complexity of her affects may contribute to an experience of distress. It is also striking that close to 43% of her tension flow attributes are in neutral flow; this is unusually high. We can see that neutral flow graphically takes a large piece of the overall TFA diagram. We wonder why Bess is having to numb herself to such an extent.[7] The load factor of 51% in neutral reflects a high degree of complexity of numbed feelings.

The gain:expense ratios in animated (421:291), neutral (290:195), and the total (711:486), are quite skewed in the direction of excessive controls as opposed to spontaneous qualities. In contrast, the 438 TFAs are quite comparable to the 429 TFRs. So, while the overall abundance of needs and impulses ("drives") is more or less equal to the abundance of safety-danger affects, the nature of Bess's affective experience is in the direction of inhibiting spontaneity. We see this even further in the bound:free ratios (70:221A, 81:114N, 151:335T), where she shows us that she is using, overall, more than twice as much bound flow as free flow. We can conclude that Bess is using excessive constraint.

Our interpretive strategy would likely be influenced by the prevention (and not clinical) context in which she was seen, as well as by her constrained affect pattern in tension flow attributes; the findings thus far (after looking at TFRs and TFAs) leave us with some concern. We would turn to movement elements that directly provide the structure for the patterns we just examined, and can be directly considered in terms of matching and mismatching with these patterns. Hence, we will turn to bipolar shape flow and then to unipolar shape flow.

### III. Bipolar Shape Flow (Diagram 5)

Bipolar shape flow has been linked to affects that pertain to comfort and discomfort, and following Kestenberg and Borowitz (1990; Kestenberg and Sossin, 1994), this cluster of symmetric shape flow patterns has been linked to the psychoanalytic construct of primary narcissism. The expansion of growing in bipolar shape flow is, in relation to psycho-analytic constructs, the physical basis of primary narcissism. From bipolar patterns, one can assess feelings of well-being, and the degree to which one seeks narcissistic supplies. Ideally, a caregiver grows into the child as the child grows into the caregiver; in the absence of such responsiveness, and mutuality of interaction, the child may show an excessive growing out into the world, i.e. showing an excessive degree of narcissistic neediness. Physical illness will often give rise to bipolar shrinking (as in the bipolar shortening in colic, the bipolar narrowing in asthma, or the bipolar hollowing in disorders involving much regurgitation).[8]

Shape flow patterns are a manifestation of plasticity (the inherent pliability of our bodies to alter body contours); it's basic elements are the growing and shrinking of body shape, and it serves interaction with, and especially affective relations to, stimuli and objects in the environment (i.e. Balint's "environmental objects"). We refer to neutral shape flow when plasticity is lost, and expressions or movements appear more anesthetized or frozen. On the right side of the diagram are shrinking, closed shapes, specifically narrowing, shortening and hollowing, and on the left side of the diagram are their growing, open counterparts: widening, lengthening and bulging. As with the other shape flow-shaping (System II) patterns, the postulated developmental order of horizontal, vertical and sagittal determines the order. In general, growing patterns reflect comfort and shrinking patterns reflect discomfort.

*Interpretive Considerations*   As we have described, each diagram is accompanied by statistical information including the number of actions, the percentage of the load factor (complexity factor), the gain:expense ratio, and the flow ratio (in this diagram, pertaining to symmetric growing and shrinking). Note that in comparison to the very complex affects (TFA, LF = 54%) pertaining to safety and danger, Bess's affects pertaining to comfort and discomfort (as reflected by the bipolar shape flow load factor) are considerably less complex (LF = 40%).

Though, all by itself, this simple comparison of load factors is not definitive, we might pause and wonder what meanings might be suggested. From what we've outlined so far, we could state that the complexity of the dynamics of affective changes related to anxiety and freedom from anxiety is notably greater than the affective changes related to states of comfort and discomfort (or to our "affective relationship to environmental objects," Kestenberg, 1985). Complexity is not simply a good or bad feature. If too small, we might be concerned as to whether there are enough integrative resources in that dimension of personality; if too large, we might be concerned that excessive exertion is involved in struggling to accomplish such integration, at some cost to the regularity and smoothness of function. In the case of Bess, we would make note of the difference, and perhaps generate a tentative hypothesis: Bess is currently more affectively absorbed in feelings more directly related to need states (i.e., drive–derivative affects) than in feelings related to confidence, sense-of-self, and overall body-image. At this point in conjecture (only considering these two load factors), we do not know whether these latter feelings are diminished (and thus of concern) or simply incorporated into more ego-controlled patterns of relating evident in other (shaping) patterns.

The highest proclivity Bess shows in bipolar shape flow is a growing pattern, the horizontal pattern of widening. However, the overall shrinking patterns, taken in total, equal the growing patterns. There is an absence of bipolar bulging.[9] This suggests that Bess does not seem to feel "filled" and gratified from within, nor, with minimal lengthening, do we infer that she feels particularly proud of herself. Moreover, we see that there is a comfort expressed in the widening, which may be in attunement with her baby's needs to grow into her as a mother.

If we look further at the matching/mismatching and balance/imbalance between bipolar shape flow and tension flow attributes, what we see is a general imbalance between the indulging TFAs and the growing bipolar shape flow elements. It would appear that the dynamics expressed and felt in graduality and low intensity have limited structure available from their bipolar affined patterns, lengthening and bulging. In other words, the safe feelings expressed in graduality and low intensity do not have directly corresponding feelings of high self-regard to support them. In a specific imbalance, there is much widening (i.e., offering much structure) without much flow adjustment (i.e., demonstrating little feeling tone).

We are again reminded that the KMP is a "summary statement" that can sometimes suffice for diagnostic inference, but very often raises questions that can only be answered by looking again at the raw data (e.g., examining specific combinations, phrasing, etc.). Does Bess widen with low intensity and graduality? Or does Bess widen with high intensity? Many such questions, which are highly relevant for interpretation, cannot be answered by the KMP data alone. However, we can conjecture that as Bess grows bipolarly in the horizontal, for instance, to welcome and greet her baby, she does not use corresponding tension flow adjustment in free flow which would equip her to feel that she could be safe (adapting to her child's tension flow changes), and sufficiently able to take care of her own needs while she takes care of her baby's. Is Bess's growing in widening vacuous, insincere, or aimless? This is the type of question or speculation that can be generated, but should not be answered or drawn conclusively unless it fits coherently with the entire profile, and with review of observations of the parent–child interactions.

We also note that while even flow and high intensity appear well matched with narrowing and shortening, it does not appear that there is enough hollowing to give sufficient structure to abruptness (though we can see that there is much more hollowing than bulging). Even though, as discussed in Chapter 5, we usually see the least amount of sagittal bipolar elements in comparison with the other dimensions, we would still wonder how this mother and child are growing together without much sagittal bipolar bulging (compared to the large amount of graduality in tension flow attributes). In this case, we are reminded that we can draw relatively few conclusions about the mother–child relationship by only looking at one KMP, and that, if our questions pertain to the functioning of the dyad, we need to compare the KMPs of each. Such an assessment approach provides an instrumental springboard to effective infant-parent psychotherapy (see Chapter 10).

### IV. Unipolar Shape-Flow (Diagram 6)

Unipolar Shape-flow[10] brings our attention to another realm of affective experience, having to do with attraction and repulsion (going towards and away), especially in relation to stimuli that are distinct. The entire shape flow-shaping system pertains to relationships, and in that vein, unipolar shape-flow, pertains to reactions to numerous objects, ranging qualitatively from wholesome to noxious. Kestenberg (1975) suggested that approaching others with unipolar shape flow expresses an individual's relationship to another that is based upon dependent and passive needs (e.g., to be fed and protected, as one was by the mothering caregiver).[11] Such a need satisfying relationship based on growing toward the other to satisfy one's needs, and shrinking away from the other when needs are met, expresses the nature of "anaclitic" relationships. In combination with tension flow attributes, unipolar shape flow patterns evince qualities that have been related to secondary narcissism.

Kestenberg (1985) reminds us that "in order to give structure to adaptive movements and efforts, the child shapes his or her body in multidimensional configurations, which are reproductions of the object in relation to the child's self" (p. 141). Bipolar shape flow movements are made in response to the environment as a whole. With unipolar shape flow, we respond to specific objects. With growing we express attraction to or comfort with someone and with shrinking we express repulsion or discomfort.

*Interpretive Considerations* We consider the data above the diagram as a first step in interpretation. The load factor indicates that there is a moderate complexity in attraction–repulsion affects, only slightly greater than that of bipolar shape flow and within expectation—still notably lower than that of tension flow attributes. This can be interpreted to mean that Bess more readily combines her affects when they pertain to safety and danger than she does when they pertain to either comfort and discomfort or to attraction and repulsion. We can't yet say why that might be so, but perhaps Bess's emotional experience as it relates to her own needs (pertaining to both pleasure and displeasure) is more complex than her emotional experience as it is related to her sense of self and to her primary attachment figures.

There is a fair balance between growing and shrinking factors. There are slightly more "closed" shape flow elements than there are "open" shape flow elements, This would appear contradictory. It is possible to combine a growing movement with a closed shape. Bess has a high frequency of lengthening down movements in which she is growing toward what is gratifying but at the same time she is closing herself off in some fashion. In fact, this may be a common phenomena in early caregiving, wherein the parent tends to the smaller (often lower-placed) child.

In general, we see a diagram that suggests to us that Bess grows and shrinks in unipolar shape flow more often in the vertical and sagittal dimensions than in the horizontal. We note that this corresponds to her overall body attitude. There are relatively few narrowing (horizontally inward) movements, and there are, similarly, relatively few bulging forward (attraction to what is ahead) movements.

Comparing data from bipolar and unipolar diagrams we find that Bess is more apt to express her self-feelings of comfort and discomfort (bipolar) in the horizontal dimension through expansion and constriction, while she is more apt to express her relational feelings to primary others (unipolar) in the vertical and sagittal dimensions. She expresses self feelings of comfort and generosity in widening bipolarly. In unipolar shape flow she expresses good cheer with lengthening up or becoming downcast with shortening down; she is more likely to express feelings of rejection with hollowing back than feelings of gratification with bulging forward.

Appraising the matching/mismatching and balance/imbalance between unipolar shape flow and tension flow attributes indicates that Bess uses the caudal patterns of lengthening and shortening down to structure high intensity and hollowing, and bulging back (posterior) to structure abruptness. When she is suddenly surprised by someone or feels impulsive in her interaction with others, she can use well-matched patterns to express her feelings (hollowing back with abruptness). However, to an unusual degree, her often-exuded equanimity, evident in a low-keyed (low-intensity) style and contemplative/forbearing manner (graduality) is often unstructured by corresponding self- or relational feelings (except when looking up or elated).

When an appropriate structure for a feeling is meager, it is difficult for onlookers to recognize the affect. It is possible that an individual can herself experience her feelings in an amorphous manner when she does not structure them appropriately. In Bess's case we see that her poise and composure often become compromised by de-animation, perhaps associated with a lack of distinctness of feeling, leading to limpness and inertia. She stays more "lively" when quickly responsive, and it is then that she expresses her feelings in relation to another, but quite possibly in a manner that highlights a sensitivity to rejection as seen in frequent hollowing back.

There is a reasonable degree of harmony available between low intensity and up (cephalad) movements. She can clearly express feeling pleasantly elated or satisfied with herself. Also there are similar amounts of lateral widening and flow adjustment with which she can connect in an accommodating manner. Overall, as we generate hypotheses, we are struck that in relation to those from whom she might seek gratification and need satisfaction, there is more recoil than there is attraction.

### V. Precursors of Effort (Diagram 3)

Pre-efforts refer to defenses and learning styles. If we think about how we approach new things, we realize that we do not employ movement patterns that reflect mastery (efforts), but rather ones which reflect extra exertion, caution, or hesitation (i.e., attempts at adaptation that do not supersede the tension flow qualities the way efforts do). The defenses that are addressed by pre-efforts are defenses which are related to how we defend against inner impulses (drives), wishes, needs, states, and feelings. These are the kinds of defenses that correspond to Anna Freud's (1936, 1965) framework, such as "isolation" (seen prominently in channeling) and "reaction formation" (seen prominently in gentleness). Of course, interpretation is complicated because psychic defenses and movement patterns do not simply share one-to-one correspondences. Needless to say, not all gentleness is paralleled by ongoing reaction formation.

Developmentally, precursors of effort evolve from related tension flow attributes and they transform into related effort elements (Kestenberg, 1985). Individuals use pre-efforts when they attempt to change the external environment through their control of tension flow attributes (Kestenberg and Sossin, 1979). From the perspective of structural theory within psychoanalysis and/or ego-psychology, precursors of effort reflect the ego's non-mastery level of adaptation, i.e., it is an attempt to do, perform, or accomplish, but the affect-laden tension flow is as present as the attempt at adaptation in the movement (see Chapter 3).

*Interpretive Considerations* What we see on this KMP diagram is a lower complexity load factor than in any other diagram. This reflects Bess's simple style of learning and of defending against inner impulses. She demonstrates a fairly balanced use of movement qualities. Her greatest proclivity (by a small margin) is in the direction of gentleness which, as discussed, suggests access to, if not necessarily an inclination toward, reaction formation. We note that this goes along with the high degree of low intensity (consonant patterns) and inner genital indulging. Generally, she seems to have adequate supplies to employ other defenses as well, except that the low complexity (lack of combining elements) may hinder their efficacy. This is further suggested by noting the greater complexity of affects evidenced in tension flow attributes (54%) than of defenses evidenced in pre-efforts (38%). We also observe that the flow factors used with pre-efforts are twice as heavily loaded toward constraint (bound) as they are toward license (free), which corresponds to the tension flow findings themselves. In all, Bess's use of precursors of effort appear fairly uniform, suggesting access to a range of defensive and learning styles, without one mode far outdistancing others. We will consider them more in relation to shaping in directions.

## VI. Shaping in Directions (Diagram 8)

We now go across the Profile to shaping in directions, where we see how an individual projects her body dimensions outward in a linear fashion, and how she tends to localize objects in space. Loman and Merman (1996) note: "These spoke-like and arc-like movements are used to create bridges to people and things in space (such as pointing to someone) and to form protective boundaries used in defending oneself" (p. 36). It is essential to consider shaping in directions in comparison to precursors of effort; both sets of patterns relate to defensive styles and both relate to styles of learning new skills that are later mastered (Kestenberg, 1985). Shaping of space with directional movements forms linear pathways in space, and offers us some indication of the individual's mode of attaining and relinquishing contact with others, of creating boundaries and modes of protection from others, in cognitive processes, and in the service of learning.

Shaping in spatial directions involves linear movement through the mover's kinesphere. Laban (1966) in his development and study of choreutics (or space-harmony), conceived of a "dynamic crystallography of human movement" (p. 103), in which he followed the dimensional directions and their deflections into their "scaffolding" forms, from the cube through various polyhedral contour-tracings to the more spherical icosahedron. In concerning himself with the practical purposes of movements, and in studying rituals and rules associated with various activities, such as fencing,[12] Laban associated projections of body dimensions into space with essential manners of defense.

In the prototypical defensive action, we use closed-shaped linear movements to bar access (create a boundary) to the body, and open-shaped linear movements to depict the exterior limits of approach to the body. We defend against others most clearly by using closed-shaped movements, but we also appease by opening up boundaries, and this can serve defensive purposes too.

*Interpretive Considerations* We notice the proclivity Bess demonstrates for downward directional movement. Such a pattern might have different meanings for different individuals, with varying repertoires of movement behavior. For Bess, I would first consider a contextual matter, which is her state of relating to her child in caregiving circumstances at a still relatively early parental phase of her life. Remember that directional movements not only make for protective boundaries, they also make for contact with others. Review of videotaped material does indicate that a significant proportion of the downward movement appeared to be in relation to her child or another child below her. However, to the extent that downward movements are not completely explained by her caregiving role, we may posit that when Bess is defending against others, she closes off vertically, perhaps protecting her trunk more than her head. Other movement elements in this diagram are fairly well balanced although there is relatively limited use of the horizontal dimension, especially across.

Comparing frequency of directional movements with frequency of pre-efforts, we find that Bess shows over 60% more shaping in directions than precursors of effort. This suggests that Bess is more preoccupied with defenses and learning associated with relating to others in specific ways than she is with the defenses and learning that pertain to trying to change the external environment. The shaping in directions load factor shows more complexity than does the load factor of pre-efforts. It appears that the manner she has of relating and making contact with others is more amalgamating of varied aspects than her dynamics of defense (against drives), which are relatively simple and less likely to combine and blend.

We can now consider the specific matches and mismatches between elements in pre-efforts and elements in directional movements. From this perspective, Bess may be barring access to her body (with across) insufficiently to support her frequent employment of isolation (channeling), but this might be expected of a still-nursing mother. She shows a well-matched and sufficient capacity to escape in a rush (as reflected in backward and sudden movements). Bess appears quite inclined to look ahead and proceed with tasks or approaching people (as in her forward movements), though she is not highly inclined toward postponement (as reflected by her minimal degree of hesitation). Bess's high frequency of down directional movements is not comparably matched by amounts of vehemence or straining in pre-efforts. If we were analyzing conjoint parent–child profiles, we might wonder if Bess's daughter shows a complimentary degree of upward movement in relation to mother's downward movement.[13] Another potential meaning of the vertical/weight comparison in Bess may indicate that she puts others down, and is perceived as doing so, beyond the degree to which she calls on defensive aggression.

Considering matching and mismatching from the perspective of learning style, we could deduce that Bess is quite prone to explain issues (down) but somewhat less inclined to attack the problem (vehemence).[14] Her manner (reflected by a relatively small degree of up) is to seek little in the way of advice or guidance from others, at least not submissively. However, she shows a higher degree of gentleness which reflects her capacity to be sensitive and mild, possibly drawing upon reaction formation at times. She may be able to employ gentleness from "on high"—as a mother, a teacher, boss, or even as a professional relating to those she serves, but she is an unlikely supplicant to those who consider themselves above her.

While Bess may define issues (as through channeling), she does less to make distinctions, and she does not seem especially prone, though able, to show displacement and generalization (as per sideways and flexibility). She may have a reasonable capacity to gain insight from past experiences (as might be reflected in well-matched sudden/backward combinations), though she is not highly engaged in this. Her dedication to getting ahead or progressing (forward) appears more developed than her readiness to make step-by-step decisions (as reflected in twice the forward as compared to hesitation).

## VII. Effort (Diagram 4)

Use of effort movement qualities reflects attitudes toward space, weight, and time that convey an ego-laden level of functioning toward mastery of skills and coping strategies (see Chapter 4). In the study of efforts, we look for both gestures and postures. Postures are those patterns which involve the whole body; parts may perform different functions, but each part is serving a common effort action. Psychodynamically, these postural patterns incorporate all the psychic agencies (speaking in psychoanalytic structural theory terms), including the superego. This allows us to look at how a person might function on an ego-level of functioning (effort gestures) as compared to how they might function on a super-ego level (postures).

As efforts mature, the developing individual begins to adapt to space by paying attention directly or indirectly, to gravity by expressing intent with strength or lightness, and by making decisions through acceleration and deceleration (Kestenberg, 1985). Effort elements, and the attitudes and adaptive functioning that they reflect, are viewed in conjunction with the structure provided for them by shaping in planes elements, but are also viewed as developmentally emerging from precursors of effort and the tension flow attributes that preceded them.

*Interpretive Considerations*  We notice that a  comparison of gestures and postures finds 105 gestures to 10 postures, suggesting that commitment can be, but is not readily engaged.[15] On the other hand, once it gets engaged, Bess's commitment and total involvement can be complex, reflected by her high load factor of 60% in postures. We see that the spatial and time efforts are well represented, with much less in the way of weight efforts. In comparison, there was a greater proportional contribution of weight precursors of effort and of the intensity factor in tension flow attributes. It appears that some developmental snag has hampered the evolution of these earlier patterns into strength and lightness. This lack may leave Bess not feeling very centered in her expression of intentionality.

Overall, we could posit that Bess may be able to investigate and attend (direct and indirect), as well as make decisions (acceleration and deceleration) and perform effectively, but she may not be able to clearly show her intention (strength or lightness) or muster her determination. The question arises as to whether these are long-standing issues, or whether her intentionality lessened in her current maternal role. She may have operated differently in her professional role that preceded the present. There are some questions we can raise (such as this one) and not be able to answer conclusively from the single KMP. Such questions can usefully be explored by conducting longitudinal KMPs that allow us to look into the effects of life course changes, experiences, and/or interventions.

Looking specifically at postures, we see that Bess uses a great deal of postural indirect, direct, and acceleration; the postural indirect stands out in that it significantly exceeds the proportional degree of gestural indirect. Apparently, only when committed is she able to pay attention to the periphery and "take it all in."

## VIII. Shaping in Planes (Diagram 9)

What we expect to see in shaping in planes is something about the quality of relationships. These three-dimensional concave and convex shapes which our movements sculpt in space serve our rapport and manner of connecting and relating to others, whom we represent internally in multidimensional ways. The spatial configurations that are "constructed" through the elements of shaping of space in planes give structure to efforts and their dynamics.

Developmentally, we note that the infant moves in all planes in early infancy (Kestenberg, 1985). However, it is in the horizontal plane that the infant practices reaching, grasping, and taking in through enclosing, while exploring space through spreading. It is later, more or less in the second year, that the toddler tends to confront people in the vertical plane, while climbing and demonstrating things using descending and ascending. Later still, in the third year, the child approaches and withdraws from people in increasingly complex ways, as evident in the sagittal, advancing and retreating. We look for matching and mismatching patterns in System II as well, as there are natural affinities, as between widening and spreading, lengthening and ascending, and bulging and advancing.

*Interpretive Considerations*    In Bess's case there are slightly more postures relative to gestures in shaping in planes than in effort; however, Bess's postural shaping in planes actions are of minimal complexity compared to the extremely high complexity of the postural efforts. There is considerable mismatching between postural efforts and postural shaping in planes, especially in the horizontal. While Bess is fully committed to paying attention (with direct and indirect postural efforts), she does not demonstrate a sufficient structure for paying attention with postures in spreading or enclosing. This suggests a potential problem with regard to Bess's maternal role. She may be fully committed to paying attention, but not to structuring that attention into her relationship with her child. Postures in shaping in planes reflect the ego-ideal aspect of the superego. Thus we can assume that Bess's ego-ideal is not sufficiently engaged to offer inspired caregiving. Bess may not see herself as one who wholeheartedly embraces others or shares herself with others. On the other hand, there is considerable correspondence in the amount of horizontal shaping in gestures compared to spatial efforts. This suggests that she is able to provide caregiving and nurturing but without full involvement of her whole self.

Looking across the time-sagittal axis in gesture, we can see that Bess's acceleration does not get adequate structure from retreating. There is a good gestural correspondence between deceleration and advancing, but her high degree of postural advancing is not sufficiently matched in postural efforts of deceleration. In moments of commitment, Bess is, in terms of shaping in planes, descending and advancing.

In gestures, Bess shows notable matching between her manner of paying attention as reflected in spatial effort and her exploration, as reflected in horizontal shaping. However, in posture, when committed, Bess pays both direct and peripheral attention without adequate exploration proclivities. We might suggest that her superego (effort postures) gets her paying better attention, but her ego-ideal (shaping in planes postures) is not sufficiently involved or engaged to aim that attention toward any particular aspirations.

Bess's ego-ideal is most involved in anticipating the consequences of actions and initiating actions, as well as in confronting others and requiring cooperation from others. This latter style of aspiring to garner cooperation is done without adequate determination (as per the lack of both gestural and postural strength). There is some indication that Bess is quite prone to rush into unambiguous decision-making while anticipating the consequences, but she is not as likely to be anticipating these consequences from past experience.

## IX. Integration of Findings

It is the evaluator's challenge to pool all the information gleaned and hypotheses generated by the KMP data, and to integrate these findings into an intelligible, meaningful, and constructive synthesis that lends insight into our understanding of an individual.

The visage that the KMP offers us about Bess at this time might be described as follows: Bess is a highly intelligent, resourceful woman who is currently involved in considerable accommodation, experiencing her own feelings without sufficient clarity. Amongst the various defenses she employs, she is relying particularly on de-animation (numbing), and does not show enough resilience for her current circumstances. She may lack the ability to adjust her mood as well as she might need to. A picture emerges of a woman who may be experiencing too little pride and sense-of-self in her current role, inhibiting the search for gratifications that are not available to her. We take note that a few months after this observation was made, Bess began to complain quite directly that she was not enjoying motherhood as much as she wished, and that she found it depleting, and she missed her former professional sources of gratification.

The utility of the KMP is reflected in the predictive and accurate insights it revealed. Perhaps these movement observations and their interpretation could have anticipated significant distress that emerged in Bess's life, as she felt she was appeasing others at the expense of her own happiness. She began to feel drained and unfulfilled in her mothering.

In retrospect, movement interventions could have been employed to raise her level of aspirations, which seemed diminished in postural shaping. Similarly, the KMP suggests that spreading, ascending, and the weight efforts (lightness and strength) are all too diminished to sustain her sense of fortitude and her capacity to explore while maintaining multiple relationships (as per spreading), and to allow for admiration of others, as well as to develop an ability to confront others with her own aspirations (as per ascending).

Unfortunately, Bess's lack of determination and clear intentionality appear to be part of a depressive state, further reflected by her high proportion of neutral flow attributes and her lack of gratification (as highlighted by her lack of bulging). Given her resources, Bess's depression may be reactive to life circumstances, in which she is feeling immobilized. Bess's state poses a risk, as well, to the nature of the mutual attachment between her and her daughter.

## Notes

1. In current psychoanalytic discourse, there is much consideration about the greater suitability of drive, ego-psychological, object-relational, self-psychological or other alternative perspectives. Much of this discourse pertains to the general superiority of one "orientation" or another, as reflected in interpretive power or technical efficacy. Integrative clinical theorists, such as Pine (1990) seek to fit the most suitable framework to the clinical situation. We might suggest that the Kestenberg body of work, reflected in the KMP, constitutes a theoretical paradigm that incorporates at least the aforementioned four psychologies (Sossin, 1990). The breadth and depth of this system of thought requires further delineation and comparative examination.

2. Resemblance is again borne to Rorschach interpretation. Exner (1993) stresses the interpretive search for all Rorschach protocols should not follow the same routine. He states: "In such a format, the first bits of data that are evaluated should provide some information concerning the core elements of the personality structure and/or response styles of the subject. Thus, the decision about which cluster of data to use as the starting point is important because the yield should for a centerpiece in the network of descriptive statements that will ultimately be generated. In turn, the first cluster selected usually should provide direction for the order by which the remaining clusters will be

reviewed" (Exner, 1993, p. 347–348). Similarly, in the KMP, the most salient findings immediately evident from a survey of the KMP statistically and/or graphically will give rise to the most logical interpretive search strategy. Though we are generally agreed in noting our application of such search strategies dependent upon the initial data we have yet to empirically demonstrate their discriminative power and utility.

3. Over the bulk of time that the KMP has been used, developmental subphases, and hence, the rhythms associated with them, were labeled as "libidinal" or "sadistic." These terms were spawned from psychoanalytic terminology pertaining to psychic "energy," in which "libidinal" pertained to sexual, erotic or life-instinctual drives and "sadistic" pertained to a mixture of aggressive and libidinal drive components. On a conceptual level, pure libidinal patterns could be conceived, but no purely aggressive rhythms were deemed likely; the aggressive-laden but nonetheless animate rhythms were deduced to reflect this mixture dubbed "sadistic." Absolutely no connotation of hurtful-intent or perversion was implied in the use of this term, only the admixture of libidinal and aggressive. However, use of the terms was certainly misunderstood outside psychoanalytic circles. Use of this terminology reflected Kestenberg's general adherence to a dual-drive (libidinal and aggressive) theory, and this was controversial even within psychoanalysis. Such adherence was not especially relevant to the specific observable rhythmic patterns, and hence the names were changed to the already used "indulging" and "fighting" terms that differentiated efforts. Readers of this text might want to know of this terminological shift so that they can turn back to earlier writings about the KMP and recognize the language used.

4. In fact, Bess became notably sad and distressed a few months after these observations were made. She then began to verbalize that she missed her career and she missed having a life of her own and that she felt that she could not maintain her well-being and continue to give so much. Using her as a case in point, perhaps the high skew was of sufficient magnitude to lead us to have this concern earlier, fostering more preventative work in the early stages to allay what otherwise became a very painful time for her, when she became acutely aware of her "over-adaptation," and she became notably more searching of her own definition and gratification of needs. There are other indications in the profile, as well as in other data we have available, that Bess was a highly motivated individual. This appeared masked in her tension flow rhythms at this time. This could have alerted us to some conflict, leading to more effective early intervention.

5. The Gain : Expense ratio indicates the degree to which there is a gain in attributes or elements over the expense through simple fluctuations in flow (Kestenberg and Sossin, 1979). In these general terms, this ratio potentially applies to each diagram-cluster on the profile, with the exception of tension flow rhythms. The interpretation of this ratio would be specific to the cluster considered, always stated in terms of the relative relation between a certain kind of control and certain types of affective spontaneity. Our current appraisal of the Gain : Expense ratio, pertaining to tension flow attributes as well as to other diagrams, is that it is conceptually defensible and useful, but that in current practice, technical demands (e.g., always notating changes in flow factors alongside changes in attributes and elements) make the ratio susceptible to error. Caution must be applied in interpreting the Gain : Expense ratio until further reliability work is applied, and/or until notational changes are employed.

6. As emphasized throughout this text, a thorough-going normative study (in progress) has not been yet completed that would permit us to discuss such percentages with proper regard for essential statistical properties such as the nature of the distribution,

the mean and the standard deviation, which, in turn, will clarify and fine-tune approximations of "within the normal range" or "beyond the normal range." However, the numbers presented in the text are those that long-standing notators and KMP analysts have been applying based upon cumulative experience. It may be that they are correct for many but not all individuals. Further study may reveal that gender or age or other determining features influence the distribution against which an individual's frequencies or percentages need to be compared.

7. Perhaps what we are seeing here is the beginning of an effort to defend against disconcerting, undifferentiated needs with over-compensatory anesthetizing of the expression without sufficient adjustment resources. Perhaps this was the very beginning of her unhappiness that developed to significant proportions.

8. There is a developmental progression from bipolarity to unipolarity. In unipolar shape flow, the growing and shrinking is asymmetric—in relation and response to more distinct stimuli (Kestenberg and Sossin, 1979; Sossin, 1983). If a noxious stimulus was localized to the left, then one might narrow (i.e., withdrawing from it) only with the left shoulder. Likewise, the child grows toward the mother who helps him or her. We speculate that unipolar shape flow patterns evolve from spinal reflexes, and then become embedded into a system of extending bodily dimensions into the surrounding space.

9. It must be noted that it has been observed that "bipolar bulging" may not be as reliably notated as other shape flow patterns; there may also be a tendency to underestimate its frequency. This seems to be a function of the perspective of the observer: generally horizontal and vertical actions are more readily seen than sagittal ones, unless a side-angle view is maintained. One can readily see that facial affects involving bipolar widening and lengthening are more readily visible than bipolar bulging, which requires a "third dimension." Much effort has gone into training notators to see symmetric sagittal movement, and Bess's total lack of such movements is seen as reflective of her, and not just of notational difficulties.

10. There is some intricacy to interpreting unipolar shape flow: (1) because there are 10 elements plotted, but 12 are conceptualized, and (2) because of changes made to keep open shapes together on one side of the diagram and closed shapes together on the other side. One might consider each bipolar shape flow pattern being split in half. For instance, bipolar lengthening involves a lengthening upward (cephalad) and a lengthening downward (caudal). Shape flow involves the three continua of lateral–medial, cephalad–caudal, and anterior–posterior. Conceptually (and anatomically) there are lateral shrinkings and medial widenings, however these are more internal-process shape flow patterns that cannot yet be reliably notated, hence two points are plotted in horizontal unipolar shape flow, but four patterns are plotted in each of vertical and sagittal unipolar shape flow. While bipolar lengthening creates an open shape, the case is not so simple with unipolar lengthening. Lengthening up makes an open shape, but lengthening down generally creates a closed shape. Since it was decided to keep all the closed shapes, and pre-directional patterns, on the right side of the diagram, lengthening down (a growing/closed pattern) and shortening down (a shrinking/closed pattern) are plotted cumulatively [see Figure 1 and Chapter 6]. Sagittal frequencies are treated in an analogous fashion.

11. As suggested in the text and in the previous footnote, there are many conceptual questions that pertain to the plotting and organizing of unipolar shape flow because of the issue of "intrinsic clashing." For instance, we know that growing is affined with free

flow and shrinking is affined with bound flow. So, is shortening up affined with bound flow or free flow? In one pattern, we see that the shortening bears affinity to the bound flow, but the up factor does not. The choice was made to organize the frequencies around the pre-directional factors more than around the primary growing–shrinking factors. Such considerations call for careful appraisal of unipolar shape flow. Especially if one is using an interpretive approach of graphic comparison, then one needs to consider the component contributions to the overall diagram and not just the overall gestalt and outermost plot points.

12. In his delineation of sequences and scales in space, Laban (1966; cf. Bartenieff, 1970) drew from the "parrying" of fencing to conceive of basic movements of defense, and counterpart movements of attack. This led him to consider the spatial orientation of both attacker and defender, and the manner in which their respective kinespheres inter-related with each other. Laban associated special movements to six inherently vulnerable regions on the body. He wrote:

   (1) The defense of the head necessitates raising the right arm upwards vertically;
   (2) The defense of the right flank demands a lateral movement downwards;
   (3) The left jugular vein is protected by a movement of the right arm across to the left;
   (4) The right jugular vein is protected by forcing the aggressor's weapon sideways to the right;
   (5) The left flank is guarded by a backward movement across the body fending off the aggressor's weapon;
   (6) The abdomen is shielded by an advancing movement, repulsing the aggressor (Laban, 1966, p. 37–38).

   Hence, in vertical, horizontal, and sagittal order, Laban linked the essential directional pathways we classify as shaping of space in directions as essentially anchored in organic vulnerabilities intrinsic to human architecture, and thus, as linked to defensive maneuvers.

13. As indicated, complimentary patterns shown by parent and child in shaping in directions sometimes reflect how they relate to each other. In addition, we might learn from such an analysis that a child has a significant degree of a pattern, such as forward, and the mother has little; such a finding might suggest that the mother, in this case, is less able to follow her child when the child uses a particular pattern not as accessible in her repertoire. In a prevention context, such a finding might give rise to a "re-training" approach, wherein the mother would be assisted in developing more capacity for the lacking pattern, because it otherwise creates an arena wherein the mother does not have the tools to bridge facilitative contact.

14. Though the KMP attempts to delineate stable personality traits, no doubt it sometimes identifies more contextually-influenced features. For instance, this KMP was taken when the subject had taken a long leave of absence from professional work to care for her child, hence, "explaining" might go well beyond "attacking a problem." However, if back at work, and regularly involved in problem solving, we might expect changes in both precursors of effort and shaping in directions.

15. The KMP approach differs somewhat from the approach of Lamb and Watson (1979), which was incorporated into action-profiling and movement pattern analysis. Lamb and his colleagues came to focus on the special meaning of the PGM, the posture–gesture merging; in fact, they observed that individuals are characterized by signature-like PGM patterns, that they interpreted in terms of core, distinctive aspects of the mover's

personality. The KMP notation includes the observation of phrasing (sequences of movement that can be identified in terms of the introduction, main theme, and transition or end), and this involves gesture–posture and posture–gesture mergings. But the KMP itself does not identify the PGMs, rather, it only shows the plotted frequency distribution of postures and frequency distribution of gestures. Whereas Lamb might find meaning in the gesture only against the background of the posture, the KMP sees the gestures as meaningful in their own right, reflecting ego-level adaptations and attitudes, though commitment and conscience are evidenced only by postures. The KMP's treatment of gestures and postures is thus designed to highlight harmonies and conflicts between gesture and posture in each system and between systems.

## References

Bartenieff, I. (1970). Laban's space harmony in relation to anatomical and neurophysiological concepts. In I. Bartenieff, M. Davis and F. Paulay (Eds.), *Four adaptations of effort theory in research and teaching*. New York: Dance Notation Bureau.

Bartenieff, I. and Lewis, D. (1980). *Body movement: Coping with the environment*. New York: Gordon & Breach.

Berlowe, J., Kestenberg, J. *et al.* (1995). *Training manual for the Kestenberg Movement Profile, revised by Loman*. Keene: Antioch New England Graduate School.

Brazelton, T. B. (1992). *Touchpoints*. New York: Guilford.

Davis, M. (1985). Nonverbal behavior research and psychotherapy. In G. Streiker and R. H. Kiesner (Eds.), *From research to clinical practice*. New York: Plenum Press.

Exner, J. E. (1993). *The Rorschach: A comprehensive system, Vol. 1: Basic foundations (Third Ed.)*. New York: John Wiley & Sons.

Freud, A. (1936). The ego and the mechanisms of defense. In *The Writings of Anna Freud, Vol. 2*. New York: International Universities Press, 1966.

Freud, A. (1965). Normality and pathology in childhood: Assessments of development. In *The writings of Anna Freud, Vol. VI*. New York: International University Press.

Freud, W. E. (1971). The baby profile: Part II. *Psychoanalytic Study of the Child, 26*, 172–194.

Kestenberg, J. S. (1965). The role of movement patterns in development, I: Rhythms of movement; II: Flow of tension and effort. *Psychoanalytic Quarterly, 34*, 517–563.

Kestenberg, J. S. (1967). The role of movement patterns in development, III: The control of shape. *Psychoanalytic Quarterly, 36*, 356–409.

Kestenberg, J. S. (1975). *Children and parents*. New York: Aronson.

Kestenberg, J. S. (1980). Ego-organization in obsessive–compulsive development: A study of the Rat–Man, based on interpretation of movement patterns. In M. Kanzer and J. Glenn (Eds.), *Freud and his patients*. New York: Aronson.

Kestenberg, J. S. (1985). The role of movement patterns in diagnosis and prevention. In D. A. Shaskan and W. L. Roller (Eds.), *Paul Schilder: Mind explorer*. New York: Human Sciences Press.

Kestenberg, J. S. and Borowitz, E. (1990). On narcissism and masochism in the fetus and the neonate. *Pre- and Perinatal Psychology Journal, 8*.

Kestenberg, J. S. and Sossin, K. M. (1979). *The role of movement patterns in development, 2*. New York: Dance Notation Bureau Press.

Kestenberg, J. S. and Sossin, K. M. (1994). Movement patterns in infant affect expression: Exploration of tension- and shape-flow features of the IFEEL pictures. Presented at the Fifth Kestenberg Movement Profile Conference, Sponsored by Antioch New England Graduate School, April, 1994.

Kestenberg, J. S., Sossin, K. M., Buelte, A., Schnee, E. and Weinstein, J. (1993). Manifestations of aggression: An exploration of movement patterns. In T. B. Cohen, M. H. Etezady and B. L. Pacella (Eds.), *The vulnerable child, Vol. 1.* Madison, CT: International Universities Press.

Laban, R. (1960). The *mastery of movement*. London: MacDonald & Evans.

Laban, R. (1966). *The language of movement: A guidebook to choreutics*. Boston: Plays, Inc.

Lamb, W. and Watson, E. (1987). *Body code*. London: Routledge & Kegan Paul.

Levy, L. (1963). *Psychological interpretation*. New York: Holt, Rinehart and Winston.

Loman, S. (1990). Introduction to the Kestenberg Movement Profile. In P. Lewis and S. Loman (Eds.), The *Kestenberg Movement Profile: Its past, present applications and future directions*. Keene, NH: Antioch New England.

Loman, S. (1995). The case of Warren: A KMP approach to autism. In F. Levy (Ed.), *Dance and other expressive arts therapies*. New York: Routledge.

Loman, S. and Merman, H. (1996). The KMP: A tool for dance/movement therapy. *American Journal of Dance Therapy, 18*, 29–52.

Mahler, M. (1971). Excerpts from a discussion by Margaret Mahler: New York Psychoanalytic Society Meeting February 23, 1971. In J. Kestenberg, *Children and parents*. New York: Aronson, 1975, (pp. 210–213).

Pine, F. (1990). *Drive, ego, object & self*. New York: Basic Books.

Schilder, P. (1935). *The image and appearance of the human body*. London: Kegan Paul, French, Trubner & Co. (Reprinted, New York: International Universities Press, 1970).

Schilder, P. (1951). *Psychoanalysis, man and society*. New York, Norton.

Sossin, K. M. (1983). Movement patterns of infant and mother and the ontogenesis of aggression in the first year of life. *Dissertation Abstracts International 45*. (University Microfilm # 8405489).

Sossin, K. M. (1987). Reliability of the Kestenberg Movement Profile. *Movement Studies, 2*, 23–28.

Sossin, K. M. (1990). Metapsychological considerations of the psychologies incorporated in the KMP System. In Lewis, P. and Loman, S. (Eds.), *The Kestenberg Movement Profile: Its past, present applications and future directions*. Keene, NH: Antioch New England Graduate School.

Sossin, K. M. and Loman, S. (1992). Clinical applications of the KMP. In S. Loman (Ed.), *The body–mind connection in human movement analysis*. Keene, NH: Antioch New England Graduate School.

Stolorow, R. D. and Lachmann, F. M. (1980). *Psychoanalysis of developmental arrests: Theory and treatment*. New York: International Universities Press.

Winter, D. (1992). Body movement and cognitive style: Validation of action profiling. In S. Loman (Ed.), *The body-mind connection in human movement analysis*. Keene, NH: Antioch New England Graduate School.

## CHAPTER 15

# Interpreting a KMP of Carlos, a Three-and-a-Half-Year-Old Boy: An Illustrative Case

Janet Kestenberg Amighi and Susan Loman

### Introduction

In this chapter we will offer a sample Kestenberg Movement Profile of a three-and-a-half-year-old child and take the reader through the process of making initial interpretations and formulating hypotheses. In this KMP analysis we will illustrate how to interpret the KMP using a developmental framework. We will not link this interpretation to any particular theoretical framework *per se* but use this as a model for a movement-based assessment. More specialized types of interpretation can be used by profilers in keeping with their own orientations.

This three-and-a-half-year-old boy, Carlos, falls within normal limits for a child of this age. His KMP helps us identify his areas of strength as well as those areas of developmental challenge. Through KMP analyses we see that there is much individual difference in movement repertoires, even among children of the same age group. The KMP reinforces the uniqueness and complexity of each individual. One of its values as an assessment tool is that it highlights health and wellness as much as it describes weaknesses and vulnerabilities. The information outlined by a KMP provides a ready-made treatment plan. It is apparent by analyzing the data obtained from the KMP which movement qualities are predominant, overly used, adequate, or limited. Parents and teachers can use this data to better understand the child. Therapists can determine which movement qualities are well-integrated in the client and how those qualities can be used as the medium for relationship and growth.

This KMP will include all diagrams except for shape flow design. As discussed in Chapter 7, shape flow design presents difficulties in notation accuracy and in achieving inter-observer reliability. Readers should refer to Figure 17 while reading this chapter to have a visual representation of what is described in the text.

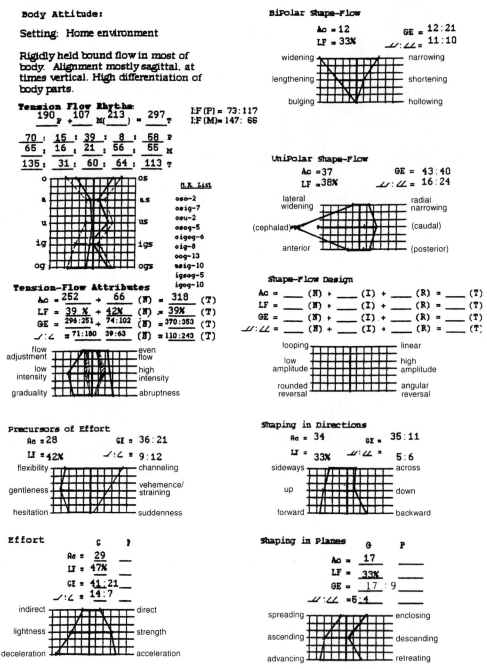

**Figure 17.** KMP of Carlos.

## Setting

This profile was made while the subject, Carlos, was playing with three other children in his home. His mother was also present. He appeared comfortable with the observer and in his environment.

## Body Attitude

Carlos displayed a high degree of differentiation of body parts. There was a prominence of mildly held bound flow in most of his body, both at rest and in motion. He seemed low-key in his manner. His alignment was slightly more sagittal than vertical, but both were present.

## Carlos's Tension Flow Rhythm Diagram

*I. Pure Rhythms*

### A. Predominant Pure Rhythms in the Diagram

Pure rhythms reflect the basic needs, impulses, and desires which often involuntarily drive one's actions. For example, when one bites one's fingernails or chews on pencils one is responding to influences of oral fighting rhythms. The pure rhythm portrait tells us which phase a person is functioning in and to which predominant needs they are responding. The pure rhythms in the diagram are represented by solid lines.

One can see by looking at the diagram that Carlos's most prominent rhythm is *os*, followed closely by *ogs* and *us*.

1. Oral rhythms (*o* and *os*) are frequently the most predominant even in diagrams of adults because needs for incorporation remain strong throughout life.
2. A high frequency of *us* indicates impatience, competitiveness, and/or irritability.
3. A prominence of *ogs* is appropriate for a child in the transition from one phase to another or in the *ogs* phase.

The fighting rhythms are integral to the differentiation process necessary to shift phases.

We can picture Carlos as a child who snaps, darts here and there impatiently, acts competitively, and at times uses focused aggression. He appears to be frequently irritated, and interrupts with a sharp edge. However, most of his aggressive rhythms are the ones which do not have a very forceful impact, even though they are aggressive. There is no one particular rhythm that is dominant or exaggerated.

### B. Least Common Pure Rhythms

*1. Fighting rhythms* The two least common fighting rhythms here are *igs* and *as*. Among the fighting rhythms, *igs* is generally the least frequent. It is a large rhythm, primarily associated with the birth process, and in every day life it usually occurs only in small segments. The *as* rhythm, not quite so large, tends to occur more frequently than *igs*, but still not so frequently as shorter rhythms such as *us* and *os*.

In the case of Carlos, *as*, which helps give organization and a stubborn type of assertiveness, covers almost one plot point in the diagram. This suggests that he does not have sufficient resources for organization and persistence. In other words, he has a minimal ability to stick to projects and follow through. Note that this tendency to have few *as* rhythms is typical for this phase. As a child becomes infused with outer genital rhythms, organization is undermined. However Carlos demonstrates an even lower than average amount of *as* for his age.

*2. Indulging rhythms*   One is first struck by the low frequency of all indulging rhythms. It is especially significant that Carlos only has one plot point in outer genital indulging, the phase which a child of almost four years would be entering.

Aside from *o*, all pure indulging rhythms are extremely low. This means that Carlos does not tend to twist and tease, passively let go or drift along, nurture, or act in an exuberant jumping manner. He moves more in the mixed form of *og*. Without using much *og* in its pure form, Carlos has difficulty jumping and thrusting himself forward. At this age, we would expect him to be showing off physically. Even in gross motor activities, he tends to become derailed and uncoordinated.

Likewise we see that use of the rhythm *u*, which promotes fluidity and letting go, is very minimal in Carlos's movement repertoire. Such a low frequency of *u* suggests a disinclination to be passive, to drift and wander without limits, allowing pleasurable experiences to just happen.

Finally, we must note that for a boy of three-and-a-half transitioning from the inner genital to the outer genital phase, he exhibits remarkably few *ig* rhythms. We are concerned about his difficulty integrating and following through.

## C. Indulging : Fighting Ratio

Just above the frequency diagram, one can find the I : F ratio in pure rhythms. It is preferable to see a relatively balanced ratio with a slightly higher amount of fighting rhythms. Aggressive rhythms, by their nature, are differentiated and clear and express differentiated needs. In the case of Carlos the ratio is 73 : 117. This suggests that when Carlos satisfies biological drives (and their psychological derivatives) he tends to do so using fighting rhythms. The ratio summarizes the data presented in the diagram.

## *II. Mixed Rhythms*

Mixed rhythms derive from exposure to external influences (such as a parenting style) and from one's own proclivities or personality. For example, someone who has a proclivity for anal twisting rhythms adds the quality of teasing to many of her actions. Someone who has a proclivity towards inner genital rhythms tends to add nurturing qualities to many behaviors and interactions. Mixed rhythms are represented in the diagram by dashed lines.

## A. Common Mixed Rhythm Patterns

To the right of the rhythm frequency diagram is a list of mixed rhythms. The list in this example only includes the most frequent combinations. Less frequently used combinations may be omitted from the KMP for space reasons, but can be found in the raw data.

With a frequency of 10, the most common mixed rhythm here is *igog*. This combination is sometimes labeled a Hershey rhythm. Blending *ig* with *og* makes the *og* rhythm less intrusive and more accommodating. Carlos also frequently combines *ig* with *as* and *o*. An *asig* combination suggests that he organizes and asserts himself in an accommodating way. One could interpret the frequent use of *ig* in mixed rhythms as the result of the influence of a person continually trying to nurture himself and others, perhaps assuming a caregiving role.

The frequent combination of *o* with *og* and *ig* suggests immaturity and/or neediness. Noting that there is an infrequency of *og* as a pure rhythm (*og* appears mixed with *o* and *ig*) we may wonder whether Carlos is having difficulty moving from early dependency needs (*oog*) and maybe an overprotective or over-dependent parental figure (*igog*) into a more mature boyhood (*og*). We might venture a hypothesis that there is a caregiver who tries to keep him childlike and pleasant (non-aggressive) and that he uses aggressive rhythms to separate and differentiate. His personal style may be more accommodating.

## B. Indulging : Fighting Ratio in Mixed Rhythms

In the mixed rhythms category, we like to see an approximately 2 : 1 ratio of indulging to fighting rhythms. Indulging rhythms ameliorate and tame fighting impulses. In contrast, mixing together two fighting rhythms is hyper-aggressive.

However, in Carlos's case, the ratio of 147 : 66 indulging to fighting is 3 : 1. What does this mean? This ratio means that Carlos's personality or character is inherently indulging and accommodating. The influence of significant caregivers can also impact his ratio of indulging to fighting.

### III. General Findings

Carlos's low frequency of *as* and *ig* in pure rhythms indicates that he has little foundation for organization, persistence, and integration. Chronologically we would expect Carlos to be entering the outer genital phase. When we look at the pure rhythms, we see that Carlos only shows a total of three plot points of outer genital indulging and fighting. In children of this age, we would expect to see many more pure *og* rhythms.

## Carlos's Tension Flow Attributes Diagram

### (1) Predominant Attributes

On the face of it this is a fairly balanced diagram. Carlos frequently uses low intensity tension flow, suggesting a mild temperament. If one notes that a significant proportion of his neutral flow is in high intensity, which approximates animated low intensity, his mildness is even more prevalent than the diagram suggests. This finding might lead us to question whether he has sufficient muscular tone.

### (2) Least Frequent Attributes

Carlos uses flow adjustment and high intensity least frequently, suggesting a limited ability to adjust moods and express intense feelings. He can maintain steady feelings for short periods of time. Regarding transitions from one feeling to another, he is able to change his feelings either abruptly or gradually. For example, when provoked, Carlos may become angry immediately (abruptly) or may gradually develop anger. In contrast, Carlos is less able to playfully adjust his feelings or accommodate his moods to frequently changing situations. Overall, it appears that Carlos is a low-key, mild child who rarely expresses intense feelings such as exuberance or rage.

*(3)  Neutral Flow*

Although the statistic is not given, we can calculate that Carlos uses neutral flow about 21% of the time. This is at the lower end of the satisfactory range of 18–30%. Use of neutral flow at a level lower than 18% means that one is not able to deaden or de-animate strong feelings well. Very high levels of use of neutral flow means that one is too often deadening one's feelinqs, and probably is depressed.

*(4)  Load Factor (Calculated in Animated Flow, Neutral Flow,*
*      and Total-Animated plus Neutral)*

A low-average load factor of 39% in animated flow and total attributes indicates that he only occasionally combines qualities of emotions to create mixtures and shades of feelings. In the neutral zone, we find slightly more complexity in the mixture of emotions.

*(5)  Gain : Expense Ratio (Calculated in Animated Flow,*
*      Neutral Flow, and Total-Animated plus Neutral)*

The gain : expense ratio is the ratio of elements of tension flow to the sum total of free and bound flow changes. Carlos shows a gain in maturation and in use of defined elements (which structure emotions) in animated flow at the "expense" of spontaneous energy in flow changes used. In neutral flow Carlos reverses this trend having a low gain : expense ratio, engaging in more flow changes and indicating spontaneity and less control over his emotions while he is in a dazed state. Carlos's total (animated plus neutral) gain : expense ratio has slightly more elements than flow changes and indicates a tendency overall toward more clearly defined and regulated emotions.

*(6)  Free : Bound Ratio (Calculated in Animated Flow,*
*      Neutral Flow, and Total-Animated plus Neutral)*

Carlos exhibits a more than 1 : 2 ratio of free to bound flow (71 : 180) in animated flow. This suggests that he is highly constrained, perhaps anxious and fearful or angry. Although somewhat less extreme, there is considerably more bound flow in the neutral zone as well (39 : 63) creating an overall total of 110 : 243.

*(7)  Number of Attribute Actions: Number of Rhythms*

Since we use the same tension flow notation lines to score both rhythms and attributes, in general we expect to see somewhat similar numbers. However, in very young children, we often see more rhythms than attributes reflecting a repetitive and simplistic use of flow patterns to respond to impulses. With maturation, we expect the relative number of attributes to increase, reflecting the ability to modulate the way one responds to impulses.

In Carlos, there is a fairly equivalent number of total rhythms (297) and the total number of attributes (318), suggesting a balance between expression of impulses and their modulation through affects. The slightly larger number of attributes reflects his developing maturity.

## Carlos's Pre-Efforts Diagram

Carlos has a fairly well-balanced use of pre-efforts with the notable exception of the limited use of suddenness. The significant usage of flexibility is surprising given that Carlos had a scant amount of twisting rhythms and flow adjustment (which both provide a foundation for flexibility).

Ideally we like to see advanced patterns evolving on the basis of earlier foundational patterns. When an advanced pattern occurs frequently but without a proper substrate, we must question whether this advanced pattern is properly integrated into the individual's movement repertoire or rather is imposed and artificial. As an analogy, this might be like a student using a vocabulary word without knowing its full meaning.

### (1) Predominant Pre-Effort Elements

The most predominant element in Carlos's diagram is channeling. As a defense mechanism, channeling is used for isolating and dividing. In learning, channeling is often used to isolate oneself from inner distractions and impulses. Carlos frequently tries to keep on track and keep disruptive impulses under control. He probably combines channeling with bound flow (bound flow is also a preferred movement quality of Carlos's. See Diagram 2 Chapter 2).

Carlos also makes considerable use of the three indulging pre-efforts. Flexibility (a first year pre-effort) allows him to skirt difficulties and/or meander in his thoughts. As a defense, flexibility is used to avoid continuing on with the same thing. As a learning mode, flexibility is used to make associations to other thoughts or ideas. Gentleness is also an important part of Carlos's pre-effort repertoire. As a defense, gentleness can serve as a reaction formation against the use of aggression. In learning, gentleness creates the ability to learn with ease. Carlos uses hesitation, which permits procrastination and dawdling. Hesitation is a delaying defense. In learning it supports taking one step at a time.

Carlos uses vehemence or straining only to a moderate degree in comparison with most of the other pre-efforts. Vehemence/straining is an identification with the aggressor defense and often functions to use aggression in an ineffectual way (e.g., as in a temper tantrum). In learning, vehemence/straining can be used in attempting to overcome frustration in mastering challenges.

### a. Learning Strategies

Thus, as the diagram shows, Carlos is more likely to hesitate, touch gingerly (using gentleness), or avoid (using flexibility). He can strain or vehemently attack problems and can subdue inner distractions with channeling.

### (2) Least Common Elements

Carlos rarely uses suddenness to escape his fears or anxieties. The low level of suddenness also suggests that he is unlikely to gain sudden insights or learn things in a flash. Perhaps, as his high degree of bound flow (see Diagram 2, Tension Flow Attributes) suggests, he is too anxious and too constrained to be able to free up his thought patterns in such a way.

### (3) Number of Actions

About 28 actions in pre-efforts are commonly found in a one-hour viewing of a mover. In Chapter 4 we compared the number of pre-effort actions with the number of effort actions.

If pre-effort actions are much more frequent, this suggests that the person is heavily defended, which can interfere with his ability to cope with the environment (which involves using efforts—see Chapter 4).

### (4) Load Factor

At 42%, Carlos has a moderate degree of complexity in his use of defenses and learning strategies. This means that at times he is able to combine defenses.

### (5) Gain : Expense Ratio

Carlos shows a gain : expense ratio of 36 : 21 demonstrating a gain in maturation and in the use of defined elements (which structure defenses and learning modes) at the "expense" of spontaneous energy in flow changes used.

### (6) Free : Bound Ratio

Carlos exhibits a 9 : 12 ratio of free to bound flow. This suggests a tendency toward constraint and anxiety in learning and in defending against undesirable urges.

### (7) General Interpretation of Carlos's Pre-Effort Diagram

Carlos favors the indulging defenses, controlling his impulses more often in accommodating ways. The only exception is his frequent use of channeling, which is a fighting defense.

## Carlos's Efforts Diagram

Diagram 4 shows that Carlos's effort diagram is well-balanced and ample in the time and weight dimensions. Carlos's spatial dimension is somewhat balanced but minimal in terms of quantity.

### (1) Prominent Elements

Carlos uses acceleration and deceleration most frequently of all the efforts. He copes well with time, able to fight time with acceleration and indulge in time with deceleration. We would expect that he would be a good decision-maker. Secondarily, he has a good balance in and a reasonable amount of weight elements. He can use a light touch or a firm (strong) one and make evaluations lightly or seriously with equal ease.

### (2) Least Common Elements

Carlos uses direct and indirect efforts to cope with space infrequently. This suggests that he does not pay much attention to things around him, focus well on specifics, or communicate effectively.

### (3) Number of Actions

There are 29 effort elements scored. This is about the same as the number of pre-efforts (see Diagram 3). This suggests that Carlos's ability to take on the challenges involved in learning new tasks (which includes defending against his vulnerabilities) supports effective problem-solving patterns. We like to see a fairly equal number of efforts and pre-efforts. If there are many more pre-efforts, it suggests that the person is highly defended and this may interfere with the individual's ability to cope with the forces of the environment. On the other hand, if someone has many fewer pre-efforts than efforts, then he may be poorly defended and poorly prepared to deal with the difficulties and anxieties involved in learning new tasks. Therefore, he may only attempt tasks which he can master easily.

To further illustrate the relationship between efforts and pre-efforts, note that in Carlos's case where the pre-efforts are the strongest (in the first year, i.e., flexibility and channeling) the effort pattern is the weakest (i.e., direct and indirect). This suggests that Carlos's defenses may be holding back his ability to cope efficiently with space in a direct or indirect manner.

If Carlos is often using channeling to isolate himself from maternal influences and using flexibility to avoid contact, then he is too inwardly- oriented to be focused outwardly in dealing with space or ideas. For example, when faced with a problem, he is less likely to be attentive (direct) or use his imagination (indirect) and more likely to avoid the situation or channel himself off.

### (4) Load Factor

A load factor of 47% indicates frequent use of two efforts elements in combination which points to an ability to cope with the environment in a creative manner. Thus Carlos appears to be quite intelligent, though we would expect that he does not make full use of his abilities because of the deficit in space elements.

### (5) Gain : Expense Ratio

Carlos shows a gain : expense ratio of 41 : 21 demonstrating a gain in maturation and in the use of defined elements (which structure coping skills) at the "expense" of spontaneous energy in flow changes used.

### (6) Free : Bound Ratio

Carlos exhibits a 14 : 7 ratio of free to bound flow. This suggests that Carlos expresses feelings of ease and safety while confronting environmental challenges twice as often as he expresses feelings of caution and anxiety.

### (7) General Interpretation of the Effort Diagram of Carlos

In sum, Carlos can weigh his intentions and act on them, but does not seek out sufficient information upon which to base his intentions, evaluations, and commitments. An adult with minimal space elements (direct and indirect) is unable to attend to new information and thus have a basis for reformulating or expanding ideas.

### The Developmental Line: Vertical Affinities in System I

Looking at the vertically-affined line of development, we expect to see each element which is prominent in early development provide the foundation for later maturation of similar qualities. For example, *os* contains some even flow which then provides the foundation for channeling, which in turn serves as a precursor for direct. This developmental pattern does not always occur. In Carlos's case we see some marked discontinuities. For example, while Carlos has a fairly high frequency of *ogs* usage and a high frequency of abruptness (a quality of *ogs*), he rarely uses suddenness. Looking further down at efforts, we see that despite the near absence of the precursor suddenness, acceleration is a frequently used pattern. How can we explain this? Carlos can use time in response to feelings (getting angry or happy abruptly) and he can accelerate in the accomplishment of tasks. Apparently, Carlos learns with hesitation, but once a task is mastered or his anxieties are overcome, he is able to proceed with acceleration. Discontinuities, such as the one described here, suggest a developmental issue which may warrant some attention. With the near absence of a precursor we may question the solidity of the more mature pattern.

## Carlos's Bipolar Shape Flow Diagram

### (1) Prominent Elements

There is a clear predominance in the horizontal dimension; Carlos widens almost twice as much as he narrows. Widening can be interpreted to mean that one feels comfortable, trusting, and generous, expecting that good things will come. Narrowing expresses discomfort, but also it provides a time for coming back to oneself and finding trust and comfort inside. A good balance of widening and narrowing reflects the feeling that the whole world loves you and will be there for you and that you love yourself as well.

When, as in Carlos's case, widening is not well-balanced with narrowing, it may indicate that he is widening in response to expected attention and love, but is not receiving it. If this happens frequently, the person may become frozen in the expectant attitude. We also see children who rarely narrow because they only receive attention when they are expressing comfort through widening.

Carlos lengthens more than he shortens, suggesting that he feels pride in himself more than he feels unsure and insignificant. However, lengthening three times as much as he shortens may suggest that Carlos is seeking a sense of pride rather than simply expressing it. We should take into account that Carlos is entering the outer genital phase where we frequently see the "jumping bean" child lengthen, show off, and feel that she can conquer the world. A good balance in shortening and lengthening gives stability in the vertical dimension.

### (2) Least Common Elements

Carlos rarely uses the sagittal qualities of bulging and hollowing. Low levels of sagittal elements may be explained partially by the fact that it is the most difficult dimension to observe. In the case of this diagram we also question its validity since only twelve actions were recorded. Based on this given, we can say that the absence of any bulging or hollowing prevents Carlos from expressing the feelings of self-confidence, contentment (fullness) or depletion (emptiness).

### (3) Number of Actions

There are only 12 actions in bipolar shape flow. This means that Carlos's global body image does not change often to express variation in self feelings.

## (4) Load Factor

With a load factor of 33%, Carlos does not combine elements. He expresses his self-feelings and moods in the simplest ways.

## (5) Gain : Expense Ratio

The gain : expense ratio compares the complexity of use of shape flow elements with the number of growing and shrinking changes. Since Carlos shows a higher number of growing and shrinking changes relative to shape flow elements (12 : 16), he is showing slightly more emotional expression than control over moods.

## (6) Growing : Shrinking Ratio

Carlos grows almost twice as often as he shrinks. Growing generally is associated with comfort and positive self-feelings. However, so much growing without a balance of shrinking becomes an expression of neediness and seeking comfort without an ability to express discomfort clearly. An excess of growing shape flow potentially puts the mover at risk by reacting openly in dangerous environments.

## (7) Comparing Bipolar Shape Flow with Tension Flow Attributes

Bipolar shape flow provides the structure for the expression of feelings, while tension flow attributes offer the dynamic aspect of feelings.

Looking over at tension flow attributes we see that Carlos uses bound flow more than twice as much as free flow, suggesting that he often combines growing shape flow with bound flow. This combination of movement qualities is considered a clash. Carlos may be searching for nurturing supplies with considerable caution or anger. A person may widen, expecting pleasant things to come to her, but when they do not, she may become angry or anxious. Similarly she may lengthen expecting praise, but if praise is not received, she may become overly assertive. Also note that there is no bipolar structure for graduality and abruptness. Often observers do not recognize emotions clearly when the appropriate structure for their expression is absent.

On the other hand, sometimes there is more structure than dynamic. In Carlos's case, he widens much more often than he uses flow adjustment. His widening sometimes occurs without an appropriate feeling tone. This confirms previous interpretations and indicates that he may have difficulty adjusting his moods to new conditions.

However, as noted above, when dealing with a small number of actions (under 20) one must be especially cautious about making interpretations.

## Carlos's Unipolar Shape Flow Diagram

Unipolar shape flow changes are made in response to specific stimuli. Note that the unipolar diagram is structured somewhat differently than the others. As mentioned earlier, in order to show the continuity between responding to stimuli from above and the later pattern "up" we place both shortening up and lengthening up on the left side of the diagram. We call these **cephalad** or "towards the head." Likewise, downward movements (shortening down and lengthening down) are placed together on the right side of the diagram and termed **caudal** or "towards the tail." The same procedure is followed with bulging and hollowing. Hollowing back and bulging back are both movements towards the posterior and placed together on the right side of the diagram. Hollowing forward and bulging forward are both movements towards the anterior and are placed together on the left side of the diagram.

Of all diagrams, unipolar shape flow is most affected by context. A mother with a small child will be likely to lengthen down frequently and the small child relating to her mother will be likely to lengthen up often. These vertical patterns must be judged in context. In addition, the presence of noxious or attractive stimuli within the setting will also affect the diagram.

### (1) Prominent Elements

Carlos shows a fairly evenly balanced diagram with the exception created by the extraordinary frequency of cephalad movements (primarily shortening up) but also by a good deal of lengthening up. Shortening up may occur frequently if a person is often occupied with picking things up from the floor, though we might expect to see a commensurate frequency of lengthening down. Carlos may be shortening up in the shoulders trying to pick himself up. In expressive gestures we may see a shrug or a disgusted shortening up of the lip or a withdrawal from unpleasant stimuli (combined with hollowing back). The combination of using much shortening up and lengthening up suggests that he is frequently relating to stimuli above himself. He may lengthen up to try to be bigger than someone else.

### (2) Least Common Elements

There are few shortening down, hollowing back, or bulging back movements. Carlos does not appear to be shrinking from noxious stimuli above him, nor does he respond much to stimuli behind him.

### (3) Number of Actions

37 actions suggests that Carlos is very responsive to specific stimuli in the environment and responds in an expressive manner, i.e., he has an emotionally-laden involvement with people or things around him.

a. Unipolar:bipolar actions Carlos has three times as many unipolar as bipolar actions. Bipolar reflects global feelings. Unipolar reflects feelings about specific stimuli. Carlos more often uses unipolar shape flow to reach out, extend himself, or withdraw in relationship to people or things in the environment. This proportion is slightly above the expected range.

b. Comparing the number of actions in unipolar to the number of effort actions, we find that Carlos is more likely to respond to an object in the environment by approaching or withdrawing from it rather than coping with the forces of space, weight, and time. We see this from the number of effort actions viewed during the same observation period (29 efforts, 37 unipolar actions). In adults we often see that there are more effort elements than shape flow elements not only because adults may be more adept at coping with the environment, but also because they tend to be less emotionally expressive than children. A much higher number of unipolar actions to effort actions would indicate a person who is extremely emotional and perhaps overstimulated. A very low number of unipolar actions in comparison to effort actions reflects a person who is minimally responsive to stimuli in their environment.

## (4) Load Factor

Carlos has a load factor of 38% which suggests that the complexity of his response to stimuli is low to moderate.

## (5) The Gain: Expense Ratio

The gain : expense ratio compares the complexity of use of unipolar shape flow elements with the number of growing and shrinking changes. The higher the number of elements to growing and shrinking changes (43:40) indicates slightly more control over responses to stimuli than emotionally expressive movements.

## (6) Ratio of Growing: Shrinking

The ratio of 16:24 indicates that Carlos withdraws from stimuli more often than he approaches them. This ratio suggests the possibility of a somewhat noxious environment.

## (7) Comparing Tension Flow Attributes with Unipolar Shape Flow

Both bipolar and unipolar shape flow may provide structure for tension flow attributes. Bipolar shape flow provides a structure in relation to global self-feelings while unipolar shape flow provides a structure in relationship to feelings towards specific objects or people.

### a. First Year Line

We can compare unipolar shape flow to the tension flow attribute diagram and see that unipolar widening and narrowing provide some, though not sufficient, structure for the amount of flow adjustment and even flow. In comparison, bipolar shape flow provides more structure. This suggests that Carlos is able to structure his adjusting or persisting feelings with symmetrical widening and narrowing (self-contained moods) more often than with unipolar widening and narrowing (seeking and withdrawing from stimuli).

### b. Second Year Line

Low intensity of feelings is given more than sufficient structure by both bipolar lengthening and unipolar shortening and lengthening up. This means that at times Carlos uses the structure of vertical shape flow without the appropriate dynamic of low intensity. For example, when Carlos lengthens up for help, he lacks an accompanying mild, appealing manner.

The small amount of high intensity in attributes is matched with a small amount of unipolar shortening down. This is a good match, but the infrequency of these patterns does mean that Carlos may have difficulty both feeling and demonstrating intense feelings such as rage.

### c. Third Year Line

The third year attributes, graduality and abruptness, are given a sufficient amount of structure through unipolar bulging and hollowing. If a change in tension flow is not accompanied by a matching change in shape flow, observers will have difficulty recognizing the emotion expressed. As the reader may recall, Carlos did not have bulging or hollowing in bipolar shape flow. This would mean that Carlos's change in global feelings of satiation and depletion may be difficult for others to recognize, though such feelings in relation to specific objects or people would be more clearly expressed. Carlos cannot gradually fill up with feeling (welling up with tears, or bulging with contentment) nor abruptly let go of feelings (as in an abrupt sigh or cry of despair).

## Carlos's Shaping in Directions Diagram

This diagram shows that Carlos favors the open shapes (there is a 2 : 1 ratio between open shapes and closed shapes) and emphasizes the sagittal dimension.

### (1) Most Prominent Elements

There are healthy amounts (plot points between 3–4) shown on the diagram for sideways, up, forward, and backward.

### (2) Least Prominent Elements

Down and across are the least common elements, but are not lacking. In general, one could say that Carlos defends himself against objects and people more frequently using open-shaped forms of defense than closed ones. He is more likely to appease or elude than he is to shut himself off (using across or down). In learning patterns he may be less adept at defining and barring distractions, but overall he has a fairly well-balanced use of directional movements.

### (3) The Number of Actions

34 actions suggests that he is active in defending himself against objects or people in the environment (this number will be compared with the number of shaping actions below).

### (4) Load Factor

The low load factor of 33% tells us that he defends or learns in an overly simplistic rather than complex fashion. He may have difficulty protecting himself from objects which approach him from a diagonal.

### (5) The Gain : Expense Ratio

In the gain : expense ratio, the total number of directional elements is compared to the total number of growing and shrinking qualities. The high ratio of directional elements to shape flow changes (35 : 11) indicates that most directional movements were mechanical in quality.

### (6) Growing : Shrinking Ratio

Whereas there is always an element of growing or shrinking in bipolar and unipolar shape flow, in directional movements growing and shrinking can be absent. Out of 35 directional elements, 11 have a growing or shrinking component in Carlos's case. This means that about one-third of these movements have an accompanying emotional component. In older adults the shape flow component tends to decrease considerably.

### (7) Comparing Directions and Pre-Efforts

When we compare directions with the pre-efforts diagram, we observe a certain lack of coordination. Channeling, Carlos's most frequently used pre-effort, is given inadequate structure by the direction of across. This suggests that as he attempts to isolate and channel his feelings, he does not have sufficient structure to contain those feelings or protect himself from distractions. We also see that he moves backwards but without the matched use of suddenness. Thus he may withdraw from unpleasant situations using hesitation, suggesting conflicting feelings about those things or people who make him feel uncomfortable. This mismatch also reveals an inability to quickly extricate oneself from danger.

Carlos does not have quite enough down to accompany his vehemence/straining pre-efforts, indicating that he may have some difficulty showing his frustration either in learning contexts or in regards to his aggressive feelings.

Flexibility and sideways are well matched, suggesting that Carlos can combine eluding and avoiding well in defensive maneuvers. In learning, this combination permits Carlos to open up his mind to make new associations, connecting one idea to another. The match of forward and hesitation is another strength Carlos has. This combination allows him to make step-by-step progress in learning and to enter new situations carefully.

## Carlos's Shaping in Planes Diagram

From this diagram it is evident that Carlos has clear preferences in his use of certain shaping elements to the exclusion of others, which limits his options in relating to others.

### (1) Most Prominent Elements

Carlos encloses about three times more frequently than he spreads. This suggests that he seeks one-to-one relationships and is more comfortable in intimate spaces. In the vertical plane there is a pronounced preference for ascending over descending. Carlos ascends to others, aspiring to be like them. In the sagittal plane, we see that he advances to others slightly more often than he retreats. With advancing he can look ahead and anticipate how things will be in the future. He tends to advance more often than he reviews past experiences through retreating.

### (2) Least Prominent Elements

Carlos spreads infrequently. This suggests that he has difficulty relating to more than one person or idea at a time. With scanty descending he will have difficulty confronting, demanding, and being grounded.

### (3) Number of Actions

There are only 17 actions in shaping in planes in comparison with the 34 we found in directional movements. This suggests that Carlos tends to relate to people in a defensive, protective, and simplistic manner rather than in multifaceted ways.

## (4)  Load Factor

The low load factor of 33% suggests that when Carlos does relate to others, there is no complexity in the way he approaches and relates.

## (5)  The Gain:Expense Ratio

The gain : expense ratio compares the complexity of use of shaping in planes elements with the number of shape flow changes. Carlos uses a higher number of shaping elements to shape flow changes (17:9) revealing more control over social interactions than emotional expression.

## (6)  Growing:Shrinking Ratio

The ratio of 5:4 is balanced. There is a total of nine elements in growing and shrinking, contributing emotional tone to the 17 actions in shaping in planes. Thus when Carlos encloses, for example, he is likely to do so with narrowing (adding feelings of self-containment), or when he ascends, he is likely to also lengthen (indicating pride), thus giving the movements more expressiveness.

## (7)  Comparing Shaping in Planes with Efforts

Here we find a considerable lack of fit with the efforts diagram. When we compare load factors we see that Carlos demonstrates creative intelligence when dealing with space, weight, or time (load factor 47%) but a low degree of social intelligence and social skills (load factor 33%). Secondly, he doesn't use enough direct attention to give dynamics to the much larger amount of enclosing. Therefore, he may be able to enclose a person or idea, but not be able to pay enough attention to it. It is often an empty type of relating and communicating. When he explores, he tends to do so in small, enclosed areas, but without the effort direct he will not be detail-oriented. Thus he may be possessive, enclosing people, things or ideas, but not be able to attend to his "possessions."

We see also that he has strength in efforts, but little structure for it in shaping. He can marshal strength, but not structure it to show his determination. His strength therefore does not serve social functions well.

Regarding Carlos's positive abilities, we see a good match between ascending and lightness, i.e., he can express his intentions and aspirations in a lighthearted manner. He can admire and ascend to someone with appropriate, easy acceptance. He also matches advancing with deceleration, which suggests that he can approach others without overwhelming them. Carlos can progress through tasks well, giving himself time to anticipate and plan. His retreating, however, is insufficient to structure all the acceleration, so he may tend to rush ahead at times. And finally, when he does spread to take in more ideas, people, or information, he is able to use indirectness to attend to a full array of things. It is not used frequently, but when it is used, there is good matching.

Note: Discussion regarding matching and mismatching must be modified when we are interpreting the profile of a young child. We do not expect to find adequate matches until latency.

## (8)  General Interpretation of the Shaping in Planes Diagram of Carlos

Carlos seems like a child who finds a role model or a best buddy whom he encloses, admires, and advances with toward shared goals. He can evaluate best with praise and admiration (ascending) and rarely grounds himself or stands up to others (descending). He seems to have an emotional investment in his relationships (growing and shrinking) but the relationships are simple (33% load factor).

## The Developmental Line: Vertical Affinities in System II

Carlos shows the most consonance in the developmental line from lengthening bipolarly, to lengthening up, to up, and finally, to ascending. All of these patterns have plot points of 3–4 on the diagram. Thus he has a solid foundation in early patterns which lead to well-developed advanced patterns. There is also some degree of consonance from narrowing bipolarly through enclosing.

However, elsewhere in the diagrams, we find that there is little shape flow to serve as an under-structure for later shaping in directions and shaping in planes patterns. For example, Carlos's forward/advancing and backward/retreating are not supported by sufficient amounts of bulging and hollowing. This lack of under-structure may affect his sense of security and balance when running and operating.

In contrast, if the foundational movements are present, it is often not so difficult to culti-vate the development of more mature patterns which are only minimally present. Perhaps with support Carlos could develop some of his self-feelings of generosity (seen in bipolar widening) into the capacity to spread his attention to others using spreading shapes.

## Overall Conclusions

Carlos's KMP reveals considerable areas of strength. First of all, his high load factor in efforts shows good adaptation to the environment and good problem-solving skills which we have termed "creative intelligence." He has abundant amounts of intention and decision-making qualities. He has good affinities with open directions and indulging pre-efforts. He has a broad movement repertoire of movement choices available to him as seen in the balance in most of his diagrams.

Regarding areas of concern, in System I we note his low number of pure indulging outer genital rhythms for a child of his age, his high level of bound flow, and his proneness to anxiety. He shows impatience or irritability in his high amount of urethral starting/stopping rhythms and interrupting with his *ogs*. He shows abruptness in attributes, but skips over suddenness and shows high amounts of acceleration. We would question his lack of suddenness in this developmental line. He is quite defended in terms of his impulses, stressing indulging qualities. He may not wish to make mistakes in decision-making or make sudden learning connections when he is not sure of himself. We see this lack of self-confidence in the total absence of bulging in bipolar shape flow. We are also concerned about his limits in spatial efforts and how that will affect his ability to communicate and pay attention effectively.

As demonstrated in this interpretation of Carlos, the KMP provides a developmental framework for assessing an individual's strengths and areas in which further growth could be fostered. This comprehensive tool for appraisal can provide a thorough basis for treatment planning.

# CHAPTER 16

# Outline for the Clinical Interpretation of the Kestenberg Movement Profile with Adults

Penny Lewis

## Introduction

This outline integrates the psychoanalytic, ego psychological, and object relations orientation of Dr. Judith Kestenberg with modern theories of recovery from abuse, addictions, and outmoded childhood survival patterns. In addition, this profile is suitable for use with adults without organic impairment. Thus the following chapter represents a clinically-oriented outline for interpreting the nine formulated diagrams in the Kestenberg Movement Profile. Prospective KMP analysts are referred to the Training Manual for the Kestenberg Movement Profile (Berlowe, Kestenberg *et al.*, 1995) for the specifics on how to translate the notation of observed movement into the graphed diagrams. The focus of this outline is on possible maladaptive or pathological findings based upon a European/Euro-American orientation to normal development.

Since the formation of personality, including the precursors for survival and repetitious behaviors, evolve in the first few years of life, indicators for maladaptive behavior are more heavily loaded in the non-ego-based flow systems. These systems develop earlier and are more unconscious and pre-verbal. Psychoanalytic language identifies them as id-based while recovery language identifies them as expressions of the inner child or inner children (multiplicity which occurs when the internalized self is ontogenically fragmented due to trauma occurring over several developmental phases). Thus more ego-based movement parameters will only be minimally discussed here. Regardless of the emphasis of the flow factors over the efforts and shaping, it is vital to view the KMP in its entirety. In this way the psychotherapist has not only an understanding of past abuse and the resultant behaviors, but also a grasp of the direction toward a more accurate expression of self. It is recommended that the KMP, like other personality evaluation tests and procedures, should be used in conjunction with other diagnostic indicators to insure greater substantiation of assessments.

## The Clinical KMP Outline

### *I. General Information*

A. The essential data should include the name, date of observation, age, and sex of the subject or subjects, and circumstances under which the observation was made.

B. States or Activities Being Done

In the general description of the activity, the KMP analyst employs colorful adjectives to describe the subject and the body movement. The clinical description may include colloquial expressions which will paint a moving picture of this individual's character and personality.

### *II. Body Attitude*

Comprising what Irmgard Bartenieff (1980) conceptualized as the "body attitude" is a gestalt of factors such as a person's characteristic standing and sitting body position, use of body parts, typical phrasing of movement, carried body shape, and readiness for certain patterns to emerge. These generalized factors may reflect body image, self feelings, object relations, collective culture and gender, and socioeconomic factors as well as the individual's present reaction to the environment and events which are occurring. It is the somatic core of the individual's presentation of the body which changes with each developmental phrase. Basically it represents that which the KMP analyst can observe without having to engage in movement notation; often the analyst will make hypotheses regarding earlier childhood and care-giving. Indications of early training can be targeted here. Fixed survival patterns may be frozen in the body or in readiness to be reactivated at a moment's notice. Gender and cultural preferences of body planes, shape, and alignment, the available use of the whole body, or restrictions to potential movement of certain body parts or certain relationships to space, gravity and time can be gleaned at this time as well.

### A. Body Part Movement Identification

*1. Uses Total Body Primarily*   The observer notes if there is a predominance of the whole body participating in most of the movement.

*2. Uses Part of the Body Primarily*   An indication here would denote that during the observation only one part of the body was moving. This would occur, for example, if someone were sitting in a relaxed position while talking. If the sample observation had been taken at different times requiring diverse movement adaptation and the individual still remained in a limited gestural pattern we might, after ruling out physical impairment and socio-cultural factors, assume a lack of development or relationship between the ego/inner adult and superego/inner parent. This level of limitation is seen in psychotic individuals and those who have been profoundly physically abused.

*3. Uses Body Segments*   An emphasis placed here indicates that body segments, such as shoulder-arm or knee-ankle, are used in movement but there is no sequential gesture-posture merger of these segments with one another. This phenomenon can be seen in its extreme in the body fragmentation of schizoid personalities, severely traumatized individuals, and autistic children. In severe pathology erratic postural shifts can be observed as well as segmentation in which body parts are moved in a non-sequential isolated fashion. This can be seen, for example, with the finger and palm hyperextension found in autistic children or isolated, disorganized weight shifts with those reacting in hypervigilence.

*4. Specify Leading Body Part* This category focuses on which body part moves first in movement sequences. This factor may have significance if we see that movement evolves solely from the periphery of the body without any movement originating from breath-supported torso movement and proximal joints. Dance therapists have assessed this phenomenon to be related to the storage of repressed drives, affect, and/or trauma in the torso area. Typically this results in a frozen shape and bound flow which can include the shoulder girdle and hip joint. The premise for this lack of central movement is that primitive defenses (tension flow attributes and bipolar shape flow) are inhibiting movement near the body block so as to not disturb the material stored there.

## B. Body Posture: Shape Flow-Shape Subsystem

*1. Body Alignment*
  a. Horizontal plane: Individuals who function primarily out of the horizontal tend to lean to the side while sitting (e.g., tilting the head or leaning on either arm). This is the plane of listening, exploring and communication. Individuals fixated in this plane literally collapse out of the vertical as if pulled downward toward the horizontal. Standing, the classic S-shaped curve can be detected: the weight of the body is on the heels, the back is swayed back with the pelvis forward and the belly emptied or hollowing back. The jaw is tilted forward and movement is generally initiated by the head. These sagittal plane adjustments are due to an inability to achieve verticality due to being clinically fixated or stuck in the earlier developmental horizontal plane. This posture gives the impression that individuals "can't" do what needs to be done in order to be proactive and move forward in life. They appear lifeless and frequently the muscles and effort expression is underdeveloped. This S-shaped curve may be slight or severe.
  Clinically speaking, since developmentally we are first in the horizontal, i.e., the lying down plane, we can posit that this individual may have unresolved issues from the first year and a half of life. These issues may stem from lack of appropriate primary care-giving, typically due either to abandonment (denoting psychodynamically a negative fixation) or smothering (positive fixation) or both. These individuals can be identified as oral characters.
  b. Vertical plane: Individuals who function primarily in the vertical (up/down) plane tend to sit upright in an unsupported/ or self-supported manner. They typically exhibit a bipolar shaping of their body in the vertical. This is true in standing position as well. This is the plane of presenting, assertion, power, and control. Developmentally this dominants during the toddler phase of the "terrible twos" which begins at about eighteen months. Clinically speaking, if an individual remains in this position no matter what the adaptive context, we may notice tightly contracted arches, over-developed calf muscles, quadriceps, and hamstrings. The pelvis is tilted forward frequently with contracted external rotator buttocks muscles resulting in a widened second position (ballet) or duck-like stance. There is often a strong muscular development with an expansive chest and low back tension frequently resulting in chronic pain. The message of the vertical personality shifts to "I won't". This posture can be typically seen in the classic state trooper's stance or salesmen presenting persistently without communicating. This anal character frequently has anger stored in the lower back area and can hold down for periods of time followed by rage explosions not unlike the temper tantrums of a two-year-old.
  c. Sagittal plane: Individuals who function primarily in the sagittal (forward/backward) plane tend to sit forward or retreat backward. They typically narrow bipolarly so that the body has an arrow-like penetrating appearance. If forward in the sagittal they often have to keep

busy "doing" to avoid feeling deeply. They may appear officious, impatient, and work-addicted. They may also demonstrate a held upper torso shift forward or backward. Clinically, this plane can be detected in the histrionic personality and incested or molested post traumatic stress individuals both moving forward in the upper torso and holding back in the pelvic area. Along with this stance can be seen frightened eyes and elevated shoulders. Their behavior can include a sexualization of relationships, occasionally with a coquettish flirtation.

## 2. General Shape

General shape category identifies which specific body parts are held in shape flow. The shape can be bipolar, involving a symmetrical held response such as widening on both sides, lengthening up and down, or bulging forward and backward; or conversely narrowing bipolarly, shortening up and down, or hollowing backward and forward. The former produces an open orientation to the environment; the latter a closed response. The general shape can also denote unipolar or asymmetrical movement. This can be seen in lengthening the shoulders upward as was described in the histrionic personality or the hollowing backward of the horizontal oral character. General shape often will be viewed as a childhood relational imprint. This shape gestalt relates how the individual responded to his childhood environment. The KMP analyst can almost mentally draw the surrounding primary care-givers in dramatic family-sculptured relationship to the subject and thereby develop hypotheses about the individual's early childhood. For example, if an individual is seated in a held, expanding, grandiose bipolar widening, lengthening, and bulging position, the analyst might imagine an enmeshed, adoring posture of an empty mother who lives off the greatness of her unrealitivized offspring.

## C. Body Action Attitude: Tension Flow Effort Subsystem

### 1 Tension Lines

Since the writings of Wilhelm Reich (1949), therapists have been aware of tension spots. These so-called dead spots indicate previously emotionally charged areas in an individual's body. These areas store childhood memories of abuse and affect—laden split-off parts of the self. Frequently, there are also constellations of held bound flow in various parts of the body which have an interrelationship to one another, such as with the anal sadistic (fighting) character. These individuals tense their arches, gastrocnemius, quadriceps, and hamstrings in their legs. Their external rotators and pectoral muscles are over-developed along with the muscles in the lumbar and cervical area in their torso. Triceps are also held and are in contracted conflict with the antagonist biceps.

Various areas frequently carry specific clinical meaning. For example, if an individual's lower torso is frozen, this may indicate cultural influences such as Euro-American and Northern European heritages, but if truly locked into a one-unit torso, sexual abuse or the fear of such may be involved. Because women's power resides in their hips and thighs, held tension may indicate cultural or family-of-origin messages that full expression of strength and assertion is not permitted in women.

Tension in the belly area, easily assessed by a lack of shape flow alteration, indicates that the internalized sense of self or inner child is split off, damaged, or not developed. Its location in the belly is due to an initial oral enteroceptive sense of self. Tension in the chest is also detected by a lack of shape flow changes in breathing. This phenomenon is typical of white males in the West who have been given the message that vulnerable, heart-related feelings such as hurt, pain, and sadness are "unmanly" to have.

Low back tension, as mentioned before, frequently addresses blocked anger, sexuality and/or assertion. Upper back tension is quite common in the West as it is a favorite storage place for the superego or inner critic. Neck tension results in a body/mind split which may serve to separate feelings and drives and stored trauma from consciousness. This tension also inhibits vocal expression. Tempro-mandibular joint tension (TMJ) also stops speaking out as well as orally receiving.

Tension in the agonist and antagonist muscle systems in the legs and arms indicates a body conflict between the desire to stamp one's feet, kick out, or move forward or reach out, bar access, or aggressively punch out respectively.

### 2. Frozen Effort and Flow Patterns
An individual's effort and tension signature is also imprinted in her body. These frozen feeling responses to the environment can also tell the analyst about the subject's primitive feeling-charged survival mechanisms which are also the support for ego defense mechanisms (pre-efforts). For example, even flow could suggest a person whose family role was to smooth things over or not bring attention to oneself; abrupt flow could indicate a hyper-vigilant response to an abusive family of origin.

A readiness for certain effort patterns to emerge from a resting state can also be identified by the KMP analyst, and used to identify ego strengths.

### 3. Effort Phrasing
The most frequently used effort sequencing in movement is delineated in this section. Here the typical effort or flow preparation with employed body parts is identified, followed by the main action or theme and the resolution of the movement phrase. Favorite transitional efforts are also noted.

## D. Sketched Standard Positions

Finally, the observer is asked to make schematic drawings of the subject lying supine and prone (if available or appropriate, as with infants) and sitting and standing with children and adults. This visual image can frequently summarize the written material and is useful particularly for those of us who are more visual thinkers and learners.

## III. Tension Flow Rhythms:
### Apparatus for the Discharge of Drives (Diagram 1)

From a structural perspective these drives are unconscious and emerge from the id. Utilizing recovery theory language, these rhythms stem from the inner child's needs and wants. These rhythms may also be stripped of the Freudian language and identified based on their functional physiological purpose:

| Age | Freudian Drive Theory | Physiologic Function |
| --- | --- | --- |
| 0–6 mos | Oral libidinal (indulging) (o) | Sucking |
| 6–9 mos | Oral sadistic (fighting) (os) | Snapping/biting and chewing |
| 9–18 mos | Anal libidinal (indulging) (a) | Twisting |
| 18–24 mos | Anal sadistic (fighting) (as) | Strain/release, defecation |
| 2–2.5 yrs | Urethral libidinal (indulging) (u) | Running/drifting, uncontrolled flowing out |
| 2.5–3 yrs | Urethral sadistic (fighting) (us) | Starting/stopping, bladder control |
| 3–3.5 yrs | Inner genital libidinal (indulging) (ig) | Swaying uterine and scrotal moves |

| 3.5–4 yrs | Inner genital sadistic (fighting) (igs) | Surging/birthing |
| 4–5 yrs | Outer genital libidinal (indulging) (og) | Jumping, out of bounds |
| 5–6 yrs | Outer genital sadistic (fighting) (ogs) | Spurting/ramming, thrusting-penetrating |
| Adult | Genital (igog) | Coital and orgasmic |

## Flow Regulation

The **modification of rhythm** in which one rhythm is altered through interpersonal attunement is also crucial. This can be seen when a mother mirrors in synchrony the sucking rhythm of her infant. A modulation of the outer genital rhythm with the addition of the inner genital rhythm (igog) may occur after male genital penetration so that sexual partners may join in rhythmic coital synchrony. The "melody of movement" may be regulated by the redistribution of rhythms in order to converse in synchrony with another. Not only do infants thrive with attunement, but adult clients, too, feel joined, congruent, and understood better when their rhythmic sequences or melodies are joined.

### A. Dominant Rhythm

With adults and age-appropriate children, all rhythms need to be present in pure form in order for the drive to be sufficiently differentiated. If a rhythm is absent, it may be due to the fact that they have not developmentally arrived at the phase or it may be that the drive has been repressed because it is considered unacceptable by the family, culture, or gender-specific attributes. If a pure rhythm is clearly dominant it indicates the developmental level at which the individual is fixated. In recovery theory this would identify the age of the inner child.

Related developmental themes summarized:

*1. Oral Libidinal (Indulging) Rhythm Dominance Symbiosis*, described by object relations theorist Margaret Mahler (1968), is the initial relational stage between mother (object) and infant. When good enough attunement of the sucking rhythm occurs, the infant's primary narcissistic experience of being undifferentiated from a loving, need-satisfying environment occurs. This self-object dual unity promotes several phenomena: basic trust and sense of safety in the environment, a sense that the self-environment matrix can satisfy needs, a positive body image, and a developing sense of fullness of self, all in conjunction with shape flow. The latter develops from an enteroceptive or belly sense of fullness which comes from an ease or satiation of the need for nourishment. In recovery theory this process addresses the development of an inner child (corroborative evidence can be seen when patients are asked to imaginally enter their bodies and locate their inner child. Invariably they put their hands on their stomachs, denoting where the child within resides).

If the mother is not able to attune to the infant's sucking rhythm, the infant will not be able to successfully feel empathy or feel that fundamental needs and wants can be met.

In other instances due to organic problems such as severe developmental delay, attention deficit hyperactive disorder, autism, or congenital anomalies (cleft palate, colic, allergies, etc.) the infant himself may have difficulty achieving or sustaining the oral sucking rhythm. In these instances organization of the rhythm may need greater encouragement over a longer period of time.

Individuals who have an overabundance of oral libidinal (indulging) rhythms in their movement are said to be orally fixated. Oral rhythms may appear in different parts of the body, manifested in constant rocking, hand to face gestures like hair twirling, head nodding, and soothing foot movements; or in addictive behavior as with compulsive thumb sucking, cigarette smoking, or constant drinking. Oral rhythms will frequently be the most employed mixed rhythm component. These patterns go along with the oral character described earlier in the section on body attitude. Often these individuals demonstrate a desire for merger through longing eye-to-eye contact, reflection of others' tension flow as seen with codependent individuals, and a general disinterest in engaging in anything which involves standing or ambulating for long periods of time.

When other rhythms are present primarily in mixed form with oral rhythms, these rhythms and their associated drives and object-related derivations are not sufficiently differentiated. In addition, since the oral libidinal (indulging) rhythm reduces aggression, the consistently merging oral rhythm could inhibit needed aggression, resulting in a diminished capacity to discriminate (oso) or stand up and assert oneself (oas).

Some individuals will demonstrate dysfunction through a profound diminished use of the oral rhythm entirely. Since the presence of this (and any other pure) rhythm is needed in order to meet basic needs, it can be assumed that although they may be able to consume food, derivatively such individuals may be fundamentally incapable of soothing themselves. This may result in their inability to receive narcissistic supplies, to maintain sustenance for a full and realistically positive sense of self, and to feel that they are capable of trusting that the environment is safe and can satisfy their needs.

*2. Oral Sadistic (Fighting) Rhythm Dominance*: This rhythm is crucial in Mahler's first sub-phase of separation and individuation (differentiation of the infant from the primary object). The same biting rhythm is used in patting and tapping the infant's self and the environment. Self-patting helps establish the needed body boundary. Tapping the environment establishes its material presence and otherness.

This same rhythm intrapsychically aids in the formation of an ego boundary thereby enhancing the individual's capacity to distinguish inner from outer reality and assisting ego formation by promoting a holding container for its developing mediational functions.

There sometimes appears an over-dominance of the oral sadistic (fighting) rhythm. When this fixation is present individuals will be seen tapping their hands and feet, talking with a quickened, sharply enunciated tone, along with a heightened tension in the jaw and neck. They may constantly chew gum or food, bite their nails, and suffer from TMJ (Tempro-mandibular Syndrome) or nocturnal teeth grinding. Their eyes are frequently glaring. They tend to be critical and hold on to ideas or relationships, unable to let go. These individuals have a biting or snapping personality. They are not cuddlers and when hugged are quick to give a differentiating pat or tap to the other person's back indicating that they are uncomfortable and want to separate. Relationally it is always safer for them to speak to how they or their ideas are different from the other person's. These individuals are typically the ones who suffer from childhood abuse of the omnipresent, undifferentiated smothering or a boundaryless, invading mother; or they may have had mothers who were themselves fixated at the oral sadistic (fighting) stage and therefore demanded heightened boundaries. Whenever people stay in close physical or emotional proximity with one of these individuals, they eventually receive the negative mother transference and a heightened separation dance occurs.

If the mother is unable to separate from the infant, dysfunctional survival patterns develop. This could occur if a mother had an insufficient sense of self either through improper parenting by her mother or through cultural or gender devaluing of her worth. She may unconsciously project her undeveloped self into the *in utero* and neonatal merged phase and then not support normal separation. This phenomenon produces the smothering, enmeshed, or engulfing mother who unconsciously through tone and movement gives the message to the baby that it isn't OK to separate. The image of the devouring witch mother who wishes to consume the child's nascent sense of self is present here. This form of abuse of curtailed development can be seen when the mother wants the infant "in her lap" or fills the child with anxiety about the environment when they begin to separate.

Other mothers utilize their children as narcissistic extensions of themselves. They therefore only mirror their children's primary narcissism and maintain the children's view that they are the center of the universe and everything must reference them and their well-being. This would result in the maintenance of a grandiose sense of self and in the demand for perfect, undifferentiated mirroring and continuous nurturance in the form of narcissistic supplies.

In contrast, some mothers may demand mirroring from their children and do not allow them to separate. They can be given the message that to act on one's own needs and wants is to be selfish and that one must care about the other first. This is particularly taught to females in our culture and is typical in many ethnic Catholic families. This frequently results in mirroring and caretaking, resulting in the presence of more libidinal (indulging) rhythms and few sadistic (fighting) ones. Oral aggressive responses are unheard of. In its extreme form some females are taught never to hold onto anything and to continuously let the other take it.

In other cases the infant may be abandoned by the primary object and thus never be able to sufficiently separate because there was no one there from whom to choreograph differentiation. In these situations the derivative use of oral sadistic as well as all other separating, [i.e., sadistic (fighting)] rhythms may not be present as the individual struggles to receive enough primary parenting. Without the derivative use of oral sadistic rhythms individuals will have difficulty maintaining protection of themselves. Due to their lack of body boundaries they may find themselves repeated victims of physical abuse. In addition, the intrapsychic lack of ego boundaries may result in the ego being flooded with unconscious material or bombarded by inner constellations such as the inner shamer, critic, or judge. They will frequently swallow what another person says about them through introjection as they will be without the capacity to discriminate, i.e., to spit out what doesn't apply and internalize what does.

*3. Anal Libidinal (Indulging) Rhythm Dominance*: This addresses Mahler's second sub-phase of separation and individuation: *practicing*. During this phase toddlers "practice" leaving mommy and returning for "refueling" and "customs inspection" of the primary care-giver to reassure themselves that she is still there. The parents respect and value the anal product and emphasize that it is the toddler's and not theirs nor produced for them. This reinforces in toddlers the sense that they can produce something of value and can identify and feel pride in it—a vital foundation for the capacity to work.

Mothers who either leave the toddler when the toddler practices moving away or withhold their positive regard when the child explores separation will often bring forth a fixation or excessive presence of the anal libidinal (indulging) rhythm. In these situations toddlers feel they can't leave and become more self-sufficient because with the former, mother won't be there if needed, and with the latter, mother will emotionally abandon them if they engage in this natural ambivalent phase.

Individuals who have an anal libidinal (indulging) fixation don't know whether they should hold on or let go, be in a relationship or leave it. They can neither commit nor sustain a relationship. If they become intimate the negative engulfing mother transference typically gets constellated and they move away and diminish contact. When the hopeful partner finally gives up, they then place the abandoning mother transference in them and begin moving closer again through phone calls, dating, or resumed sexual intimacy. They will be unable to stand on their own two feet for any long periods of time. They will shift back and forth in an anal rhythm. Assertion is unavailable and they may at times have a whining ambivalent tone to questions requiring self statements.

*4. Anal Sadistic (fighting) Rhythm Dominance*: In terms of object relations this parallels the third subphase of separation and individuation: *rapprochement.* Relationally, toddlers have internalized enough of a sense of self that they feel ready to stand up and test the authority of the parent. In adulthood they can then stand up for themselves and what they believe in. In terms of recovery theory they have a healthy external boundary which is neither wall-like nor leaky. They are able to ensure that no one violates their personal space and consequently give off the non-verbal message that they are not potential victims.

The parent who gives the message that it is not OK to have personal needs and wants or to stand up for them will frequently deny their children the right to integrate the anal sadistic (fighting) rhythm. Here we will find an absence of the derivative use of the rhythm or its presence in mixed form with libidinal (indulging) rhythms used to "tone down" the intensity. These individuals are unable to stand up for themselves and are pushovers for others.

Conversely, some individuals decide to identify with their rageful or otherwise over-controlling parents and develop anal sadistic (fighting) characters (described in the **Body Attitude** section under **Vertical plane**). These are individuals who make sure they are in positions of power and control. The anal sadistic (fighting) rhythm is held in their body. Instead of straining and releasing downward they strain and hold upward, producing clenched gluteal and external rotator buttocks muscles. Holding their feces (which may symbolize unexpressed childhood anger), they explode periodically in rage attacks at spouses, children, and other vulnerable individuals. This retroflexed rage also produces uncommunicative, determined, perfectionist, productive, obsessive-compulsive styles. Culturally, males are more condoned for this type of behavior while females are disdained for such "witchy" attitudes. In recovery theory these individuals are called "rage addicts."

*5. Urethral Libidinal (Indulging) Rhythm Dominance*: This adult will flow everywhere without a responsible sense of time. Body boundaries become libidinally (indulgingly) softened, their gentle flowing nature may put them in harm's way or result in their obliviously pouring into another person's personal space.

If a family's message is that one must do something in order to be loved or that indulging in free-floating, revitalizing reverie is a sign of sloth and laziness, then this rhythm may not be derivatively present in an individual's repertoire. Conversely if there is a predominance of urethral libidinal (indulging) rhythms, an individual may have difficulty doing anything. Complete oblivion regarding time and task completion may result in an individual's inability to maintain a job or get anywhere on time. They may have a dazed look about them and be identified as "space shots," "zoned out," "New Agey," or "not on this planet".

Fixation in the urethral phase is often a result of an unwillingness to be fully present in the world. Potential child abuse will need to be focused upon with the additional goal of their feeling safe enough to let go of a survival pattern which keeps them at least two inches off the ground.

*6. Urethral Sadistic (Fighting) Rhythm Dominance*: With a beginning internal sense of self and other, this character can leave mommy but mentally feel they have taken her with them. With the integration of the capacity to operate and get things done comes the development of the capacity to work.

Parents who want to keep their children tied to them frequently instill anxiety or judgment in them regarding doing. For example, "Oh, don't run too fast—you might fall" or "Oh, that's not good enough for me." Other mothers will literally take everything the child does and claim it so that the child gets the message that nothing they do is for themselves. In these instances this operational rhythm is curtailed and absent in their repertoire. They will come to therapy complaining that they can't ever complete a task or feel good about what they are doing.

Parents who produce narcissistically disordered children can also curtail the joy in doing with the message that unless you are the best or do the greatest things immediately you will not be the "wonder person" I have told you you are. The person, fearful of being "just like everyone else," does nothing.

Positive fixation is the result of work-addicted families who convey the message that they are not worth anything unless they do things. Others have a predominance of urethral sadistic (fighting) rhythms as an adaptation in order to attract attention and win the love they never got. Their view is, "Well, if I keep doing things, maybe then I'll be acceptable and cherished." These individuals are always running with many tasks to do at once and never have time for refueling or real relationships. Culturally, the Protestant work ethic has produced many urethral sadistic fixated work addicts who even "work at play" and have a diminished ability to employ urethral libidinal (indulging) rhythms.

*7. Inner Genital Libidinal (Indulging) Rhythm Dominance*: These inner sensations are more subject to primary process thinking. In terms of object relations mothers are identified with by both sexes for her capacity to create. This is vital if individuals are to experience themselves as creative in adult life.

The inner genital rhythm with its graceful, caressing, swaying, lyrical movements is society's stereotype for the female gender, thereby curtailing the full androgynous instinctual expression of both males and females. Males may feel uncomfortable being tender if they were shamed for playing with dolls or doing things "girls do" during this phase.

*8. Inner Genital Sadistic (Fighting) Rhythm*: These deep, high intensity undulations can be seen when an individual is embodying a birthing process.

*9. Outer Genital Libidinal (Indulging) and Sadistic (Fighting) Rhythms Dominance*: In the same way the graceful inner genital rhythm has been stereotypically assigned to females, the outer genital, ballistic rhythms have in the past been assigned to males. Feminist outrage has now expanded sports and military duty to include women who utilize these rhythms. Aggressive women are still discouraged in business where competition and hierarchical ranking requires outer genital rhythms.

*10. Genital Rhythm Dominance*: The combination of the inner and outer genital rhythm results in the experience of medium—to high-intensity rhythms of gradually rising and falling tension. These rhythms dominate in adult life and are utilized in sexual gratification in the movement during coitus and the powerful contractions during orgasm. Interpersonally the presence of this rhythm demonstrates the capacity of the individual to be vulnerable with protection, to bring forth their ideas and also hear others and to join together in consensus.

Males or females who have an over abundance of inner or outer genital rhythms need to claim the drive that they deny within themselves. This appears in their gender-based attraction or repulsion of others via projection onto an individual or a group via prejudice. Frequently the instinctually-based tension flow rhythms appear in dream and authentic movement images as animals, children, and/or impulsively volatile characters. Snakes and cats (domestic and wild) can house the inner genital rhythms and mobsters, rapists, and grizzly creatures can express the outer genital waiting to be confronted, embodied, and claimed. In this process they are humanized, civilized, and transformed as the ego mediates the genital drives. When they appear as children they can grow and develop through active imagination embodiment. The union of contrasexual sides can occur via creative improvisation, producing adult gentility and a balanced inner feminine and masculine side.

## B. Drive Derivative Behavior
It is helpful to reiterate which drive-derivative behavior may also be absent. If the individual does not have oral sadistic and anal sadistic rhythms in pure form this may suggest faulty boundary formation pointing to potential early child abuse. Dysfunctional ego and body boundaries may be demonstrated with a lack of oral sadistic (fighting) and dysfunctional external boundaries may be demonstrated with a lack of anal sadistic (fighting) rhythms.

## C. Ratios of Rhythms to Each Other: Oral: Anal: Urethral: Inner Genital: Outer Genital
These ratios are mentioned particularly if they elucidate a loading of a rhythm in pure and mixed components. If there is a heavy loading this statistic gives further evidence that the individual is fixated at a particular phase.

## D. Pure to Mixed Ratio
It is expected that rhythms become more differentiated as the person moves into adulthood. A 3 : 1 ratio for an adult is appropriate.

## E. Dominant Mixed Rhythm, Mixed Rhythms Present, and Mixed Rhythm Components
Maladaptive over-usage of a particular mixed rhythm component with an absence or diminished amount in pure form is another indication of lack of sufficient differentiation. If the dominant component is also the dominant pure rhythm, then a case can be made for an increased level of fixation of the individual.

The dominant mixed rhythm is often indicative of a primitive form of sublimation and can be discussed as such. Two rhythm mixes may allow for more harmonious behavior, but large mixtures point to psychic disorganization.

## F. Libidinal: Sadistic (Indulging: Fighting) Ratio
Both libidinal (indulging) and sadistic (fighting) rhythms are needed to support higher adaptive functioning. But this factor will tell the analyst whether the individual will respond more aggressively or receptively.

There should be a 1 : 1.2 ratio in pure rhythms and a 2 : 1 ratio in mixed rhythms for ease in adaptive behavior.

## G. Presence of Localization of Rhythmic Drive Expression
Drives need to be localized in the specific bodily zone they serve. If, for example, the anal sadistic (fighting) rhythm is present only in the oral region, the ego will not be able to sufficiently control and mediate the drive, nor will the drive fulfill derivative needs such as assertion. The analyst will need to take notes on which body parts are being used as the data will not appear directly in the profile.

## H. Characteristic Flow Sequence
Returning to the data, the analyst identifies any typical sequencing of rhythms. This may be helpful process information for therapists. If certain rhythms back up and support others which need development, the therapist can employ these in therapy.

*I. Pathological Features*
1. Derailed rhythms denote disorganization and immaturity. This can occur when one rhythm interrupts another.
2. Fragmentation occurs when several rhythms occur at once, as sometimes observed in autistic children. It can also be seen when the rhythms appear erratic.


### IV. Tension Flow Attributes (TFA): Feelings and Affective Reactions to Safety and Danger (Diagram 2)

These "affective potentials" (Kestenberg, 1971) relative to the autonomic nervous system and the affective centers of the primitive brain, address motor inhibition and discharge. With regards to the former, stopping, delaying, diminishing, or reversing movement becomes the basis for fear responses which form the foundation for such defensive patterns as denial, repression, isolation, and splitting. With regards to the latter, the continuity of movement becomes the basis for responses of comfort or fight/flight responses which form the foundation for displacement, acting out, identifying with the aggressor, manic flight, and projection as well as ease in coping with the environment.

One of the beginning functions of the ego is to regulate unconscious and id-based material. Tension flow rhythms, stemming from the id, need to be regulated by the ego. Thus the capacity for the mobilization and immobilization of rhythm is fundamental in development.

Tension flow attributes (TFA) function as affective need-regulatory mechanisms. If free or bound flow is brought to the extremes, the former can result in unrestrained behavior while the latter can result in body blocks and rigidity. If there is a lack of range between free and bound flow, the individual may be said to have lost elasticity and be in neutral flow, which is a result of flat affect denoting depressive or schizoid features. Very low intensity neutral free flow creates a rag doll-like flaccidity seen in suicidal patients. High bound neutral flow produces brittle non-adaptive personalities and, in its extreme, catatonia. If neutral flow is predominant, the individual appears to be "uninhabited." If the family of origin environment is repeatedly abusive, TFA fight or flight childhood patterns will develop and become habitual survival patterns which continue into adulthood. Although these survival modes were useful in childhood, a time when there is frequently no way out of abusive situations, they become detriments in later life. These archaic affective responses which were once used for protection now keep the person from being fully present in the moment and appropriately responding to the situation.

Clinically speaking, an over-use of free flow could indicate a lack of boundaries. Without ego boundaries the psyche could be swamped with unconscious material, unmediated drives, or negative internalized objects. Without body boundaries one may not be able to contain his feelings and be subject to physical violation. Without external boundaries the individual can affectively give off the message that his personal space can be encroached— thereby setting him up as the perfect victim. By avoiding bound flow the individual is basically expressing that everyone and everything is safe to be with.

With an overuse of bound flow, wall-like boundaries develop, blocking on an ego level the individual's access to her own feelings, wants, and needs. On a body boundary level she will be unable to express her feelings or receive affective responses of others. With rigid external boundaries, she will send out the message, "Don't approach me," thereby isolating herself from the possibility of experiencing a more benign world.

## A. Tension Flow Attribute Presence

All TFA's should be present, thereby indicating the capacity to vary affective response. Note should be made if there appears to be an absence of a tension flow attribute element.

## B. Over-Dominance of a TFA

The dominant TFA tells the analyst either the fundamental temperament of the individual or, with those suffering from early childhood abuse, it can give insight into how the person emotionally responded to danger. The presence and preponderance of characteristic TFA primitive responses to danger can help the analyst target the existence of early child abuse. A preponderance of fighting or aggressive TFA's in response to frustration and caution and an abundance of elements in neutral flow can alert the analyst that early childhood was not safe. A sense of ease, satiation, playfulness, or relief is seen with the presence of indulging TFA's

*1. Even Tension Flow:* A clinical maladaptive overabundance of even flow may denote someone who had the role of the "smoother-over" in the family, i.e., keeping everything on an even keel. With even flow as a primitive survival expression, nothing flusters this individual, even when it should. If even flow is in bound flow the associated survival pattern demonstrated is one of wary caution. These individuals may bind their flow so as not to attract attention in a volatile family with potentially explosive parents. If they have identified with the aggressor and become an abuser themselves, this attribute could denote a predatory, stalking capability to their personality.

When combined with neutral flow the flight response becomes even more dramatic as the individual is seen to de-animate, disassociate, depersonalize, and figuratively leave his body. An individual who sustains this behavior is living in continuous shock, usually due to a form of physical abuse, e.g., beatings, sexual assaults, major surgery, or physical accidents.

*2. Flow Adjustment:* Clinically, individuals who have a maladaptive habitual overabundance of flow adjustment may have used it as a primitive survival mechanism. They may have needed constantly adjusting feelings as they may have been trained to meet other individuals' moods and needs before addressing their own. These individuals have been identified as co-dependent and in severe cases they may not even know what they feel or need. When flow fluctuation is combined with bound flow, these adjustments in temperament are influenced by caution. They qualify their mood and that of others with various concerns. Clinically, these individuals have a form of hypervigilence, looking around, feeling uneasy about the environment. Their family of origin may have abusively violated their spatial boundaries, e.g., a physically abusive or over-protective, controlling, smothering mother. These individuals will describe a "yucky, queasy feeling" in their stomach. Their movement, constantly unsettling, delivers an uneasiness to those who observe them.

If high intensity is added these individuals become predisposed to disorganization. Adding the time factor of abrupt changes in flow, personality fragmentation will occur. When combined with neutral flow their affective responses become loose-jointed. They may give in to expressing deeper levels of the unconscious. Bizarre twisting gestures such as tics and autistic-like features develop.

*3. High Intensity:* When the majority of muscle fibers contract, the individual can be said to be moving in high intensity bound tension flow. These people are able to express strong needs and drives and feel deeply about life. They also can feel elated, exuberant, deeply upset or ragefully angry in temper tantrums. When combined with free flow they

easily excited and can derail and lose control. Clinically, these individuals may
..eeded boundaries to contain the extremes of their emotion. Codependents and
rage or love addicts describe being on an emotional roller coaster ride. DSM IV denotes
these individuals as histrionic personalities, having poor impulse control with a possibility
of antisocial behavior. Individuals with narcissistic personalities also exhibit this attribute
combination in their grandiosity and rages at not being perfectly mirrored. When combined
with bound flow the intense feelings are held and restrained, producing a "time bomb"
feeling around these potentially explosive individuals. Frequently it is anger that is stored
in the body, as the up-tight individuals tend to be negative and furious. Clinically, these are
the classic anal retentive personalities who hold their rage and then burst forth in abusive
ways. The childhood pattern of identifying with the aggressor creates little bullies and later
child abusers and wife beaters. Because their rage is retroflexed, i.e., turned back inward
on themselves, they are frequently masochistic with shame-producing inner critics.

When neutral is added, the core of their inner child is surrounded by deadness. Here the
adult ego remains split off from the child-self or from the split bad self which occurs during rapprochement (Lewis, 1993a). When the adult ego continues to banish the child self
into a neutral dead zone, the inner child remains held in a frustrated deanimated state until
the individual accesses this split part of the self. These individuals have been described as
wooden, heavy, inert, "like molasses," and can be passive-aggressive.

4. *Low Intensity:* Clinically, the individuals who use low intensity as a survival expression
are seen to respond with little feeling to trauma which may have befallen them. Instead of
being hurt or angry they can often be seen smiling. These individuals who are afraid of their
anger or the anger of a parent may neutralize their feelings. Their voice is in the high register
with minimal amplification. Clinically, when low intensity is combined with bound flow this
individual may be afraid to feel too deeply but when deep feelings come close to the surface,
they may need to bind up and avoid the flow of expression lest any enters ego consciousness.
When individuals combine neutral flow with low intensity, they have drifted so far away
from their real feelings that they no longer care about anything. Their bodies are fluid but
weak. They have given up feeling that what they want and need can matter in the world.

5. *Abruptness:* Users of a predominance of abruptness can be volatile and labile in their
survival expression, but are typically alert. When combining abruptness with free flow,
these individuals tend to be impulsive about their feelings and are quick to uninhibit-
edly be filled with feeling or collapse in relief. Clinically, these individuals have poor
impulse control and cannot sustain attention. They can frequently be seen in anxious manic
flight, looking to flee as if the present environment were as abusive as their childhood.
Organically-based attention deficit hyperactive disorder (A.D.H.D.) is slotted here. These
individuals describe not being able to feel deeply or pick up affective cues from others as
they cannot sustain time long enough to sensitize themselves. With a lack of control, they
often violate other's boundaries without being aware. Coordination becomes difficult and
they leave a wake of chaos in their path. Frequently combined with flow fluctuations, they
are literally all over the place emotionally and otherwise. When abrupt change is combined
with bound flow, these individuals can move quickly into restraining their expression or its
reverse in decrease of caution. Clinically, these individuals are jumpy, having come from a
family of origin in which they never knew where or when the attack would come. This
form of hypervigilance would allow them to quickly freeze if they needed to so as to not
draw attention to themselves as a potential victim.

6. *Graduality:* With a preponderance of graduality, clinical concerns develop when the
individual needs faster transitions in situations when flight responses may be required.

They are said to have "slow reflexes." This may result from a dysfunctional family in which any abrupt changes might have affectively "set someone off" into abusive behavior.

When combining graduality with bound flow individuals are cautious and become less intense in a restrained manner or conversely become more and more affectively charged like someone who has a "slow fuse" (they gradually begin to boil with anger or effervesce with excitement). Clinically speaking, these slow fuse individuals are often difficult to calm down, especially when even high intensity flow is added, they stay adamantly locked in the intensity of their feelings and in impressing them on whomever is around, unable to adjust and adapt to other's affective expressions.

When combined with neutral flow, a gradual disassociative spacing out occurs as these individuals leave their bodies during flashbacks of severe physical abuse.

## C. Ratio Between Attributes in Animated and Neutral Flow

The dominance of attributes in neutral flow is potentially indicative of depression, schizoidal splitting, depersonalization, and de-animation. 18%–30% in neutral flow is considered normal range.

## D. Presence of Functional Flow Factors

Kestenberg pointed out that the capacity to provide an affective foundation for attention requires the underpinning of acquiring even flow and flow adjustment. The capacity for the affective foundation for intention requires the integration of high and low intensity and the capacity for the affective foundation for decision-making requires the integration of abrupt and gradual tension flow.

## E. Load Factor

The load factor pertains to the complexity of feeling within each TFA action. The more attributes used in a single action (three is maximum, one minimum) the higher the load factor. If all actions had three elements the load factor would be 100%, denoting a highly complex expression of affect. 33% or only one element per action depicts an individual with very simple, unsophisticated affect.

## F. Gain : Expense Ratio (GE)

The GE addresses the ratio of control to spontaneity and is measured through the ratio between the amount of attributes of tension flow and the total of changes in free and bound flow. A higher amount of attributes indicates more affective modulation. A high level of free to bound flow would indicate less modulation of alternations between feelings of safety and danger and more spontaneous expression.

## G. Free to Bound Ratio

This ratio will point to the relationship between feelings which are based upon motor discharge or continuity of affective expression with free flow or feelings addressing inhibition, delaying, diminishing, or stopping affective expression altogether with bound flow. Here a balance is looked for in affective preparation for the vicissitudes of life's stimuli.

## V. Bipolar or Symmetrical Shape Flow (Self Representation and Object Relations; Undifferentiated Response to the Environment) (Diagram 5)

Bilateral shape flow can identify an individual's level of comfort or discomfort in a given situation or atmosphere. The individual's self-in-relation to others is expressed in shape flow. Shape flow thus provides for the motor apparatus for the flow of libido and aggression between self and other. Through this structure body boundaries are aided along with an internalized sense of self and other as described in the theories of object relations and self psychology. Bipolar shape flow gives three-dimensionality to an individual's sense of fullness of self and serves healthy narcissism or the capacity to feel that one is worthy, lovable, and has a right to be considered.

### A. Dominant Shape Flow Attribute

In combination with other attributes, it tells the analyst the individual's sense of self-in-relation to the undifferentiated primary object. Thus it indicates the type of early nurturing or abuse the individual received and the resultant sense of self.

*1. Widening Dominance*   is an object-seeking response which suggests that the initial relationship with the primary care giver was one in which there was a physical availability and affection. It is expected that with a healthy amount of widening in an individual's repertoire, the individual would be able to receive. With a sustained dominance of widening, however, a narcissistic omnipotence may be present. In this case, the individual would require perfect mirroring from the environment. This phenomena is present due to the fact that widening in the horizontal is associated with the first developmental phase of symbiosis. In this oral phase the relation to the environment is a merged one as self-object or the infant/mother dual unity is seen as encompassing the entire surroundings. Those who have a dominance of widening often feel that unconsciously everyone is "mother" and therefore should dote on their every word and wish. Without the balance of shrinking in the horizontal (narrowing) their grandiosity is not relativized in reality. This typically occurs with one of two mother–child scenarios: either when the mother, empty of a sense of worth and a connection to her own self or inner child, sustains the symbiotic phase of undifferentiation with the infant and places all her unmet compensatory monumental fantasies in the child or, when a child compensates for feeling less than in relation to his primary care-givers by acting like he is "better than."

Widening is associated with free flow and the tension flow attribute of flow fluctuation. When mismatched with bound flow, the individual may be manifesting a fear of falling apart resulting in an outer manifestation of the inner split or fragmented self.

*2. Narrowing Dominance*   is seen when the rib cage contracts and moves toward the body center, drawing the arms back in adduction to the torso. This gives the message that in childhood it wasn't OK to expand oneself, to reach out to another, or to take what one needed. These self-contained individuals don't know how to get what they need or be sensitive to the needs of a significant other. They constrict their interactions with the environment and give the message that it wasn't safe for them in their childhood. They tend to shy away from social interaction. They can feel defeated, powerless, and helpless to reach for anything they need. If their arms are also showing neutral or limp levels of tension flow, it could be assumed that they were severely abused or abandoned by the primary object during infancy. If high intensity bound flow is present in their arms they can be seen as being in conflict (i.e., wanting to extend but the antagonist muscle contracts, holding them back).

This might indicate a volatile or abusive object, in which case the individual may also be turning her own aggression back in on herself. Narrowing is matched with even flow of tension and oral sadistic (fighting) biting rhythms associated with the differentiation sub-phase of separation/individuation in object relations theory.

A natural balance between widening and narrowing reflects the individual's capacity to experience trust and mistrust appropriately, a vital developmental foundation for life. Without it they are unable to sustain intimate relations or have faith in themselves and their capacity to get what they need in life.

*3. Lengthening Dominance*   gives one an experience of being tall, becoming bigger hierarchically in stature and status in relation to others. Our culture has reinforced bipolar lengthening due to its patriarchal competitiveness, where being the "alpha" or top dog is associated with one's own sense of well-being, differing from the horizontal, more self-in-relation feminist networking model. Bound lengthening suggests someone who is filled with anal level rage and/or someone who is compensating for feeling "less than" by a false persona of being "bigger than."

*4. Shortening Dominance*   is seen with individuals who shrink in stature, frequently feel inferior to others due to low self-esteem, and living with a core of shame surrounding them from an abusive childhood. Culturally, certain groups of oppressed individuals can be seen shortening their height in order to suggest submission. There was pressure on African–Americans in the South prior to W.W. II to adopt this pose.

Object relationally and in terms of recovery theory, if individuals, without cultural precedence, frequently present themselves in a shortened position it gives the impression that they are waiting for someone to dominate them and/or take care of them. These individuals may be co-dependent, dependent personalities, or raised to be victims of another's abuse. Countertransferentially, the therapist might be aware of growing taller and feeling a demand to "fix their problem," mother them, or even be controlling.

If bound flow combines with sustained shortening an individual may figuratively be all tied up inside. When both lengthening and shortening are utilized appropriately, an individual can be said to have stability, balance, and self control.

*5. Bulging Dominance*   is associated with feelings of fullness, saturation, and gratification. In terms of object relations if bulging is present at a healthy level the individual may be said to have a strong sense of self. Exaggerated bulging or bound flow bulging can give the appearance of someone bursting with feelings. This body shape flow occurs in food and alcohol addiction when individuals strive to fill an empty relational void with oral cravings.

*6. Hollowing Dominance*   is suggestive of a lack of internalized sense of self in object relations and a lack of connection with the inner child in recovery theory. These individuals frequently feel rejected and unlovable. They often do not know what they need and want, deferring to others or cultural stereotyping to tell them what they should want. The individual can secretly hunger for relationship but feel so depleted they have no idea how to get what they need. A natural balance between bulging and hollowing provides a natural sense of confidence which is associated with object constancy and a realistic sense of self.

## B. Load Factor (LF)

The load factor tells the analyst the level of complexity of mood and self feelings. These feelings range from feeling expansive to feeling small and insignificant.

### C. Growing to Shrinking Ratio

Less growing and more shrinking points to the amount of potential abuse and the resultant low or empty sense of self. The reverse is suggestive of narcissistic compensatory response. This ratio should be within a balanced range.

### D. Gain Expense Ratio

The GE indicates the ratio between the elements of shape flow and the sum total of growing and shrinking. If there is a much higher amount of shape flow elements over growing and shrinking then the individual demonstrates control over their spontaneous expressions of self and object related feelings.

### VI. Unipolar or Asymmetrical Shape Flow (Individual's Response to Internal and External Stimuli) (Diagram 6)

Unipolar shape flow addresses an individual's response to discrete stimuli, originating internally or externally. Structured channels are thus created for tension flow rhythms and their object-related expression. The capacity for more discrete responses to the environment now serves secondary narcissism. The child recognizes that the mother is not undifferentiated but is localized in space.

### A. Dominant Unipolar Attributes Employed

This feature gives the analyst a more defined version of the individual's early object relationship entailing widening or narrowing to one side, lengthening or shortening upward or downward, or bulging or hollowing forward or backward.

### B. Growing to Shrinking Ratio

As with bipolar shape flow, this factor can indicate the level of abuse if individuals have a much higher loading of shrinking than growing. If the reverse is true, they may be seeking the object everywhere. Clearly a balance is needed.

### C. Load Factor and Gain Expense

These factors are viewed in the same way bipolar shape flow is, except with the understanding that the responses are more discrete and serve secondary narcissism. This factor points to potential overstimulation and survival patterns of hyper-responsiveness. (See Chapter 6 for general information on unipolar shape flow.)

### VII. Shape Flow Design (Diagram 7)

This movement category is not part of this analyst's profiles as it is more an indicator of cultural diversity than clinical issues. (See Chapter 7 for more information on shape flow design.)

### VIII. Pre-efforts (Modes of Learning, Ego Defenses Against Drives and Cognitive Distortions) (Diagram 3)

Through supplementing and controlling affective reactions to safety and danger, and defending against primitive drives, pre-efforts serve as the motor apparatus for defenses.

Pre-efforts address inner sources of frustration and outer danger with fighting or more passive indulging behavior.

## A. Dominant Pre-Efforts

This feature tells the favored modes of learning and mediation between internal drives and external reality. Pre-efforts can also be activated if therapeutic interventions prove to be too invasive.

*1. Channeling*: As a mode of learning it aids in maintaining an undistracted focus and is a vital component for good attention. This focusing also helps in pinpointing, honing, discriminating, and defining issues.

As a mode of defense channeling is employed to assist in isolation, insulation, and disconnection via focusing away from the drive or external fearful stimuli. An individual may also channel toward the potentially dangerous stimuli as well as when someone narrows her focus and stares at the potentially dangerous individual. This is done to aggressively deal with danger through "staring them down."

*2. Flexibility*: As a mode of learning flexibility assists in learning through searching inner memory banks for something with which to associate the new learning. Flexibility also supports generalizing so that new learning can occur.

As a mode of defense, it aids individuals who tend to move into their head as a way of defending. Cognitive distortions such as intellectualization, rationalization, generalization, dichotomization, and other avoidance strategies such as displacement, projection, and transference can employ flexibility. Use of fantasy and the obsessive ruminations employed in love addictions also utilize flexibility often in conjunction with vehemence.

*3. Vehemence* uses high intensity of flow in weight or gravity. It is the precursor of the effort of strength. As a mode of learning it aids in overcoming frustration through straining to maintain concentration. Here learning is literally attacked with force in service to conquering a lack of understanding about something.

As a mode of defense, vehemence can be seen in exaggeration or those who identify with the aggressor and become acting-out bullies, individuals who have to have control over everything and everyone to feel safe, or in extreme, rage addicts and batterers. Bound vehemence (straining) can also be employed in denial and repression by keeping feelings and memories stuffed down away from conscious awareness.

*4. Gentleness*: As a mode of learning, gentleness serves to open the individual to new ideas or actions with ease and without resistance. It can be seen in individuals who move away from having intense feelings such as rage as a mode of defense employed in service to denial and minimization. It is also seen in reaction formation in the prevention of dangerous needs and drives reaching conscious expression, such as seen in individuals who might act prim and proper to avoid their own sexual urges. Individuals also use gentleness in attempts to control the potential rage in others. These individuals frequently speak in soft, child-like voices and give the message that they are too delicate to attack and should be treated with care.

*5. Suddenness*: As a mode of learning, suddeness is found in individuals who have intuitive flashes in which understanding is acquired in its entirety. As a mode of defense in conjunction with forward, it is seen in those individuals who employ a counter-phobic reaction to danger. Instead of proceeding with caution, they rush into dangerous situations. Males in Western culture are typically rewarded for this behavior.

*6. Hesitation*: As a mode of learning, hesitation incorporates pauses, uncertainty, and time for reflection in a deliberate, slow-paced, methodical manner. As a mode of defense it is seen in those individuals who defensively postpone decisions and actions with questions, concerns, and literally anything they can think of to put in the way of moving forward. This delaying may contain an obsessive or compulsive quality (e.g., the performance of personal rituals before beginning the feared task) or seen as passive-aggressive.

## B. Load Factor

The load factor tells the analyst the level of complexity of learning behaviors and defenses. For example, time and weight pre-efforts can be utilized together for more sophisticated denial and repression mechanisms.

## C. Gain Expense Ratio

The gain expense ratio indicates the ratio between the amount of attributes and the sum total of tension flow changes. This could indicate the level to which the individual employed ego defenses against drives and forbidden affect. The higher the amount of flow charges the more emotionally and instinctually uninhibited the individual is. In extremes the individual is childlike and emotionally impulsive. If the reverse is true, he will appear to be very disconnected from his drives (needs and wants) and feelings.

## D. Relationship Between Libidinal (Indulging) and Sadistic (Fighting) Pre-Efforts

Gives an indication as to whether the individual utilizes more aggressive types of defenses such as vehemence and channeling over softer, potentially more victim-like defenses such as gentleness and flexibility.

## IX. *Gestural Efforts (Ego Adaptation) (Diagram 4)*

Efforts denote methods of adaptation and favored ways of mediating drives with external reality. They address ego adaptation to space, weight, and time. The ego translates the id will (tension flow rhythms) into actions (efforts). Efforts then subordinate tension flow in order to get instinctual needs met. Thus the presence of efforts denotes the presence of an ego. Gestural efforts occur in one or more parts of the body without encompassing the whole body.

## A. Dominant Efforts Employed

*1. Direct*  is the focused, fighting spatial effort of attention. Direct (along with indirect) is concerned with where things are and is associated with the thinking function of personality typology (Laban, 1960). Individuals who have an overdominance of directness can only attend to one thing at a time, and if combined with bound flow they have difficulty considering any other possibilities other than the one they hold onto. These people can be blunt and often lack the relational skills which can temper words and actions with grace.

*2. Indirect*  is the indulging spatial effort which allows one to attend to many different things at once. When used in abundance, indirect may prevent individuals from staying focused.

*3. Strength*  is the weight-fighting effort which addresses intention and the "what." It is associated with sensate personality types. An overabundance of strength can be seen in hyper-authoritative individuals who are focused upon power and control. Thus they are unable to really hear other people or to defer to anyone else.

*4. Lightness*  is the indulging weight effort which is used in fine touch. An over-abundance is seen in airy individuals who are ungrounded in reality. Slang terms such as "flaky," "air head," and "head-in-the-clouds" denote these individuals who, with the combined use of flexibility, frequently have artistic or inspirational sides to their personalities but are unable to take a stand and commit themselves to task.

*5. Acceleration*  is the fighting effort which contends with time in an urgent manner. Accelerators are concerned with "when" and are associated with intuitive personalities. A preponderance of quickness can be seen with individuals who are so busy trying to complete a task that they forget very important elements. They may assume that the means always justifies the end and find themselves having to double back and redo a task. They may tie their identity to doing and thus lose their sense of self-worth if they aren't doing something.

*6. Deceleration*  is the indulging effort used to adapt to time by slowing down. An overabundance in an individual's repertoire can result in being so slow to take action that they "miss the boat." Unable to keep up with the commitments and decision making of others, they are left behind.

## B. Effort Attitudes: Two Motion Factors Combined in Space, Weight, Time and Flow:

Incomplete efforts are actions in which only two efforts from space, weight and/or time are performed (66% load factor). Laban (1960) felt that these combinations revealed inner attitudes. They can be seen as fleeting "shadow movements," preparations for three-effort combinations, or as frozen effort signatures (discussed in II. **Body Attitude**). Clinically, it is important to notice if these inner attitudes are being used in lieu of three effort externalized drives. A lack of capacity to combine three efforts at a time reduces the load factor, suggesting limited intelligence or more typically, a reluctance to interact dynamically in the external world. For example, if a person needed to assert herself to confront a colleague's racist, sexist, or ageist comments, use of direct, strength, and deceleration might be required. If strength supported by high intensity tension flow is not available due to childhood experiences with an authoritative parent, then the person would be left with direct and deceleration lacking the needed "umph" to let the other know "they really meant it."

*1. Awake State*  employs space and time efforts, such as the use of direct and acceleration in an alert, sharp, changing focus filled with attention and the capacity to make non-impulsive thought-out decisions—vital characteristics for functioning in a fast-paced work world.

*2. Present State*  employs weight and time, producing earthy, rhythmic qualities such as strength and acceleration in forceful assertiveness or lightness and deceleration in a soothing, peaceful presence. Regardless of the favored qualities it is easier to more fully experience the moment when this combination is available.

*3. Stable State*  employs weight and space, producing a steady, balanced quality such as the combination of strength and direct in commanding firmness, or lightness and direct in gentle focus.

*4. Dreamlike State*  employs weight and flow, producing qualities which can create hazy fantasies, as with the use of lightness and free in a buoyant, flying quality. With the flow factor replacing more externally-oriented effort qualities, the individual will be unable to maintain attention or make decisions based upon external factors.

*5. Remote State* employs space and flow, producing a pensive quality, such as using indirect and bound flow to create a wringing-like movement. The flow quality draws people inward, pulling them back into primitive childhood patterns and subverting their capacity to be fully present in the moment.

*6. Mobile State* employs time and flow, such as with bound flow accelerating in manic flight. Without attention to the events of the outer world and lacking in intention or commitment, the person may appear as a bobber on a fishing line responding only to pulls from the liquid deep of the unconscious.

## C. Effort Drives: Three Motion Factors Including Flow as One of the Potential Factors

*1. Action Drives,* mentioned earlier, have space, weight, and time factors. These basic effort actions are present when an individual is fully engaged and interacting in reality. The adaptive use of action drives (punches, slashes, wrings, presses, floats, glides, dabs, and flicks) are the sign of a healthy, adaptive individual, particularly when they are carried out through the entire body. When flow is considered an active element and is exchanged with an effort element, transformational drives occur. The flow brings with it the capacity for transformation as it accesses and can affect the unconscious imaginal realm (Lewis, 1993b). The awareness of the potential for the use of transformational drives is important for dance and drama therapists who utilize embodied movement in the therapy process.

*2. Passion Drives* utilize weight, time, and flow. They produce emotional qualities such as being excited, or driven. This combination can prove highly destructive. Rage addicts, unreasonable and out of relational control, can lash out without a sense of spatial awareness, abusing themselves and others. However, with the use of indulging efforts of lightness and deceleration, a detached, often childlike embodiment can be seen when free flow is added. In any case the ability to deeply care for oneself or another requires access to the drive.

*3. Spell Drives* utilize space, weight, and flow, producing qualities such as persuasion and fascination. This timeless drive is employed to seduce and induce others and can be utilized in guided imagery experiences.

*4. Vision Drives* utilize space, time, and flow, reducing the sensate bodily involvement producing qualities of abstraction. This drive allows an individual to enter into childhood memories as if they were being experienced in the present, an important ability in recovery work in psychotherapy utilizing drama therapy. However, this weightless quality of recreating the past through accessing the unconscious using the element of flow can become maladaptive if the person is unaware that they are engaged in such a process. Additionally, in this weightless drive a person is able to envision the future and experience it in body enactment without being inhibited by his present state of affairs. However, in order to get to the future, one needs effort attributes of weight in order to take the steps needed to progress.

## D. Adaptive Presence of Efforts

All efforts should be available in an individual's movement repertoire in order to be employed when needed in adapting to space, weight, and time. Since efforts subordinate vertically-affined tension flow rhythms to their adaptive aims, all attributes are needed as all drives and their derivatives need mediation in adulthood for adaptive functioning. For example, if an individual needs to assert himself in a situation, anal sadistic (fighting) drive discharge is required, but it must be mediated with strength (otherwise, the individual will appear to be childlike in authority). In addition, in terms of external reality, if the attributes are lacking this may demonstrate faulty attention (spatial efforts), intention, determination, and commitment (weight efforts), or capacity to make a decision, carry out a task or operation (time efforts). If there is an absence of pre-efforts, efforts, directional shape, and shaping, there is no presence of a functioning ego. This may occur in individuals with severe psychosis, retardation, or organic dysfunction, such as in the final stages of Alzheimers disease.

### E. Load Factor in Efforts

The load factor tells the analyst the level of complexity of ego adaptations. This factor appears to parallel IQ and indicates a person's capacity for problem solving and creative intelligence. 33% is felt to be low, 40% medium and 55% high creative intelligence. As children mature they will have a greater capacity to synthesize and combine attributes of ego adaptation. A low LF for an adult often correlates with emotional pathology in as much as the individual is functioning with minimal ego adaptation, suggesting a primitive or weak ego.

### F. Gain Expense Ratio

This indicates the ratio between effort attributes and the sum of tension flow alterations between free and bound. This ratio pertains to elasticity or the level of mediation of affect and spontaneity. $2:1$ (two times as many attributes as flow changes) shows that the individual's affect is highly differentiated and lacks spontaneity. $1:4$ (four times as many flow changes to effort attributes) shows an extremely childlike character. They will be very spontaneous but will be ingenuous, e.g., an adult who "jumps for joy" when happy.

### G. The Amount of Indulging Efforts: Fighting Efforts

This factor points to whether an individual is more receptive or pro-active in their external engagement.

## X. Postural Efforts (Punitive Superego)

### A. Dominant and Present Postural Efforts

Postural efforts are actions which involve a continuous adjustment of every part of the body with consistency in the process of variation (Lewis, 1986). Postural efforts are written on the same diagram as gestural efforts and express the punitive superego, inner judge, or inner critic. The use of postural effort qualities identifies the collaboration of all psychic agencies including the superego, which approves of the individual's actions. If the dominant postural effort qualities are on the fighting side of the diagram then the analyst can assume that the individual may have a fairly assertive inner critic. If only indulging postural efforts are used, the inner judge may be more "understanding," but may not be able to provide the needed "punch" to get the person into pro-active engagement when needed.

### B. Load Factor in Postural Efforts

This factor addresses the level of complexity of the punitive superego. The more attributes per action the more dominant and sophisticated the superego.

## C. Gain Expense Ratio in Postural Efforts

The ratio of postural effort qualities to tension flow changes points to the ratio of the motoric expression of punitive judgments to spontaneous affect-based movement. In terms of transactional analysis and recovery language a 2 : 1 ratio would suggest the inner parent overrides the inner child. 1 : 4 would suggest the reverse (i.e., the child has dominance).

## XI. Directional Shape (Modes of Object Related Learning and Defenses Against Objects) (Diagram 8)

Kestenberg and Sossin (1979) state that directions are projections of body dimensions into space providing a bridge between the self and objects. Shaping in directions is an ego function which addresses external reality. Whether these linear movements remain within **personal space** or extend into **reach space**, they address external objects. Providing a structure for pre-efforts, these movements are utilized in object related learning and in defenses against external stimuli through barring access to the body in **closed shapes** or by extending external boundaries with **open shapes**.

### A. Dominant Directional Shape Attributes

This factor indicates the types of favored object related defenses and interpersonal learning skills.

*1. Across*   contributes to learning via preventing distractions and learning to weed out extraneous information for clearer definition. As an object related mode of defense, it serves to bar access to the body such as with crossed arms or legs.

*2. Sideways*   contribute to learning via association and generalization. As an object related mode of defense, it serves eluding through displacing projecting, or transferring onto another object and avoiding via generalizing. It also serves in the function of extending external boundaries by extending the arm to keep others from torso contact.

*3. Down*   contributes to learning via moving down to the heart or essence of the matter and learning to explain. As an object related mode of defense, it serves to "put someone or something down" that another does or says.

*4. Up*   in the vertical dimension contributes to learning via seeking guidance from the teacher. Individuals may employ this object related defense when moving up and away from a grounded connection to someone. This behavior may represent an object related reaction formation position used to ward off their own downward high intensity tension flow expression of rage or aggressive assertion.

*5. Backward*   contributes to learning by remembering and backtracking. As an object related mode of defense, it is seen in escaping and withdrawing, as when individuals move backward out of a family or group therapy session.

*6. Forward*   contributes to learning via "learning to make step-by-step deductions with proper sequence and anticipating the consequences" (Berlowe, Kestenberg *et al.*, 1995). As an object related mode of defense it is used to approach objects in a counter phobic response to danger.

### B. Load Factor in Directions

This factor addresses the level of complexity of the object related defenses and learning styles. A high load factor (55%) shows a sophisticated defensive apparatus used for protection from other individuals, and may suggest childhood relational abuse. It may also show an individual who can learn in relation to others, connecting to material already known. Movement in one directional shape at a time is an indication of a rigid character. This also may be seen in individuals with minimum or no ego functioning, as with psychotics. It is important not to confuse organic or physical dysfunction with functional difficulty. Individuals with Parkinson's disease or those in severe pain may only move in one direction at a time.

### C. Gain Expense Ratio in Directions

The Gain Expense is the ratio between the amount of directional shape qualities and shape flow changes. This factor elucidates the level of plasticity in an individual's relationship to external objects. If there are more flow changes, the individual can be said to respond to the world based upon early object relations. The more directional shape the individual uses, the less access to her fundamental responses to the environment. Where there are few shape flow changes and bound held torsos, individuals have a rigid mannequin or wooden soldier-like appearance. Somewhere in childhood or in severe disciplinary training they were given the message that it is not okay to express self-feelings, or show any signs of comfort/discomfort or attraction/repulsion.

### D. Growing to Shrinking Ratio

This ratio gives the analyst some idea as to the fundamental response to the environment (i.e., is there more of a predominance of feeling comfort and pleasure, as with growing or withdrawal, or discomfort, as with shrinking).

### E. Relationship Between Open Shapes and Closed Shapes

This factor will tell the analyst the degree to which the individual puts up barriers in relation to other objects, internalized or external, or chooses to expand his external boundaries as a means of protection. Analysts are encouraged when the patient does the latter, as the presence of external boundaries suggests a higher developmental stage (rapprochement phase). Using only closed shapes could suggest that only body boundaries are present or developing (differentiation phase).

### XII. Shaping in Planes in Gestures (Ego Apparatus for Complex Relationships with External Objects) (Diagram 9)

Shaping in planes, often referred to as "shaping," are multi-dimensional spatial configurations which give complex designs to relationships. These movements sculpt space in complex relatedness to the object. Including the flow factor, these correspond to the three effort orientations:

| *Shape* | *Effort Orientation* |
|---|---|
| Horizontal | Space |
| Vertical | Weight |
| Sagittal | Time |
| Growing | Free flow |
| Shrinking | Bound flow |

Shaping in the horizontal plane is used for **exploration**, in the vertical plane for **confrontation**, and in the sagittal for **anticipation**. **Closed gathering**, or **concave** shapes, are enclosing, descending, and retreating. **Open scattering**, or **convex** shapes, are spreading, ascending, and advancing. Without shaping an individual would be described as aloof. In Western culture women typically utilize more shaping in planes and men in directions when relating to others.

## A. Dominant Shaping Attributes

This factor indicates the favored styles of relating to the external world.

*1. Enclosing:* Enclosers tend to relate to a small exclusive group or to one person at a time. They tend to be the gatherers or takers. If unbalanced with its polar opposite (spreading), enclosing can "straitjacket" individuals, as they continually wrap space around themselves.

*2. Spreading:* Spreaders are like the proverbial sower of seeds. They open to include all points of view, all ideas. They can frequently have very creative ideas but can also spread themselves too thin. They are the givers and often are addicted to relationships in which they codependently take care of other's needs and wants to the exclusion of their own.

*3. Descending:* Descenders are very down to earth; they challenge and confront situations and individuals head on. They are forthright and realistic. With an overabundance of descending, individuals cannot get their feet off the ground. They descend into depression and gravely respond to those around them. Sinking into the depths, they can't seem to see the light, or with deceleration, may appear old before their time.

*4. Ascending:* Ascenders resist pressure. They can rise to any occasion and inspire those around them. They are often charismatic and can make the worst situation sound like a blessing. An overabundance of ascending and the individual's head is stuck in the clouds. They can't ever commit to anything nor can they see any of their ideas or relationships come to fruition.

*5. Retreating:* Retreaters can see perspective and terminate. They pull space back with them. In extreme they are reticent about everything. They back away from relationships, new ideas, and activities. Caught in their own history, they cannot extricate themselves nor can they experience the present.

*6. Advancing:* Advancers are forward-looking, far-sighted, and anticipate the future. They can be seen sitting almost out of their chairs, ready to move at a moments notice. If they have too much advancing, these individuals are always in the future and can never experience the moment. They can never fully live their lives and may have difficulty "backing off" of situations.

## B. Adaptive Presence of Shaping Factors

The ability to communicate and investigate relies on shaping in the horizontal plane. Presentation and confrontation would be unavailable if there were no shaping in the vertical plane, and anticipation of consequences, operating, and proceeding to carry out a task would be difficult without shaping in the sagittal plane.

## C. Load Factor

This factor addresses the level of complexity in ways of relating in the external world and could point to an individual's level of social skills. In U.S. culture women are seen to have a higher load factor than men because they are raised to be more relational.

## D. Gain Expense Ratio

The Gain Expense is the ratio between the total amount of shaping qualities and shape flow changes. This factor addresses the level of plasticity in complex relating.

## E. Growing to Shrinking Ratio

This ratio gives the analyst some idea of the fundamental response to the environment when engaging in complex relating to the external world.

## XIII. Shaping in Planes in Postures (Superego Apparatus for Ego-Ideal)

### A. Dominance and Presence of Postural Shaping

Postural shaping is written on the same diagram as gestural shaping and addresses the individual's ego ideal, or how they most want to present themselves in the world in relation to others. This parallels the concept of persona.

### B. Load Factor

This factor addresses the level of complexity or adaptive possibilities of the ego ideal. The higher the loading the more variety of persona; the lower the loading the more limited an individual's internalized sense of how he should respond to others.

### C. Gain Expense Ratio

The ratio of postural shaping elements to shape flow changes points to which is more dominant: what the superego dictates (how the person should respond to others) or self feelings of comfort or discomfort.

Once each of the nine diagrams and related data has been individually discussed, the profile can be analyzed in a number of different ways:

*1. Intra-systemically:* A vertical comparison of diagrams within either System I or System II. This is a developmental approach. Do the earliest elements support and match later developmental elements?

*2. Inter-systemically:* A horizontal comparison of diagrams which are closely interrelated. Do the diagrams of System II provide the structure for and match with the diagrams of System I? Looking specifically at the elements of each diagram one asks, for example, if there is enough enclosing to create a structure for the element of direct.

*3. Psychic structures: Id, ego, and superego-related diagrams*
   a. Id-related diagrams (TFR, TFA, Bipolar, and Unipolar Shape Flow)
   b. Ego-related diagrams (Pre-Effort, Gestural Efforts, Shaping, and Directional Shape)
   c. Superego-related diagrams (postures in efforts and shaping in planes)

Analysts are concerned with finding sufficient presence of all elements and attributes. When comparing diagrams, analysts search for matches or affinity, suggesting intrapsychic syntonia, and/or clashes suggesting conflict. The following are definitions of frequently employed terms for these comparisons.

### *XIV. Affinity and Clashing*

**A. Affinity** is a KMP concept based upon the compatibility of the elements in the nine diagrams. If the diagrams are affined, they will have roughly the same visual shape. Affinities can occur both vertically (within each of the two subsystems) or horizontally (across developmentally parallel effort and shape graphs). When corresponding movement elements are horizontally affined, it is called **matching**.

**B. Clashing** is seen when elements as viewed on the diagrams are not the same visual shape. Clashing diagrams often appear as mirrored images of each other. Clashing demonstrates conflict and affinity demonstrates support, syntony, and systemic agreement. This can occur vertically within a system and/or horizontally across the subsystems within the id, ego, and superego. When corresponding movement elements exhibit horizontal clashing, it is called **mismatching** .

### C. Vertical Affinities and Clashing

*1. Within System I : Tension Flow-Effort*

*a. Affinities*

*The General Pattern: Tension Flow-Efforts:* Angry and cautious feelings (TFA) are affined and harmonious with aggressive and sadistic rhythms (TFR), which are affined with aggressive defenses (P-E) and fighting efforts. Likewise, pleasant and safe feelings (TFA) are affined with libidinal rhythms (TFR); TFR are affined with placating defenses, and P-E are affined with indulging efforts.

*Vertical affinities* (also called "consonance") exist when an early pattern, such as even flow (TFA), is continued with similar emphasis in the developmentally more advanced related elements, such as channeling (P-E) and direct (E).

For example, preferred modes of learning seen in pre-efforts need to correspond to modes of ego adaptation (efforts). The more internally-oriented systems (TFR and TFA) support the more external reality-oriented and developed efforts when they are present in fairly equivalent proportions.

*b. Clashing*

*Vertical Clashing* (also called "dissonance") occurs when elements from the id, ego, or superego are not affined. For example, a predominance of flow adjustment (TFA) is dissonant with a predominance of channeling (P-E) and direct (E). While flow adjustment promotes turning this way and that, channeling and direct promote a singular focus.

Wherever there is dissonance, there is conflict. This type of "genetic" conflict indicates that the developmentally higher psychic structure (i.e., either the ego or superego) is not supported by the more primitive feelings and basic drives of the id.

*c. Discussion of Clashing*

If there is a dominance of libidinal rhythms and fighting efforts, there would be no avenue of adapting need gratification for nourishment, elimination, sexual gratification (and their derivatives such as self-esteem building, playful letting go, or gender expression in reality) other than feeling one has to fight and attack in order to get what one needs. This pattern is sometimes found in abusive individuals.

If there is a dominance of aggressive rhythms with indulging efforts, there would be no avenue available for modifying and "civilizing" one's aggressive impulses. If effort patterns are present without similar levels of related tension flow patterns, then the adaptation is there without the support of or access to the feelings and drives which give emotion and passion to a person's life. If such a pattern is pervasive, individuals would have flat, unavailable affect and appear machine-like. They may be so rational and emotionally unavailable that they lose connection to the childlike spontaneity and potential joy in life.

More specifically, if a tension flow pattern does not have a supportive base in a related pre-effort pattern (i.e., there is a lot of high intensity but little vehemence) there is little possibility for ego defense or sublimation of this strong feeling. If the effort of strength is only minimally present in an adult, this hampers the mediation of drives and high intensity feelings in service of coping with reality. Thus a lack of impulse control might exist if there are sadistic (fighting) TFAs without matching fighting P-E and E patterns. This lack of ego corresponds to the adult leaving and the child taking over as expressed in recovery theory.

### 2. *Within System II: Shape Flow-Shape*
#### a. *Affinities*
In general, opening and moving towards uni- and bipolarly (S-F) is affined to opening access to one's body (D-S) and approaching relationally (shaping in planes). Closing and moving away uni- and bipolarly (S-F) is affined to defensively barring access to one's body (D-S), which is affined to withdrawing relationally (shaping in planes).

More specifically, an affinity or consonance exists when the qualities of symmetrical shape flow, such as widening bipolarly, support the more discrete relationship to the environment, such as widening unipolarly towards something or someone. Looking at directions and shaping in planes, modes of object related learning must support complex external interaction. Thus, barring access with across (D-S) is a supporting precursor of the more relational gesture of enclosing (shaping in planes).

#### b. *Clashing*
Clashing or dissonance occurs when growing shapes in uni- or bipolar shape flow predominate along with closed shapes in directions and shaping in planes, or when shrinking shapes of uni- and bipolar shape flow are met with open shapes of direction and shaping in planes. This type of conflict indicates that the higher psychic structures used in relationships are not supported by object related responses to comfort and discomfort and self feelings. For example, a woman may move forward to greet someone (D-S) but she may be hollowing backward in unipolar shape flow. She may be attempting to bridge in the external world to another, but her earlier history with her primary object and her sense of self may have left the bodily message that either she or the object now transferred onto everyone else is not safe.

### D. Intersystemic Matching and Clashing: Comparing System I and System II

In general, the right side or shape side of the KMP Diagram Sheet provides the structure or container for affect, drives, and dynamic ego adaptations of the left side of the KMP. In addition, the right side relationally bridges the expressions of the left side. A balanced matching of these diagrams is an important indicator of health and intra- and interpersonal functioning. Each diagram of the left side of the KMP is particularly closely related to a specific diagram on the right side of the KMP. If these two related diagrams are similar, we say that they are matched. If they are very dissimilar, we say that they are clashing.

*1. Conceptual Examples of Horizontal Affinities or Matching: Within the Id Psychic Structure: Between TFA and S-F*

    a. In horizontal affinities there is matching between libidinal drives (TFR) and feelings of safety (TFA) and comfortable, attracting, open self-object and environmental responses (S-F).

    b. There is also matching between aggressive rhythms (TFR) and feelings of caution and danger (TFA) and discomforting repelling, self-object and environmental responses (S-F).

*2. Within the Ego: Between (P-E) and (E) and (D-S) and Shaping in Planes*

    a. There is matching between placating defenses (P-E) and opening up and extending external boundaries in D-S. There is also a match between an indulging adaptation to reality (E) and approaching relationally (shaping in planes) and

    b. There is matching between aggressive defenses (P-E) and barring access to one's body (D-S) and in a fighting adaptation to reality (E) and withdrawing relationally (shaping in planes).

*3. Within the Super Ego: Between Postural Efforts and Ego Ideal*

    a. There is matching between the fighting critical side of the punitive super ego (postural efforts) and the relationally closed part of the ego ideal (postural shaping in planes).

    b. There is also matching between the positively supportive indulging side of the punitive superego (postural efforts) and the relationally open part of the ego ideal (postural shaping in planes).

## E. Broad Matching Patterns

*1. Tension Flow and Shape Flow*

When the patterns of tension flow attributes and shape flow are well matched with supportive tension flow rhythms, the capacity for trust, stability, and confidence emerges.

| TFR | TFA | Shape Flow | Quality |
|-----|-----|------------|---------|
| Oral | Flow adj./even | Widen/narrow | Trust |
| Anal | Low int./hi. int. | Lengthen/shorten | Stability |
| Urethral | Graduality/abrupt | Bulge/hollow | Confidence |

*2. Pre-Efforts and Directions*

When pre-efforts and directions are well matched, defenses against internal feelings as well as against external objects are supported. This match also creates the potential for effective learning patterns. For example, when the fighting pre-effort of the first year, channeling, is matched with the closed directional shape across, the individual is able to learn and define issues while preventing distraction (see Table 10, Chapter 8 for a description of all of the matches).

*3. Efforts and Shaping in Planes*

Matching between efforts and shapes demonstrates harmony in coping with the environment and relating to objects. Ego syntony occurs when there is homogeneous affinity and balance in all patterns.

| *Efforts* | *Shapes* | *Quality* |
|---|---|---|
| Indirect/direct | Spreading/enclosing | Communication/ investigation |
| Lightness/strength | Ascending/descending | Presentation/ confrontation |
| Deceleration/ acceleration | Advancing/retreating | Operation/ decision |

## F. Clashes or Mismatches

1. When tension flow patterns do not have matching shape flow patterns, a lack of structure for the inner feelings results.

2. When shape flow patterns are not matched with affined tension flow patterns, there is structure but not sufficient affect or drive, i.e., a lack of related expressions of bodily needs. Thus there is a lack of dynamic impact.

3. *Efforts without affined shapes:*   If an effort is predominant without a corresponding expression of shape, there will be little relational bridging for ego adaptation. This poor connection to external objects can give the impression that individuals do not expect that others will respond or be affected by what they do. They appear aloof, distant, having diminished interpersonal skills. This may be due to the individual's belief that people wouldn't respond in an appropriate way due to past abuses or non-related experiences in their family of origin. They may have been abandoned or ignored, given the message that "nothing you do matters, you are worthless, and not worth being related to" or due to abandonment deprived of relational socialization to stimulate the development of shape. They often don't know how to touch another or relate. They may have been physically abused, which gave them the message that their fighting efforts should not be matched with affine shape or they would be severely beaten. They are thus unable to bridge their aggression to the world. If sexually abused, their indulging efforts may not have open shape affinities for fear that the generalized perpetrator might be further stimulated.

4. *Shaping without affined efforts:*   If a shaping pattern is not well matched in efforts, there is little ego adaptation to provide the reality-based "substance" for the relational structure. There is no action or coping with the environment which can support relationship. If, for example, individuals have predominantly closed shapes (such as enclosing or descending) and few fighting efforts, they would not be able to directly fight for what they want. It may look like they are assertive, but they will appear empty of the qualities they need. By the same token, if individuals have predominantly open shapes (such as spreading or ascending) but few indulging efforts, they will look like a posed mannequin without any dynamics.

5. *Load factors:*   A high load factor suggests a complex use of elements in adapting to the external environment (efforts) or to others (shaping in planes). A low load factor suggests a more simplistic and less effective pattern of adaptation. A higher effort load factor suggests that adaptation of feelings and needs has a greater impact on behavior. A higher load factor in shaping suggests that relationships have more importance. If one follows the self-in-relation model, one would predict that women would tend to have a higher load factor in shaping in planes than men would, reflecting a greater complexity in women's modes of relating with others.

## G.  Postures and Gestures: Clashing and Matching

When a gestural effort precedes a postural it is seen by Kestenberg as a preparation or "try-ing out" of movement. When a gestural effort follows a postural effort these actions can be seen as continuing the movement without over-stressing the body.

*1. Efforts*
   a. When gestural and postural efforts share the same effort qualities, this phenom-enon is referred to as **posture–gesture merger** (PGM) or **gesture–posture merger** (Lamb, 1965). Lamb feels that the more PGM's which occur, the more the individual can be said to be acting in accordance with the real self. Kestenberg and Sossin (1979) describe gestural efforts as ego adaptations and postural efforts as expressions of an individual's punitive superego (the "inner critic" or "inner judge" in recovery theory language). A posture–gesture merger indicates that the punitive superego goes along with the ego adaptation.
   b. If there is a clash between gesture and posture in efforts, this indicates an ego and superego conflict. For example, if there are many gestural fighting efforts but few postural fighting efforts, this suggests that the punitive superego does not support an assertive, confrontative adaptation to the world.

*2. Shape*
   a. If there is a gesture–posture merging in shaping, this indicates that the ego's mode of relating is congruent with the ideal self-image of the superego.
   b. Where there is mismatching between gestures and postures in shaping, the ego ideal image is not in agreement with the ego's mode of relating to others. If there are many gestural open shapes and few postural open shapes, then the ego ideal is one which views being closed to others as the ideal mode of relating (e.g., a male should be more macho and unavailable). If there are many gestural closed shapes and few pos-turally closed shapes, the reverse is true (i.e., the superego feels that the individual should be more open).

## H.  Id–Ego–Superego Match

There is a full match when the (a) id-based feelings, needs, drives, self and object relations, and responses to safety and danger are consonant with (b) ego-based modes of learning, defenses, ego adaptation, and interpersonal relationships, all of which are (c) consonant with the punitive superego and ego ideal.

The interpretations offered in this chapter reflect the perspectives gained by the author over twenty-five years of clinical experience, and an attempt to integrate KMP material with that of recovery theory. The KMP is open to varied theoretical perspectives which accept as a common denominator a focus on movement as a key to understanding human behavior.

## References

Bartenieff, I. and Lewis, D. (1980). *Body movement: Coping with the environment.* New York: Gordon and Breach Publishers.

Berlowe, J., Kestenberg, J. *et al.* (1995). *Training manual for the Kestenberg Movement Profile, revised by Loman*, Keene: Antioch New England Graduate School.

Kestenberg, J. (1956). On the development of maternal feelings in early childhood. In *The Psychoanalytic Study of the Child XI*. New York: International Universities Press, pp. 275–291.

Kestenberg, J. (1971). *The role of movement patterns in development I*. New York: Dance Notation Bureau.

Kestenberg, J. and Buelte, A. (1977). Prevention, infant therapy and the treatment of adults, I. Toward understanding mutuality, and II. Mutual holding and holding oneself up. *International Journal of Psychoanalytic Psychotherapy. VI*: pp. 339–366, 367–396.

Kestenberg, J. and Sossin, M. (1979). *The role of movement patterns in development II*, New York: Dance Notation Bureau.

Laban, R. (1960). *The mastery of movement*. London: MacDonald and Evans.

Lamb, W. (1965). *Posture and gesture*. London: Gerald Duckworth.

Lewis Bernstein, P. and Singer, D. (1983). *The choreography of object relations*. Keene: Antioch New England Graduate School.

Lewis, P. (1990). The Kestenberg Movement Profile in the psychotherapeutic process with borderlines. In P. Lewis and S. Loman (Eds.), *The Kestenberg Movement Profile: Its past, present applications and future directions*. Keene: Antioch New England Graduate School, pp. 65–84.

Lewis, P. (1984). *Theoretical approaches in dance movement therapy Vol. II*. Dubuque: Kendall Hunt Pub.

Lewis, P. (1986). *Theoretical approaches in dance movement therapy, Vol. I*. Dubuque: Kendall Hunt Pub.

Lewis, P. (1987). The expressive arts therapies in the choreography of object relations. *The Arts in Psychotherapy Journal, Vol. 14*.

Lewis, P. (1993a). *Creative transformation: The healing power of the arts*. Wilmette: Chiron Publishing Co.

Lewis, P. (1993b). Kestenberg Movement Profile interpretation: Clinical, cultural and organizational application; In *Following our dreams: dynamics of motivation*. Columbia: American Dance Therapy Association.

Lewis, P. (1994). *The clinical interpretation of the Kestenberg Movement Profile-work in progress*. (Available through Dr. Penny Lewis 978-388-3035.)

Lewis, P. and Loman, S. (1990). *The Kestenberg Movement Profile: Its past, present applications and future directions*. Keene: Antioch New England Graduate School.

Mahler, M. (1968). *On human symbiosis and the vicissitudes of individuation*. New York: International Universities Press.

Melody, P. and Miller, A. W. (1989). *Recovery from codependency*, San Francisco: Harper & Row.

Reich, W. (1949). *Character analysis*. New York: Farbar, Straus, and Giroux.

Sossin, M. (1990). Metapsychological considerations of the psychologies incorporated in the KMP system. In Lewis, P. and Loman, S. (Eds.), *The Kestenberg Movement Profile: Its past, present applications and future directions*. Keene: Antioch New England Graduate School.

APPENDIX

# The Body Attitude and Interpreting KMP Diagrams

Janet Kestenberg Amighi and Susan Loman

## I. The Body Attitude

Humans and all social animals observe and analyze the movements of others in order to judge their emotional/cognitive states and probable actions. From the observation of movements of familiar persons, one creates an image of how a person characteristically moves, and then uses this image to make an assessment of the person's persistent or core style of behaving. For example, during a conversation, a man may hold himself rigidly, creating the impression that he is resistant to the idea being proposed. If this way of holding himself pervades most contexts, one might form the impression that this is a generally rigid individual.

This persistent and characteristic way of moving and holding oneself is called the "body attitude." Before beginning formal notation, the observer describes the setting, the persons involved, and the general context of the observation. Then the observer writes a short qualitative description of the mover, focusing on the preferred movement patterns for which there is readiness at rest and which can be easily discerned during movement (Kestenberg and Sossin, 1979). Only what is "readily observable" without quantification or systematic notation is described. Typically the observer includes a description of body alignment (horizontal, vertical, or sagittal), body shapes, characteristic phrases, tension spots, and areas which are devoid of elasticity of movement. For example, one might note:

The mover usually has tension in his shoulders and walks and sits with a hollowed back chest. He often looks as though he would sink down or fall backward. He is typically sagittally aligned. He has a lot of neutral flow (dead spots) in his chest, but is more animated in his hands.

The characteristic way of holding oneself and moving described in the body attitude reflects body image, self feelings, and influences of gender, culture and development. Body attitude is the somatic core of the individual's presentation which changes with each developmental phase, until it reaches a certain degree of stability in adulthood (Kestenberg, 1975). However, even in adulthood changes continue as one ages physically and emotionally (Erikson, 1950; Levinson, 1986).

Body attitude is discussed in detail in Chapter 16.

## II. Interpreting KMP Diagrams

### *Interpreting Tension Flow Rhythm Diagrams*

#### Definitions: Pure and Mixed Rhythms

The ten rhythms shown in Diagram 1 are called *pure rhythms*. *Pure rhythms* are motor expressions of specific needs. They are directed to satisfying needs in a fashion that is clearly organized and adapted for functioning in their zones of origin. Thus, the sucking rhythm, which originates in the oral zone, is adaptive for nursing and satisfying nutritional needs, though it is used in other activities as well.

*Mixed rhythms* tend to reflect individual predilections and adaptations to specific contexts. Such mixtures may reduce optimal functioning or may help adjust the way a need is met. For example, an infant who is temperamentally impatient, or influenced by an abrupt caregiver may often mix starting/stopping rhythms into the soothing sucking rhythm, coming up with an individual blend or mixed rhythm.

Note that the solid lines reflect the frequency levels of each of the ten pure rhythms (snapping and biting are diagramed together) and the dashed lines reveal the frequency of use of each of these rhythms in a mixed form.

*(1) Pure rhythms*   After pure rhythms are recorded, they are classified, counted up, and plot points for a frequency diagram are calculated. Solid lines connect the plot points and the resultant diagram illustrates the frequency of each pure rhythm relative to the whole repertoire of rhythms of the mover.

To make a developmental assessment based on the diagram, the age of the person observed must be taken into account. For example, a three-month-old infant would be expected to show a high frequency of sucking rhythms; we would be concerned if the infant had more snapping rhythms than sucking rhythms. We look to see that children have sufficient quantities of rhythms appropriate to their developmental phase so that they can fully meet their developmental needs. In adults and older children we find that rhythmic preferences reveal the kinds of needs which are more powerful and influential in a person's life.

There are some common norms with which the movement profiler should be familiar in order to be able to interpret rhythm diagrams. For example, we know that the first year rhythms (sucking, snapping, and biting) tend to persist as important rhythms for most people throughout life.

We also find that certain fighting rhythms (starting/stopping and spurting/ramming) often become pronounced for a short time during the transitions from one phase of development to the next. It is also common that starting/stopping rhythms increase with irritability which may or may not be short term. For example, such urethral phase rhythms could increase due to a bladder infection, a recent clashing with a parent, or frustration related to need satisfaction. Also, a toddler who is frequently interrupted while straining to stand up, assert herself, or defecate, may become suffused with starting/stopping rhythms, expressing irritability.

*(2) Mixed rhythms*   blended or combined rhythms, such as "*oas*."

*Mixed rhythms and their components* collected from the recorded tension flow lines data are counted up separately, converted into plot points, and added onto the diagram using dashed lines (in contrast to the solid lines used for pure rhythms).

All mixed rhythms (left as whole rhythms and not broken up into components) are listed separately on the KMP diagram form. This list indicates which rhythms are mixing together and in what frequency.

Mixed rhythms generally reveal individual proclivities. For example, if we see a person who *frequently* combines sucking rhythms "*o*" with jumping rhythms "*og*" written as "*oog*", we infer that the person has an oral influence which inhibits a more dynamic explosive way of dealing with tasks and meeting needs. If we find a lot of twisting rhythms " *a*" mixed in with strain/release "*as*", this may indicate a person who begins to concentrate on a task, then wavers in concentration and finally ends the activity. We form hypotheses based on data from one diagram, gather more information from other diagrams and use clinical data, when available, to find confirmation or modification of our hypotheses.

In mixed rhythms, one rhythm may cover up, derail, interrupt or blend with another. Some blends may be very functional. For example, in blending a swaying rhythm "*ig*" with a strain/release rhythm, "*as*," the hard edges of the assertive rhythm become softer and more compromising. This may or may not be adaptive. For example, one may begin with a soothing remark "*o*" and it may sharpen into a biting comment "*os*", becoming a blended "*oso*". Although more research is needed to confirm these clinical findings, KMP analysts have discovered that some mixtures may be linked with diagnostic categories. For example, when an individual displays an overabundance of the mixture "*usogs*", we are concerned about the possibility of conditions of overexcitability in the brain, such as epilepsy since those two fighting rhythms express excessive irritability. Other mixtures which concern KMP analysts if seen in excess in the child are combinations of adult rhythms such as "*igsogs*", "*igogs*" or "*igsog*". We would wonder why such a young child would be displaying so many rhythms usually seen in adolescents and adults. We would not make a conclusion on this data alone but would want to explore the possibility that the child may have been sexually abused or exposed to sexual material.

Here we will discuss briefly the meaning of the statistics included in the tension flow rhythm diagram (Diagram 1). More indepth interpretations based on case analyzes will be offered in Chapters 14–16.

*(3) The ratio of pure:mixed rhythms* compares the total number of pure rhythms scored with the total number of mixed rhythms scored. The higher the frequency of pure relative to mixed, the stronger the drive to meet clearly defined needs. A person with more pure rhythms is generally strongly organized and directed to fulfilling needs. A person with a higher number of mixed rhythms is less organized or less focused on meeting specific needs. Needs are often blended, confused and/or derailed. This is particularly disruptive when the person freauently combines more than two rhythms, e.g., "*oasaog*" or "*asusuigog*."

*(4) Equations* The very top equation, ——P+—— (——)M =—— Total, tells us how many pure rhythms and mixed rhythms the individual mover used. The components (——) are derived as the sum of all the mixed rhythm parts contributing to make up the whole mixed rhythm (e.g. "*oig*" is one mixed rhythm but has 2 components and "*oigog*" is one mixed rhythm with 3 components). If 200 mixed rhythms have 420 components, this indicates that most mixed rhythms consisted of 2 components, but that some had more. The mixed rhythms are listed next to the diagram. The most frequently occurring combinations are generally highlighted for emphasis, and as a cue for interpretation.

*(5) The total number of rhythms* is calculated by adding pure and mixed rhythms together. This total will be compared to the total number of attributes (to be discussed later) to give us an indication of how driven a person is in meeting her needs versus being focused on feeling states.

*(6) Ratios* The three 5-part ratio equations show the number of each phase-related rhythm (for each phase, indulging and fighting subphase types are combined). The top line represents pure rhythms, the second line, mixed rhythms and the third line represents the

total rhythms in each phase. These ratios display numerically which phase was most favored by the individual, which was the next favored and so on. Most often we see that the highest number is found in oral rhythms because most people use these versatile rhythms for many functions. The second highest number reflects the child's phase of development or the rhythm which the adult prefers to use. In clinical populations, an excess amount of a rhythm may indicate regression to an earlier phase of functioning.

*(7) The ratio of indulging to fighting rhythms (I : F) in pure and mixed rhythms* is calculated by first adding the total number of pure indulging rhythms together (o, a, u, ig, og) and then comparing it with the total number of pure fighting rhythms (os, as, us, igs, ogs). The same procedure is followed for the mixed rhythms. The optimal ratio of indulging:fighting for pure rhythms is a reduced ratio of approximately 1:1.2. Slightly more fighting rhythms in the pure category supports the ability to assert oneself and get needs met. In mixed rhythms, the desired reduced ratio is about 2:1. Combining more indulging than fighting rhythms suggests the ability to be adaptable and tame needs rather than combining two or more fighting rhythms which leads to becoming irritable and overly aggressive.

## Interpreting Tension Flow Attribute Diagrams

Tension flow attributes are scored using the same tension flow lines data used to identify tension flow rhythms (Chapter 1). The profiler constructs a diagram which displays the relative frequencies of the six tension flow attributes, plus the use of neutral flow and rebounds in each of these six categories. The method for scoring and diagraming is given in the KMP manual (Berlowe *et al.*, 1995). In addition to the diagram itself, there are other types of associated data which help shed light on the individual's pattern of affect expression.

### Diagram Organization

Diagram 2 and all subsequent diagrams are organized such that each movement pattern is plotted across from its polar opposite pattern. The order of placement from the top line down to the middle and third line of the diagram corresponds to the developmental sequence experienced by the child. Elements represented on the top line become prominent in the first year of life, elements on the middle line become prominent in the second year and elements in the third line become prevalent in the child's third year of life.

In System I diagrams, the three lines of the diagram reflect a developmental progression from a focus on space, to weight and to time respectively in the first three years of life. In System II diagrams, the three lines reflect a developmental progression from a focus on the horizontal to the vertical and finally to the sagittal dimension or plane.

*1. The diagram* The TFA diagram is really a composite of three separate diagrams. The outer plot points include neutral flow (inner shaded area), rebounds (diagonal lines extending from the neutral section), and finally the attributes in animate flow extending from rebounds to the outer edge of the diagram.

*2. Equations* We identify in the top row the number of actions that are neutral, the number that are animate, and the number of total actions. Similarly, we identify the load factors for those actions in animated flow, neutral flow and for the total. Two primary ratios, the gain:expense and free:bound ratios are identified for those elements and/or actions that are in animated flow, neutral flow, and the total.

*3. Total number of attributes versus total number of rhythms*  The total number of attributes can be compared with the total number of rhythms.

  a. If the total number of rhythms is more than the total number of attributes, we can say that the subject is driven by needs with less focus on the regulation of feelings.

   Rhythms are motoric responses to needs, i.e., the need to eat, to soothe oneself, to nourish, to discharge excessive energy, etc. People who engage in repetitive rhythmic patterns tend to have a higher number of rhythms than attributes, since we do not score continuous repetitions of attributes, but we do score repetitions of rhythms. A higher frequency of rhythms indicates that a person frequently gives in to his or her needs and impulses in a relatively uncontrolled fashion.

  b. Attributes are qualities of affects. They regulate the expression of needs. If there are more attributes than rhythms, this suggests that the person is using attributes to regulate and begin to exert some control over needs. We like to see a fairly even balance between TFA and TFR totals.

  c. In general small children have a higher ratio of rhythms to attributes. Maturation brings more regulation of needs and thus a lower ratio of rhythms to attributes.

*4. Neutral flow*  The profiler calculates the percentage of time the person observed was in neutral flow by dividing the number of actions in neutral flow by the total number of attribute actions. From our data so far, it appears that a normal range for the use of neutral flow is 18–30%. The number of actions in neutral flow and its percentage is written out and is also plotted on the graph as discussed in the manual. The area of the diagram is shaded to indicate the relative frequency of specific qualities (e.g., high intensity, gradual etc.) used in neutral flow.

If there is a high frequency of neutral flow (i.e. more than 30%), one might hypothesize that the person is depressed and numbing her feelings. Alternatively, there could be an organic problem. The hypotheses which we form are checked when we view the whole profile and clinical data (see Chapters 14–16). If there is a very low frequency of neutral flow the profiler might hypothesize that the person is highly emotional and perhaps lacks the ability to occasionally use numbing to dull feelings. One would want to look at what other defenses and coping mechanisms are used.

*5. Load factor*  (calculated in animated flow, neutral flow, and total-animated plus neutral)
The load factor is a measure of the complexity of movement patterns. It designates the average complexity of each action (i.e., how heavily each action is loaded with elements within one movement category).

*An element* is an individual attribute (even, abrupt, etc.).

*An action* is any movement which contains one, two or three attribute elements.

If only one element is used in an action, then the action is loaded with one of the three possible elements and has a 33% load factor. If there are two elements used in an action, e.g. tension flow adjustment and graduality, then there is a two/thirds or 67% loading. If three elements (e.g. flow adjustment, low intensity and graduality), are used in one action, then the action is fully loaded or has a 100% load factor.

If a person frequently uses only one tension flow attribute element in each action, this means that his emotional expression is quite simple. This person rarely combines feelings together, for example, using even flow which is neither of high nor low intensity. The feeling expressed is a steady and unchanging emotional state that is not combined with shades of other feelings. If a subject often combines two elements in an action, this creates a more complex emotional situation. We might see high intensity and abruptness combined together in a person who often expresses angry feelings with no warning.

Load factors of about 33–37% represent the most simple use of emotional expression. Moderate complexity would be shown by a load factor of 38%–45%. Load factors of over 45% indicate a complex mixture of emotional qualities (i.e., mixed feelings).

*6. Gain: expense ratio*   (calculated in animated flow, neutral flow, and total-animated plus neutral)

The gain: expense ratio is the ratio of elements of tension flow to the sum total of free and bound flow changes. The "gain" refers to the gain in maturation and in use of defined elements (which structure actions) and the "expense" refers to the expense of energy in flow changes used. Someone who has a low gain: expense ratio engages in a lot of flow changes and has a lot of spontaneity. Someone who has a high gain: expense ratio has more elements than flow changes and thus has more clearly defined and regulated emotions.

*7. Free flow: bound flow ratio*   (calculated in animated flow, neutral flow, and total-animated plus neutral)

The totals of the number of times free flow and bound flow changes were notated are recorded as whole numbers and placed in a ratio. The ratio of these two totals indicates whether there is a balanced use of free and bound flow or whether there is a greater use of one or the other. The desired ratio is approximately 1:1. If there is considerably more bound flow than free flow, this indicates that the person has a tendency to be anxious, controlled and cautious. If there is considerably more free flow than bound flow the person tends to be spontaneous and uncontrolled.

### Interpreting Pre-effort Diagrams

*1. The diagram*   Diagram 3 shows the relative frequency of the six elements of pre-effort. Pre-efforts reflect the mover's defenses against impulses in response to anxiety provoking situations or in trying to master new tasks. Reviewing the diagram one discovers a mover's preferences and areas of limitation. For example, one mover may use excessive hesitation but meager amounts of suddenness revealing a proclivity towards dawdling and postponement of action. The reader is reminded that the two pre-efforts of strength, vehemence and straining, are plotted together on the right side of the second line of the diagram. In order to know which combinations of pre-efforts are used, and in what context, one must go back to the raw data.

*2. Number of actions*   The number of pre-effort actions is recorded. This figure will later be compared with the number of effort actions to see whether there is more focus on dealing with the environment (efforts), or with inner control (pre-efforts).

*3. Load factor*   The load factor indicates the complexity of the learning styles and defenses against impulses used in various situations. For example, when tackling a difficult problem, one might use both flexibility and hesitation. This combination offers a more complex approach than if one employed only flexibility. The load factor thus reflects the complexity of the strategies in defense and learning.

*4. Gain: expense ratio*   The gain: expense ratio is obtained by comparing the total number of pre-effort elements with the total number of free and bound flow changes. The number of elements is associated with the gain, and the number of flow changes is associated with the expense. Many free and bound flow changes without changes in pre-efforts is associated with spontaneity, but also with less control in defensive processes. The use of more elements relative to flow is indicative of a more mature and controlled way of regulating defenses. This ratio is usually found in KMPs done by experienced notators who calculate bound and free flow changes along within their pre-effort actions. If few bound and free changes have been recorded, this ratio will have less significance.

*5. Free : bound ratio*   The free : bound ratio compares the individual's feelings of safety with feelings of anxiety and constraint. We would like to see a balance of a 1:1 ratio. This ratio will be less significant if the notator did not score bound and free flow with the pre-effort actions. Some bound and/or free flow will be scored if the mover uses any vehemence/straining movements since bound flow is scored with straining and free flow is scored with vehemence.

### Interpreting Effort Diagrams

1. *The diagram*   The effort diagram displays the relative frequency of use of effort elements. Efforts are used to cope with tasks related to the external forces of space, weight and time. The profiler focuses on most common or least common effort patterns.

2. *Actions*   The raw score of total effort actions is calculated and can be compared with the total number of pre-effort actions. If there are many more pre-efforts than efforts in a person older than five years of age, we can hypothesize that the person is overly defended and/or in a learning mode. She may feel threatened and insecure. Such a focus on defending against internal states and feelings often interferes with adaptation to outer reality.

If a person uses many more efforts than pre-efforts one can hypothesize that the person observed is under-defended, and with little protection against her own emotions. Her main orientation is toward coping with the external environment.

3. The *load factor*   indicates, on the average, how heavily loaded effort actions are, i.e., what percentage of the three possible elements were involved in effort actions. An effort action may consist of one, two, or three effort elements. The higher the loading, the more complex the action. A load factor of 33% indicates that a person uses only one effort element (out of three) in each action. A high load factor (between 45–60% ) means that a person is frequently using two and sometimes three elements (such as strength and acceleration) in a single action (such as a swing or a punch). This means that the mover attends to and utilizes elements of space, weight, and time in various combinations. This is interpreted as a high level of creative intelligence. (Since work tasks often employ full efforts, a profiler must make sure that the sampling of movements includes varied types of activities.)

4. The *gain : expense ratio*   of effort elements to total number of flow changes indicates the ratio of control to spontaneity. Flow factors (bound and free flow) must be scored in order for this ratio to have significance.

5. The *free : bound ratio*   representing the ratio of feelings of ease to feelings of caution, is calculated and presented. Bound and free flow are not considered effort elements in the KMP system as they are in Labananalysis; they are called "flow factors." Flow factors must be scored in order for this ratio to have meaning.

6. *Notating effort phrases*: Novice notators may write down single effort actions. With practice, however, one is usually able to observe a whole phrase of effort actions and then transcribe them onto paper using the effort symbols and surrounding the sequence with parentheses to indicate a phrase. Notators can examine the data later to find characteristic patterns of phraseology used by the person observed.

7. *Notating postures*: When an effort posture is observed it is indicated by notating the effort symbol (as is done for the effort gesture) and then drawing a box around the symbol. Postures are scored separately and form the basis for a distinct diagram of postures superimposed over the effort gesture diagram. The gesture diagram is connected by dashed lines and the posture diagram is connected by dotted lines. Postures in shaping in planes

(see Chapter 9) are also diagramed. Postures are only notated for efforts and shapes. In general, for both efforts and shaping in planes, gestures are considered trial actions and postures are considered actions which require total commitment and wholehearted involvement. By adulthood, individuals move with recognizable phasing of gestures and postures. Using more gestures than postures helps to create transitional movements.

### Interpreting Bipolar Shape Flow Diagrams

1. *The diagram*   The shape flow diagram is constructed in developmental order (as are other diagrams). However, in System II, the diagrams show development from focus on the horizontal dimension or plane to the vertical dimension or plane to the sagittal dimension or plane. Bipolar shape flow reflects moods, global self-feelings of comfort–discomfort, and the body image.

2. The *total number of bipolar shape flow actions*   reflects the degree of expressiveness and responsiveness to the global environment. The number is expected to be higher in small children than in adults. Elderly people typically exhibit few bipolar shape flow changes. They generally are less expressive of emotions and less responsive to global changes than are younger people.

3. The *load factor*   reflects the degree of complexity in the way moods are expressed and the way people feel about themselves and the environment.

4. The *gain : expense ratio*   compares the complexity of use of shape flow elements with the number of growing and shrinking changes. The higher the number of growing and shrinking changes relative to shape flow elements, the more emotionally expressive the person's movements.

5. The *ratio of growing : shrinking*   represents the total number of growing shape flow (counted automatically with each open shape element such as widening, lengthening and bulging) compared with the total number of shrinking shape flow (counted automatically with each closed shape element such as narrowing, shortening and hollowing). This ratio reflects the balance between comfortable and uncomfortable self feelings. The desired ratio is 1:1.

### Interpreting Unipolar Shape Flow Diagrams

1. *The diagram*   Particular care is required in interpreting unipolar shape flow diagrams due to the following disjuncture. The two horizontal dimension unipolar shape flow qualities are plotted on the first line of the diagram as expected. However, the vertical dimension qualities, lengthening down and shortening down are both placed on the right side of the diagram because they are both precursors of downward directional movement. Likewise, shortening up and lengthening up are plotted together on the left side of the diagram as precursors to upward movements. In the same fashion, we place bulging forward and hollowing forward together and bulging back and hollowing back together.

Thus, we focus on unipolar shape flow as a precursor of directional movements. One can also compare the growing and shrinking aspects of unipolar shape flow by comparing shortening with lengthening and hollowing with bulging. This is possible because an individual plot point value is indicated for each of the ten elements included on the diagram. Thus it would be possible to compare specific types of responsiveness and to locate the direction away from or toward which a person most frequently responds.

2. The *number of actions*   in unipolar shape flow reflects the degree of responsiveness of an individual to external and internal stimuli. Generally the number of unipolar shape

flow changes in a child should be twice that of efforts (2:1). In an adult the ratio of shape flow : efforts should be approximately 1 : 1. Thus if there were 50 efforts in an adult, an average unipolar would be between 40 and 60. Lower numbers of shape flow would reflect a high threshold to stimuli and higher numbers would reflect a low threshold.

3. The *load factor* in unipolar shape flow reflects the complexity of responses to specific stimuli. A high load factor would be found in an individual who responds to specific stimuli in complex ways.

4. The *gain : expense ratio* compares the complexity of the use of shape flow elements with the number of growing and shrinking changes. The higher the number of growing and shrinking changes relative to shape flow elements, the more emotionally expressive the person's movements.

5. The *growing : shrinking ratio* suggests the degree of comfort versus discomfort in the individual's feelings in relation to stimuli around him. It is desirable to have a 1 : 1 balance in this ratio. An imbalance in the ratio would indicate a person who is either overly attracted to stimuli or a person who is overly repelled by stimuli.

## Interpreting Shaping in Directions Diagrams

1. The *number of actions* in directional movement gives an indication of the frequency with which defensive (and learning) actions are taken. One could compare the number of defenses against inner impulses (pre-efforts) with the number of defenses against objects (directions). This is a rough estimate since not all directional movements or pre-efforts are defensive.

People who do not have many pre-efforts or directional movements find it difficult to handle learning situations. They may avoid any activity in which they do not quickly excel. They may avoid interacting with people who are not familiar to them and may not be able to cope well with aggressive people.

2. The *load factor* is an indication of the complexity of the defenses and learning strategies used. Note that a frequent use of directions in combination indicates a more complex relationship to objects in space. However, since the movements are still linear, the relationship defined continues to be one dimensional and defining rather than able to capture complexities and nuances.

3. In the *gain : expense ratio* the total number of directional elements is compared to the total number of growing and shrinking qualities. A high ratio of directional elements to shape flow changes (growing and shrinking) indicates that most directional movements were mechanical in quality. A fairly balanced ratio suggests that there was an emotional component in the directional movements used. Growing and shrinking must be notated in order for this ratio to have meaning.

4. The *growing : shrinking ratio* indicates whether there were more growing or shrinking movements taking place. This suggests the degree of comfort or attraction to stimuli or discomfort or aversion to stimuli experienced. The notator must score growing and shrinking along with the directional movement in order for this statistic to have significance.

5. *Matching: directions and pre-efforts* In older children and adults we expect that pre-efforts will often match with corresponding directional movements, reflecting harmony between dynamic defenses and learning modes and the structures for them. (See Table 8, Chapter 8.) Where instead opposite qualities tend to be combined, this reflects a clash between dynamic defenses and learning modes and the structures for them.

### Interpreting Shaping in Planes Diagrams

1. The *diagram* itself reveals individual styles of interacting, operating, and processing information. One might initially check to see if the individual has a clear preference for movements in one plane or another. The horizontal plane is diagramed on the first line, the vertical plane is diagramed on the second line and the sagittal plane is diagramed on the third line. Qualities within the plane can be further analyzed by considering which of the two movement patterns of the plane is used more frequently.

2. The *number of actions* in shaping in planes compared with the number notated for shaping in directions indicates the degree to which one is involved in complex relationships versus simple and more defended ones. If a person is very defensive, i.e., uses a lot of directional movements, this may interfere with the formation of good social relationships. If, on the other hand, a person has a large number of shaping actions relative to directional actions, she may not be defending herself enough. Such a person would be particularly vulnerable.

3. The *load factor* reflects the degree of complexity in one's relationships and cognitive patterns. One might interpret the load factor in shaping in planes as a partial measure of social intelligence just as the load factor in efforts is a measure of creativity in coping with space, weight, and time. One might also suggest that a high loading may occur in people who are able to see things from many different perspectives (Goldman, 1992).

4. The *gain : expense ratio* compares the complexity of use of elements with the number of shape flow changes. The higher the number of shape flow changes relative to shaping elements, the more emotionally expressive the person's movements. Growing and shrinking must be notated for this statistic to be relevant.

5. The *growing : shrinking ratio* suggests the degree of comfort to discomfort experienced while moving in multidimensional planes. Growing and shrinking are notated with the shaping in planes action. The desired ratio is 1:1.

6. *Notating shaping in planes phrases*: Novice notators may write down single shaping in planes actions. With practice, however, as with efforts, one can observe a whole phrase of shaping in planes actions and then transcribe them onto paper using the shaping symbols and surrounding the sequence with parentheses to indicate a phrase. Notators can examine the data later to find characteristic patterns of phraseology used by the person observed.

7. *Notating postures*: When a shaping in planes posture is observed it is indicated by notating the gesture symbol and then drawing a box around the symbol. Postures are scored separately and form the basis for a distinct diagram of postures superimposed over the shaping in planes gesture diagram. The gesture diagram is connected by dashed lines and the posture diagram is connected by dotted lines. As in efforts, shaping in planes gestures are considered trial actions and postures are considered actions which require total commitment and wholehearted involvement. By adulthood, individuals move with recognizable phasing of gestures and postures which repeat themselves and become part of the movement repertoire. Adults use more gestures than postures which help to create transitional movements.

8. *Matching: shaping and efforts:* When shaping in planes occurs without a paired effort, the movement loses its dynamic content. It becomes somewhat empty and mechanical. For example, descending without strength or lightness, i.e. with no effort element, is confrontational without being clearly serious or light hearted about it.

When efforts occur without shaping, they lose their relational component. Madden (1993) suggests that shaping creates context, meaning, structure, and organization. For example, without shaping, one may see strength, but have no clue as to its meaning in relationship to others. With descending, strength defines and confronts authority; with ascending, strength challenges authority. Together, efforts and shaping in planes offer the dynamic, coping aspects of movement, structured in ways which create relationships to people and objects. The profiler compares shaping and effort diagrams to evaluate how well they are matched and where clashes occur. We do not expect well-matched diagrams in young children but by latency matches usually emerge. Preliminary studies suggest that extensive clashing between efforts and shaping and pre-efforts and directions diagrams in adults may be seen in individuals with borderline personality disorder.

## Understanding Interpersonal Relationships by Comparing Profiles

In the same way that we evaluate how well System I movements match with System II movements within one person's KMP, we can also look for matches and clashes between KMPs of two or more people. For example, we might find that one member of a couple uses abruptness and high intensity frequently while the other uses graduality and low intensity. This interpersonal clash may disrupt the relationship in various contexts. Mutual understanding may arise when patterns between people harmonize through the use of interpersonal matching.

If interpersonal alignment is shared, (i.e. two or more people are using the same plane), the foundation for a shared experience which enhances the formation of relationships is created. When efforts and shaping in planes are matched, they form the basis for effective interpersonal communication in the horizontal plane, presentation and evaluation in the vertical plane, and operation in the sagittal plane.

## Conclusion: Interpreting the KMP as a whole

We do not usually discuss each and every movement quality separately, but instead focus on affinities, clashes, balances, imbalances, matches, mismatches and other comparisons. While we usually begin with rhythms and attributes, in clinical or research situations, the sequence of analysis is often determined by the diagnostic or research questions.

In general, when an individual does not present a problem clinically, the evaluator usually begins with TFRs and continues down "vertically" through System I and then from bipolar shape flow "vertically" down through System II to shaping in planes, to be followed by an examination of matching and mismatching between related diagrams and movement patterns. However, as imbalances or mismatches are discovered, or other hypotheses generated, the evaluator is guided along a more specific path of interpretation. The ability to interpret a KMP depends on understanding normative patterns and theoretical prescriptions (need for balance and for access to sufficient resources), as well as understanding of how each element fits into the whole.

## References

Berlowe, J., Kestenberg, J. S. *et al.* (1995). *Training manual for the Kestenberg Movement Profile, revised by S. Loman.* Keene: Antioch New England Graduate School.

Erikson, E. (1950). *Childhood & society.* New York: W. W. Norton & Co.

Goldman, E. (1992). Personal communication.

Kestenberg, J. S. (1975). *Children and parents: Psychoanalytic studies in development.* New York: Jason Aronson.

Kestenberg, J. S. and Sossin, K. (1979). *The role of movement patterns in development. Volume II.* New York: Dance Notation Bureau.

Levinson, D. (1986). A conception of adult development. *American Psychologist. 41(1).*

Madden, P. (1993). *Shaping motion and movement.* Unpublished Manuscript.

# Subject Index

# Author Index